Dig That Beat!

Dig That Beat!

*Interviews with Musicians
at the Root of Rock 'n' Roll*

SHEREE HOMER

Foreword by SMILIN' JAY MCDOWELL

McFarland & Company, Inc., Publishers
Jefferson, North Carolina

LIBRARY OF CONGRESS CATALOGUING-IN-PUBLICATION DATA

Homer, Sheree, 1978– author.
Dig that beat! : interviews with musicians at the root of rock 'n' roll / Sheree Homer ; foreword by Smilin' Jay McDowell.
      p.   cm.
Includes bibliographical references and index.

ISBN 978-0-7864-7446-2 (softcover : acid free paper) ∞
ISBN 978-1-4766-2046-6 (ebook)

1. Rhythm and blues musicians—United States—Biography.
2. Rockabilly musicians—United States—Biography.
3. Country musicians—United States—Biography.
4. Rock musicians—United States—Biography.
5. Musicians—United States—Interviews.   I. McDowell, Jay.
II. Title.

ML394.H664 2015   781.66092'2—dc23   2015009665

BRITISH LIBRARY CATALOGUING DATA ARE AVAILABLE

© 2015 Sheree Homer. All rights reserved

No part of this book may be reproduced or transmitted in any form or by any means, electronic or mechanical, including photocopying or recording, or by any information storage and retrieval system, without permission in writing from the publisher.

Cover image © Patterson Graham/ThinkStock

Printed in the United States of America

*McFarland & Company, Inc., Publishers
Box 611, Jefferson, North Carolina 28640
www.mcfarlandpub.com*

For the fans,
thanks for keeping the music alive!

Table of Contents

Acknowledgments ix
Foreword by Smilin' Jay McDowell 1
Introduction 4

One. Rhythm and Blues and Doo-Wop Legends 7
    Dale Hawkins 7
    Big Jay McNeely 18
    The Orlons 22

Two. Rockabilly Pioneers 28
    Clyde Stacy 28
    Al Ferrier 32
    Rusty York 34
    Don Woody 38
    Bobby Crown 41
    Alvis Wayne 44
    Janis Martin 48
    Ray Campi 52

Three. Sun Stars 60
    Glenn Honeycutt 60
    Alton and Jimmy 63
    Sleepy LaBeef 68
    Eddie Bond 71
    Andy Anderson 76
    Vernon Taylor 82
    Ace Cannon 88

Four. Country Hit Makers 92
    Conway Twitty 92
    Billy Swan 100

Leroy Van Dyke   103
Buck Owens and the Buckaroos   109

Five. Pop Sensations   116
Dodie Stevens   116
Robin Luke   122
Carl Dobkins, Jr.   127

Six. Roots Revivalists   130
The Four Charms   130
Ronnie Mack   138
James Intveld   144
Rosie Flores   153
Eddie Angel   158
Billy Hancock   162
The Paladins   165
Jerry King and the Rivertown Ramblers   170
Jai Malano   175

Seven. International Rockabilly Performers   180
Junior Marvel   180
Mars Attacks   183
Lil' Esther   185
Jack Baymoore   187
Miss Mary Ann   191

Selected Discography   193
Chapter Notes   223
Bibliography   227
Index   229

Acknowledgments

Without God, this project would not have been possible. Words cannot begin to thank Him enough for introducing me to the wonderfully talented, generous, and kind folks that I have met in the rock and roll community and for blessing me with both the talent and the opportunity to tell their stories. Music has always been my sanctuary. Listening to it and writing about it gives me inner peace and solace when the world around me gets too crazy. Music is as essential to me as breathing. This book encompasses my favorite genres: rockabilly, rhythm and blues, traditional country, and 1950s pop.

Many thanks to my mom, who introduced me to rock and roll and for being the best mom anyone could ever hope for. Your unconditional love and support have always encouraged me to pursue my dreams. I cherish the times we spend together attending concerts.

Thanks, too, to my brother Gary, who helped me and my mom through several rough patches. We wouldn't have survived without you. You came to the rescue when we needed you most.

Extra special thanks to all the singers, musicians, and notables for providing my book with rare photos and invaluable insight into your lives and careers. It is both a privilege and an honor to tell others about your talents. Much appreciation is due to Vernon Taylor and his wife, Brenda, James Intveld, Allen Harris, Kent Vikmo, Eddie Angel, Jimmy Sutton, Frank Marquez, Ronnie Mack, Alton Lott, and Jerry King for answering follow-up questions.

Jay McDowell—I am grateful to you for writing my foreword. You provided insight into both rockabilly and your own career. I hope to someday visit you at the Musicians Hall of Fame and Museum in Nashville. Thanks for all the hard work you do in helping to preserve the music.

I owe my gratitude to those individuals who helped me gather contact information, research materials, and/or provided photos, or who gave love and encouragement: Dominique Imperial Anglares, Joel Aparicio, Bruce Berenson and XM Radio, Bo Berglind, Steve Bonner, Steve Bowers, Marc Bristol and *Blue Suede News* magazine, Sonny Burgess, Ken and Lorraine Burke, Trevor Cajiao and *Now Dig This* magazine, Stuart Colman, Jim Dawson, Neil DelParto, Loretta Doles, Alex East, LeeAnn Enns, Buster Fayte, Kevin Fennell, Ana Fernandez, Steven Ferrier, Paul Freeman, Hans Goeppinger, Ken Haskins, Liz and Lou Holly, John Hopkins and *UK Rock* magazine, Tracey K. Houston, John Karay, Ken King, Michael MacDonald, Don Mason, Jenni Mayes, Adrian Mazar, Kent McCombs, Carolyn McDonald,

Rockin' John McDonald, JD McPherson, Marc Mencher, Bob Miner, Dave Moore, Sue Moreno, Nashville Musicians' Union, James L. Neibaur, Randy Poe, Rita Posselt, Don Rieck, Jeremy Roberts, Shawn Roux, Jim Shaw, Shreveport Musicians' Union, Joe Sixpack, Bob Timmers and the Rockabilly Hall of Fame, Janet VanDeelen, Gladys Van Dyke, *Vintage Rock* magazine, Nick Willett, Lew Williams, Martin Willis, and Linda York.

Adriaan Sturm and Tony Wilkinson—Although they are no longer with us, my book wouldn't be complete without mentioning my friends and two of the biggest supporters of the roots scene. Both were always willing to assist if I needed contact information or research materials. The community is forever indebted to your unending love and support. We all miss you and feel the void that your absence has left behind. Wish everyone was as dedicated as you both were.

Last, but certainly not least, much appreciation is due to all the roots singers and musicians who are still rockin' today, both contemporary and legendary; the fans, the festival and club promoters, the disk jockeys, the record labels, the writers, the magazines, and anyone else who help keep the flame alive.

Foreword
by Smilin' Jay McDowell

For a kid growing up in the '70s and '80s, the Midwest was a bit of a musical wasteland. The local radio station offered a really slim cross section of Top 40 rock. The first music you are exposed to is typically from your parents. In our household, luckily, it was a heavy dose of guitar driven rock and roll mixed with country and blues. My dad would put on a Johnny and the Hurricanes record and then follow it with Merle Haggard or the Rolling Stones. I was getting a good foundation of a range of styles. Finding out that there was more out there than what was being fed to us by the radio programmers opened up a whole new world to me.

My father surprised me one day at school. He came into my third grade classroom and said, "Come with me." He signed me out, and we went to see *The Buddy Holly Story*. I didn't know anything about Buddy Holly. I did recognize a song or two but I didn't know how, or when, he died. After I saw the movie, I wanted to find out more about the Crickets, and I learned more of their story from books and liner notes. Fast forward to 1995. I was asked to play bass on a Crickets album, and I got to hang out with them at drummer Jerry Allison's house. This was like a dream. While I was there, Jerry got a phone call. He had been told that there was going to be a new Beatles release called *Anthology*, and it would include "That'll Be the Day." Jerry was co-writer on that particular song. I can still see Jerry looking around his house with a big grin on his face, saying, "I think I'll put in a wine cellar...."

The early Beatles records were probably my gateway to rockabilly. Some of my earliest memories are jumping around the living room as "Roll Over Beethoven" or "Little Child" was blaring out of the speakers. I was drawn to the guitar. I wanted to learn how to play like George Harrison. I read somewhere that his favorite guitar player was Carl Perkins. It then became apparent that the "Perkins" who had been credited with writing "Matchbox," "Honey Don't," and "Everybody's Trying to Be My Baby" was the man himself. I started rooting around looking for more by this mystery man. The fact that we can click a mouse now to find five generations worth of information blows my mind. In 1981, it took a little more work. I was asking my father about Carl Perkins, and he told me all about Sun Records and some of the other artists that I might appreciate.

I got Elvis Presley's *Sun Sessions*. This was NOT the Elvis that I knew. I was more familiar with "Kentucky Rain" and "In the Ghetto." Hearing this early stuff, it sounded like a different singer entirely. And the guitar ... it was like it was from outer space. I was able to get all of the early Gene Vincent and the Blue Caps albums. I love the mixture of sweet innocence and back alley danger. It's like part country and western, part jazz, and part old-fashioned American standards. You can tell that there wasn't really a rulebook they followed. They all seemed to be chasing the success that Elvis was having, but the Blue Caps certainly weren't just copying Presley's formula in the recording studio. They had their own thing going on. I had bought a greatest hits cassette by Eddie Cochran when our family was on vacation in England in 1982. To find out about his untimely death made it all the more impressive. He had crammed so much into his few years in the studio.

From there, Johnny Burnette and the Rock 'n' Roll Trio, Ricky Nelson, Billy Lee Riley, Johnny Cash, Chuck Berry, Jerry Lee Lewis, Little Richard, and Bill Haley. I was looking for anything that had a bit of twang to it. I was falling down this rabbit hole, and it was becoming apparent that none of my friends knew any of this music. I couldn't relate to anyone. They were all still listening to Supertramp and Pat Benatar. I was in my own world. The only kids at school with whom I felt any affinity with were the punks. I could relate to them. They, too, were listening to stuff that nobody else knew. They appreciated artists like the Cramps and Robert Gordon.

Duane Eddy has always been a huge figure in my life. My father had grown up listening to his music and became involved with the Duane Eddy Circle, a fan club that was started in the 1970s. We went to Nashville in 1986 and visited Duane and his wife, Deed. Duane was always interested in what I was doing musically. He has always encouraged me. He told us about a project that he had been involved in with a young guy named Jerry Dale McFadden. I had heard Jason and the Scorchers, and this was similar. In fact, Warner Hodges even played guitar on it. This was the kind of music I was looking for. It made me want to move to Nashville. I wanted to be in a band like that. When I eventually moved to Nashville, I searched out Jerry Dale, and we are good friends to this day. He related to my situation of growing up with alien musical tastes.

I joined a band that played nightly in a little western wear shop/bar. We clicked immediately. BR5-49 was like a rocket ship that took off. We never looked back and played together constantly. The pinnacle for me was one night when Duane and Deed Eddy showed up. The table up front where our girlfriends were sitting was vacated and they were offered the seats. Duane was watching us intently. We went into "Waiting for a Train" by Jimmie Rodgers. Duane, grinning ear to ear, closed his eyes, threw his head back and started playing air guitar along with us. It hit me right there. How many kids had played air guitar along with Duane Eddy records growing up? And here he was, "playing" along with us.

Suddenly, we were making records and traveling all around the world. We continued to find pockets of rockabilly fans everywhere. Every town has that small group of people who feel they don't belong. They are all searching for that community that accepts them. When we came into town, we were getting support from the mainstream country radio stations. The fact that we played rockabilly, and it was showing up between Brooks and Dunn and Shania Twain, gave me more than a little satisfaction. Every night, people would tell me, "I don't like country music, but I like you guys." That still makes me proud.

Towards the end of our song "Even If It's Wrong," Chuck Mead plays a riff that is stolen from Paul Burlison of the Rock 'n' Roll Trio. CMT regularly played a video. On a rare off night for BR5-49, Ronnie Dawson was playing in Memphis. My wife and I made the three-hour trip to see him. We got to the bar and staked out a table. An older couple walked up and asked if they could take the two unused seats at our table. I immediately recognized Paul Burlison. I introduced myself and told him what a big fan I was. He said something to the effect of "Yeah, I'm a big Ronnie Dawson fan, too." I told him that I was referring to being a big Rock 'n' Roll Trio fan. He was flattered. He asked, "What do you do Jay?" I replied that I played bass in the country band BR5-49. He turned to his wife and said, "That's the band I saw on TV today that played my riff!" I couldn't believe it. I was meeting one of my idols, and he was excited to meet *me*! We talked all night and after the show, Paul invited us to come out to their house for breakfast. Now, my wife and I were planning on driving back to Nashville that night, but we changed our plans and got a hotel room so that we could take him up on the offer. We ate breakfast, and Paul showed me his guitars and amplifiers as well as his record collection. He told me that Stevie Ray Vaughan used his guitar to record "The House Is Rockin'." He told me the stories of when he played with Howlin' Wolf on the radio in Memphis in 1954. Paul and I stayed in touch until he died. He was one in a million.

I also got to spend quite a bit of time with Ronnie Dawson. We ended up playing a lot of the same festivals, and I would find myself with a night off in some city that he was playing. I'd go see him any chance I got. He was really encouraging. Ronnie always had time to sit and talk about what I was up to. I never have met anybody who had a bad thing to say about Ronnie Dawson. The last time I was with him, we went to the Pancake Pantry in Nashville with Kevin Smith, and he wanted to know all about what I was working on. I wanted to hear his stories, but he wanted to hear mine. It's really hard when these guys pass away.

When I stopped traveling with BR5-49, I made the transition into the film and video world. I became a full-time video editor. In 2007, I started working with the Musicians' Hall of Fame and Museum. As the multimedia curator, I get to be surrounded by the instruments that were involved in some of the most iconic songs from different genres of music. We honor the sidemen and studio musicians who contributed to the hits that everyone knows. If you aren't familiar with the Funk Brothers of Motown, you should look them up. Each recording center had their circle of go-to session guys: the Swampers of Muscle Shoals, Alabama; the A-Team in Nashville; the Memphis Boys; Booker T & the MGs, etc. Our museum collects instruments as well as recording consoles and other items that were used to record the songs that we all grew up listening to.

I was walking through the museum with Scotty Moore one day as he reminisced about some of the old photos of Elvis and the Blue Moon Boys. He said to me, "I've forgotten a whole lot of stuff, but, when I come here, I remember." I get chills even now when I think about that moment.

As I read Sheree's book, I was reminded of a lot of those people that I had crossed paths with on the road: James Intveld, Eddie Angel, the Paladins, Sleepy LaBeef, Dale Hawkins, Jimmy Sutton, Buck Owens, Rosie Flores, and more. It became really obvious that we all do it for the same reason. We all put up with the traveling, the crazy hours, the crooked business people, and the time away from loved ones. We do it because something grabbed us at an early age and hasn't let go. I'm glad to say that rockabilly is alive and well. Right now, there are some kids out there who are just finding it and feel all alone. But they will follow a path that we all did, and hopefully this very book will help them on their quest.

Introduction

My first book, *Catch That Rockabilly Fever: Personal Stories of Life on the Road and in the Studio*, was a tribute to the troubadours and revivalists of rockabilly music. I felt it was important to give credit to a genre that is not recognized nearly enough. In this book, I write about more rockabilly artists but also feature others that represent my love of all roots music—traditional country, 1950s pop, doo wop, and rhythm and blues.

Dale Hawkins is one of those artists. I became a fan of his in 2001 when I heard "See You Soon Baboon" on Chicago's WJMK-FM during disc jockey Dick Biondi's *Forgotten Oldies* segment. I am sure I was familiar with "Susie-Q," but it didn't capture my attention the way this tune did. It was different from anything I had ever heard. The Tarzan yell inserted into the intro and outro really stood out. It was a catchy tune, similar to Bill Haley's "See You Later Alligator." My mom and I then wanted to hear more of Dale's music, so I went online and purchased *Oh! Suzy-Q, The Best of Dale Hawkins* from eBay. After that, we wanted to see whether he was still performing. As luck would have it, I found an announcement stating that he would be participating in the 2002 Ponderosa Stomp in New Orleans. My mom and I bought tickets, and we attended the two-day festival. In fact, we went two years in a row, simply because Dale was on the bill. Both years, he brought James Burton onstage to play guitar for him on "Susie-Q." I am so glad we got the opportunity to witness that historic moment. We saw other rockabilly performers during the festival, and they included Joe Clay, Rocky Burnette with the Rock 'n' Roll Trio's guitarist Paul Burlison, Elvis Presley's original guitarist Scotty Moore and original drummer D.J. Fontana.

I was introduced to rock and roll by my mom. She was a teenager in the 1950s and fell immediately in love with Elvis Presley. His hip shaking, rousing rendition of "Hound Dog" on *The Milton Berle Show* was the first time she ever laid eyes on him. When my mom was pregnant with me, she said that she played his music, along with the music of Fats Domino, Jerry Lee Lewis, Chuck Berry, and Little Richard. I liked it even then since she mentioned that I would move around a lot. If I had been born a boy, my mom would have named me Elvis. Instead, I was named after Marilyn Monroe's character in the movie *Bus Stop*. When I was three years old, I wore Elvis T-shirts and butterfly cowboy boots while dancing to my favorite song at the time, "Shake, Rattle, and Roll/Flip, Flop, and Fly" from the *This Is Elvis* movie soundtrack. I'll always regret that I wasn't born earlier, to possibly have known Elvis personally. As I grew older, I heard other artists, including Wanda Jackson, Buddy Holly, and Brenda Lee, whose 45s were played whenever my first cousin Jennifer came to visit. I was bullied in school, so I never let my love for rock and roll shine through. I was afraid of being further chastised. Most people didn't even know I liked Elvis until high school.

A turning point came in my musical education when I helped my mom re-organize her 45 rpm record collection. I was sixteen at the time. As I assisted in re-numbering the singles, we played many of the tunes. It was through this process that I became a fan of Ricky Nelson, Carl Perkins, LaVern Baker, Jackie Wilson, Ray Charles, Bobby Darin, the Everly Brothers, Dean Martin, and Eddie Cochran. It wasn't until 2001 that I discovered rockabilly music. I purchased *The Sun Records Collection*, a three-CD box set, mostly because I recognized tunes by Elvis, Carl Perkins, and Jerry Lee Lewis. As I tuned into each individual track, I stumbled upon "Red Headed Woman" by Sonny Burgess and the Pacers. I had never heard a song so rockin' in my life. I loved its raw intensity and wild abandon. It still sounds as exciting to me today.

After five years of education at the University of Wisconsin–Parkside, I still didn't have a clue what I wanted to do. Thankfully, by the time I graduated, I figured out what my career choice would be. The Ponderosa Stomp in 2002 was the first music festival that we ever attended, and it ended up changing my life. I had wondered how many people knew who these artists were. At that time, I wasn't aware that there was a rockabilly subculture that spanned generations and crossed oceans. My peers had no idea who Dale Hawkins was, let alone any of the other performers. I figured that was the same mind-set of most of mainstream America. I was determined to change that and give recognition to those artists who had been struggling in the music business for fifty years. Therefore, it was easy for me to make a vocational decision; I would combine my journalism degree with my passion for music.

Even though I didn't know anything about starting my own magazine, I did just that in September 2002. The first artist I spoke to was Dale Hawkins. I wound end up interviewing him on four occasions. The last two were for an article featured in *Keep Rockin' Magazine* shortly before his death. I am very grateful that he not only got the opportunity to see it but also be pleased with it. My magazine, *Rockabilly Revue*, didn't last long, only eight issues. I found it too difficult to try to do everything on my own even with assistance from my mom and a friend, Roger Moser, Jr. It wasn't cost effective to continue, especially considering I had few subscribers and no advertisers. However, it was a good learning experience. In two years' time, I had amassed hundreds of interviews. Those would come in handy later as I started to write biographies.

In 2006, my mom and my good friend Ken Burke suggested that I should take those interviews and write a book. Books preserve histories for generations to come. I am glad that the artists' stories were told since a few of them are no longer with us, and that number has unfortunately grown with this second volume. I am going to mention Dale Hawkins again and relate a story. My mom and I not only loved his music but considered him a dear friend, and we miss him every day. For Dale's birthday in 2009, my mom bought him an animal print dress shirt from a high-end men's shop. (Incidentally, she was notorious for buying him gifts.) We saw the shirt and thought it would be ideal since he sang "Wildcat Tamer." My mom purchased it, but then later thought about getting him something else. We tried to return the shirt, but the store wouldn't give us a refund—only a store credit. Therefore, the shirt was given to Dale. He wore it at the Billy Lee Riley memorial tribute, and afterward he emailed my mom to let her know how everyone had complimented him on the shirt. Dale said those were the most comments he had ever received about something he had worn. As fate would have it, we weren't meant to get that refund. Not only was the shirt a hit at the show, but a few months later, when Dale passed away, he was buried in it. His manager/longtime friend Flo Murdock emailed me and said, "Be sure to tell your mom that Dale was buried in her shirt. I thought it was the right thing to do." My regret is that Dale isn't here to see his profile in this book. I hope that he would be proud. Like so many others, he was underrated and should have been a much bigger star. His legacy is so much more than "Susie-Q."

In this book you won't find any tabloid fodder about the artists' personal lives. I write biographies concentrated on their music, either told by the artists themselves or musicians/producers who have worked with them. I conducted numerous interviews, read various books and magazine articles, and researched websites. The Rockabilly Hall of Fame and the Rockin' Country Style online discography were especially helpful. Stories about recording in the studio, their signature tunes, and life on the road can be found within these pages. I enjoyed hearing all the stories as each one was unique. The legends' tales gave me a key to the past. I wish I had grown up in the 1950s, and if I could time-travel I would go back to Sun Studio in Memphis.

It's also important to help support the music scene. Buy the CDs, read the magazines and books, and go to the shows. Without you, the singers and musicians can't continue. Thanks to all those who continue to showcase their talents. But my life wouldn't have been the same without you.

Chapter One

Rhythm and Blues and Doo-Wop Legends

Dale Hawkins

Dale Hawkins established swamp rock boogie, which added a whole new dimension to rockabilly music. He had a knack at choosing top notch session men, such as James Burton, Roy Buchanan, Joe Osborn, Scotty Moore, and D.J. Fontana. As a performer, he scored four Top 40 hits, while as a producer he excelled with nine, which included "Western Union" by the Five Americans. Hawkins' signature tune, "Susie-Q," was named one of the songs that shaped rock and roll by the Rock and Roll Hall of Fame. His original peaked at number twenty-seven, while Creedence Clearwater Revival's 1968 revamped version scored a number eleven position. In 1999, Hawkins recorded his first album in thirty years. *Wildcat Tamer* earned a four star review by *Rolling Stone* magazine, proving to the world that Hawkins was still a force to be reckoned with.

Delmar Allen Hawkins was born on August 22, 1936, in Goldmine, Louisiana. His father, Delmar Sr., was a musician who played a wide array of instruments in local hillbilly bands. However, his main instrument was the stand-up bass. When his father couldn't make a living as a musician, he pursued farming. Music ran in the bloodlines since Dale's first cousin Ronnie Hawkins was a rockabilly singer, and Dale's younger brother, Jerry, had three record releases in 1958 and 1959. In fact, Dale wrote one or two of those songs and produced the sessions. Unfortunately, the siblings never had the opportunity to sing together.

When Hawkins was three years old, his parents divorced. Around that same time, he sang his first songs a cappella, which were "You Are My Sunshine" and "White Cliffs of Dover." Shortly after, his mother, Estelle, who worked at a military defense plant, sent her two sons to live with their grandparents and other relatives in Mangham, Louisiana, a town just south of Shreveport. At a young age, Hawkins picked cotton and shined shoes. Music was also an integral part of his environment. He recalled, "My grandfather was marshal of a parish out in East Louisiana, and I got to go with him sometimes on Saturday nights. We'd run up and down the street and listen to the music."[1] He added, "[Sometimes at the same venue], you'd hear Elmore James in the back and Hank Williams, Sr. in the front. They had a Pentecostal church just down the street, and I loved to hear 'em play and sing. [On occasion], I got to go up and sing with 'em."[2] The styles that had the greatest impact on Hawkins were blues and bluegrass: "Bluegrass music was a love of mine," especially Bill Monroe, Jimmie Rodgers, and Hank Williams, Sr. Hawkins and his brother hitchhiked to see Flatt and Scruggs play in Monroe and Rayville, Louisiana. As far as the blues, Hawkins loved Lightnin' Hopkins, Jimmy Reed, and Lonnie Johnson. Inspired by the music he heard, a seven-year-old Hawkins picked up his Stella guitar, got a Wayne Raney/Lonnie Glauson harmonica code book, and learned chord progressions.

In the mid–1940s, after Hawkins' mother remarried, he and his brother returned to her care. At the time, she worked at Miss Gertrude's, a small café where Hawkins regularly hung out and listened to their jukebox. At fourteen, he dropped out of school because he hated it. Hawkins then delivered newspapers and bagged groceries to make a little extra money. As soon as he got his first paycheck, the teenager ran away from home, first to Houston, then to Dallas. Both times, Hawkins ended up returning home. The Dallas police had forced him. He had wanted to relieve his mother of some of her financial responsibility. Hawkins conveyed, "We had a church, and I'm so grateful for it, because growing up the way I had to, it saved my life many times." In February 1953, Hawkins joined the Navy. In June 1954, he was "honorably discharged after severely injuring his back in an ammunitions misfire while aboard the USS *Maddox*."[3] Hawkins spent all summer in the hospital recuperating. While there, he spent a lot of time soul-searching and praying for a way out of the housing projects. Thoughts of playing music weighed heavily on his mind, but he didn't know how to pursue it. To please his mother and because the Navy paid his tuition, Hawkins continued his education. For seven months, he attended Norton Business School. Hawkins then tried regular jobs such as clerking at a creosote mill and later at a railroad station, but those vocations didn't speak to him the way music did. Later, when he made the transition to singing, his mother was supportive: "She knew the elements because my dad was a musician. She wasn't too happy [with my decision] but proud."

Dale Hawkins is known as the pioneer of swamp rock boogie. His signature tune "Susie-Q" influenced generations, including a young John Fogerty (author's collection).

About 1955, Hawkins and his brother took jobs parking cars for the Municipal Auditorium, home of the *Louisiana Hayride*. Fifty cents was the fee, and that money went to the *Hayride*. Hawkins remembered, "When their parking lot got full, we took the cars and parked 'em in the public parking lot and still charged them." It was a bit of a scam since the patrons were unaware that the parking lot was actually free and open to the public. In fact, one night the police came, and it scared the Hawkins boys: "They hollered at us, and we took off. I hit a clothes line, and it flipped me, but we got away with it." Around that same time, he made friends with Sonny Jones, a popular singer in the area. Hawkins made a point of seeing him live several times. In late 1955/early 1956, Hawkins took a job as a singing sales clerk at Stan's Record Shop on Texas Street in Shreveport. The store had opened on June 22, 1947, and specialized in rhythm and blues records that catered to a mostly black clientele. Before Hawkins had gathered enough courage to ask for the position, he hung out there frequently, studying their stock with "feverish intensity." He declared, "That's why I landed the job because I knew every one of them [records]."[4] The store owner, Stan Lewis, admitted, "Dale was a kid, just looking for a job, so I hired him. He had a lot of personality and knew all the rhythm and blues songs and artists, which were assets for a salesman. If a customer mentioned two or three words out of a song, Dale knew what it was."[5] Lewis was impressed by that knowledge. Hawkins added, "I worked at the store in the afternoon when I could and on Saturdays. Black people would come in and not know the titles of songs. I'd tell them, 'Sing me a little bit.' They would, and bam [right away] I knew who it was and when it was cut. That's how I got to meet B.B. [King]. He is a good friend of mine." The customers affectionately knew Hawkins as Del. After work, he went to the back of the shop and mastered the rhythm and blues records note for note. Hawkins would also sometimes participate in jam sessions with younger musicians or sit in with a black vocal group. Together, they would sing tunes by The Clovers and Clyde McPhatter and the Drifters.

Soon after, he met James Burton, who became a student of the blues, thanks to Hawkins' vast knowledge. On a Saturday night in 1956, Hawkins worked his first gig with guitarist Sonny Jones and bassist James Kirkland at the Horseshoe roller rink in Plain Dealing, Louisiana. Hawkins commented, "James was the best, really particular in wanting to do it right the first time. He could really slap that bass." The trio, using only one amp and two microphones, played rock and roll and rockabilly songs of the day, like Chuck Berry's "Maybellene." That experience helped boost Hawkins' confidence as he fed off the audience reaction. He was particularly enthralled by the females. Some of those early gigs were rough for Hawkins: "You had to have chicken wire up to keep them from throwing things at ya."

Hawkins yearned for a record that sounded unique compared to the records he sold at the record store. In early 1956, he recorded a demo version of "Susie-Q" at radio station KENT in Shreveport. Even though, the song was not rehearsed in the studio, the band had played it many times in nightclubs on the Bossier strip over a five month span. Burton was still underage, so he had to be sneaked in through the bathroom. One night while setting up for a gig, "Hawkins' drummer [A.J. Tuminello] started warming up by hitting his drum and cowbell simultaneously."[6] The young vocalist told him to remember it for later. As it turned out, that accident became the intro to "Susie-Q." Merle Kilgore engineered, and the demo version had both saxophone and guitar solos. Shelton Bissell was the alto saxophonist. "If You Please Me" was also recorded at the session. Hawkins remembered, "The original 'Susie-Q' [relied] heavily on blues in its orientation. It took a while to get the blues feel together. I am a perfectionist, so I put James through boot camp. He played [the riff] over and over until it was the way I wanted it to sound. I don't think anyone else could have done it but James [Burton]. 'Susie-Q' would not be nearly as good as it is if it hadn't been for James' playing." In 1997, Norton Records issued the unreleased track along with other Hawkins rarities on an LP called *Daredevil*.

Hawkins had originally wanted "Susie-Q" to be his first release, but when "See You Later, Alligator" became a number six hit, his plans changed. He paid engineer Bob Sullivan twenty-five dollars to cut "See You Soon Baboon" and "Four Letter Word (Rock)" at radio station KWKH: "The session was [held] to get the contract with Chess, which was never really finalized. I said if Bobby Charles can do it, I can." Charles had written and originally recorded "See You Later, Alligator." However, it was Bill Haley's version that was flying off the shelves at Stan's Record Shop. Lewis, who was Hawkins' manager, had encouraged him to write a song that was similar in content and aimed toward teenagers. "See You Soon Baboon" was born from that idea. Sonny Jones played guitar, A.J. Tuminello played drums, while Allen Harris was the featured pianist. Lewis sent the demo tape to Leonard Chess, who frequently visited Stan's Record Shop. Before issuance, Chess made a few changes. They added the ape call intro and outro, which had been provided by disc jockey Gene Nobles, and removed Hawkins' name as songwriter. This fact naturally upset Hawkins, who commented "You're trying your best and not getting paid."

Due to a misunderstood phone call, the label renamed their new artist Dale Hawkins. When he had said his name was Del, his Southern accent had made it sound like Dale to Leonard Chess. On July 7, 1956, the 45 rpm single "Four Letter Word (Rock)" b/w "See You Soon Baboon" hit store shelves. Unfortunately, only a few copies sold. Despite low sales, on December 16, 1956, Chess signed Hawkins to his Checker record label. Hawkins disclosed, "I think the reason Leonard signed me was because he thought I was black."[7] It also didn't hurt that Lewis was the biggest distributor for Chess and Checker Records in Louisiana. However, Hawkins didn't see his next release for another ten months.

On February 14, 1957, Hawkins and Burton rode their bicycles to KWKH to record the released version of "Susie-Q." KWKH was located on the second floor of the Commercial National Bank in downtown Shreveport. The actual size of the studio was 35 × 40 square feet with a high ceiling, which was conducive for good sound. Engineer Bob Sullivan remarked, "Stan Lewis had called and said, 'I got a kid I want to record. Let me know what night we can do it.' I said, 'About any night.' I had been recording country stuff with Jim Reeves and Slim Whitman, so I assumed it was another country artist. Instead, here comes Ronnie Lewis with his drums, and I thought, oh boy, this is a problem because I had never recorded drums in my life. I didn't have enough microphones, only had but four. After he got set up, I walked around and listened to him play, found the spot that I thought would sound the best and hung the mike there. [It ended up being] the best drum sound I ever got. They were trying to figure out how they were going to kick it off. They never could get it right, so they said, 'Well let the drums do it.' [A.J. Tuminello couldn't make the session, so Lewis played the intro instead.] When James Burton hit that guitar lick, it knocked me out; I never heard anything like that."[8] Hawkins recalled, "The only time that we could get in there to record was at one o'clock in the morning. We only had an hour. We had four microphones and the old RCA pods that they used for radio." Hawkins produced while Sullivan engineered using "an aging Collins broadcast board with no equalizer and no echo."[9] The board only had two turntables and a Magnecord mono tape recorder. During recording, Sullivan took out part of the tape and fed it back into the recorder to create slap back. He stated, "We mixed as we went along." They cut four takes of "Susie-Q," and Hawkins ultimately chose which one would be used. Sullivan revealed, "He took the wrong cut; that was one of the earlier ones. I was trying to get a balance when I happened to notice he was singing. I then eased the mike up. If you listen to the record, you hear Dale come in singing Q real weak and then the next time he's real loud. I guess it had the energy and spontaneity [that he wanted]. Dale later joked, 'Ole Sullivan was asleep at the mike and didn't turn it on.'" There are differing reports on who provided the handclaps. Even though Maylon Humphries and Gene Scudder have been credited in liner notes, Sullivan remembered that it was three black men. Most likely, it's the same trio that sang backup on "Don't Treat Me This Way." Lewis claimed it was him and two of his employees. There was a third opinion with Hawkins, who said it was Scudder and two black men. *Louisiana Hayride* staff member Sonny Trammell played electric bass: "I never knew much about Dale because he didn't come down to the Municipal Auditorium very much on the count that he didn't go for country music. Dale was a funny guy, cracked jokes."[10] One of the reasons Trammell was chosen to play on the session was because he had the only electric bass in Shreveport. According to Sullivan, Hawkins had said that Lewis got the names all messed up, listed ones that weren't on the record but in the union since the real musicians were not. That's the reason why Tommy Mandina is sometimes given the credit for playing bass. On the version of "Susie-Q" that was cut in 1956, an upright bass was used, and the player is unknown. At the same time as "Susie-Q" (1957), "Don't Treat Me This Way" was recorded. The background vocals for that particular track were provided by three young black men who used to come into Stan's Record Shop. Hawkins recalled, "We made some good, good music. We'd get out on the street corner and sing."

Hawkins was assured he had a hit. However, Leonard Chess failed to issue "Susie-Q" immediately following the session: "I had trouble getting them to release the record. It took me about three months. Nobody knows what you go through when you're dealing with these music people, and you don't know what you're doing. This disc jockey friend of mine, Chuck Dunaway, told me, 'Well, I'll tell you what we do, let's send a copy to Atlantic, and let them hear it.' [Their record executive Jerry] Wexler told me, 'Heck yeah, I want it.' I said, 'Well Mr. Wexler, Mr. Chess has got it, and I can't get him to return my calls. I need to get this out.' He said, 'Well, you tell him that I said to either sh** or get off the pot; you got a week.' I called Leonard and told him that and after about ten seconds, he said, 'I'll call you back in ten minutes.' I never heard back from him." Within three days, on May 6, 1957, "Susie-Q" b/w "Don't Treat Me This Way" was released.

Incidentally, "Susie-Q" took inspiration from The Clovers' "I've Got My Eyes on You" and its guitar riff from Muddy Waters' "Baby, Please Don't Go." A line in The Clovers' tune referred to a dance craze called the Eagle Rock just as Hawkins alluded to the Susie-Q. Three names were given credit for penning "Susie-Q": Hawkins, Stan Lewis, and Eleanor Broadwater, which was the maiden name of WLAC disc jockey Gene Nobles' wife. Chess added her name in appreciation for her husband playing Hawkins' records. Lewis claimed that the song was written about his daughter, Susan: "My daughter was born in 1955. Right after she came home, I came in the shop and said, 'Oh Susie-Q, my Susie-Q. I love my Susie-Q.' Dale and I co-wrote the song, and he put the music to it." Lewis noted that James Burton had nothing to do with writing the song. According to Hawkins, he wrote the arrangement and lyrics while the guitar lick was a combined idea between him and Burton. He felt that Burton should have gotten partial writing credit. Hawkins recalled, "For a while there, Stan was a real help to me, until I realized that I had signed everything I had away. He said that I sold him 'Susie-Q' for $125, and he was taking half of everything I made. It's bull. The man has never written a line of a song that I have ever had."[11] In 1968, when Creedence Clearwater Revival brought the song back to the charts, Hawkins only received BMI airplay royalties: "The contract I had with BMI made them my legal guardian, and they wouldn't let them take it away from me. As for sales, I never received a dime."[12]

In May 1957, Hawkins quit his job at the record store and went on tour to promote his latest platter. He appeared on *The Milt Grant Show* in Washington, D.C., and was the first white artist to play the Apollo Theater in Harlem. His appearance was three weeks before Buddy Holly and the Crickets graced the same stage. In fact, Hawkins and Holly were good friends. They hung out together in New York City: "We had a lot of fun. There's no telling how far Buddy could have gone." Hawkins also formed friendships with Gene Vincent and Eddie Cochran: "I met Eddie when we were once on tour for five days. We had a lot of respect for each other. He was a heck of a musician, a pretty smart businessman, and a good guy."

"Susie-Q" proved beneficial to Hawkins in more ways than one. Allen Harris explained, "In the summer of 1957, I was playing with Al and Sonny Jones at the Skyway Club, which was the number one nightclub in Bossier City, Louisiana. I had an old car, and it broke down, but I wanted to come home to Monroe for the few days that I had off."[13] Harris decided to hitchhike: "I wasn't out on the highway with my thumb up for [more than] five minutes when this little MG convertible pulled up. It was Dale Hawkins [who had purchased the car either with his first royalty check or with an advance from Leonard Chess]. Dale then said, 'Where you going?' I told him, and he said, 'Well, hop in.' By the time we'd gotten to Monroe, which was a two hour drive from Shreveport, he had talked me into going with him to Philadelphia to do *American Bandstand* and then on to Chicago to do a recording session for Chess Records." They then began their journey to the East Coast. Harris added, "We talked until we ran out of something to talk about. Dale started getting sleepy, so he asked, 'Do you wanna drive?' I was dying to get my hands on that little sports car, so I said, 'Yeah, I'll drive.' I got to driving but pretty soon I got sleepy, so Dale said, 'I got this little pill here to keep you awake.' I took one of those little white pills, and I could have driven to China. When we were going through Chattanooga, Tennessee, I was still driving because Dale was asleep. [All of a sudden], this cop pulls us over. He looked at my driver's license and said, 'Is this your car?' I said, 'No, it belongs to Dale.' He replied, 'Who's that guy in there?' I said, 'That's Dale Hawkins.' He goes, 'The Dale Hawkins?' I said, 'Yeah.' He said, 'The singer?' I then said, 'Yes sir, that's him.' The cop retorted, 'I don't believe that. Wake him up.' I reached over the seat and woke Dale up. The cop said to Dale, 'You Dale Hawkins?' and he said, 'Yes sir.' In the meantime, Dale's looking around, trying to get his bearings and find out where he is. The cop then said, 'Well you guys follow me.' We followed him down to the police station. Before we started in, he said to Dale, 'Bring your guitar.' The cop made Dale sing 'Susie-Q.' It satisfied him; he didn't give us a ticket, and he let us loose. On August 7, 1957, we got to Philadelphia, and Dale lip-synched 'Susie-Q' on *American Bandstand*. I met Dick Clark and sat in the audience. [The night before, Clark had hosted a sock hop where he played "Susie-Q" non-stop for twenty-one minutes]. We left there and went to New York City to do Alan Freed's television program, *The Big Beat*. I wasn't nearly as impressed with Freed. After New York City, we went to Chess Records in Chicago. That day, [Chuck Berry's piano player] Johnnie Johnson was there recording. I was tickled to death to see Johnnie play. Dale and I spent a couple of days in Chicago, but then he mentioned how he was going to stay there a while to do an album. He asked if I wanted to play on it, and of course I did, but I had to get back to my job and wife in Shreveport. I had already been gone a week, so I caught a plane and flew home." Not participating on that album is one of Harris' greatest regrets.

During the summer of 1957, "Susie-Q" took the number seven position on the R&B charts, while peaking at number twenty-seven on the pop charts. Hawkins had worked really hard to establish the song, conquering each city's market one at a time. His perseverance paid off though as the single sold 300,000 copies. Dean Mathis acknowledged, "'Susie-Q' would have been a number one song on the *Billboard* charts if Chess had played the game right. They went from market to market with that song, so it wouldn't hit the Top 10. It was a monster record, a lot bigger than number twenty-seven."[14] Chess would wait for the song to start coming down the charts before pushing it in another town. Mathis mentioned, "It was probably number one in every city."

Recording at KWKH proved beneficial for a hit single, but his next session took place on August 29, 1957, in Chicago. James Burton went to work for Bob Luman, so Hawkins recruited Carl Adams. At five years old, Adams had accidentally shot off the two middle fingers of his left hand. His injury caused him to play the guitar backwards, upside down, and left handed with picks taped to his thumb and little finger. Adams also pulled the strings instead of using a push technique. Hawkins disclosed, "Carl and I went to elementary school together. I had to have somebody I knew, that I could communicate with, and that could play what I heard." While in the studio, they cut "Baby, Baby" and "Mrs. Merguitory's Daughter." Two days prior to the session, "I went to see a Lon Chaney movie. His daughter was named Mrs. Merguitory [providing inspiration for a song]." His third single, "Baby, Baby" b/w "Mrs. Merguitory's Daughter" was issued on October 7, 1957.

Leonard Chess booked more studio time for Hawkins in December 1957. At the session, "Little Pig," "Juanita," "Tornado," "Boogie Woogie Teenage Girl," "Teenage Dolly," "Sweetie Pie," and "Heaven" were all recorded. In an hour's time, Dean Mathis had written "Little Pig," with lyrics adapted from the children's fable "The Three Little Pigs." He recalled, "I wrote 'Little Pig' for me and my brother to cut because we were a duet [like the Everly Brothers]. Merle Kilgore's name is on it, but he didn't write one word. I don't know how his name got on there, and he doesn't either. Marc and I made a demo of it at KRMD in Shreveport, with Johnny Horton on piano. Dale was going to Chicago, and he was gonna take it up there to play for Leonard. We wanted to get a recording contract. Leonard heard the song, liked it, and wanted Dale to cut it. He cut 'Little Pig,' but Leonard said, 'I'll go ahead and sign the brothers to a recording contract.'" Argo Records was their label, and they enjoyed a few releases. When Hawkins returned, he told Mathis right away that he had recorded it: "I was kind of in shock and upset about it, but after I heard Dale's record two or three times, it kind of wore off. Dale apologized, and he told me the circumstances. He said Leonard thought he oughta do the song because he thought it would be a hit for him. I understood; I wasn't naïve about it. I knew a little bit about the business. Even though, I think if he hadn't signed us to a contract then Dale wouldn't have recorded the song." Mathis added, "You can't [refer to your girlfriend as a pig]; that's why it wasn't a hit. I didn't know that, just thought it was cute because it was about the nursery rhyme. I am glad Dale cut it though. I love what Carl [Adams] played; it just knocks me out. The guitarist we used sounded nothing like that. It's a great record." Unfortunately, the demo version has been lost, even though, Mathis said that Hawkins' version was the same, except for its musical score. Marc Mathis played bass, and Ronnie Lewis played drums. Margaret Lewis and her sister Rose provided background vocals on "Juanita," while Harvey Fuqua and the Moonglows added backup on "Heaven." Adams played lead guitar on all the songs, except for "Tornado," which featured him and Kenny Paulsen. Hawkins mentioned, "I didn't have a guitar player. Kenny wanted to play some blues, so he came with me." Incidentally, Paulsen stayed with Hawkins for three years and also played lead guitar on "Liza Jane." Checker only issued one single from the December 1957 session. On April 7, 1958, "Tornado" b/w "Little Pig" hit store shelves.

The years 1957 and 1958 were busy for Hawkins. Besides playing high school auditoriums and nightclubs, he made five guest appearances on the *Louisiana Hayride* with Harris on piano. Sullivan reported, "Dale was well known, and he got a good reception." Harris recalled live appearances with Hawkins at the Skyway Club. The house band was Harris, D.J. Fontana, Fred Carter, Jr., and Al and Sonny Jones. For other gigs, Hawkins usually played with a three piece band: guitar, bass, and drums. Sometimes piano or sax would be added if someone was available. Harris recalled, "We didn't do much touring outside Shreveport because I was part of the staff band at the *Louisiana Hayride*. I had to be in town for the Saturday night broadcast." Even though, he did work with Hawkins off and on for a year. The It'll Do Club, on the Bossier Strip, was a regular booking for Hawkins. In fact, he occasionally dated the owner, if only to borrow her brand new Cadillac. Kilgore commented, "Dale was the top draw in Shreveport. He would just jam 'em in."[15] Beginning in 1958, Hawkins' road band featured guitarist Roy Buchanan, bassist Marc Mathis, drummer Melvin Rogers, and piano player Dean Mathis. Hawkins recollected how he and Buchanan met: "I went to do a record hop [the *Oklahoma Bandstand*] in Tulsa, and Roy was there. He came up and asked, 'Can I play?' I said, 'Well, can you pick?' He said, 'Yeah,' so I replied, 'Plug it in.' We had a good time." Throughout Wisconsin, Michigan, Illinois, and Ohio, the band played record hops, which were teenage dances that disc jockeys hosted at National Guard armories, high school auditoriums, and skating rinks. Dean Mathis acknowledged, "That's how Dale made his money. We'd do the show and then leave." He also revealed an occasion where two fights broke out in the same night, only twenty minutes apart: "We had played a club in Claxton, Georgia. There was another down the road with a band that somebody had said was really good. We decided to stop in and listen for a little bit. Well, when we got down there, Marc and I didn't want to get out. I was tired, and it was cold. We stayed in the car, while Melvin, Roy, and Dale went inside. They must've been in there at least an hour before Melvin came running out. He said, 'Man, y'all go in and help Dale and Roy. They're in a fight.' I never did know what the fight was about. I don't even think Dale knew." He figured Buchanan was a victim of mistaken identity "because he said first thing he knew somebody hit him. When he did, Roy came up swinging, and then Dale got involved. By that time, three or four other guys did too. That's when Melvin, who didn't want any part of it, came and told Marc and I that we needed to get in there and help. Melvin got in the car as he didn't go too much for fighting. Everything got straightened out once they found out who Dale was. They didn't call the cops, so we left. We then stopped at a restaurant where we sat in booths. Dale got up to play the jukebox. When he came back and sat down, he said something to the waiter, and I don't think the guy understood what he said, thought he was being smart. He then said something back to Dale that was smart. Dale replied with a smart comment then he started getting up out of the booth. When he did that, the guy took off running and came back with a baseball bat. He came down and hit Dale with it. [Thankfully], Dale had thrown up his arm to block it. [Therefore, the guy didn't break his arm, only gave him a bruise.] Roy then hit the waiter, knocking him straight across to the next booth. When that happened, we got up and got back in the station wagon. Melvin had run into the woods when the fight started. We drove round and round trying to find him but couldn't. Dale said, 'Well, we'll go down the road.' We took off but then spotted Melvin waving us down." The South was a rough area to play. Mathis stated, "We did a tour with Little Anthony and the Imperials and Roy Hamilton. We rode on a bus with them but when we crossed the Mason-Dixon Line we stayed in different hotels and had to eat in different restaurants. They knew we weren't racist; we didn't like it at all."

In June 1958, Hawkins returned to KWKH to record his self-penned tunes "La-Do-Dada," "Superman," and "Crossties" (co-written with Dean Mathis). On "La-Do-Dada," Joe Osborn played guitar, D.J. Fontana played drums, Marc Mathis played bass, and Allen Harris played piano. Hawkins, Dean Mathis, and Margaret Lewis overdubbed backing vocals. On July 21, 1958, Checker released "La-Do-Dada" b/w "Crossties." "La-Do-Dada" peaked at number thirty-two on the pop charts.

In September 1958, en route from Dallas to Chicago, Hawkins and Buchanan formulated the groundwork for "My Babe": "I told Roy, 'Let's just sing some gospel music. Grab that E string and leave the top one open.' [Sister Rosetta Tharpe's "This Train" was the song of choice.] At ten years old, I was singing 'Strange Things Happening Every Day' and 'Didn't It Rain.' I can't even think of how much I really appreciated her work." At the session, three different versions of "My Babe" were cut as well as "Who Can Say," "Someday, One Day," and an instrumental track, "The Hawk Walks." Willie Dixon played bass on "My Babe." Hawkins commented, "We hit it off. I had a lot of respect for Willie, and I thought he was one of the greatest bass players." In regard to "A House, a Car, and a Wedding Ring": "Marc Mathis and I drove all the way from St. Paul, Minnesota [to New York City]. We had a show the next night, so we put a mattress in the back of that '56 station wagon and took off. On the second take, I got it. Sessions like that were easy for me. They used to call me 'One Take Hawkins.' We got back in time to do the show, but I was sick as a dog." Dean Mathis disclosed, "Dale had broken the caps on his front teeth. He had a habit of taking the mike, throwing it out, and bringing it back with the cord. He misjudged, and it hit him. Dale grabbed his mouth and ran off stage. It was right at the end of the show, but he couldn't finish. Dale then went to New York City to get them fixed and while he was there he cut 'A House, a Car, and a Wedding Ring.'" For the recording, Marc Mathis played bass, while Buchanan added his guitar licks. Dean Mathis added, "Dale didn't have a lot to say onstage. He'd talk a little bit in between songs, [but for the most part] he would just stand up there and sing, take a step to the left and then to the right with the microphone. Dale would kinda bend his knees, lean back, and throw the mike up. That's about as much as you'd get out of him, but he always had the ladies' attention." On October 20, 1958, Checker released the 45 rpm single, "My Babe" b/w "A House, a Car, and a Wedding Ring." The latter tune scored a number eighty-eight position on the *Billboard* charts.

In January 1959, Checker mass marketed "Take My Heart" b/w "Someday, One Day." For "Take My Heart," Leonard Chess had urged the singer to sound like Elvis Presley. Hawkins replied, "I ain't sounding like anybody. I don't know how to imitate anybody else." On March 27, 1959, Hawkins performed on one of Alan Freed's package shows at the Brooklyn Fox Theater. Others on the bill included Fats Domino, Jackie Wilson, Duane Eddy, Bobby Darin, and Jo Ann Campbell. In fact, the July 1959 issue of *TV Movie and Record Stars Illustrated* reported that Campbell dated Hawkins and Darin at the same time. Hawkins then recorded at Sheldon Recording Studios in Chicago. On that particular visit, he paid homage to one of his heroes, Jimmy Reed, by recording "Ain't That Loving You Baby." The track featured Scotty Moore on guitar, D.J. Fontana on drums, Willie Dixon on bass, Dean Mathis on harmony vocal, and Lafayette Leake on piano. Mathis remembered, "Thomas Wayne went up just for the ride, to see Chess. He sat and watched the session. We spent the night at the hotel right across the street. Dale, Scotty, Thomas, and I went down to the bar to have a drink. When the bartender's back was turned, Thomas would reach down and grab a bottle of whiskey and then set it down on the floor. He did that about three times before he got caught. Dale had to do some talking to get him out of that because he was fixin' to call the cops." On May 11, 1959, Checker issued the 45 rpm single, "Ain't That Loving You Baby" b/w "My Dream."

Hawkins enjoyed recording in Chicago the most because of the friendships he made with his fellow label mates: "I got along good up there in Chicago, with the musicians especially. Muddy [Waters] took me aside and told me, 'You're stealing my licks.' I said, 'I ain't never heard your licks before.' He told me, 'Just be yourself, and you'll get along fine.' I didn't ask for his help, but he explained to me how I could get along better with the Chess brothers, Leonard and Phil." Hawkins revealed, "The second time I went up [to Chicago], Sonny Boy [Williamson II] was sitting in the lobby. We started talking then he reached in his case and pulled out a little flask of whiskey. He said, 'Dale, you want a little taste of this?' I said, 'Sonny, man I'd like to, but I got to go in and see Mr. Chess. We don't have enough money; that darn amplifier blew out. We got a gig to get us home, but I got to have an amp.' He said, 'Let me tell you what you do, don't sweat that. People out there in the world gonna try to get you to do all kinds of crazy things. Don't do that; just keep your little flask around and when you feel like something coming on just take you a little sip of this.' I said, 'I better not Sonny,' and as he started to put it back in his briefcase, I said, 'Give me that bottle man.' I took a big slug and went in and got my money." While recording with Hawkins, Dean Mathis recollected seeing Bo Diddley at Chess.

In 1960, Hawkins replaced Hy Lit as host of *The Big Big Beat*, aka *The Dale Hawkins Show*: "Hy was really deep into payola, so CBS took the show off [the air] because they didn't want the bad publicity. They then came and asked if I would be interested in it. I said, 'I don't know what to do.' The director said, 'Don't worry about it.' It took all week to get ready for thirty minutes. I wasn't used to being an emcee, a dancer, and a singer on the same TV show. We had a choreographer [who taught us] dance steps, which I had no problem with at all. I never took a lesson in my life, but I could dance as well as they could." There were seven other dancers besides Hawkins. The show featured guests such as Lloyd Price, Johnny Preston, The Flamingos, Ray Stevens, Little Willie John, and Connie Francis and aired on WCAU-TV in Philadelphia. Hawkins remarked, "We tried to find the master tapes, but they're nowhere to be found. I'd like to see them." That same year, Hawkins asked to be let out of his contract with Chess. He moved onto several different labels: Atlantic, Zonk, Tilt, ABC-Paramount, and Lincoln with little fanfare. In 1962, Hawkins traveled to Miami, Florida, to record a live album at the Peppermint Lounge. Roulette Records then released *Let's All Twist at the Miami Beach Peppermint Lounge.*

By that time, Hawkins' recording career had begun to wane, so he changed his focus to behind the board. He had helped Merle Kilgore and Johnny Horton master their demos of "Whispering Pines" and "Honky Tonk Man" at KWKH. Those experiences gave him invaluable lessons in production. In 1964, he went to work as an A&R man for Stan Lewis and his new label, Paula Records. Hawkins brought John Fred and Joe Stampley to Lewis' attention. Stampley had come into the record store, wanting to sing for Lewis, but he was too busy so instead told Hawkins to listen to him. Upon his recommendation, Lewis decided to sign Stampley. Hawkins produced Joe Stampley and the Uniques' "Not Too Long Ago," which peaked at number sixty-six in April 1965; The Five Americans' "Western Union," which scored a number five position in March 1967; Jon and Robin's "Do it Again a Little Bit Slower," which went to number eighteen in 1967, and Bruce Channel's "Mr. Bus Driver," which rounded out at number ninety in December 1967. In fact, Hawkins, while executive vice president at Abnak, tried to manage Channel and find him some bookings. In 1969, Hawkins once again stepped in front of the microphone when he recorded ten songs for the album, *LA, Memphis, and Tyler*: "Dan Penn and I wrote some of it together, and I did all of the arranging. I had Ry Cooder, James Burton, and Buggs Henderson on guitar, Taj Mahal on percussion, and Joe Osborn played an eight string bass." A year later, Hawkins moved to Los Angeles and became the A&R representative for RCA. According to Lewis, Osborn had gotten Hawkins the job. There he produced Harry Nilsson's "Everybody's Talkin'" and Michael Nesmith's "Joanne": "I enjoyed producing at times. It took a lot out of me because I was so focused on working on it. It's got to be right, or I don't want anything to do with it." In 2006, he produced Kenny Brown's critically acclaimed album *Goin' Back to Mississippi.*

In 1981, he entered rehab to kick his addictions to amphetamines and hard liquor. He had quit his job in Los Angeles and returned to Louisiana: "Even though I left the good money as a producer, I left to save myself."[16] After he finished his year long stint, Hawkins started an intervention program for teens in Louisiana, which he had for five years. Once sober, he made his first trip overseas to perform at a festival in Amsterdam. In 1985, he received his master's degree, mostly through correspondence school: "I was really proud of that." Ten years later, thanks to a $63,000 back royalty check from MCA, he was able to build his own studio, which was aptly named Hawk's Nest.

In 1999, Hawkins issued his first album in thirty years. *Wildcat Tamer* received rave reviews. That same year, he appeared at the New Orleans Jazz and Heritage Festival and the Chicago Blues Festival. Hawkins was then bestowed with the honor of being inducted into the Louisiana Music Hall of Fame.

In 2008, *Oxford American* magazine invited Hawkins to do a show at the Club Ground Zero in Clarksdale, Mississippi: "I never played Mississippi in my life." In 1965, he had recorded John Lee Hooker's "Boogie Chillen'": "I did it with the One O'Clock Lab Band [a jazz ensemble] out of North Texas State University. Man, we kicked it in and wore it out." In 2009, *Oxford American* released the previously unreleased track on their two CD compilation set, *10th Anniversary Edition: The Southern Music CDs*.

In April 2009, Hawkins thrilled rockabilly enthusiasts with a short set at the Viva Las Vegas Weekender. While there, he was reunited with an old friend, Harvey Fuqua from the Moonglows. He had sung background on a few of Hawkins' early tracks, including "Lifeguard Man": "I didn't know that he was even on the show. This big black man was sitting right outside the stage door. He said, 'Hey, come here.' I said, 'Okay, how you doin?' I introduced myself, and he said, 'I know who you are; do you know who I am?' He said, 'Harvey.' I said, 'Chess, Moonglows, is that you?' He said, 'Yeah, and you still got it. Give me a hug.'" They hadn't seen one another since the late 1950s.

Hawkins had aspirations of a new album and touring as much as possible: "I like to [always] have a project. It takes your mind off of thinking about things that you don't want to." Unfortunately, those plans quickly disappeared once he discovered that his battle with colon cancer was in its final stages. On February 13, 2010, Hawkins passed away. At his funeral, Bob Sullivan and Joe Stampley were in attendance while James Burton gave a note of condolence as he was on tour in London. After the memorial service, there was a jam session, which featured his brother Jerry, Maggie Warwick (formerly Margaret Lewis), and Joe Osborn. His younger sibling sang "Susie-Q." Hawkins was then interred at his family's burial plot, Hawkins Hollow, in the Ozark Mountains.

Through it all, Hawkins never strayed far from his true love, which was music. Harris related, "I remember Dale as a dashing handsome young man with a lot of personality. I liked Dale very much, and I thought he was underrated. His career didn't go anywhere near as far as I thought it should have."

Big Jay McNeely

Hypnotizing audiences with his electrifying stage show and honking saxophone, Big Jay McNeely stands apart from the legions of sax players that followed. As he transformed his style from jazz into rhythm and blues, he was often criticized by other musicians for only being able to play one note. McNeely rebuffed, "The repetition is what excites people. That's the key—no matter how many notes you play; it's how you play them."[17] His unusual technique produced hits on the rhythm and blues charts: "Deacon's Hop," which was number one, "Wild Wig," which peaked at number twelve, and "There Is Something on Your Mind," which scored a number five position. McNeely's influential career was documented in a 1994 biography by Jim Dawson entitled *Nervous Man Nervous: Big Jay McNeely and the Rise of the Honking Tenor Saxophone*.

Cecil James McNeely was born on April 29, 1927, in Watts, a neighborhood in Los Angeles, California. Musicianship ran in the family. While attending grammar school, McNeely played tunes taught to him by his brother Bob. At sixteen, he became a serious stu-

Big Jay McNeely (left) and his brother Bob (right) entrance the audience with their 1949 instrumental hit "Deacon's Hop" (courtesy Big Jay McNeely).

dent of the saxophone: "I was working at Firestone Rubber Company [eight-hour days]. The first four were cool, but [during] the last four I'd say, 'Man there has to be a better way to make a living.'" His parents were poor, so they couldn't afford to buy him a saxophone. Instead, McNeely's family gave him an alto sax that once belonged to his slain cousin. At this time, he formed a jazz band with fellow schoolmates Sonny Criss and Hampton Hawes: "They went into jazz, while I went and studied from Joseph Cadaly, who played first chair saxophone in the RKO studio orchestra. For a whole year, I became very legit [by studying theory and harmonics]. I sounded like a cello on the saxophone."

McNeely made the transition from jazz to rhythm and blues because "I didn't have a pitch perfect ear like Sonny Criss. I still love jazz, and that influence is there even in the wild powerhouse tunes [that] I play." Incidentally, his musical influences include fellow saxophonists Charlie Parker, Ben Webster, Coleman Hawkins, and Lester Young. Recording and jamming with the Johnny Otis Band at the Barrelhouse Club in Watts, a neighborhood in Los Angeles, provided him with invaluable experience. By late 1948, McNeely was offered a recording contract with Savoy Records. Its president, Herman Lubinsky, christened Cecil with a new name: "He didn't like it because he didn't think that was good enough for a professional."

Since McNeely wasn't sure what his first offering would be, he paid a visit to Pete Canard, who owned a record shop in Watts. Canard gave him a copy of Glenn Miller's "Nothing but Soul." The sock cymbal percussion on the song captured the sound that McNeely was looking for and gave him the inspiration to write "Deacon's Hop." Peaking at number one on the *Billboard* rhythm and blues charts, the single brought forth the honking saxophone phenomenon, spawning hits such as Paul Williams' "The Hucklebuck" and Hal Singer's "Cornbread." In this early incarnation of the band, McNeely had his brother Bob on baritone saxophone and his other brother Dylan on bass.

Co-owner of the Barrelhouse Club, Bardu Ali, advised the young singer that if he went on tour to promote the single he would end up broke: "When 'Deacon's Hop' was tearing the country down [in early 1949], I didn't go on the road at all. It was better because I probably would have ended up owing the government money." His stay at home attitude proved beneficial to his career. In July, McNeely and his brother Bob played Wrigley Field in Los Angeles. They were on the same bill as Lionel Hampton. McNeely recalled, "Lionel's wife was very cautious. She wouldn't let anyone steal the show from him. When she saw us playing, after Jesse Belvin got through singing, she pulled me off the bandstand and paid me off." However, Hampton then invited McNeely to play saxophone on "Flying Home." McNeely added, "My brother and I went to the bandstand, which was seated behind second base. I went past third and up into the grandstand. People were yelling 'Hometown Boy,' so I came all the way around. When I got back to the bandstand, Hampton marched his whole band out to home plate. When he got there, I lay down on second base and crawled. People were screaming and hollering. I kept on crawling down into the dugout. Then everybody followed me." The next day, the newspaper read 'Hometown Boy Steals Show': "I never worked with Hampton again."

McNeely packed clubs and schoolhouses in Los Angeles. The kids loved his wild stage show, a fact that bewildered city officials: "They couldn't stop the kids [from attending my shows], and they didn't understand why they were responding to me the way they were." The city officials assumed that the kids had to be on drugs in order to react the way that they did. The first time he incorporated lying on the floor with playing his saxophone was at a show in Clarksville, Tennessee: "The blacks didn't like you lying on the floor; they thought that was degrading, but they were the ones that caused me to do it. We had a hot band, but the people didn't respond to anything we played. After intermission, I got down on my knees, nothing happened, so then I lay on the floor. [That's when] they started going crazy." The same routine caused a sensation in Texas and Los Angeles. McNeely was eventually banned from playing in Los Angeles, "either the cops would come and shut us down, or they wouldn't give me a permit." Even big stars of the day held opposition to working with McNeely: "I was supposed to go on tour with Nat King Cole. When I was just a kid, Nat came out to the garage and said, 'You guys sound great; you'll make it someday,' but the one time I opened for him, he said, 'You'll never work with me again.'" In San Diego, McNeely was jailed for supposedly disturbing the peace since he had wandered off the bandstand and onto the street. The police arrested him in the middle of a song. The band continued playing and didn't even realize he was gone until the police called and told them to post bail.

All the other saxophonists of the day began to emulate his stage antics, so to stand out; McNeely adorned his saxophone with fluorescent paint. He had gotten the idea after witnessing a female stripper use the paint to her advantage. Besides being a show stopping performer, he also cut some wild recordings, including "3-D" for the Federal label.

In the 1950s, McNeely headlined package tours with Bill Doggett, Faye Adams, Etta James, Little Richard, and Big Joe Turner for the Top Ten Revue: "It was a tough, tough show. It was kickin'." McNeely also participated in one Alan Freed show alongside Carl Perkins and Buddy Holly.

In 1959, Little Sonny Warner was the featured vocalist on "There Is Something on Your Mind." McNeely remembered, "I carried 'There Is Something on Your Mind' to Hollywood, and nobody wanted it. Disc jockey Hunter Hancock usually put songs on the air and saw what got response before he would spend any money to release it [on his Swingin' label], but he said, 'For you, I'll put it out.' I knew I had a hit record." The recording pinnacled at number five on the *Billboard* R&B singles chart while it rounded out at number forty-four on the *Billboard* Hot 100. A year later, Bobby Marchan scored a chart topper with the single. Incidentally, B.B. King, Etta James, Freddy Fender, Gene Vincent, and Professor Longhair have also recorded "There Is Something on Your Mind."

Warner was lead vocalist on the majority of McNeely's early recordings. Other vocalists for McNeely included his wife Jackie Davis and Johnny Torres. When he returned to the limelight in the 1980s, after working as a mail carrier for twelve years, McNeely decided he would do his own singing: "I always had vocalists because I didn't think I could sing. I always wanted perfection, so I went out and hired somebody. I started singing because people relate to words. Being able to play the saxophone compliments my singing. I couldn't go out singing without my saxophone. I started to sing like I play."

One of the highlights of his show is when he treats the crowd to "Big Fat Mama." McNeely recollected, "'Big Fat Mama' was written in Australia when I worked with The Mighty Reapers. This cat, T Bone Walker, was playing real funky blues, and I just sat down and wrote 'Big Fat Mama.' When we performed that night, I didn't play the song because I just made it up for the TV show [appearance]. Some lady [came up to me and said], 'I was waiting for you to play 'Big Fat Mama.' I then started putting it into my repertoire. It is a good tune for me to play because it really gets the audience." In fact, his CD *Party Time*, which was recorded in Amsterdam and released in March 2009, features "Big Fat Mama" along with fourteen other songs.

In 1987, the National Academy of Recording Arts and Sciences allowed the first ever blues ensemble to take center stage at the Grammy Awards. McNeely joined B.B. King, Etta James, Dr. John, Koko Taylor, and Willie Dixon in a twelve minute jam fest: "When I lay on the floor, six thousand people stood up." Two years later, McNeely honked outside the Quasimodo Club in West Berlin, Germany, on the same evening that the Berlin Wall crumbled. The German press remarked that McNeely was the modern day Joshua.

In 2000, the Experience Music Project in Seattle, Washington purchased McNeely's original Conn saxophone from him at a sum of $10,000 for an exhibit, which is still on display. At eighty-seven years old, he still finds time to record and tour all over the world. McNeely knows what it takes to excite a crowd, and he sticks to that formula: "It's very impressive to dress in a white tuxedo [and wail away on a glowing saxophone]. Your appearance is a key factor. When I play rockabilly [festivals], I keep everything kicking. You can't play anything slow."

The Orlons

The Orlons were formed in Philadelphia, Pennsylvania, and its vocalists featured Shirley Brickley (born December 9, 1944), Rosetta Hightower (born June 23, 1944), Marlena Davis (born October 4, 1944), and Stephen Caldwell (born November 22, 1943). While attending high school, they often swapped gigs with The Dovells. After two releases on Cameo-Parkway, The Orlons finally struck a chord with listeners. Their third single, "The Wah-Watusi," peaked at number two on the *Billboard* charts. To promote their latest platter, they appeared on *American Bandstand*. More national hits followed, including "Don't Hang Up" and "South Street." In 1964, Davis quit the group and then Caldwell moved on in 1965. A year later, the remaining members moved onto a new label, Calla Records. By 1968, their popularity waned in the United States, so the group disbanded. Hightower became a solo artist and backing vocalist for other singers. In 1988, Caldwell and Davis reunited and performed in a reinvented version of The Orlons until her death five years later. Today, Caldwell continues to entertain audiences as the sole original member of The Orlons.

Prior to The Orlons, all four members were involved in other bands. Shirley Brickley, Marlena Davis, and Rosetta Hightower were in a quintet called Audrey and the Teenettes along with Brickley's sisters: Jean and Audrey. The pairing didn't last long since they were still in junior high school, and the Brickley's mother didn't approve of them playing in nightclubs. At the time, Stephen Caldwell was the lead singer of an all-male group, The Romeos. He recalled, "Shirley lived two doors from me; Marlena about four blocks from me, and Rosetta was about six blocks away. One Saturday after doing chores, the girls were out on the porch harmonizing when I picked up the lead on 'Daddy's Home.' From then on, we started singing and doing talent shows at school. We did about seven of them, and we often came in either first or second. [They usually competed against The Cashmeres, aka The Dovells.] Our group was unique because you had the girl groups, the guy groups, and then us (a guy with three girls). I sang lead but tried to make the girls' harmonies stand out. The talent progressed, and we continued to do little parties and got a manager. Later, we moved onto clubs. We worked a place called the Imperial Ballroom [in Philadelphia] quite often, where we did a forty minute set."[18] Song suggestions from peers, such as The Silhouettes' "Get a Job," The Miracles' "Shop Around," and Ray Charles' "Hit the Road Jack," had expanded their repertoire. The group's musical influences were Smokey Robinson and the Miracles, The Marvelettes, Ruby and the Romantics, Jackie Wilson, and Shep and the Limelites. Caldwell cited his personal influences as Brook Benton, Ray Charles, and Muddy Waters: "Those were the ones that I really felt that I could mimic."

The foursome had browsed through several books and thought of various material names before deciding upon The Orlons. Caldwell remembered, "DuPont had a fabric called Orlon. I had a black Orlon sweater, and one day, the sweater label turned up and was rubbing against my neck. I took the sweater off, looked, and it said Orlon." There was another group who attended Overbrook High School that had a material name, The Cashmeres, who later became The Dovells. Caldwell conveyed, "We were rivals and competitors but the best of friends. Performing was something that we did for enjoyment." If there was a gig they couldn't do, then they'd offer it to The Cashmeres. Caldwell added, "Lenny [Barry] always said he's

In 1962, The Orlons scored their first national hit with "The Wah-Watusi." Clockwise from left: Marlena Davis, Rosetta Hightower, Shirley Brickley, and Stephen Caldwell (courtesy Stephen Caldwell).

a black man locked up in a white man's body. He said that all through school, and I wholeheartedly believe that he felt that way."

It was Barry who arranged The Orlons' audition with Kal Mann for Cameo-Parkway Records. Caldwell related, "At our first audition in January 1960, I did four or five songs, which included 'Daddy's Home,' 'For Your Love,' and 'Hit the Road Jack.' They liked us, but they were looking for a female lead. They gave us the opportunity to come back. We took three months, and each of the girls learned two songs. That was sometimes hard because they didn't want to do it. I had to push, push, and push. Rose was the hardest because she didn't want to sing lead at all. [Incidentally, Brickley came from a musical background where she and her mother played piano, and her father played guitar. Davis just needed to be coached.] I encouraged them to do it, so we could get with the company. We went back in October, and we were signed to a contract with a six month option, three sides. If the option was picked up, the contract would be renewed for two more sides." The girls were enthused by the idea of national exposure. Since they were all minors, their parents also had to sign the contract.

Originally, Cameo-Parkway couldn't decide who the lead vocalist should be, so as it turned out, each girl had a chance at fronting the group. Davis sang the lead on their first release "I'll Be True," Brickley took over the reins for "(Happy Birthday) Mr. Twenty-One," and then Hightower had her turn with "The Wah-Watusi." Cameo-Parkway executive Dave Appell ultimately chose Hightower to be the lead vocalist because she was selling records. Caldwell acknowledged, "They were looking for a certain sound and what they called the value of talent. 'I'll Be True' was soft and mellow, and it did well locally. '(Happy Birthday) Mr. Twenty-One' did well nationally, but it still wasn't what they were looking for. In 1962, when we did the dance tune 'The Wah-Watusi,' it took off. We then felt Rose was going to be the spirit of the group. She became the star. The fame took over, and she started appreciating the fact that people recognized her as a lead singer. It made us realize we had talent and that we were able to produce for the company. That was a remarkable thing for us to have a record that sold a million copies. However, it didn't reflect in the funds that we received." Cameo-Parkway had entered a clause into the last line of their contract where they would pay for promotion, transportation, lodging, etc. upon the condition that it would all be paid back once they scored a hit. Therefore, even though "The Wah-Watusi" was awarded gold record status, The Orlons didn't see any of the two or three percent of the royalties.

"After 'The Wah-Watusi,' I had a little handle on not spending a whole lot of unnecessary money. I looked for a bargain. When we did publicity photographs, I picked the photo company." Also, instead of renting a car, they bought their own car, which sat in a garage ready to go whenever it was needed for out of town trips. Caldwell added, "They were out to make money and had a book of regulations that they went by. I opened that book and said, 'I don't like these.' I then had an option to either use theirs or use mine. I started using mine because it was beneficial to us to spend less money. They agreed upon it once I showed them that our money was not their money. When they gave us an advance, it was still our money that they gave us. I told them, 'I'm in this to make money, not pay it all back to the company.' I had married at fifteen, so I had a wife and a baby at home. It was a job to me." Caldwell declared, "Once the company sold in 1967, ABKCO could reproduce the records and sell them without paying royalties. I sued them thinking that they owned me royalties, but I found out that's not how the contract read." In 1993, "Don't Hang Up" had been used in the movie *Dennis the Menace*. No royalties were due to The Orlons if the song had only been reproduced on vinyl or CD, but if other media, such as a movie or a play, used it then they got paid. Caldwell won his case in that regard.

Besides their own songs, Brickley, Hightower, and Davis provided background vocals on Dee Dee Sharp's "Mashed Potato Time" and "Gravy (For My Mashed Potatoes)." However, they didn't receive credit and only got paid union scale, which was $18.50. Caldwell admitted, "I have to say that I raised a little hell with the label about giving Dee Dee the songs. [He felt they should have gotten the songs because they hadn't yet scored a hit.] I didn't sing on them, and I asked my ladies not to." "Mashed Potato Time" scored a number two position on the charts, while the follow-up "Gravy (For My Mashed Potatoes)" rounded out at number nine. Caldwell later vocally assisted on The Dovells' "Hully Gully Baby," which was a number twenty-seven tune, and "Bristol Twistin' Annie," which secured a number twenty-five position on the charts.

Once The Orlons became hit makers, they were booked regularly: "There was a promoter out of the South named Henry Wynn. We did his tours and then we did Dick Clark's Cavalcade of Stars. That's where we made our money. It wasn't a lot, but the more you worked on the road, your price went up. Your popularity gauged how much you made. We were working constantly, but just as quick as we would get two or three days off we were back in the studio." In July 1962, they did a Dick Clark Cavalcade of Stars tour on a non-air-conditioned bus that lasted twenty-eight days and covered the South, East, and Midwest along with Canada. Some of the other acts included Dick and Dee Dee, Paul and Paula, Chubby Checker, The Dovells, and The Tymes. Those Southern tours, called the Chitlin' circuit, were tough. At that time, segregation was rampant, especially in Little Rock, Arkansas and Chattanooga, Tennessee: "Just as quickly as we crossed the line out of Chattanooga, the sheriff pulled us over and took us to the general store. He counted the number of people on the bus and the number that went into the store. Then he went to the owner and said, 'How many people you serving here?' Everybody had to buy something, whether you wanted to or not. We had tours where we did white shows first and then white and black shows second." Dividing lines were set up between black and white audiences: "That was almost the norm. At a show in Jackson, Mississippi, we had gotten there around seven o'clock in the morning, so we were in the facility most of the day. When they opened concessions at four o'clock in the afternoon, Marlena went down to get a Dr. Pepper. She was told, 'We don't serve y'all at this time.' I saw she was in a huff, so I went down to find out what was going on. The lady told me the same thing. I said, 'What do you mean, you don't serve us at this time?' [She then gave her explanation.] I said, 'Okay,' but Marlena said, 'Get the bags and pack our stuff because we're not working.' I, Frankie Valli, everybody started packing up because we weren't gonna do the show. Then we found out that the first show was an all-white show. The second would be all whites downstairs and all blacks upstairs. I said, 'We're definitely not gonna do this under those conditions. No way. We're not used to that, and we don't put up with that.' Promoters were up in the air on what to do, but they changed their minds quickly. They ended up calling the radio station and [the disc jockey] announced every eight minutes that both shows would be open to everybody. We had two dynamite shows that night." Some of the other acts on those Southern tours included The Marvelettes, Ruby and the Romantics, and Dionne Warwick.

In October 1962, Cameo-Parkway issued the 45 rpm single, "Don't Hang Up" b/w "The Conservative." Caldwell indicated, "I did the 'no, no' in my regular voice and then on a playback I did the frog voice. We were listening to the take, and the engineer said, 'Who did that? What was that?' I said, 'That's just a voice that I do.' He then said, 'We're gonna play it back, and you put that in there.' It was just on a whim and something that I had tried to do. In doing so, my eyes watered, and my throat got sore, but I was determined. Once my eyes stopped watering and my throat stopped tingling, it was perfected. It wasn't from Clarence 'Frogman' Henry, but from watching Gene Autry and cowboys all the time." That vocal trick made the record stand out to listeners, and helped "Don't Hang Up" reach number four on the *Billboard* charts.

Caldwell was okay with being reassigned to baritone harmony instead of lead, as he explained, "With The Romeos, I had trained myself to be versatile and had learned enough about music that I could sing wherever I had to be. When it came to having to sing between the girls, I didn't have to, I just went underneath them. [As the only male member] it was rough sometimes with three young ladies with three different attitudes, trying to satisfy everyone and keeping us all on the same page. I was the road manager and the go-getter for anything that was needed. It didn't bother me because it was part of what needed to be done for the group."

The Orlons' next release was "South Street," which was originally titled "Sansom Street." According to Caldwell, "South Street had a lot of pawn shops, men's stores, and shoe stores, while Sansom was the jazz street of Philadelphia. It had the hippest people." When the song's title was changed to "South Street," that fact was mentioned, and it was the first time the word hippies was ever used on a record. "South Street" peaked at number three on the pop charts. That same year, 1963, they had two other songs hit the charts: "Not Me" at number twelve and "Crossfire" at number nineteen.

In 1964, Davis left the group and then Caldwell quit in 1965. He commented, "The ladies really decided that for me. They had set up a meeting with the manager at ten o'clock in the morning. At two in the afternoon, they finally called the office and said they didn't want to work with me anymore. I said, 'Fine.' I contacted my lawyer, and he said, 'Stephen, you got a contract until the end of November, get back and collect the money,' which I did." In 1966, Brickley and Hightower regrouped with Sandy Person and relocated to a new record label, Calla. Yvonne Young and Audrey Brickley were also members for a short time. In 1968, the group went their separate ways. Hightower went onto lead a successful solo career and backed artists such as Joe Cocker, Muddy Waters, and John Holt. Shirley Brickley was murdered by a home invader in 1973. Davis became an executive secretary. In Philadelphia, Caldwell managed three different groups of young men, was a shop steward of the bus drivers' trade union, and then became administrator and trustee for the union's legal fund. He also served on the Philadelphia Board of Education for twenty-nine years. It wasn't until 1988 that Caldwell and Davis as The Original Orlons once again graced the stage: "When the trademark for the name The Orlons expired in 1986, Jolly Joyce Agency's Norman Jacobs picked it up and put a group together. One day, [disc jockey] Hy Lit called me and said, 'Stephen Caldwell?' I said, 'Yeah, this is Stephen Caldwell.' He then said, 'How in the hell are you letting somebody come out there using your name?' I replied, 'What do you mean, using my name?' I'm thinking he's talking about my name, Stephen Caldwell. He said, 'Naw, The Orlons. I hired the group thinking it was you.' I told him, 'Well you didn't call my house like you are calling me now.' I found out they were awful. In fact, the young lady had cussed him out. I said, 'Well I didn't know anything about it, but if you can give me some information, I'll check it out.' About two days later, he called me with some dates that they were working. Marlena had said she was never going to sing again, but I grabbed her and took her down to see them. They were working right here in Philadelphia. The group was horrible, looked like they were in a burlesque show, and you would never know that they were singing our songs. Marlena looked at me, and I looked at her. She started on one side, and I started on the other side of the venue, handing out our picture of the original members and telling folks that the ones on stage never have been and are not who they are supposed to be representing." For their next imposter gig, Caldwell informed *The Philadelphia Inquirer*, the city's biggest newspaper. He wrote a letter letting them know that they were sponsoring frauds. Two weeks later, Caldwell received a phone call with a request for an interview. The Orlons garnered the front page's attention. Jacobs claimed he had tried to contact Caldwell and offered him $1,000, which he refused: "It's not about the money; it's just the idea of duping the people of Philadelphia." Davis, Caldwell, and two new recruits started rehearsing in October 1988. Coco Muhammad was a member of the ill-fated group, but Caldwell retrained her. He eventually regained the trademark, but is now listed as The Original Orlons. Davis remained with the group until her death from lung cancer in 1993.

Nowadays, Caldwell participates in fifteen to thirty shows a year. However, he hasn't performed in Europe since 1964. The Orlons' current lineup is Cynthia Powell, Coco Muhammad, Jean Brickley-Maddox, and Caldwell. Besides the group's signature hits, audiences are treated to "Higher and Higher," "Let the Good Times Roll," "Lovers Never Say Goodbye," and "For Your Love." They have a variety of fifty-five songs in their repertoire. New fans are being made thanks to movies like 2011's *The Help*, in which "The Wah-Watusi" appeared. Caldwell is proud of their legacy and the fact that he made amends with the girls: "People make mistakes."

Chapter Two

Rockabilly Pioneers

Clyde Stacy

While teenagers were going crazy for Elvis Presley, Clyde Stacy was creating a name for himself in Oklahoma. In high school, he played in a band with Buddy Holly and Waylon Jennings. By 1957, he and his own band the Nitecaps had recorded their first single, "Hoy Hoy" b/w "So Young," thereby establishing the Tulsa sound. Appearances on *American Bandstand* followed and throughout the 1960s and 1970s, he played numerous club bookings. However, it wasn't until 1982 that he toured overseas. In 2011, he performed at the Viva Las Vegas Weekender and England's Hemsby Rock 'n' Roll Weekender.

Haskell Clyde Stacy was born on August 11, 1936, in Checotah, Oklahoma. He began singing and playing guitar at an early age: "I've sung ever since I can remember. I used to sing to my five little sisters. [That way] I had a built-in captive audience."[1] Similar to most musicians from the South, he had a religious upbringing. In fact, two of his uncles and his grandfather were Baptist preachers. Stacy recalled, "If they told me I was going to sing Sunday then I'd sing." At the age of seven, Stacy and his family moved from Checotah to the western part of Oklahoma: "My dad bought a farm in a little town called Binger. We came back to Checotah when I was fourteen, but we didn't stay there too long because I had an uncle who was looking for work and heard about some in West Texas. We decided to go with him, and that's how I ended up in Lubbock [Texas]."

He attended Lubbock High School with Buddy Holly and Sonny Curtis. Stacy commented, "Sonny is one of the greatest guitar players of all-time. He is probably as good as Chet Atkins." Waylon Jennings also hung around the guys quite a bit: "Waylon went to school across town at Montclair High School. We didn't see him on a daily basis, but we saw him nearly every weekend. He played guitar or bass for Buddy. Waylon didn't sing very much at that time, and he's a good singer. I really liked Waylon. He was a great guy, what you saw was what you got. Waylon didn't take any crap from anybody."

While attending high school, Stacy befriended Holly: "Buddy was a tall gangly kid, who was very shy, especially around girls. I went to school with him for six months or a year before I actually met him. The first time I remember seeing Buddy was when I heard this kid walking down the hallway carrying his books singing 'Kaw-Liga' just as loud as he could. I told him, 'You're going to get into trouble making all that noise here in the hallway.' We then got to talking about music."

Stacy added, "Buddy and I were good friends. We worked radio stations together. I played with him in his band, had rehearsal in his garage. We'd play together at the local roller rink during intermission. We didn't get paid for it, just did it for some exposure and for something to do. Buddy was more into rock and roll and rockabilly [although they performed country music together]. Buddy loved Hank Williams, Sr." They once even competed in the same talent show: "It was a real close deal. It could have gone either way, but I beat him. He came in second. I'm a better singer, but he's a better musician. He was very cordial about it. We were just young guys. It didn't matter to us back then."

The last time Stacy ran into Holly was in 1958 when they appeared on the same television program in Baltimore, Maryland: "I was promoting my record 'You Want Love,' and Buddy was promoting 'Peggy Sue.'

While in the recording booth, Clyde Stacy takes a listen to his latest platter, "Hoy Hoy" (courtesy Clyde Stacy).

We sat backstage talking. He was plunking on his guitar and saying, 'I can't get this guitar in tune. It doesn't sound right.'" After Stacy tuned Holly's guitar, they continued their conversation: "Buddy told me that he had a tour coming up, several cities he was going to. He said when he got back, he was gonna get married [to a woman he had met in New York], which was gonna be in a couple of weeks. He was just thrilled to death." Stacy remembered, "I liked Buddy a lot, so naturally I supported him, and I was a fan of anything that he did. He was a good musician. I knew that he was going to be big."

In regard to Stacy's own musical aspirations, he started out singing country music like many of his contemporaries but soon switched to rockabilly/rock and roll: "It wasn't anything except necessary. Back in the '50's and early '60's, you couldn't sell country music. They didn't want to hear it, especially back East. I knew if I was going to do anything I'd have to go to rock and roll/rockabilly, so that's what I did. If it had been entirely up to me, and I was in a position to do anything I wanted to, I would never have done rock and roll; I would have done country. Personally I like country better." In 1955, he formed his rockabilly band, the Nitecaps.

After the transition, Candlelight Records took an interest: "I knew [Don Wallace] who was a disc jockey in Tulsa [Oklahoma], and he knew Woody Hinderling, owner of the record company. Don called Woody and got him to come down and listen to us at The Nitecap in downtown Tulsa. I talked to him for a while after the show: Don, he, and I together. Then he came back about three weeks later, and I signed a contract with him." Stacy and the Nitecaps played the nightclub five to six nights a week for a year before recording their first single, "Hoy Hoy" b/w "So Young," at Oral Roberts Studio in Tulsa. This session was the only time the Nitecaps, which included John D. Levan on lead guitar, Rick Eilerts on upright bass, and Bill Talbert on drums, were used. Once in New York, session musicians were hired. Candlelight was interested strictly in Stacy and not the band. Wallace acted as his manager locally then later Hinderling took over managerial duties: "Woody decided what I did and what I didn't do."

The 45 rpm single "Hoy Hoy" b/w "So Young," was released in June 1957. The latter song was banned by some radio stations because they felt the female backing vocalist, Pat Peyton, sounded too seductive. Despite that, the tune peaked at number sixty-eight on the *Billboard* charts. "So Young" was later released on the Argyle label. It hit number one hundred that time around. Stacy recollected: "There's a young fella here in Oklahoma that wrote 'Hoy Hoy.' [Stacy only recalled the songwriter's last name, which was Jones.] He did a home recording of it and got it played but never thought to have it copyrighted." It was originally sung in a slow blues tempo: "I heard this kid [who was probably eighteen or nineteen] doing 'Hoy Hoy' in a club. After they got through, I asked him about it. I said, 'Where'd you get that song? Did you write it?' He said, 'No that's an old blues song, comes from down in New Orleans.' He wasn't exactly right. It was an old blues song, but it didn't come from New Orleans." "Hoy Hoy" soon became a staple of Stacy's live set: "I used to do 'Hoy Hoy' everywhere because it was up-tempo. However, if I had to do it over, I would do it differently. I would do it a little slower, more like a down home southern blues type song."

Thanks to "Hoy Hoy," Stacy has been credited with creation of the Tulsa sound: "Up until that time Tulsa was pretty much a country music town. I came on the scene in '56 and actually '57 before I had any kind of recognition. We performed rock and roll songs. I had about the only band in town [doing that type of music], so they credit me as the founder." Other Tulsa sound artists include John D. Levan, J.J. Cale, and Leon Russell.

As for Stacy's own musical influences: "Actually, I don't know if I could pick one person that was my influence. My mom taught me how to play guitar. She was a guitar player, [although] not professionally. She just played around the house, and she sang [gospel]. When I first got interested in music, most of it was country: Hank Williams, Sr., Webb Pierce, Carl Smith, Marty Robbins, and Ray Price. My dad would put on the *Grand Ole Opry* every Saturday night." Stacy also really liked Nat King Cole, Arthur Prysock, and Elvis Presley: "I thought Elvis was fantastic. Every time I listened to his records, I would get mad. Nobody should be that good."

Nineteen fifty-seven turned out to be a banner year for Stacy. After a move to Scranton, Pennsylvania, he recorded his sessions at Bell Sound in New York City. He appeared on *American Bandstand*, in which he sang "Baby Shame." A second appearance would occur in 1959, in which he performed "You Want Love." Stacy also participated in one of Alan Freed's concerts at the Paramount Theater in New York City: "That was a big thrill, but I was scared to death. My manager knew Alan personally. He just called and got me on there. They had so many acts that we were only allowed to do one song." The song he chose to sing was "So Young": "I asked somebody backstage [what to sing]. The guy told me '[All the other acts will] be doing rock and roll, fast up-tempo songs, so it wouldn't hurt to do one a little slower.' I think that's why I did it, [but] they probably didn't have my best interest at heart."

Around this time, he became lifelong friends with actor Michael Landon: "I knew him really well. I met Michael in New York City in 1957. He had the same agent as I did. He was promoting his movie *I Was a Teenage Werewolf*, and I was promoting my record. We hit all the TV and radio stations [across the country]. He was a character, loved to joke around and have fun. We stayed in touch for a long time. The last time I saw him was in Detroit, and we went to see his movie since he had never seen it. I didn't see him again for twenty years. He was always trying to get me to come to California. They filmed *Bonanza* up around Lake Tahoe. He said, 'I'll write in something for ya, put you in the show.' It seemed I was always busy when he called. I regret it now. In 1989, I finally went to see him in Los Angeles. He was filming a segment for [his television series] *Highway to Heaven*. I got to talk to him for a little while during the lunch break. It was real good to see him. He was like he always was, still a cut-up. We talked about stuff we used to pull. He still remembered it. Of course I did too, but I didn't think he would. We'd do skits together. For instance, we were in a hotel in Kansas City [Missouri] back in '57, and there were people standing in the lobby waiting for the elevator. We were all going up to our rooms. Out of the blue, Michael said, 'Can I have your attention please,' so everybody looked at him. He said, 'I know you're wondering why I called you all here?' He stalled for a minute, looked around, and said, 'Darn I forgot.' We then turned around and walked away. He was always pulling things like that."

In January 1958, Columbia Records released the Collins Kids' version of "Hoy Hoy": "To tell you the truth, I never even knew they did it until I went to Oklahoma City last year." In October 2009, Stacy played at the History Center in Oklahoma City. The Collins Kids and Wanda Jackson were also featured guests.

In 1959, Stacy saw his last release on Candlelight with "You Want Love" b/w "Once in a While." Benny Goodman's younger brother Gene owned the publishing company and was part owner of the record company, G&H Records, which owned both Candlelight and Bullseye Records. After Candlelight opted not to renew Stacy's contract, he recorded for Bullseye. In total, there were four releases on Candlelight and two on Bullseye.

Between 1957 and 1959, Stacy played shows with Bobby Darin, Jerry Lee Lewis, Johnny Horton, Frankie Avalon, Conway Twitty, and Patsy Cline: "Patsy was just a wonderful singer, nice person too. I was young, and she just helped me as much as she could, by telling me what to do and what not to do on stage. She was really trying to be helpful." He toured regularly with The Four Flames throughout Canada, where his music was very popular, and had successful club dates in New York, Pennsylvania, and New Jersey: "I met up with them in Scranton, Pennsylvania. They were a quartet that was extremely good. The Four Flames worked with me on the road for several weeks [at a time]. They were Pete DeMarzo on guitar, John Cognetti on bass, Don Joseph on piano, and Sal Mecca on drums." In 1960, Stacy and the Four Flames joined forces with Vernon Sandusky and Big Al Downing and recorded eight demos. "Summertime Blues" was one of the songs they cut.

By 1961, he had signed with Len Records, which was owned by Bobby Poe and Big Al Downing. In fact, Downing wrote two songs for Stacy, "Sit'in Down Crying" and "You're Satisfied." In fact, Len issued both songs as a single. Over the next two years, recording sessions were sporadic. However, Stacy continued to perform, most notably on shows with his friend Leon Russell.

In 1982, he received a call from the owner of Eagle Records in Germany: "I didn't know [people still cared about my music] until this guy from Germany called me. He said, 'If it's okay with you, and you have no objection, I'm going to purchase all your masters. Then I'm gonna release them on an album.' He wanted me to come to Germany, meet him, and also do a show while I was there." Three years later, Stacy retired from the music business: "I quit traveling and playing regularly in '85. I could have kept playing, but I just got tired. [However], when you say you retire you don't really retire because when somebody calls, you still go and play." At the time, he and his oldest son ran a construction business: "He pretty much runs it now. I don't have much to do with it anymore.

Even though he had been out of the limelight, Stacy was still in high demand with fans eager to hear his rockabilly singles: "Hoy Hoy," "Honky Tonk Hardwood Floor," and "I Sure Do Love You Baby." In October 2009, he reemerged at the History Center in Oklahoma City with backing provided by JD McPherson and his band the Starkweather Boys. Stacy acknowledged: "JD is a good friend of mine. [The Starkweather Boys] are a great bunch of guys. I really like them. They want to record with me. If we can come up with some good material, I told JD I'm up for it." Two years later, he performed thirty minute sets at both the Viva Las Vegas Weekender and Hemsby Rock 'n' Roll Weekender. Stacy's original guitarist John D. LeVan joined him onstage in England. Stacy summed up his career by stating: "I never made a fortune, but I sure have lived a lot and met a lot of great people."

Tragically, his comeback was short-lived. On November 6, 2013, Stacy was killed when his car went underneath a five-ton crane truck. Even though he is no longer with us, his musical legacy lives on thanks to fans like the producer of AMC's *Mad Men*, who recently chose Stacy's "So Young" to be included in one of its episodes.

Al Ferrier

On April 11, 2009, Goldband recording artist Al Ferrier made his much anticipated return to live performances with an appearance at the Viva Las Vegas Weekender. Fans were treated to a fifteen minute set, which included his signature tune and personal favorite song, "Let's Go Boppin' Tonight." In 1956, Ferrier began his career with two releases on Goldband: "No No Baby" b/w "I'll Never Do Any Wrong" and "My Baby Done Gone Away" b/w "Too Late Now." Three years later, he returned to the label and recorded "Let's Go Boppin' Tonight." He performed on the *Louisiana Hayride* three times and was a nightclub staple throughout Texas and Louisiana. Once the rockabilly revival began in the late 1970s, Ferrier was one of the first artists to participate. After his 2009 re-emergence, Ferrier was overwhelmed by requests to play overseas.

Al Ferrier was born on August 19, 1935, in Montgomery, Louisiana. His parents, six brothers, and three sisters were all musicians. Ferrier remembered, "My mama played the guitar, and my dad played the fiddle. They used to go to these old timey country dances and play."[2] He added, "I started trying to play a mandolin, but one of my brothers beat me playing that. Then I started trying to pick out tunes on the lead guitar, but another brother beat me doing that. Then I started singing, and they all had to join me because nobody in the family could beat me singing. When I was ten years old, I started singing at the schoolhouse and little parties. I [also] used to go and sing at the barbershop in Montgomery." Incidentally, the first song Ferrier ever sang and played rhythm guitar on was Jimmie Rodgers' "T for Texas." Besides helping their father with the logging business, Ferrier and his brothers participated on radio shows. They started out singing country music but switched to rockabilly when the Hillbilly Cat [Elvis Presley] arrived on the scene.

When Ferrier was seventeen years old, he performed on the *Midway Jamboree* in Gaston, Alabama. Upon his return to Louisiana, he wrote "Let's Go Boppin' Tonight." In fact, that song ushered in the trend of bop music. "Let's Go Boppin' Tonight" became quite popular with the locals and when Ferrier appeared on the *Louisiana Hayride*, Elvis Presley took a liking to it: "When we got to the *Louisiana Hayride*, emcee Horace Logan introduced me to some people on the show: Johnny Cash, Carl Perkins, and Elvis Presley. He called me out in front of Elvis. [Ferrier's brother, Warren, accompanied him on upright bass while another brother, Brian, played lead guitar.] I got three encores on 'Let's Go Boppin' Tonight.' Elvis looked at me, smiled, and said, 'If you'll send that song to Sam Phillips, I'll record it for ya.'"

Ferrier declined his offer since he decided if Presley thought he could record it, it must be good enough for him to record. Unfortunately, it took until 1959 before Ferrier made a recording of it. He feels if he had given the song to Presley he would have made something of it: "He probably would have made it a hit because I can hear him singing it." After his encounter with Presley, Ferrier incorporated many of his songs into his set list along with other popular songs of the day, including Fats Domino's: "I used to sing all of the songs that he put out. I liked the way Fats pronounced his words." Presley, Carl Perkins, Johnny Cash, and Ernest Tubb were all influences on Ferrier's music.

In 1956, Ferrier traveled to Lake Charles, Louisiana, to record at Eddie Shuler's Goldband Studio: "I just took a song down there and sang it for him. He signed me with that song, 'No No Baby.' I

Elvis Presley had wanted to record Al Ferrier's "Let's Go Boppin' Tonight," but Ferrier turned down his offer and issued it himself (courtesy Al Ferrier).

always gave him half of the song." Songwriting credit to Shuler was the fee for bringing in the band. The band at that time was known as the Boppin' Billies and included Brian Ferrier on lead guitar, Ross Harbour on drums, David Gregory on bass, Joe Roy on piano, and Al Ferrier on vocals and rhythm guitar. Shuler engineered the sessions: "I learned a lot from Eddie, [i.e.] how to hold my notes longer. He used to tell me, 'You're cutting your words off too short, Al.' He sure did like rockabilly. He sold a lot of them rockabilly songs."

A year later, "I'm the Man" b/w "Hey Baby" was released on the Excello record label. Warren Storm played drums on "I'm the Man," and it scored a number three hit in Nashville. In the 1960s, Ferrier played two shows with cowboy Tex Ritter: "He came down to the E and E Club in Alexandria, [Louisiana] where we were playing. The owner, Elmore Walden, booked him, and he sang with our band. [One of the songs Ritter sang was "High Noon (Do Not Forsake Me)"]. He was booked back about six or eight months later and asked, 'Have you still got the same band that was down here with me before?' The owner said, 'Yes,' and Ritter replied, 'I'll come down there then because they know what they're doing.'" Ferrier was so well liked by the owner that he also backed Ray Price. Around this time, Ferrier started his own seafood market. He was very successful in his business for thirty-five years. Throughout the 1960s and 1970s, the singer continued to play the club circuit.

Even though Ferrier had been receiving fan mail and had exposure in various fanzines, he didn't realize his true popularity until he played a festival in Holland in 1979. After that, he came out of retirement because "I felt like I should be in there, hanging out with the guys again." Ferrier was then signed to a long term contract with his former label, Goldband. In the late 1980s, fellow Goldband recording artist Johnny Jano wrote the country tune "I'll Try One More Time" for Ferrier, which became a number one hit in Monroe and Shreveport, Louisiana. Ferrier recalled, "We got lots of bookings off of that." In 1989, Ferrier made a brief appearance as a newspaper photographer in the movie *Blaze*, which starred Paul Newman. In the 1990s, the Jazz Festival in New Orleans hired Ferrier to participate for five years in a row.

In 2004, Ferrier battled throat cancer, which derailed his performance schedule for a while since he couldn't even talk: "God healed it on me, so I'm back singing again." He played several show dates overseas, and performed in church. In 2007, he released the gospel CD *Cup of Water*. He died from Alzheimer's disease on January 6, 2015.

Rusty York

Rusty York penned sixty songs, including "Sadie-Mae," but is best known for his signature song, "Sugaree." On June 22, 1959, Chess Records released the 45 rpm single, "Sugaree" b/w "Red Rooster." It eventually sold more than half a million copies and peaked at number seventy-seven. York lip-synched "Sugaree" on the August 22, 1959, broadcast of *The Dick Clark Saturday Night Beechnut Show*. Clark also had York perform as one of the headliners at the Michigan State Fair and at the Hollywood Bowl. Later, York backed Bobby Bare on and off for five years, played guitar on a James Brown record, and produced a Grateful Dead recording session. By 1970, he quit performing to concentrate on his recording studio. In 1991, he made a return to rockabilly and continued to perform for enthusiastic crowds until his death in 2014.

Charles York was born on May 24, 1935, in Gray's Knob, Kentucky. In regard to his stage name, he recalled, "My sister gave me a guitar that had Rusty written in gold letters across it. [When I became a performer] I sat in at various places, and everybody started calling me Rusty. They thought that was my name."[3] Rusty York sounded good, so he kept it. Besides a sister, he also had a brother. York's father was a coal miner, and the family moved around frequently.

The state of Kentucky provided York with a background in bluegrass music: "I had a five string banjo that was made out of four strings. Somebody had put a thumb key in it. In 1951, I went to see Flatt and Scruggs. Earl [Scruggs] played the banjo with three picks—a thumb pick and two finger picks. I was only using two. [After witnessing that] I went back home and practiced with three. I liked to have never gotten it." York was exposed to a lot of country music thanks to the *Grand Ole Opry*, which he tuned into every Saturday night. He also listened to Knoxville, Tennessee, radio programs *Mid-Day Merry-Go-Round* on WNOX and Cas Walker's *Farm and Home Hour* on WIVK.

As a teenager, he switched from banjo to guitar: "When I was about fourteen, my father bought me a guitar for five dollars. I taught myself and started playing with the same picks I used on the banjo." Three years later, he and his family moved to Cincinnati, Ohio. At nineteen, he started singing: "My dad used to say, 'You got to learn how to sing.' My voice hadn't changed yet, so I waited until it did." Unfortunately, his father never heard him sing because he died in 1952. York then had to quit high school and go to work. First, he was employed at a restaurant then at a stockbroker's firm. Besides banjo and guitar, York could also play Dobro and bass: "I used a leather glove to play upright bass. If you used tape, you got the residue on your fingers, and it was hard to get off. When you play bass, you can get blisters very easily. With the gloves, I didn't get any."

Larry's Café, in Cincinnati, Ohio, provided him the opportunity to sit in with other musicians. He soon joined forces with vocalist and guitarist Willard Hale. They played the local nightclub circuit for five dollars a night plus tips. One of their regular bookings

Rusty York's first loves were bluegrass and country, but he did record a few rockabilly numbers—most notably Marty Robbins' "Sugaree" (courtesy Rusty York).

was the Old Hickory Café in Cincinnati. York remembered, "I played 'Wildwood Flower' and thought that I was an instrumentalist. A guy in the club used to say to me, 'When you come to the corn.'" His heckling comment insinuated that York's music was corny because he played banjo; he wanted to hear rock and roll. The audience would even yell out titles, such as "Hound Dog." One night, York performed "Mystery Train" "more as a joke, and the fans loved it. Soon they were doing mostly rock and roll songs but would still perform fifteen minutes of bluegrass nightly."[4]

After attending a Jimmie Skinner performance, York and Hale befriended him. Soon, they had a regular spot on his shows. Skinner had a radio program that he would broadcast from his music center on weekday mornings. York recollected, "Jimmie would sing, and I would engineer the records. I would also play guitar without any drums or bass. During the evenings, I worked in its mail order business—packing and shipping records." Later, in 1957, York played lead guitar on Skinner's Mercury sessions.

The young singer recorded "The Girl Can't Help It" and "Sweet Love" in 1956 for the Wright record label: "I knew that I had to cut a record. I went down to the studio and paid for it myself. They only had mono then, so they had to put the drums way, way back from my microphone." In November 1957, "Lou Epstein, who ran the music center, called and asked, 'Do you know somebody who can sing like Buddy Holly?' I said, 'Yeah.' He replied, 'Who?' I told him, 'Me.' I was kidding, but they had an audition, so I went over to King Records with my band. I sang four or five songs, including 'Whole Lotta Shakin' Goin' On.' They brought me back the next day and said, 'Okay, you're on. You'll do 'Peggy Sue.'" On December 16, King Records released "Shake 'Em Up Baby" b/w "Peggy Sue." York added, "Most of the stuff I did for King was rock and roll, and sometimes the band was Hank Ballard's Midnighters." One of York's songs that they played on was "Goodnight Cincinnati, Good Morning Tennessee." Nathan also teamed York with Bonnie Lou to record "La Dee Dah" and "Let the School Bell Ring, Ding a Ling." In 1958, he recorded a banjo instrumental titled "Dixie Strut" for Mercury Records.

York cited Maybelle Carter, Elvis Presley, and Flatt and Scruggs as his musical influences. Dean Martin and Gene Watson were his favorite singers.

In 1959, York and Hale cut three bluegrass tracks for Starday Records: "Don't Do It," "Banjo Breakdown," and "The Lock on Your Heart." The first two songs were released on the album *Banjo in the Hills* while the latter tune was issued as a single. York became associated with Starday through Jimmie Skinner: "Jimmie and his manager were real thick with [one of its owners], Don Pierce." A year later, the duo (Hale and York) along with Curly Tuttle on mandolin and Bill Lanham on guitar recorded twenty-four tunes. They were marketed as Rusty York and the Kentucky Mountain Boys, and their tracks were sold through the Jimmie Skinner Music Center.

Also, in 1959, Pat Nelson, a friend of York's, asked him to come to the King Records studio. While there, York cut a rock and roll instrumental version of "Comin' 'Round the Mountain," which was retitled "Red Rooster." Nelson suggested "Lawdy Miss Clawdy," but Marty Robbins' "Sugaree" was ultimately chosen to be the flip side. York disclosed, "I told him that I didn't know that one, but he said to just make up the words, so I did. I changed it around and made it faster too. We recorded 'Sugaree' in two takes."[5] The scream that is heard on the tune was originally caused by a microphone that had given him an electrical shock. Nelson liked the scream so well that, on the second take, it was done on purpose. The single was initially issued on Nelson's label PJ. They started with a thousand copies but kept selling out. When they reached ten thousand pressings, King Records had Hank Ballard cover the tune. Then York's version was re-issued on Note Records but mass marketed by RCA. Finally, Chess Records capitalized on its sales by making the record available nationwide. Thanks to Chess' promotion and the fact that Dick Clark played it almost daily on *American Bandstand*, the single reached number seventy-seven on the *Billboard* charts and number sixty-nine on pop and number twenty-nine on the R&B charts in *Cashbox*. York conveyed, "We kinda did it as a lark; I didn't expect it to do anything."[6]

For six months, after the success of "Sugaree," York toured the United States in first class accommodations, but those expenses were coming out of his royalties. On August 30, 1959, Dick Clark produced a package show at the Hollywood Bowl. The program featured such artists as Rusty York, Duane Eddy, Robin Luke, Annette, Frankie Avalon, Bobby Rydell, Ray Sharpe, and Jack Scott. York was the opening act and sang only one song, "Sugaree." He recalled, "We had 30,000 people in attendance, and 5,000 more trying to get in. When I stepped onstage, all the cameras were flashing. The bulbs looked like lightning bugs." York also participated in a show with Johnny Cash in Dayton, Ohio: "The guy snuck out and didn't pay us, so we went over to Little Mickey's Tavern. Johnny sang while I played guitar, just like Luther Perkins." Besides bookings, York frequented the disk jockey convention in Nashville. While there, Carl Perkins and Roger Miller dropped by his hotel room for impromptu jams.

After the hoopla died down and no interest was shown by Chess in having York record anymore for the label, he came home and continued to play the local nightclub circuit. In the early 1960s, York performed in Germany, England, Sweden, Finland, Spain, and Denmark. By 1961, he had founded his own recording studio, Jewel, in Mt. Healthy, Ohio. While producing other artists, he continued to sing on Saturdays and Sundays. Everything from rock to bluegrass, jazz, country, gospel, and classical was recorded there. Brother Claude Ely and Jean Shepard were two artists who took advantage of the studio facilities. Even the Grateful Dead cut some tracks there. Throughout the early to mid–1970s, many jingles for Kenner Toys, Huffy Bikes, the *Cincinnati Post*, and Coney Island were recorded at the studio. York mentioned, "Once I quit performing in 1970, I made the same amount of money in one day at the studio as I did in three days at the club." For many years, he did all the work on his own. Eventually, York got burned out by the daily grind, so he hired another engineer and let him run the studio. In 2008, the remnants of the studio were sold at auction.

In 1964, York was opening act and played guitar for Bobby Bare: "I went to Europe and all over the United States with him." They had met at a show and became good friends, even did some recordings together, such as "Long Black Limousine." In fact, they worked together on and off for five years, including some gigs in Las Vegas. Merle Haggard was also featured on one of the tours with Bare. One night, they had a jam session while traveling by car from Los Angeles to Phoenix. York remembered, "Merle said, 'Rusty, did you know I could imitate Lefty Frizzell?' I said, 'No' and gave him the guitar. I then asked, 'Do you know any Jimmie Rodgers' songs?' He said, 'Yeah,' so we started singing them." Incidentally, York had played a Fender Telecaster but in later years switched to a Fender Stratocaster. He actually combined the two by adding a Telecaster neck to a Stratocaster body: "I had been used to a Telecaster neck but wanted the tremolo bar of the Stratocaster." During his tenure with Bare, York managed to cut a couple of songs as a solo act. In 1961, New Star released the 45 rpm single, "That's What I Need" b/w "Just Like You."

The last time he recorded was 1973, collaborating on a bluegrass project with Lonnie Mack. QCA released the album, which was entitled *Dueling Banjos*. In 1991, York made a triumphant return to Europe with several appearances. On June 1, 1996, he was one of the featured acts at the Oldies Fest '96 in New Richmond, Ohio. Chuck Berry, Jan and Dean, Freddy Cannon, Little Eva, The Marcels, Sam the Sham, and The Outsiders were also on the playbill.

York grew to appreciate rockabilly music. One year, his wife arranged for Jerry King and the Rivertown Ramblers to perform at his birthday party. Toward the end of his life, York only participated in two shows a year, mostly festivals. He enjoyed spending time with his wife and watching westerns and old movies from the 1930s, 1940s, and 1950s. His favorite actor was Gary Cooper. York died from Alzheimer's disease on January 26, 2014.

Don Woody

Don Woody and his college roommate Paul Simmons wrote "Bigelow 6–200." In 1956, Brenda Lee recorded it for her first single. Woody had no intention of having a singing career even though he provided the vocals for the demo. However, Decca Records' producers Paul Cohen and Owen Bradley had other plans and signed Woody to a song by song contract. Unfortunately, his April 27, 1957, release "You're Barking Up the Wrong Tree" b/w "Bird-Dog" was strictly a regional hit. Among rockabilly enthusiasts, this single cemented Woody's legendary status. 2010 proved to be a banner year for this highly revered act with a solo CD release, *You're Barking Up the Wrong Tree*, on Bear Family Records, and an appearance at the Hemsby Rock 'n' Roll Weekender.

Don Woody was born on June 29, 1937, in Tuscumbia, Missouri. He began his career in show business when he was a junior in high school, as a disc jockey for KDKD in Clinton, Missouri: "It was one of those stations where we played all different kinds of music. Early in the morning, we played country music; during the day, we played pop music, and in the evening we played light jazz."[7] Around this same time, he played drums for the high school marching band. In the fall of 1955, Woody attended Southwest Missouri State University in Springfield where he disc jockeyed on KICK, a Top 40 station, for the next four years. Musically speaking, Ferlin Husky, Carl Perkins, and Jerry Lee Lewis had the most impact on the youngster.

Also in 1955, the *Ozark Jubilee* (*Country Music Jubilee*) began showcasing its country music talent on national television: "It was then produced live in Springfield, [Missouri] and starred Red Foley." By mid–1956, Woody entertained the audience before the show aired with his comedy routine: "Their band at the time was the Bill Wimberly Band, and during the summer they would tour and do county and state fairs up through Iowa, Illinois, and all around Missouri. For two summers, I toured with them, doing my comedy routine as part of their overall show. I never was out there singing with any of these bands. My friend [Paul Simmons] and I had written some songs, and as a result of being around the *Ozark*

Jubilee, we had Gary Walker act as our manager. Decca Records was looking for a song for Brenda Lee, whom they had just discovered. [Walker took some of the songs he had written along with a few compositions by Woody/ Simmons. Jay Rainwater, Lee's stepfather, liked Woody and Simmons' penned tune "Bigelow 6-200" the best.] That was the first song she [ever] recorded." Incidentally, Lee sang "Bigelow 6-200" on *The Steve Allen Show* in 1957.

Much to his surprise, Woody received a phone call from Decca asking him to come in and record his own single. He had provided Decca with the demo for "Bigelow 6-200": "As a result of singing that demo [which was recorded at KWTO in Springfield, Missouri], Decca decided to sign me to a contract. They signed a whole bunch of singers during that period of time. If your record did fairly well, then they'd extend the contract."

Don Woody wrote and demoed "Bigelow 6-200" before Brenda Lee's 1956 release (courtesy Don Woody).

Decca teamed Woody with Grady Martin and the Slewfoot Five: "Now looking back at it, I wish I had gotten more from Grady because he was such a fabulous player." In Nashville, they recorded four songs: "You're Barking Up the Wrong Tree," "Bird-Dog," "Morse Code," and "Make Like a Rock and Roll" [adapted from the saying 'Make like a tree and leave']. Woody remembered, "We went, and I sang 'You're Barking Up the Wrong Tree' like I wrote it." The song originally contained no barking sound effects. Those were added at the recording session because Patti Page had recently been successful with "How Much Is That Doggie in the Window?" The whistle was also added to "Bird-Dog." The barks and whistle gave the songs a novelty slant: "That's probably what kept them alive all these years."

After Decca released "You're Barking Up the Wrong Tree" b/w "Bird-Dog" on April 27, 1957, Woody continued with his stand-up comedy act and disc jockeying duties: "If I did any shows I'd just pick up a band, or if there was already a band playing I would go sing with them for a set." There wasn't any touring done to promote the record. Therefore, Decca did not renew his contract.

By 1958, Gary Walker, who had become successful in Nashville with his own singing and songwriting career, convinced Woody to record again: "Gary had me come down, and he paid for the session and hired the band. On those [three songs: "Not I," "Red Blooded

American Boy," and "Lesson in Love"], we had backup singers. Then Gary took those masters and tried to sell them. He got me a contract with Arco Records." "Not I" b/w "Red Blooded American Boy" was released on May 5, 1958. This single again failed to jumpstart his career, so Woody got married and received his commission as Second Lieutenant in the Army. He had enlisted with the ROTC and went to missile school at Fort Bliss in El Paso, Texas.

In late 1960, upon discharge from the armed forces, Woody returned to radio where he once again disc jockeyed before becoming program director. Soon after, Si Simon, producer of the *Ozark Jubilee*, offered him the opportunity to move to Nashville. There he would open a publishing firm for him: "I decided not to do that, and I went to work for Sears in 1961." He worked there for thirty years, first as store manager then as regional vice president. Woody traveled and played golf upon retirement from Sears then decided to become a real estate agent, which he continues to this day.

He never thought much about his short lived recording career, aside from an interview that was conducted by Capitol Radio's Roger Scott. This interview garnered attention in a 1976 edition of *New Kommotion Magazine*, thanks in part to British rockabilly band Matchbox covering "Make Like a Rock and Roll" on their first album, *Riders in the Sky*, and the MCA release of Woody's "You're Barking Up the Wrong Tree" b/w Peanuts Wilson's "Cast Iron Arm." The single peaked in the low 40s on the British charts. It wasn't until he was contacted by two young ladies, Lotta and Kitti, from Amsterdam that he realized that rockabilly had made a comeback: "I didn't know until 2002 that my songs were actually as popular as they are. They'd been trying to find me for a long time and when they finally did they told me they had a website." Promoters began contacting Woody after the launch of the site: "Tom Ingram contacted me in the summer of 2006, and I told him I just don't want to [participate at your festival in Las Vegas]. I haven't been onstage in almost fifty years. He kept coming [back] and saying, 'The band is really good, and they know your songs. We'll help you.' After about two or three months, I thought I'll just do this."

In April 2007, he made his triumphant return to rockabilly with an appearance at the Viva Las Vegas Weekender. In attendance were his two sons and grandchildren, who ultimately convinced him to participate. Woody recalled, "That was fun. Ashley [Kingman], Shorty [Poole], Carl [Sonny Leyland], and Bobby [Trimble] are absolutely fantastic musicians. They played exactly like the records. We zipped through rehearsal in about thirty minutes. They can sure make you look good. It was also amazing that the audience knew the words to all four of my songs."

Two years later, he returned to the Viva Las Vegas Weekender stage: "A young man from Paris told me that he was in an old record store and saw the title 'You're Barking Up the Wrong Tree.' He thought that sounded kind of fun, so he bought the record, took it home and claimed to me that's what got him interested and started in rockabilly. He specifically came up after the show to tell me, so that was very nice." Woody then played the first Rockabilly Bash in Amsterdam in November 2009.

The illustrious singer is very thankful for the rockabilly resurgence because he feels it is so much fun to play the shows and meet all the fans: "[Originally], singing just wasn't something that I felt like I wanted to pursue, so I decided to go in a different direction. I literally gave it up [in 1958]. I wrote a few songs over the next five or ten years and maybe made demos but never really pursued trying to sell them."

Bobby Crown

As a teenager, Bobby Crown performed country music with his father. In 1955, after seeing Elvis Presley in concert, he made the transition to rockabilly. Four years later, Crown cut his signature tune, "One Way Ticket." Today, the record is a rare collector's item and can fetch prices in excess of $800. Crown made a couple of appearances on the *Big D Jamboree* and continued to play in Texas throughout the 1960's. Besides his own bookings, in 1969, for six months, Crown backed Ray Sharpe at the Playmate Club in Fort Worth, Texas. In the 1990s, he took a break from performing for ten years. The Europeans embraced his comeback in 2003 with successful shows in Sweden and France. Since then, he plays the occasional show with usual backing from Wildfire Willie and the Ramblers.

Bobby Crown was born on March 7, 1941, in Fort Worth, Texas. His real last name is Krajca: "My grandfather came from Czechoslovakia and settled in Ennis, Texas, when he was seventeen years old."[8] Crown's father was a musician, who played upright bass for a few years in the western swing band, Ernest Winnett and the Texas Trailblazers. Crown's brother, Johnny, played drums and was featured in his band for thirteen years. In 1960, he sang the B side of an Omar Records' release, which was called "Diddley-Daddy." The A side featured "Lonely Avenue," which was sung by Crown's keyboard player, Glen Clark. Crown also has a sister named Bonnie, who sang a lot in church. At five years old, Crown started singing: "I kind of got the idea from a young guy named Kenneth 'Pee Wee' Short, who sang in the Texas Trailblazers. The first two songs I learned were 'Remember Me' by T. Texas Tyler and 'Stars and Stripes on Iwo Jimo Isle' by Bob Wills and His Texas Playboys."

Crown took an interest in guitar playing when he was twelve years old. He recalled, "My mom showed me my first chord, an open G. There was a guy about my age who lived across the street, and he showed me two other chords, E and B. The B chord was kind of hard for me to learn. I remember my dad and I used to sit on the front porch on Saturday nights; we'd sing and play guitar. My mother would fix us toasted bologna and cheese sandwiches." As The Krajcas, they got a gig on *The Cowtown Hoedown*, which aired on KCUL in Fort Worth: "We did that for a while, and then my dad got involved with another band. They were going to play the Lavida Club in Fort Worth, but the singer didn't show up. My dad came and got me, and that's when I started in the clubs." Crown and his father frequently played beer joints together: "I would sing, and my dad would play guitar. They'd give us tips, sometimes seven or eight dollars, which was pretty good back then." At this time, Crown played country music. He tuned into *The Country Picnic* TV show, which broadcasted from Dallas: "We saw a band on there, and I thought we're probably just as good as those people, so we went and auditioned. We got on and did a couple of tunes." Crown didn't transition to rockabilly until he heard Roy Orbison and Elvis Presley. He remembered, "We used to do 'Rockhouse' by Roy Orbison. I also tried to learn Elvis' songs when they came out."

Similar to other teenaged boys of the era, Crown tried to grow his sideburns and hair like Presley's. One night, a patron and his two daughters sat at a front table to watch his act. One of the girls told her father, 'Daddy, he looks like Elvis.' In high school, he was a member of the ROTC: "You weren't supposed to have sideburns, and I remember Sergeant Caldwell asked me to cut them off. I told him that it was part of my business; I was a singer." That didn't deter the sergeant's request and made it mandatory before the next federal inspection. Crown obeyed his orders but then realized it would take a while to grow them back to that length.

Crown graduated from high school when he was only seventeen because he had skipped a grade. He didn't attend football games, homecoming, or participate in any after school activities: "I was always pretty shy in school." At one of his reunions, he commented to a fellow classmate that he didn't think anyone remembered him. To his surprise, he replied, 'Everybody knew you.' Crown stated, "I guess I was better known that I thought."

In 1958, Jimmy Fields of Felco Records took an interest in Crown and mentioned that he should record some songs. Fields co-owned the label with Joe Bill, and they also produced *The Country Picnic* TV show. Bob Lumpkins had written "Your Conscience," which Fields really liked. Due to Fields' suggestion, it was at this time that the singer's name was changed from Bobby Krajca to Bobby Crown. Crown conveyed, "We went to record 'Your Conscience,' and he said, 'You got anything for the other side?' I replied, 'Well, I got a song that I wrote when I was about fourteen called "One Way Ticket."' He said, 'Let's put it on a demo and see what it sounds like.'"

On May 11, 1959, Felco Records issued the 45 rpm single "Your Conscience" b/w "One Way Ticket." Crown recollected, "The first pressing of the record had the writer's credit wrong. They had me as the writer of 'Your Conscience' and Bob Lumpkins as the writer of 'One Way Ticket.' They tried to change it and came out with a new batch of records with Bobby Lumpkins as the singer. The third time, they got it right."[9] Crown added, "When I recorded 'One Way Ticket,' I didn't know it was rockabilly. Dale Morgan arranged the song and finger picked like Chet Atkins. It sounds like two guitars, but it's actually just one." Crown's mother sent copies to her brother in Florida, who then passed them onto disc jockeys, even though "I don't think 'One Way Ticket' got played on the radio a whole lot." Only the two songs were cut for Felco despite the fact that Crown had a contract with them: "Jimmy and my dad kind of had a disagreement because my dad thought we were supposed to be making some money, and we never did."

Fields set up appearances for Crown on the *Big D Jamboree* in Dallas: "I remember when we went over there to talk to them about it. As we were going down the hallway, I saw Gene Vincent and the Blue Caps come off stage. Unfortunately, I didn't meet them." During this time, Crown also backed George Jones after a rodeo dance in Texas.

Bobby Crown signed a contract to appear on the *Big D Jamboree* in Dallas, Texas, on the same day that Gene Vincent and the Blue Caps performed (courtesy Bobby Crown).

Crown cited Elvis Presley as one of his musical influences. In 1955, Crown attended a Presley concert at the North Side Coliseum in Fort Worth. Hank Snow was the headliner. Crown remembered, "It was an afternoon show, and I was in the eleventh row. Elvis wore a white lace shirt, red jacket, and a blue pair of pants. I knew I was seeing something special. He stole the show from Hank, and I heard the country crooner said after the tour, he would never work with Elvis again. I also remember that Bill Black was quite the showman, and I watched him about as much as I did Elvis. [Incidentally] Marty Robbins was my favorite before Elvis. I used to sing his 'I Couldn't Keep from Crying' and 'I'll Go On Alone.' [Mitchell Torok's "Down in the Caribbean" and Jim Reeves' "Bimbo" were also part of his early sets.] I think I got some of my styling from Ken 'Pee Wee' Short."

Brown added, "I used to take my mother to the grocery store on Saturday mornings. I would sit in the car and listen to KNOK, which was a black station that broadcasted from Dallas. The rhythm and blues and blues influenced me too. Even nowadays, I do 'Bright Lights, Big City' while playing a little harmonica." Crown named Trick Pony, Marty Robbins, Jim Reeves, Mitchell Torok, Elvis Presley, Buddy Holly, Roy Orbison, and Carl Perkins as his favorite singers.

Throughout the years, Crown kept active in the music business but also had a regular day job. At seventeen, he had married and was in need of a steady income to support his family. He eventually went to work in the maintenance department at Texas Steel Mill. He was employed there for twenty-one years. Then he worked at Johns Manville for another twenty-one.

In 1970, Crown received a phone call from a guy who was inquiring if he had any copies of his 45 rpm record, "Your Conscience" b/w "One Way Ticket": "My wife told me that he had offered ten bucks a piece, but I didn't have any extra. I said that he must have been some kind of idiot, and I never called him back. I later found out that it is a collector's record. In fact, some people have listed it as one of the Top Ten in rockabilly [rarities]." "One Way Ticket" wasn't his sole release, as in 1960, Manco Records issued "Wait a Minute" b/w "I've Never Had a Broken Heart." Years earlier, Crown had recorded a demo of "Shake, Rattle, and Roll" b/w "Fraulein."

For thirty-five years, Crown was a mainstay on the local nightclub circuit, usually playing for four or five hours a night: "It got to be a real drag. Now, I can do a forty-five minute set and relax." For ten years, he took a break. When performing no longer occupied his time, Crown wrote songs and recorded them at his friend Mickey Moody's Ben Jack's Recording Studio in Fort Smith, Arkansas: "He gave me an outlet for my music." Soon after, Canadian fan and archivist Steve Kelemen contacted Crown about being inducted into the Rockabilly Hall of Fame. Crown recalled, "Once that happened, I started going to the record convention in Austin. There, I met some people from Europe who knew my recordings. Laurent Petit from France liked 'One Way Ticket' and had paid good money for a copy. He had asked me, 'Did you ever think about going to Europe to do some performing?' I had said, 'Well, not really.' He told me that I could make some pretty good money and have some decent backup bands. I then thought well, that might not be so bad. I think he mentioned me to Wildfire Willie." Since 2003, Crown has played several festivals in the States and overseas. Sweden's Wildfire Willie and the Ramblers normally back him: "Jan [Wildfire Willie] called and asked me about coming over. I believe he and his band were backing Huelyn Duvall at the time. I found out they were going to play the Continental Club in Austin, so I went down to hear them. Jan saw me and asked, 'Do you want to get up and do "One Way Ticket?"' I said, 'Well, I don't know. Let me give it some thought.'" After Crown discovered that they played it just like the original, he sang the tune. He disclosed, "Jyrki 'JJ' Juvonen played the guitar licks on 'One Way Ticket' as good as anyone I had ever heard." In 2006, he participated on Jan Svensson's Swedish radio program with an interview and live performance of four songs with the band: "It was the first time I had actually played on the radio." He admitted, "I am surprised that my music is still popular today. I thank my lucky stars for the night I was plunking on my old Gibson and came up with the idea for 'One Way Ticket.' At the time, it seemed so simple, and it still does. I am really thankful that I am getting a bit of recognition because I never expected it."

Alvis Wayne

Texas in the 1950s was a breeding ground for rockabilly talent and included artists such as Buddy Holly, Sid King, Lew Williams, Mac Curtis, Bob Luman, Johnny Carroll, and Alvis Wayne. Many of those same men began singing country music before Elvis Presley came on the scene and brought rockabilly to the forefront. Wayne only had three single releases, but fans never forgot him. In 1999, he was contacted by Pink 'n' Black Records with an offer to play Europe. He then toured in England, Sweden, Germany, and Finland. Over forty years since his first recording, and Wayne was finally getting recognition for his contributions to rockabilly.

Alvis Wayne Samford was born on December 31, 1937, in Paducah, Texas. Wayne had three brothers and one sister: "My sister didn't beat me up because I was the oldest, but she made it rough on the rest of the younger ones. One girl growing up in a house full of boys, she's gotta be tough."[10] As a youngster, Wayne tuned into the *Grand Ole Opry*: "That was the thing on Saturday night. When I got a little older and finally got my own room, I had my own radio. I started listening to a lot of rhythm and blues [on a radio station out of Shreveport, Louisiana] late at night. That was the only [station] you could pick up, but I enjoyed it."

At ten years old, Wayne played on a stage with Bob Wills and His Texas Playboys at a dance hall in Macdona, Texas: "We all went over there to see him. My mama talked to him, and then he called me up onstage. I only did two songs as I was trembling so bad I couldn't sing any more. I was scared to death. They all said, 'Hey man, you did a good job' and patted me on the back. That alone meant a whole lot coming from those guys."

Wayne added, "I can't remember when I wasn't [singing]." Like many of his contemporaries, he began singing in church. At twelve, "a friend of the family had a country band, and he put me to work as the lead singer. We played beer joints and honky tonks and had a live country radio show every Saturday afternoon from 12:30–1 p.m. on KBOP in Pleasanton, Texas." Around that same time, Wayne learned how to play the guitar. His first guitar was purchased from a Sears Roebuck catalog for $18.98: "One of my aunts ordered it for me. She owned a ranch, and I would go down there in the summer to work: pulling corn, picking watermelons, [whatever needed to be done], and that was my pay." He taught himself how to play the guitar, using a how-to book. He was determined to master "Goodnight Irene": "I played it over and over and over until I got the chords figured out. [I drove my parents nuts.] In fact, I was run out into the yard a few times. In 1953, my family moved to Corpus Christi [Texas], and I got hooked up with Al Hardy and the Southernaires. I was working in that band when Tony [Wayne] and I got together."

Wayne conveyed, "At the time I started recording rockabilly music, I was singing in a six-piece dance band, playing country and western swing. [Tunes by Hank Williams, Sr., Slim Whitman, Jimmie Rodgers, Bob Wills, Webb Pierce, and Lefty Frizzell were all part of his repertoire. He also incorporated some of Elvis Presley's songs into the act, such as "Baby Let's Play House," "That's All Right," and "Blue Moon of Kentucky."] A friend of mine, Tony Wayne, had found something in one of the newspapers about Westport Records in Kansas City [Missouri]. He contacted them, and they told him that they wanted rockabilly. Well, they didn't call it rockabilly then; they called it rock and roll. They told him that's the kind of music that they wanted, and if I could do that then I may have a shot at recording for 'em. I liked rockabilly, and I enjoyed doing it. About that time, you couldn't give a country song away. We put some stuff on tape and mailed it to 'em. They released the demo. I never did record it again. There were only two songs on that demo." "Swing Bop Boogie" was one of the songs with Al Hardy and the Southernaires as backing: "They didn't even play that kind of music as a rule. Tony Wayne and I had to tell them how we wanted it to sound. Their steel guitar player was a little wild Cajun, so it didn't take him long to catch on." The whole band appeared on those demos, but on the other Westport recordings, he only used certain members of the Southernaires. Those demos guaranteed Wayne the contract with Westport. It was a one record at a time contract with no set time period. Wayne explained, "When they felt like it was time to release another one, they'd contact me. We couldn't afford to drive [to Kansas City to record]. We were poor boys. We'd go to a studio in Corpus Christi, put some stuff on tape, and mail it to 'em. We then signed a contract for those songs."

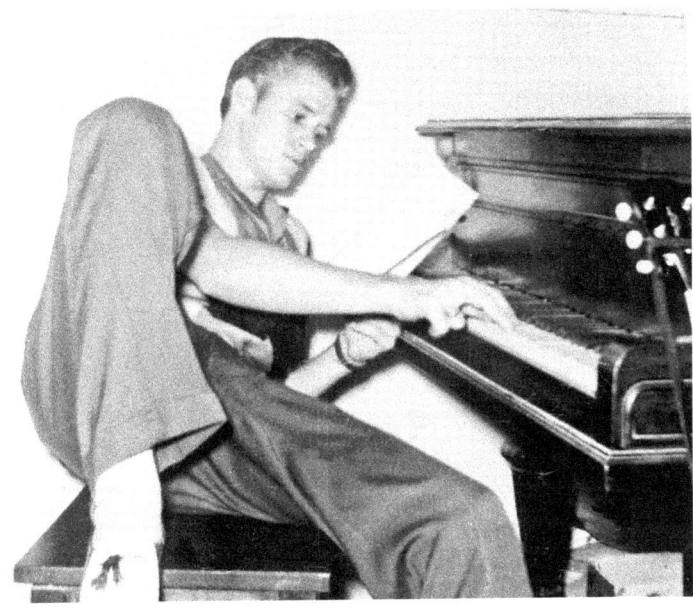

In 1957, Alvis Wayne scored a regional hit in Texas with "Don't Mean Maybe Baby" (courtesy Alvis Wayne).

Westport issued the 45 rpm single, "Swing Bop Boogie" b/w "Sleep Rock-a-Roll Rock-a-Baby" on September 29, 1956. Wayne added, "It was a real small label. Actually Westport Enterprises was a real estate company, and Dave Ruf, the guy that owned it, had kids that were playing music. He started that record label, so he could put out some of their records.

Then they picked up a few other artists like Mac Curtis." Wayne revealed, "I didn't make the [transition] completely to rockabilly. We recorded those songs, but I kept working in Al Hardy's band. After the record was released, that's when we started trying to promote it and booking jobs. [I even dropped out of high school to do it]. I did some teenage things like sock hops, mostly right there in Corpus Christi. Out on the road, we were just booking nightclubs. We weren't known well enough to draw a huge crowd. Nobody ever heard of us. It didn't work out that well. We finally had to give up and come back home because we were about to starve to death."

There were two more sessions after they recorded the demo songs. "Lay Your Head on My Shoulder" was recorded in Houston with studio musicians: "I didn't know any of them. We had all the music on paper, and I sang the song four or five times. Each one of them figured out his part." "Don't Mean Maybe, Baby" b/w "I'd Rather Be with You" was released on November 11, 1957 while "Lay Your Head on My Shoulder" b/w "You Are the One" hit shelves on September 15, 1958. In regard to "Don't Mean Maybe, Baby": "At the time it came out, that was probably the favorite of the three records. It was number one in South Texas for about four or five weeks." "Swing Bop Boogie" was also a regional hit.

Wayne enjoyed the opportunities to appear on both the *Big D Jamboree* and the *Louisiana Hayride* and then on many of the Hayride's road shows: "They'd put together these package shows with five or six artists. That's how I got to work with Johnny Horton. He was my idol and a real fine guy." Besides Horton, Wayne also listed Carl Perkins, Johnny Cash, Elvis Presley, Bob Wills, Eddy Arnold, Slim Whitman, Webb Pierce, and Hank Williams, Sr., as musical influences.

Backstage at the *Louisiana Hayride,* the girls pushed Wayne, who was trying to have a conversation with Presley, out of the way: "After the show was over, they'd let all these pretty girls backstage. They were lined up to get their kiss and autograph from Elvis." He worked with Presley a few times and also Johnny Carroll and Bob Luman on occasion: "My kid sister used to follow me around all the time. She flipped her lid over Bob. Every time he came anywhere close, she had to go see him. Usually when that happened, we were both on the same show." One such gig was a Hayride package show in Corpus Christi in 1957. It was Luman's last before going to California to film *Carnival Rock*. Incidentally, "Butch White, Bob's drummer, was my drummer before Bob ever heard of him. Butch and I went to high school together. He, Kenneth Whit, and I all started out. That was our band, and Kenneth and I stayed together a long time after that. Hank Thompson was looking for a drummer, and somebody told him that I had a knocked out fine drummer, so he came to listen and hired Butch right on the spot. He was Hank's drummer for a while before he went to work for Bob."

Wayne's parents, especially his mother, were supportive of his musical endeavors but "my grandparents and a whole lot of my aunts and uncles didn't think much of it. [My grandparents were very religious]. They said things like, 'You're wasting your time picking that guitar.' Of course, when I started playing in them honky tonks and beer joints, most of the rest of the family all but disowned me. There for a while I was the black sheep of the family. They didn't think much of it until I started amounting to something, then they all came around."

It was difficult making a living in the music industry, and Wayne knew his name was next on the draft board, so he enlisted: "In 1960, I went into the Air Force and was stationed in Warner Robins, Georgia. A friend of mine, who was a recruiting officer for the Army, had called. He asked how I was going to like being a ground pounder. I told him that I didn't think I was going to like that very much. He said, 'Well, if you don't want to be in the Army, you better hurry up, go down, and join something because your name's on the list.' I ran down and joined the Air Force." During his enlistment, the young soldier was sent to Florida in case extra troops were needed during the Cuban Missile Crisis: "We were ready to go, but thank God we never had to." He spent four years building communication towers in Florida; Puerto Rico; Goose Bay, Labrador; and Iceland.

Upon his discharge from the Air Force in 1964, Wayne quit performing: "I was having a hard time getting back into the music business. Everybody had already forgotten about me, or so I thought. I was married, so I had to get a job. First I went to work for a neon sign company and then for some car dealerships, selling cars. I tried to be a door to door salesman, selling vacuum cleaners, encyclopedias, and toothbrushes. That didn't work out. I liked to starve to death there too. I finally went to work for Braniff International Airlines. I started out loading airplanes with airfreight and then I got promoted to agent. I finally [worked my way up] to management at Love Field in Dallas, [Texas]. I stayed there until they were about to [drive] me nuts, and I had to quit."

In the early 1970s, Ronny Weiser, owner of Rollin' Rock records, set up a show in Austin, Texas, which included Ray Campi. In 1974, for Rollin' Rock, Wayne cut three new sides, just him singing and playing acoustic guitar. Those songs were "I Wanna Eat Your Pudding," "It's Your Last Chance to Dance," and "She Won't See Me Anymore." All three were overdubbed with extra instrumentation and eventually released. Weiser also had the hindsight to purchase the rights to Wayne's Westport recordings, including an unissued track, "I Gottum." In 2000 and 2001, Wayne cut two albums for Weiser: "I went to Vegas to record at his home studio." Fellow rockabillies Mac Curtis and Mack Stevens made guest appearances. *Rockabilly Daddy* was issued on Rollin' Rock in 2000 while the other, *Proud of My Rockabilly Roots*, saw the light of day eight years later.

Originally contacted by the owner of Rollercoaster Records, Wayne turned down his offer of performing again. Then in 1999, John Kennedy and Perry Williamson, owners of Pink 'n' Black Records, called: "They asked if I would be interested in coming to Europe to do a show. I said, 'Yeah, I sure would.' I didn't know what was going on over there before that. In fact, I really wasn't even interested in doing a whole of music at that time." Wayne continued to perform at local beer joints and dance halls including VFW Clubs.

Wayne played the Hemsby Rock 'n' Roll Weekender and then the Viva Las Vegas Weekender and finally back to England and Germany. Wayne commented, "We pulled in the driveway at Hemsby, and there were people waiting for us. The fans started stuffing things through the window to get my autograph before I even got out of the car. When we left, it was the same way. We had to ease through the crowd to get out. [The whole experience] was like being in a time machine. I walked around half the time with my mouth hanging open. I couldn't believe it. Never saw anything like that before. I went to Sweden in 2000. After Sweden, I made a trip to Finland. Most of the bands, including Wildfire Willie and the Ramblers, knew my songs better than I did. In fact, one time at a rehearsal, we kicked off a song, and I started singing when the guitarist stopped me. The whole band stopped playing, and he said, 'Alvis, that song doesn't go like that.' I said, 'Whaddya mean?' He said, 'It goes like this.' He was waiting to do it exactly like I had done on the record. I don't ever do that, but that's the way they wanted to do it because that's the way they learned it. I don't expect them to do it exactly like it is on the record because like on 'Swing Bop Boogie' I used a double neck steel guitar. There ain't anybody in rockabilly that's got one of them."

His last trip overseas was in 2003: "I'm not physically able to do it. I'm just not up to making that trip anymore. It's hard on you when you're in good shape. I know all the bands around here, and if they're playing somewhere close I'll sit in and sing a few songs, just to satisfy my own ego." In 2007, he had an accident while working in his backyard: "I got into a den of fire ants. They bit me on both legs that morning. That night, I was running a fever. The next morning, my left leg was swollen and looking bad, so I went to the emergency room. My right leg had healed, but my left had an infection. They wound up cutting part of the leg off, right below the knee." He then had to be fitted for a prosthesis.

On July 31, 2013, Wayne passed away at his home in Bacliff, Texas. Rockabilly fans around the world were saddened by the news, but they can take solace in the fact that Wayne enjoyed performing and loved meeting them: "I've had a lot of fun being a musician. That's what I was supposed to do, sing songs."

Janis Martin

Janis Martin played tent shows and enjoyed success on the *Old Dominion Barn Dance* before she ever set foot in a recording studio. She had several nicknames: The Female Elvis, Little Miss Elvis, The Girl with the Golden Voice, The Queen of Rockabilly, and Little Miss Hillbilly. RCA Records signed Elvis Presley in January 1956 and Martin in March. It was the label's idea to christen her with the moniker The Female Elvis. At first, Martin had a hard time accepting the title. In fact, she absolutely refused to be promoted that way: "I wanted to make it on my own."[11] That was until she saw Presley perform live in concert. The vocalist then discovered the natural comparisons. That same year, *Billboard* gave Martin extra publicity when they named her "Most Promising Vocalist." Her career flourished, but RCA was unaware that Martin had wed at the tender age of fifteen. When that news was discovered, it shattered the record label's teenage image that they had been showcasing to the public. In 1958, Martin was dismissed from her RCA recording contract. A few more recordings on Palette followed, but it wasn't until 1982 that she reappeared on the rockabilly scene. Martin has legions of fans because she was feisty with a voice to match. Contemporary songstresses Kim Lenz, Rosie Flores, and Martí Brom have all sung her praises and have cited her as a major influence.

Janis Martin was born on March 27, 1940, in Sutherlin, Virginia. Her parents were fans of country music, especially Eddy Arnold and Hank Williams, Sr. Her father and uncle were both musicians. The latter played guitar and emulated Marty Robbins. After dinner, they'd sit around the table to play guitar and sing. She was always surrounded by music. Martin recalled, "There was a black church up the road, and we would go out on a Sunday afternoon, hide in the weeds and listen to some of the prettiest singing. Oh, I loved it."[12] At age four, Martin started strumming the guitar. Within two years, she had learned all the elementary chord progressions. Beginning in 1948, her mother entered the youngster in numerous local talent contests. Martin's first competition scored her a second place finish.

By 1951, Martin enjoyed a stint on the *WDVA Barn Dance* in Danville, Virginia. She toured with Jim Eanes and performed on the same bill as Ernest Tubb at a tobacco festival in Virginia. In 1953, Martin played a show with Cowboy Copas and Sunshine Sue. The latter vocalist was so impressed with Martin's talent that she invited her to join the *Old Dominion Barn Dance* on WRVA in Richmond, Virginia. That show was telecast every Saturday night on a CBS affiliate, and its guests included The Carter Family, Jean Shepard, Hawkshaw Hawkins, Sonny James, and Martha Carson. Martin remembered, "We traveled from South Boston [Virginia] to Richmond each Saturday. [One day] I was fiddling with the radio trying to find something I liked, and I ran upon this song of Ruth Brown's, 'Mama He Treats Your Daughter Mean.' I said, 'That's it! That's it!' Pretty soon, I was doing Ruth Brown's music on this old country show. At first, I think people looked at me and thought, 'Well this is strange,' but they loved it. They would just tear the place down."[13] She gravitated toward rhythm and blues and rockabilly. Tunes by LaVern Baker and Dinah Washington also became part of her set lists. Incidentally, Ruth Brown was her biggest musical influence. She also paid attention to the artists who were on Sun Records.

The female Elvis, Janis Martin, broke 1950s conservative stereotypes by singing barefoot (courtesy Dominique Imperial Anglares).

The *Old Dominion Barn Dance* had given her exposure and also the opportunity to play with some of the biggest names in country music: "I had Hawkshaw Hawkins, Sonny James, and Jean Shepard telling me to pursue a music career."[14] Carl Stutz, a staff announcer at WRVA, requested that she sing a song that he had co-written, "Will You, Willyum." A demo was then made and sent to Nat Tannen, who presented it to RCA Records' producer Steve Sholes. RCA was very interested, and Chet Atkins called her with an offer to sign with the label.

In March 1956, Martin traveled to Nashville for her first recording session where she cut four songs: "Will You, Willyum," "One More Year to Go," "Drugstore Rock and Roll," and "Let's Elope Baby."

The session musicians were Chet Atkins, Hank Garland, and Grady Martin on guitar, Floyd Cramer on piano, Bob Moore on bass, Buddy Harman on drums, and The Jordanaires, who provided background vocals. RCA had requested original material. In only ten minutes, she wrote "Drugstore Rock and Roll." On April 7, 1956, RCA Records released the 45 rpm single, "Drugstore Rock and Roll" b/w "Will You, Willyum." It was stated in her contract that "she had to make ten public appearances for each record."[15] Thanks to guest spots on *American Bandstand*, *The Tonight Show*, and the *Ozark Jubilee*, the single sold 750,000 copies and hit the *Billboard* Top 10 for a week.

Carl Stutz and Carl Barefoot, who had written "Will You, Willyum," penned "Little Bit" and "Barefoot Baby" for Martin's next session, which occurred on May 11, 1956, in New York City. Different musicians were used, and she recorded two other songs as well—"My Boy Elvis" and "Ooby-Dooby." June 16 saw the release of "Ooby-Dooby" b/w "One More Year to Go." On September 1, RCA released "My Boy Elvis" b/w "Little Bit." Both sides did very well in France and South Africa. Before the end of 1956, one more 45 rpm single, "Barefoot Baby" b/w "Let's Elope Baby," hit store shelves.

By this time, publicity agent Brad McKuen had seen her live performances and had told A&R man Steve Sholes that Martin's stage delivery was similar to Elvis Presley's. She was then pegged as The Female Elvis. Even though, she was popular with promoters, the teenager had to deal with criticism from the public. Other girls chastised her for being compared to Presley; while the adults considered it vulgar to sing rock and roll tunes and move on stage like she did. According to Martin, "I was considered a rebel because I sang barefoot onstage."[16] She added, "Doing that kind of music, it just wasn't natural for me to stand up there and tap my foot. I'd get up there with a guitar and move all over the stage."[17] Initially, Colonel Tom Parker and Elvis Presley were fine with the idea of Martin being promoted as The Female Elvis. In fact, Parker had expressed interest in becoming her manager. Thankfully, her mother had read about the toll Parker's management was taking on Presley in the newspapers and politely declined his offer.

Martin wanted to explore the rockabilly field, but the record label constantly booked her on package shows with various country stars, such as Hank Snow, Porter Wagoner, and Faron Young. She explained, "I couldn't stand the tours. They put you on a train or bus and treated you like cattle; it wasn't for me."[18] She was pleased, though, to share the stage with Carl Perkins. Her strangest show was with Pat Boone, "who had an orchestra backing him and plenty of rehearsal time. When she came on with no sheet music and performed a stunning rendition of 'Will You, Willyum,' the crowd went crazy. Pat Boone asked that she not be booked with him again."[19] Eventually, she formed her own band, The Marteens, and toured extensively in the United States and Canada. MGM screen tested her for a movie role, but nothing ever materialized.

In January and June 1957, she put down vocals on several songs, including "Love Me to Pieces," "Love and Kisses," "I'll Never Be Free," and "Half Loved." Unbeknownst to RCA, she was married. While on a European tour of USO bases with Jim Reeves, her paratrooper husband made conjugal visits. The tour manager alerted RCA, and they were furious. When Martin arrived back in the States, she was pregnant. It was strongly suggested that she have an abortion to ratify the situation. When Martin refused, RCA immediately stopped promoting her. During the October session, she was eight months pregnant but managed to record "Good Love," "Cracker Jack," "Billy Boy, Billy Boy," and "All Right Baby." Martin recollected, "Steve Sholes was standing in the control room, and tears were rolling down his cheeks. The guy had really gone all out with publicity for me."[20] RCA Records issued three singles that coincided with the session dates: "Two Long Years" b/w "Love Me to Pieces," "Love and Kisses" b/w "I'll Never Be Free," and "All Right Baby" b/w "Billy Boy, Billy Boy."

The record label had become disillusioned with Martin's mass market appeal. On July 7, 1958, as a RCA recording artist, Martin entered the studio for the last time, where she sang "William," "Bang Bang," "Please Be My Love," and "Love Me Love (Cha Cha)." In August, the 45 rpm single, "Bang Bang" b/w "Please Be My Love" was issued.

Once Martin's contract was dissolved, RCA sent her a bill claiming that she still owed $3,300 for session and expense fees. She refused to pay, so the label released an album entitled *Janis and Elvis* to try and recoup their money. It was only seen on the shelves for one day in South Africa before Colonel Tom Parker got word and insisted that it be pulled. Today, it is a highly prized collector's item that sells for top dollar.

In 1960, Martin got divorced. She then tried to pick up the pieces of her musical career by signing with Belgian label Palette. In June, four songs, "Cry Guitar," "Teen Street," "Here Today and Gone Tomorrow," and "Hard Times Ahead," were recorded at Owen Bradley's Recording Studio in Nashville. In 1960 and 1961, fans were treated to two new releases, "Hard Times Ahead" b/w "Here Today and Gone Tomorrow" and "Teen Street" b/w "Cry Guitar." Martin didn't stay with the label for long because her second husband demanded she stay at home. In 1967, he presented her with an ultimatum, either him or the music. That time, she chose domestic life. However, the music was so deeply rooted inside that she suffered a complete nervous breakdown: "It was like part of me was missing. I didn't know what to do with myself."[21] For thirteen years, she had stayed committed to the marriage, but then again her husband asked her to choose. Martin couldn't deny her musical impulses any longer and dissolved the union. She conveyed, "You cannot change a person's entire life and all they have known. I tried, but the music was too strong inside."[22]

In 1975, Ed Bayes called Martin, who was working at the sheriff's department in Danville, Virginia, with an offer to appear on *The Larry Angelo Show*. Three years later, the rockabilly pioneer told Chet Atkins that she wanted to be in the spotlight once again. He replied that the music business had drastically changed, but that a rockabilly resurgence was happening in Europe. That was the first time she had become aware of her popularity overseas. Also, in 1978, she married for a third time. Luckily, this husband, Wayne Whitt, was supportive of her musical endeavors. In 1982, Rockhouse Records contacted Martin and asked her to participate in a show. On her forty-second birthday, she combatted her nerves and got onstage in Holland.

Martin continued to perform occasionally and then Rosie Flores recruited her to participate on a duet of "Blues Keep Callin'." It was released on Flores' 1995 album, *Rockabilly Filly*. In later years, Martin stayed busy as manager of a country club in Danville, Virginia, but also performed at various venues throughout the United States and overseas. In Europe, she always opened her set with "Drugstore Rock and Roll." Enthusiastic fans came by the thousands to attend Martin's concerts. It was a mutual love affair since she adored meeting and greeting the fans, happily signing autographs and posing for photos.

Martin acknowledged, "It's really just a kick for me to go to Europe a few times a year and be a 'star' again."[23]

In November 2006, Flores again contacted Martin. This time, she wanted to produce an entire album on her. It had taken Flores many years of trying to convince Martin to record again. Flores remembered that she kept saying, 'Well, maybe someday, I'm not really ready now, but let's keep it in mind.'[24] Then, an album magically fell into place: "Rosie, along with Bobby Trimble, sat down and listened to hundreds of songs and then sent Janis sixty songs at a time. She listened to them but didn't like most of them."[25] The exceptions were Dave Alvin's "Long White Cadillac" and Ronnie Dawson's "Wham Bam Jam." Songs were selected, and musicians were compiled, which featured Trimble on drums, T Jarrod Bonta on piano, Dave Biller on lead guitar, Sarah Brown on electric bass, Beau Sample on upright bass, and Flores on background vocals. Incidentally, Trimble co-produced the two day session that produced eleven songs. Flores added, "I really wanted her to have a chance to do a whole record because she hadn't recorded in thirty years. When we first got into it, she was really nervous. I then realized that I had a positive effect on her by making her comfortable in the studio. I noticed how I was able to get her to smile, relax, and really record well. She got to hear the songs because we recorded the record in two days and on the third day, we mixed them. Janis got to take home some very good sounding rough mixes."[26]

Martin was excited about the prospects of a new album and touring to promote it. Unfortunately, she wouldn't get the chance to see the finished product nor play any gigs that showcased the new material. To everyone's shock and dismay, Martin passed away from lung cancer on September 3, 2007. Martin was unaware of how ill she was at the time of the recording. Flores disclosed, "Janis had mentioned that she felt really lousy. I told her that she probably didn't have cancer but that she should go to the doctor and check the lump she had on her back. I suspect that it started in her lungs. She liked to smoke, drink, and rock and roll. Janis always wanted to let people know that she did it her way, and she wasn't gonna make any amends for who she was."

Flores tried to find a label that was interested in releasing Martin's final recordings, but to no avail. In 2011, she created a Kickstarter campaign to raise funds for production, distribution, and promotion costs. Once Flores had collected enough money, she collaborated with Cow Island Music. A year later, *The Blanco Sessions* was released. Since then, Flores and Martí Brom have traveled around the country showcasing Martin's life story through pictures and song. Their appearance at the Rock and Roll Hall of Fame was a sold-out success. Flores added, "The greatest thing is that Janis has been recognized as somebody who is pretty amazing and legitimate from that era."

Ray Campi

Even though Ray Campi had a few single releases in the 1950s, it wasn't until Ronny Weiser re-discovered him that his popularity soared. In 1977, he made his first appearance overseas. Campi commented, "It was just unbelievable [that they remembered me]. It's still shocking when I go over now."[27] Music has always been just a hobby since Campi has had several jobs throughout the years, primarily as an English teacher. One of his other hobbies is collecting classic cars. He currently owns ten different models including 1962 and 1963 Lincolns, a 1966 Cadillac Eldorado convertible, a 1960 Cadillac convertible, Cadillac 1978 and 1979 Coupe de Villes, and a 1959 Chrysler Imperial.

Ray Campi was born on April 20, 1934, in New York City, New York. At age nine, he and his family moved to Austin, Texas. "My dad was a distributor for Armstrong Flooring in New York City. We lived in Yonkers, and he had to drive into downtown every day. My dad also didn't like the winters. He had been pretty busy during the war years, but in 1943, he decided to have a different kind of lifestyle. The Armstrong dealerships were pretty rare in Texas. A fellow dealer had moved to Houston, and he had written my dad and said, 'This state of Texas is wide open. It's gonna grow. A lot of construction is gonna be happening.' My dad then bought a home trailer, and we hooked it onto our 1941 Dodge. In early September 1943, we went to Houston and stayed about a week there. We didn't like it because of the humidity. He had a talk with the fellow dealer, and he said there were a lot of other cities in Texas that would be good spots." They made a tour of Texas—Laredo, San Antonio, and then back to Austin: "My younger brother, Harvey, and I liked Austin and said, 'Let's settle here.'" Campi's father stayed with the flooring business for about a year and then got involved in the grocery business. Later, he changed vocations to real estate.

At twelve, Campi developed an interest in singing and playing guitar: "The first songs I ever sang on stage were at the Austin Civic Theater in 1949. They had acts perform in between scenes of *The Drunkard*. We had a hillbilly act with Betty Jo Gregory. I played the guitar, and Joe Bill Hogan played the washboard. We sang Grandpa Jones' 'Old Rattler,' and for an encore we did Wayne Raney's 'Why Don't You Haul Off and Love Me.'" Campi's cousin, Harold Layman, had taught him how to play guitar. The first song he ever learned on steel guitar was "My Bonnie Lies over the Ocean": "I sure got bored quickly with that, but I learned how to hold the bar and put the finger picks on."

While in junior high school, Campi started recording: "I had a friend, Jack

Many of Ray Campi's early songs were unknown—until Rollin' Rock Records' founder Ronny Weiser discovered him and issued the songs twenty years later (courtesy Ray Campi).

McGraw, who would bring his Audio Disc cutter over to my cousin, Harold Layman's house. I cut one song after another. Those are the first songs I ever wrote, from 1949–1951. They have not been released since they are just too amateurish."

Layman was a musician as well. He was taught how to play the button accordion by his father Hector: "We'd have parties where there'd be three button accordion players who performed polkas and waltzes." Campi's mother also played. In 1951, Campi and his cousin attended a Hank Williams, Sr., concert. In fact, the young singer got Williams' autograph on a songbook. They also saw Maddox Brothers and Rose twice when they came to Austin for a Four Star Records' Show and Hank Locklin.

The rockabilly legend stated that Hank Snow, Carl Perkins, Jerry Lee Lewis, Elvis Presley, Johnny Cash, Chuck Berry, Hank Williams, Sr., Lefty Frizzell, and Gene Snowden were his musical influences. Campi commented, "Hank Snow is my favorite singer, songwriter, and guitarist of all-time. My cousin, Harold liked to buy records, and that's where I heard Hank Snow for the first time." He also became affiliated with King Records (Grandpa Jones, Merle Travis, and The Delmore Brothers) thanks to his cousin's record collection. Years later, Campi recorded tunes from the King Records stable, which are available on *Ray Campi Favorite Country Kings*. Campi added, "I also always liked rock and roll." Every night, he tuned into Albert Lavada Durst's "Dr. Hepcat" radio program on KVET in Austin. That's where he first heard Fats Domino, Little Richard, and Chuck Berry. Campi recalled, "The first songs I did were inspired by black rhythm and blues singers. I really liked Lightnin' Hopkins. I recorded 'Scrumptious Baby' and 'I Didn't Mean to Be Mean' at home with just two guitars—Fred Taylor and myself."

Campi's first band, Ramblin' Ray and the Ramblers, featured Campi on lead/rhythm guitar and vocals, Douglas Burton on fiddle, Burt Riviera on steel guitar, and Leon Hankins on rhythm guitar. The vocalist met Riviera on the first day of high school. Hankins and Burton were friends of Riviera's. Ramblin' Ray and the Ramblers' first gig was at Rudy's Drive-In in Austin. They then played local dances whenever possible. Once the band gained in popularity, they established themselves on radio with two different programs—one on KNOW in Austin, which was a thirty minute show every Saturday morning, and the other on KTAE in Taylor, Texas. Recording soon became a priority. According to Campi, "I hired Pee Wee Faury, who was not in my band, and we recorded six songs in the radio station at the University of Texas [in Austin]. [It was equipped with microphones, engineers, and tape recorders]. He brought his bass and started taping his fingers. I said, 'Whatcha doing?' He said, 'Oh, I haven't played in two or three days. I have to get my fingers strong, protect them.' My voice hadn't changed, so it was still kind of high. However, the recordings were fairly professional sounding. Each guy in the band got a copy of the songs that we did. A couple of years ago, a few of the discs got misplaced. Fortunately, one of my buddies, who was in the band from '51–'52, Leon Hankins, had three of them." In total, there were six one-sided acetates: "Toe Tapping Rhythm," "I Love to Love You," "Won't You Love Me Darling," "Rolling Along," "Hawaiian Chimes," and "The Rambling Rag." They have all been transferred to CD and released on Enviken Records in Sweden.

In 1957, Campi's big break came or so he thought: "The TNT record ['Play It Cool' b/w 'Caterpillar'] was heard by Hal Fine through my cousin, who was his babysitter. It turned out he owned a publishing company, Roosevelt Music. He kind of took me under his wing, but I was only in New York City for two or three weeks. While there, I used to sing my songs to Jesse Stone, who was my mentor. I did a promotional tour [which included appearances on *Ted Steele's Bandstand* and *American Bandstand*], where I lip synched my Dot record, 'It Ain't Me' b/w 'Give That Love to Me.'" Campi couldn't stay because he didn't have a job and ran out of cash. He disclosed, "I was in the National Guard, and I was missing meetings. They kept calling and saying, 'You better come. You're gonna get kicked out if you don't.' They weren't paying me at Roosevelt. Hal was very successful and very wealthy, so he didn't understand a guy like me, who had no money." Back in Austin, Ray and the Snappers opened a show for Gene Vincent, Bob Luman, and Sonny James. According to Campi, "That's what Dot Records called my band because we had that finger snapping on our records."

In 1958, the night before Elvis Presley's deployment to Germany, Campi met him briefly in Killeen, Texas: "I knew Elvis was stationed at Fort Hood because of my friend, Bobby Reed, who had played piano on my Dot Record. He had made friends with Elvis the year before, and he told me, 'Elvis is gonna go to Germany; you oughta meet him.' When I got there, Elvis wasn't home. His dad answered the door and said, 'They [Elvis, Gene Smith, and Lamar Fike] are out driving around.' When they got back, all these women and their daughters came up to the house for autographs. I met him though." Then a couple of years later, Campi spent four days on the set of *G.I. Blues*: "Actor Jim Drury was a friend of mine. One night, he and his family were at my house for dinner, and he happened to mention, 'Elvis is coming back to Paramount tomorrow. You wanna go and see him?' I said, 'Yeah, I met him a few years ago.' We went, and I immediately went to the production office and introduced myself to Colonel Tom Parker. He told me, 'Go to Stage 25. Elvis is gonna be there. He's rehearsing.' Elvis sat down next to me, and we talked a little bit, but he was involved with his work. He did all the songs on the soundtrack, and I also saw them do some screen tests on a couple of people, who were in *G.I. Blues*. I thought Elvis was great, and I admired his records."

In September 1958, Campi paid a visit to Norman Petty's Recording Studio in Clovis, New Mexico, where he recorded "Unchained Melody." Unfortunately, the track has never been issued, and he doesn't know if it even still exists. Petty was instrumental in getting Campi in touch with Buddy Holly. Campi acknowledged, "I told him, 'I got a couple of songs I'd like Buddy Holly to hear.' He said, 'Oh Ray, I have to tell ya; Buddy Holly left me. I'm not associated with him anymore.' Buddy had started his own publishing company. In November, I recorded 'My Screamin' Screamin' Mimi' b/w 'With You' for the Domino label. I called Buddy since Norman had given me his phone number. I told him, 'I saw you play last year at the Brooklyn Paramount with Little Richard. I'm gonna send you my new record on Domino.' Years later, when Sotheby's [Auction House] sold Buddy's record collection, my record was in it."

The first tribute songs dedicated to Buddy Holly, Ritchie Valens, and The Big Bopper were recorded by Campi. He recollected, "In the 1950s, Jerry Green was a disc jockey and singer/songwriter in Austin. It was his idea [to write the songs]. 'The Man I Met' is sort of a musical copy of 'Chantilly Lace,' and it talks about a guy who meets The Big Bopper and is inspired by his showmanship. 'Ballad of Donna and Peggy Sue' is about two girls who lose their boyfriends." On February 9, 1959, D Records released "The Man I Met (A Tribute to The Big Bopper)" b/w "Ballad of Donna and Peggy Sue."

That same year, Campi moved to California to try to make his way in music. He admitted, "I never played music for a living as it's always been a struggle. I had other jobs. In 1967, I became an English teacher at Baldwin Park High School. I had a degree, went to the University of Texas." Surprisingly, music was not his major but rather drama: "You have to be skilled in at least two subjects in California. Drama is never a sole study, so it is usually part of the English department. I taught stagecraft. I did Christmas plays, and I taught English too."

Campi tried to make his drama classes interesting for students. He conducted three hundred audio interviews with various movie stars, western stars, and country singers. Hank Snow, Rose Maddox, Tom T. Hall, Joe and Rose Lee Maphis were among the interviewees. Campi revealed, "I had a friend, Mike Marx, who worked for Rogers, Cowan, and Brenner Inc. as a publicist, so he had books full of phone numbers. I interviewed Larry Fine of the Three Stooges at the Motion Picture Home in Woodland Hills, California. One of my student's mothers volunteered there, and she said, 'If you want to meet him, go out to the home.' She set it up and also one with Moe Howard. We went out to Moe's house. I used to listen to the *Louisiana Hayride*, so I spoke with many of its stars too: David Houston, Tillman Franks, Webb Pierce, and Faron Young."

Mae West was another eager participant, and eventually she and Campi became good friends. He recalled, "Mae was easy to find because at one time she owned this big apartment building called Ravenswood in Los Angeles, and she still lived there. I just called her like I did many, many others to see if I could do an interview. I used the reason that I was a drama teacher, and my students would like to hear your life story. Mae was bored and not doing anything [so she agreed]. She wanted to do something for her sister, Beverly, so she gave me the publishing on six demos that Beverly had recorded in the mid–1950s. I arranged a deal with Ron Weiser. We stretched the songs by repeating the vocals and adding a muted trumpet. Billy Zoom played lead guitar. The songs were re-conditioned, and Ron put out an EP on Beverly Arden. By working on that project, that's how I became friendly with Mae. I could then go see her any time I wanted."

Their friendship blossomed. One of the stories she told Campi was that "she didn't want to do a film with W.C. Fields because he was a drunk. When she did *She Done Him Wrong*, it was a movie that saved Paramount Studios. They were going out of business. The movie was a big, big hit, so they wanted to do more movies with her. They came up with the idea of *My Little Chickadee*. Fields was known to be a drunk. He used it a lot in his act as part of his persona. They talked Mae into doing it and said, 'It'll be a good movie. You'll have fun and total control over it. He promises he won't drink.' She said, 'Well, if he comes on the set, and he's drinking; I'm leaving.' She said he wanted a special director to direct his scenes, so he could drink. She told me, 'I went on the set one day, and I saw he had gin. I turned around and went home.' Mae went to Europe, and the movie was only half-made. They kept calling her, saying, 'C'mon finish the movie. He promises he won't drink.' She came back and finished it, but the movie wasn't a big hit."

On April 14, 1973, Campi helped West organize a roast at the Masquers Club. Michael Landon and George Raft were two of the key speakers, while West sang with a piano player and drummer. Fifteen years later, it was released on a CD, *The Masquers Club Salutes Mae West—Mae Day*, on Bacchus Archives. Campi and Johnny Legend paid tribute to her in the song, "Mae West Made Us Laugh": "I wrote it with the idea of telling the life story of Mae." The song is available on the CD, *Ray Campi with Friends Along the Way—Austin to L.A.* West's version of "Caterpillar" is also included in its tracks.

When Campi became a teacher, he quit music. It wasn't until 1972 when he met Ronny Weiser and rented a room in his house that Campi's urge to record and perform was re-ignited. Campi explained, "I was married in my first years of teaching and completely detached from music. I didn't do anything as I lived on a ranch with horses. Then the marriage dissolved, and I had to have somewhere to live. In Europe, Ron had heard my Dot record, 'It Ain't Me' b/w 'Give That Love to Me.' Somebody told him, 'That guy, Ray Campi, lives in Los Angeles. You might find him.' He found my number listed in the phone book, called, and said, 'Do you have any tapes?' I said, 'Yeah, I got a dresser drawer full of stuff that's never been out.' He released the '50s material first. At that time, Ron had the Hollywood Fan Club. He met Gene Vincent and had him record four songs. Jimmie Lee Maslon and I provided the music. Shortly thereafter, I started writing songs again and recording. Ron founded Rollin' Rock Records and discovered other artists: Mac Curtis, Jackie Lee Cochran, Tony Conn, and Johnny Carroll to record again."

Under Weiser's tutelage, Campi learned how to play a new instrument: "I never played bass in the '50s. I played guitar and mandolin, and I could play some slide guitar. For Rollin' Rock, the first records I made were 'Tore Up' and 'If It's All the Same to You.' Then Ron said, 'I wanna buy an upright bass, and I want you to learn it.' We went to North Hollywood Music. I thumped the basses, and the one with the lowest sound was chosen. I knew the notes, but there are no frets on a double bass. I listened to records, and by listening I learned how to slap and pop back. Your fingers bleed, and you get big blisters. Sometimes the blisters popped and blood flew all over the bass. You have to get your fingers hard way down inside, which takes about six months of playing every day. I don't play a lot; never have, so I tape my fingers."

In 1977, Campi and the Rockabilly Rebels traveled to England for the first time: "Colin Winski and I had to get some good clothes, so we went to Turk—the original Rodeo tailor. He made two pairs of pants for me—one red and one blue. I still have the blue pants even though I ripped the seat out a bunch of times." They returned in 1979. One of their performances is featured in the musical *Blue Suede Shoes*.

During the 1970s, Weiser released several new Campi tracks on Rollin' Rock Records. "Hollywood Cats" was written by Steve Roosh, who was a friend of Ronny Weiser's. "Rockabilly Man" was written by Rip Masters. In fact, he recorded it first for Rollin' Rock. In regard to "Rockin' at the Ritz," Campi penned that tune after a show at the Ritz Theater in Austin, Texas in 1978: "It was the first time I had gone back to my hometown to play. When I was a kid, I used to go to the Ritz to see cowboy movies. Jim Franklin had bought the theater and made a nightclub out of it. There were some other acts on the show, and we had a lot of problems. It rained, and the roof leaked. The whole thing was kind of a disaster. When I got back to L.A., I told Ron Weiser, 'You get me in some difficult situations sometimes, [but] I'm gonna get a song out of it.' In the lyrics, I told of some of the things that happened. [He also mentioned some of the cowboy stars he used to see in the movies at the theater, like Lash LaRue and Johnny Mack Brown]. The song got pretty popular with the rockabilly people in Europe, England especially. It's still a song they all know."

Radar Records wanted Dave Edmunds to produce a record for Campi, but he refused:

"I stuck up for Ron and made everybody angry. Ron ended up producing it, and we got it on Radar. They put out 'Caterpillar' b/w 'Play It Cool' as a bonus single. They were real nice people, but they wanted to cut Ron out. I'd never heard of such a thing. There was always dissention in my band—a tug of war between Jerry Sikorski, Colin Winski, and myself."

The Blasters also recorded for Weiser: "When Ron manufactured their album, he took it to Shakin' Stevens, who was staying at the Beverly Hills Hotel. Ron told him, 'There's a song on here, and if you do it, I think it would be a hit.' He heard 'Marie, Marie' and said, 'Let's do it.' It made him a superstar. The Blasters quit Ron because some big Hollywood manager said, 'You shouldn't be with this tiny label. You're wasting your time.' The Blasters didn't get on Warner Bros. right away but rather on Slash. They weren't supposed to record or release the same material for ten years or so [but they did anyway]."

They played the Palomino Club in North Hollywood but so did Campi. He sometimes had James Intveld, Ronnie Mack, Bill Bateman, and Rip Masters in his band. In 1988, Campi performed six songs on *Austin City Limits* with Ronnie Mack and the LeRoi Brothers. Bonnie Raitt and Sleepy LaBeef also had segments: "I met Bonnie because she rehearsed in a little building in North Hollywood where I parked two or three old cars. She played every night, and I'd go watch her sing. We became friends. One night, she says, 'We're gonna go to Austin and do *Austin City Limits*, you wanna be a guest? We got Sleepy LaBeef too. We'll take your bass in our van and take it down to Austin.' Two days after that television performance, my brother said, 'There's a TV series being done here called Dixie's Bar and Bus Stop. It's all live. You wanna do that on Monday?'" That show, which is entitled *Rockabilly Man*, is available for purchase on DVD, and it includes twenty-four songs.

In 1996, Rose Maddox was invited to play a rockabilly show in France by their Rock and Roll Society. Campi remembered, "I had played for them the year before. They called and said, 'Can you get us in touch with Rose?' I said, 'Yeah, she lives in Oregon, and I got her number.' They called, and Rose said, 'You know I don't speak French, and I'd be a little lost over there by myself.' They then called me back and said, 'Do you want to come over and sort of be a companion to Rose and help her out with anything she needs?' She wasn't in good health, so I said, 'Sure.' She had to re-learn all those rockabilly songs because she hadn't sung them since the 1950s. I was standing in the wings when all of a sudden, she yelled to me, 'C'mon let's do a song.' They just about pushed me out there. She knew all Hank Williams, Sr.'s [tunes], so we did a duet of 'You're Gonna Change or I'm Gonna Leave.'" The video clip can be seen on YouTube.

Campi has also shared the stage with his brother. One time, they sang "Christmas Cheer" at a show in Branson, Missouri. He disclosed, "Harvey is a better singer than most people in the world, but he never had success as such." His songs are available on iTunes, listed under *The Best of Harvey Campi*. The two brothers even appeared together on a few of Ray Campi's tracks, including "Let Go of Louie (When You're Dancing with Me)."

As far as recording, Campi prefers modern technology: "I like the vocals to sound bright and clear. About three years ago, I recorded two Gene Snowden songs, 'I'm the Son of a Railroad Bum' and 'Angel Darling,' with a band that had fiddles. Wildfire Willie tried to record it on a little tape recorder, but it would stop in the middle. We'd then have to play the song again since there was no editing. It took a long time to get those two songs. They haven't been released. I have copies, but I don't own them."

Even though Campi officially retired from teaching in 1999, he is still regularly called to substitute: "Students like to have me come into the classroom." He also still performs, which sometimes includes acrobatics atop his bass: "I have the bass set up to where it kind of balances itself. My left hand sort of lays it down, but then I roll on the floor, so it looks like I fell. I've never gotten hurt because it's a planned fall, almost like gymnastics." Kevin Fennell lines up bookings for him and has played guitar in his band for the past thirty-seven years. Campi added, "I have brought Kevin to Europe six times because they were willing to pay for his airfare and hotel. He's a good friend and has put out sixteen CDs of his own. Kevin is very loyal and so is Rip Masters." On April 12, 2014, Campi celebrated his eightieth birthday with friends and fellow performers Glen Glenn, Rip Masters, and Rocky Burnette at the nightclub Viva Cantina in Burbank, California. Journalists have given Campi the moniker "The King of Rockabilly." However, he begs to differ and retorts, "I never call myself that, and I don't know who started it. Carl Perkins is the King of Rockabilly as far as I'm concerned."

Chapter Three

Sun Stars

Glenn Honeycutt

In 1957, Sun Records owner Sam Phillips was going to allow Glenn Honeycutt's "All Night Rock" to be heard but was afraid its lyrical content would prevent it from radio airplay. Therefore, Honeycutt only had one Sun Records release, which featured two slow tunes. The young singer quickly became disenchanted with the music business even though he had a few other releases, including one on Fernwood Records in 1964, "Tombigbee Queen" b/w "Campus Love." A year later, he quit performing regularly and didn't reemerge until the 1980s. It wasn't until 1999 that he traveled overseas and played to a crowd of rockabilly enthusiasts.

Glenn Honeycutt was born on May 2, 1933, in Belzoni, Mississippi. Incidentally, his real name is Harold. Honeycutt has two sisters and comes from a musical background: "My mother played guitar and sang, [but] she never sang publicly. She could read music and helped me, but I also learned how to read music out of the hymnals at church. [My father] died when I was two years old. My stepdad didn't play or sing."[1] At five years old, Honeycutt started singing: "'When It's Nighttime in Nevada' was the first song that I knew some of the words to." He also sang in church and was even a song leader. Two years later, his family moved to Memphis, and he frequented the movie theater once a week to watch westerns starring his favorite cowboys: John Wayne, Tex Ritter, Wild Bill Elliott, Johnny Mack Brown, and Red Ryder. At thirteen, "I started learning how to play the guitar. For three or four hours a day, I'd sit and practice. [Two years later] I went to parties where there would be jam sessions for attendees to create a band."

In 1952, Honeycutt joined the Army for three years: "I was in the medics as a core man in a mental ward." Upon discharge, he formed his own band, The Rhythmaires: "The first time I ever played in public was at a little grille on Thomas Street in Memphis. Johnny Bernero played drums. [The pay was all they could drink, and they were allowed to pass a cigar box for tips.] That didn't last long. I had in mind to play schools, but it just didn't work out as I didn't have any credentials. During that time, I went to see Sam Phillips with some country songs. He told me, 'Nashville has country' [which showed his disinterest]. I started working in a band with the owners of Fernwood Studio, Jack Clement and Ronald "Slim" Wallace. I worked with Slim Wallace and the Dixie Ramblers on and off for three years. Slim was the bandleader and booked the jobs, and I was the singer. Jack played drums and could also play guitar and sing. In nightclubs, I was doing a lot of rock and roll. [He also sang country and pop songs of the day, by artists such as Teresa Brewer and Johnny Ray.] I never did my own songs. It was called rock and roll back then. As far as I know, that term rockabilly didn't come up until the 1970s."

Honeycutt added, "In 1956, Slim [Wallace] and Jack [Clement] built a studio behind Slim's house on Fernwood. Billy Lee Riley was around then. He cut ['Think Before You Go' and 'Trouble Bound'] in that little garage studio. [Clement gave the tapes to Sam Phillips], and then Billy Lee made a deal with Sun. Jack and Slim had me do something out there too. That's how I got on Sun." Clement was already producer and engineer.

The songs Honeycutt took to the small independent label were "All Night Rock," "I'll Wait Forever," and "I'll Be Around," which were all ready for release. However, Phillips had him re-cut the tunes with guitarist Roland Janes, drummer JM Van Eaton, pianist Jimmy Wilson, and backup vocalists The Miller Sisters: "I don't remember how much we rehearsed. At the time, they were going to put out 'All Night Rock' and one of the slow songs. Then Sam Phillips told me that he'd have trouble with the copyright office. He might have thought it was too risqué. At the time, the lyric rock all night might have had a little different meaning for some people." In 1981, the tune was released on an LP in England but as "Rock All Night": "I don't know why it was ever changed [to that]. When I wrote it, it was 'All Night Rock.'"

Although the tracks were cut, Phillips shelved them for months: "It was really hard waiting because I wanted to be a big star and make money. The record was just about dead in the water before it ever came out." On April 20, 1957, Sun Records finally released "I'll Be Around" b/w "I'll Wait Forever." Honeycutt acknowledged, "Both of them were slow tunes, which was a strange thing because that's when rock and roll was going pretty good. My record probably was never really promoted. Sam may have had more artists than he had resources to promote. I know at the same time it was released, Sun also [issued singles] by Roy Orbison ['Sweet and Easy to Love' b/w 'Devil Doll'] and Sonny Burgess ['Ain't Got a Thing' b/w 'Restless']. I only got paid for eighteen hundred copies," which wasn't much.

Honeycutt added, "Recording at Sun was just a dream. At work, that's what I thought about, becoming a big time singer. I did my job, but I'd go around with little pieces of paper. If I'd get an idea for a song or a couple of lines I'd write them down and stick them in my pocket. I'd get home from work and have all kinds of little pieces of paper. I actually wrote quite a number of songs. I would go up to Sun now and

Glenn Honeycutt's best-known song is often incorrectly titled "Rock All Night." The proper title is "All Night Rock" (courtesy Glenn Honeycutt).

then. I remember one day I was just sitting there going through a bunch of songs. Well, some of that stuff is what came out overseas. Some of the songs weren't even finished [as they were demos]. I got a little song called 'Be Wise, Don't Cry' that I love, and they put that out. I hadn't heard it for years."

While at Sun, he ran into several of its stars, such as Billy Lee Riley, Johnny Cash, Roy Orbison, and Jerry Lee Lewis: "I didn't know any of them that well. We just met." Honeycutt, Orbison, and a couple of others made a commercial for country sausage. In it, Orbison played the harmonica and recited humorous lines. Another time, Honeycutt, Clement, and Lewis chatted over some coffee at Taylor's Café, which was next door to the studio. In Arkansas, Honeycutt even did a radio spot with Billy Lee Riley and the Little Green Men.

Honeycutt cited another of his label mates, Elvis Presley, as a musical influence, along with Marty Robbins, Hank Williams, Sr., Carl Smith, Little Jimmy Dickens, Little Richard, and Chuck Berry. Honeycutt is a distant cousin to Elvis Presley: "I never met Elvis, but my grandfather was Elvis' great-grandfather's brother." His favorite singer, which is Luciano Pavarotti, might come as a surprise: "I admire and respect classical singers so much. They can hit those high notes time after time and hold onto them."

In 1958, Honeycutt got a job as letter carrier at the postal service: "I retired after thirty years." The performing he did at that time was at nightclubs and dance halls, mostly on weekends. In 1965, he quit playing regularly and didn't reemerge for twenty-five years. Upon his return, he was booked at a schoolhouse.

In 1981, "I got a call telling me that they had released 'All Night Rock,' over in England. That was a surprise as that was the first I had ever heard about it. Then throughout the years, somebody with a little fanzine might come over for an interview. However, I didn't get invited [to do a gig] until 1998." A year later, Dave Travis brought Honeycutt over to play the Hemsby Rock 'n' Roll Weekender in England.

In 2004, Ralph Braband and Rhythm Bomb Records had Honeycutt come to Germany to record: "Randy Rich recommended me. We [Randy Rich and the Poor Boys and I] did a session over there, and I swear it was terrible. I had a sinus condition before I left, and it didn't get any better. I carried lemon juice around with me, but I got so bad that some fellow took me to the doctor. I couldn't even do a show that I was supposed to do in Sweden. I went over anyway, and there was a guy who knew 'All Night Rock.' I went out on the stage with him for a little while, but he did the song. I did sign autographs though. [I feel] the CD, *Mr. All Night Rock*, suffered on the account of my sinuses. On two or three of those songs, one can hear the scratch in my voice. I can do a lot better but just couldn't at the time."

With his local band, Honeycutt doesn't perform his rockabilly sides: "There's not much rockabilly going on around here. Bluegrass is pretty prominent, but I don't play that. Country music is still good. I do a lot of the old rock and roll like Jerry Lee Lewis. It's still hard to play to a young audience, so I don't even try. I like to do the older country, rock and roll, and standard pop like 'Misty.' One of my all-time favorite songs is 'Harbor Lights,' and I love to sing it. 'Unchained Melody' is also a wonderful song that I do. That's stuff that a lot of the kids probably never even heard. I'm happiest whenever I'm playing to a fifty [plus] crowd." Every Friday night for two years they played a dance in Saratoga, Mississippi: "I really thoroughly enjoyed that. We could please the crowd with the music that I liked." Honeycutt admitted, "I never made a living playing music, just a little extra money."

Alton and Jimmy

Alton Lott and Jimmy Harrell are first cousins. Harrell acknowledged, "We thought alike. We could anticipate what each other was about to say. It was an incredible relationship."[2] For three years, they performed together as the singing duo Alton and Jimmy. The Delmore Brothers and The Everly Brothers were both cited as influences. Harrell stated, "We loved them and everything they did. We didn't copy them per se, but we really liked their harmony." Even though Alton and Jimmy recorded for Sun Records, their success was regional. They were set to return to the studio to cut more tracks when Harrell re-enlisted in the Navy. Lott was devastated but went home and continued with other bands. In 2011, they re-emerged on the rockabilly scene with an appearance at the Viva Las Vegas weekender. Since then, they have released a new album entitled *Still Shakin',* and have played other festivals around the world. Harrell is very surprised that their music is still popular: "I didn't think it would amount to anything, although 'No More Crying the Blues' is a classic."

Alton Lott was born on June 17, 1940, in Hillsboro, Mississippi. There were two more boys and two girls in the family. Lott conveyed, "My sister, Mickie, also sang rockabilly and appeared on the *Louisiana Hayride*. In fact, Johnny Horton was really knocked out by her. Mickie recorded a song at Sun, and RCA wanted to sign her, but she turned them down as she didn't want to be involved in the music business."[3] While in the third grade, Lott started singing, and the first tune he sang was "If I Had a Nickel." He disclosed, "On a country station in Bainbridge, Georgia, I did three radio shows a day with my mom and dad. [They had a country band]. I would sing at six in the morning, and then they would come get me at school during the noon hour, and finally we had another at six o'clock."

At fourteen, Lott began playing guitar, which was a 1947 Gibson 235 that originally belonged to his mother. The first songs he strummed were by Bill Haley. Both his mother and father were very supportive: "They loved it. We would sit around and play." Lott recollected that for the celebration of graduating from the ninth grade, "our class had a swimming party at the Legion Hut in Jackson, Mississippi. Andy Anderson and the Rolling Stones played it. I watched them, and I was just awestruck. That's when I knew that's what I wanted to do. That day I discovered rock and roll, and I discovered girls had legs. I guess I thought they walked on air."

When Lott was fifteen years old, he heard Elvis Presley for the first time at his friend Eugene Barrett's house: "'Mystery Train' sent chills down my spine. There was no other music like that. I would listen to Scotty Moore on guitar and try to copy everything he did." Around that same time, Lott got his first professional gig: "A guy called me to play the NCO Club in Jackson, Mississippi. I told him I could play [the following songs]: 'Honky Tonk,' 'Ooby Dooby,' 'That's All Right,' and 'Blue Moon of Kentucky.'" Lott and his friends would frequent specific drive-in restaurants just to hear certain songs on their jukeboxes. One in Clinton, Mississippi, specialized in Little Richard tunes. Lott was especially keen on Sanford Clark's "The Fool" and Dale Hawkins' "Susie-Q," listening to both over and over again: "I learned to play James Burton's guitar licks." He also loved any song by Jack Scott.

Lott named Scotty Moore, Bill Haley, Lefty Frizzell, Elvis Presley, and Carl Perkins as his musical influences. In regard to Moore, Lott remarked, "I still cannot play 'Shake, Rattle, and Roll.' I tried to get him to teach it to me in 1961, but we got busy recording at Phillips International in Memphis, and I didn't get a chance." Lott was there with Howard "B.B." Boone. Moore engineered. Lott recalled, "I was very nervous to play in front of Scotty." He added, "My favorite artist of all-time is Ray Charles, whom I got to see several times in concert. He was the very essence of music and soul."

Jimmy Harrell was born on November 16, 1936, in Forest, Mississippi. His musical talent was inherited: "My father was a musician, who played guitar and fiddle and sang. He actually won a state fiddling contest in Mississippi. He and Alton's mother were brother and sister. They were big country fans, so the two groups of parents took Alton and I to a Delmore Brothers' concert in the late 1940s. We went backstage, and Alton's daddy told Alton Delmore that Alton was named after him. He pulled out a brand new shiny fifty cent piece and handed it to Alton."

To support the family, which included two other boys and one girl, Harrell's father was a farmer, who grew corn, hay, and cotton: "I used to come home from school, get my sack, and head to the field. I picked a lot of cotton. We'd come home and have to take care of the hogs and cows. Then I'd have to do my homework by a kerosene lamp because we had no electricity."

Harrell started singing in church. As a teenager, his father taught him a few chords on the guitar: "When I went into the Navy, I bought a Martin guitar at a music store in San Diego. When I got out, I sold that Martin for twenty bucks. I remember saying, 'I just don't want to have to take it on a bus back to Mississippi. It's excess baggage.'"

His parents were very supportive of his musical endeavors: "In high school, I had a little stint as a singer in a gospel quartet. Our group, The Mississippians, was in Future Farmers of America, and we entered a gospel singing contest. It started

In 1958, Sun recording duo Alton and Jimmy briefly backed Nanette Workman, famous for her background vocals on the Rolling Stones' "Honky Tonk Women" and "You Can't Always Get What You Want." From left: Nanette Workman, Jimmy Harrell, and Alton Lott (courtesy Jimmy Harrell).

off locally, and if you won you got to go to the district, and then to the state [competition]. In 1955, we tied for first place in the state contest, where we sang 'Looking for a City.'" Unfortunately, they didn't win a prize but did get recognition. Harrell revealed, "We got to appear with The Blackwood Brothers in Starkville, Mississippi. They were impressed, so they asked us to be on another show with them at Ellis Auditorium in Memphis. We were backstage with them and The Statesmen." Years later, The Blackwood Brothers' Jackie Marshall commented to one of Harrell's fellow vocalists that after the show in Starkville, they had told each other on the bus, 'We're gonna see those guys a lot.' They really thought we had it and would stay with it. That's quite an honor to hear one of the original Blackwood Brothers say that."

In 1954, Harrell entered the U.S. Navy and was stationed at Camp Pendleton in Oceanside, California. He heard Elvis for the first time when he was home on leave. Harrell declared, "I went back to California and told my shipmates about him. They hadn't heard Elvis. We got in the car one weekend and drove to a bus stop to play 'That's All Right' on their jukebox. I was already very excited about that sound and then in 1956, I heard 'Be-Bop-a-Lula' on the radio. Lo and behold, there was an announcement that Gene Vincent and the Blue Caps were coming to San Diego. My two friends and I went to the concert. There was no seating, just a wide open ballroom. We were able to stand in front of the stage, right at his feet. Gene did a few songs, and then he said, 'Okay, ladies and gentlemen it's time to sing the song.' Then he did 'Be-Bop-a-Lula.' That was an amazing thing to see and hear. We looked at each other and said, 'We can do that. We wanna do that.'" Vincent's performance was very inspirational, and after that night, Harrell took his music more seriously: "My buddies and I had been fooling around with music a little bit. One of them played lead guitar, and we taught the other how to play bass. It was a stick with a string attached to an old galvanized metal washtub. Then we finally rented a standup bass. We started playing around the San Diego area. That group was called the Jimbobs because the other two were named Bob Allen and Bob Cohen. We entered a talent show and won second place. There was a country music radio show out of Tijuana, Mexico. We went and did a couple of songs live. Shortly after that, I got out of the Navy and came home to Mississippi."

Elvis Presley and Gene Vincent were his musical influences. Much of the music that was being played on the radio in the late 1940s and 1950s also inspired him. Harrell added, "Living in Hernando [Mississippi], I listened to disc jockey Dewey Phillips on WHBQ in Memphis. He played all the rhythm and blues people like Muddy Waters, Big Mama Thornton, and B.B. King. That affected me greatly. I was also influenced by my father and Alton's mother. They'd go to my grandpa's house and play and sing in the living room. They would let Alton and I join in occasionally, and we used to just eat that up." Harrell cited Ricky Nelson, Carl Perkins, Gene Vincent, Roy Orbison, Elvis Presley, Carl Mann, Warren Smith, and Billy Lee Riley as his favorite rockabilly singers.

Harrell was in the Navy for three years before attending college: "We all were gathered at my grandpa's, and they were asking me, 'What are you doing since you got out of the Navy?' I said, 'Essentially nothing' since I was going from one little job to another. Aunt Peggy, Alton's mother, said, 'Well, why don't you come down to Jackson? There are a lot of jobs. You can stay with us.' That's what I did, packed up the car, and lived with them for almost a year. Alton had a job with his dad doing construction, and I got a job at the University of

Mississippi Medical Center. In 1957, we started kicking around in Hernando, Mississippi. After work and on weekends, all we did was music." They really hadn't sung together prior to that. Harrell recalled, "It was something that we had each done separately and when the family got together, but it wasn't planned [for us to start a duo]. We were together all the time, [so it was only natural]."

Before recording for Sun Records, Alton and Jimmy cut two unreleased songs for Ace Records. Harrell commented, "We met [its founder] Johnny Vincent and auditioned for him. In September 1958, he took us down to Cosimo Matassa's studio in New Orleans. Huey Piano Smith played on the session. We recorded two songs: 'I Got It Made (in the Shade)' and 'Looking for Someone.'" Harrell enjoyed recording "I Got It Made (in the Shade)" and declared, "We had a lot of fun with it."

Then they made an appearance on the *Louisiana Hayride*. Lott remembered, "Our manager, Melvin Cox, had an in, so he took us to Shreveport, [Louisiana]." Harrell conveyed, "We auditioned for Tillman Franks on a Saturday afternoon, and that very night he put us on the Hayride. We sang The Delmore Brothers' 'Blues Stay Away from Me.' Johnny Horton, Jim Ed Brown, and Carl Belew were also guests. Tillman had gotten on the phone to Sam and said, 'I have some boys here that I think you oughta listen to.' Sam gave us a date and time to show up at Sun. We were in such awe of where we were and what we were doing that I don't remember much that was said in the lobby that day. Our knees were knocking. We thought we were going up for an audition, but Sam came out, shook our hands, and asked his secretary where the contract was. She pulled it out and laid it in front of us on the desk. We signed it right there. He had never heard us, just went on Tillman's word. We were shocked."

In 1959, Alton and Jimmy first recorded at Sun Studio. Lott remembered, "We got there a little early. Sam had to leave, so he said, 'I'll be right back. Go next door.' We had hamburgers with Jerry Lee Lewis and Billy Lee Riley [at Taylor's Café]. We wouldn't talk as we were so intimidated." Once Sam Phillips returned, they got to work on material. Five songs were recorded at Sun ("No More Crying the Blues," "Have Faith in My Love," "I Just Don't Know," "What's the Use," and "The Longest Walk"), but none were released from the second session. According to Harrell, "Alton hasn't gotten the credit he deserves as a rock and roll/rockabilly guitar player. He played lead on those sessions. Roland [Janes] was there, but he played rhythm. Billy Lee Riley played bass on our first session, but he didn't show up for our second." Stan Kesler replaced Riley on bass while JM Van Eaton played drums. Harrell remarked, "Most of those guys were really quiet and shy, Roland particularly, and I don't think JM said a word. It was just another eleven dollar session for them." Lott recalled, "There were just a couple of songs that I played lead on, but using the same microphone that Elvis used was quite a thrill." Incidentally, Lott used a 1956 Gibson Les Paul Gold Top guitar on the recordings. Regretfully, he eventually traded it for a 1960 Fender Stratocaster: "My Gibson didn't have any value then, and they were really heavy. A Strat weighed a lot less." On July 20, 1959, Sun issued "No More Crying the Blues" b/w "Have Faith in My Love." Today, Lott has two original copies of the 45 rpm single signed by all those that participated in the recording: Harrell, Phillips, Janes, Riley, and Van Eaton.

According to Harrell, the song, "What's the Use," was written about heartbreak: "Alton had broken up with his girlfriend, and he was all torn up about it. We were driving in the car one day, and I said, 'Well, why don't you call her, go back and talk to her?' He said, 'What's the use, Jimmy? She's through with me.' We started that song in the car and had it pretty much finished by the time we got home." Lott remarked, "Sam would tell us what to do and what not to do, like 'You don't need to play the guitar right there.' At the end of 'What's the Use,' we went, 'Bomp, bomp, bomp.' Sam stuck his head out the door and said, 'Girls, there will be no cha, cha, cha.'"

Lott will never forget recording at Sun Studio. "Sam had a knack for seeing things that other people couldn't. For some reason, Sam really liked me and Jimmy. He really thought that if we kept going that we would wind up doing okay." Harrell added, "Sam Phillips was very nice to us."

Their success was regional. According to Lott, "At that time, Sam was running out of money. He didn't do a lot of promotion. We continued to appear around the area, playing sock hops. We also did some radio shows, which included the *Louisiana Hayride*." The Collins Kids appeared with them on the program. Harrell reflected, "I could not believe Larry could play the guitar like he did at that age. When I was stationed at Camp Pendleton, I used to go to Compton to watch Larry and Lorrie Collins and Joe and Rose Lee Maphis on *Town Hall Party*."

Alton and Jimmy were slated to return to Sun Records to record some more tunes, but unbeknownst to Lott; Harrell had married and signed up to re-join the Navy. Lott recalled, "I was totally devastated. I went to Sun Studio, and Sam was just beside himself. He really thought we were on our way. I really thought that we had something since we were good at writing. 'No More Crying the Blues' is almost like a cult standard now. If you were going to Sun Studio to record in those days, that was it. That was the very essence of rockabilly." After Lott realized that the duo would not be continuing, he went back to Jackson [Mississippi] and started playing with some other bands: "If I had gone to Memphis and had done like Sam Phillips told me, Elvis would have recorded my song, 'Why Do I Love You.'" Years later, Lott's version with Bill Justis on saxophone was released: "It's actually a pretty good tune."

Throughout the years, Lott continued to work with various artists: "I recorded 'Brand New Baby' with Murray Kellum. Then I worked in a band with Buddy Rogers, Wray Hixson, Bill Tackett, and Jimmy Whitehead. Our regular booking was the Arena Club in Jackson [Mississippi]. I also did some stuff with Andy Anderson. I played guitar for Charlie Rich and Gene Simmons at the Wagon Wheel in Jackson and Jerry Lee Lewis at the City Auditorium in Jackson. One night, Roland [Janes] didn't make it for the show, so all of a sudden Jerry had to have somebody. He came up to me and said, 'I'll watch you play this first set. If I think you're good enough, then I'll let you play with me.' He turned around to walk away, but I grabbed him and said, 'Whoa, wait a minute. Let's just get the record straight here. I don't have to play for you.' He kind of looked at me then walked away. As I played, he was over in the wings giving me an A-okay sign. That first show I did with him, the Hammond organ was half a step flat on the hammer. It was a packed house, and he kicked off with 'Down the Line.' I realized that I was half a step off, and I had to tune real fast. He didn't say anything. I knew all the licks. He was kind of surprised since we hadn't rehearsed. Jerry actually paid me a compliment as he told the crowd that I just jumped up there and knew everything. He was quite a character, fun to work with though."

Lott also worked with The Faux Pas, in which he originally played bass: "I went on the road with them, and we wound up letting the guitar player go. I then took over as leader of the band and played guitar. We all dressed alike and could play for five hours without ever repeating a song. I was with that band for thirteen straight years. We toured up and down the East Coast, New Orleans, Miami, Chicago, and Las Vegas playing pop, Top 40, and show tunes." It wasn't until 1973 that Alton and Jimmy saw one another again. According to Lott, "I was playing in Hagerstown, Maryland. Jimmy got wind of it, and he came to watch me and my band play."

Four years later, Lott quit the music business because it was just too hard to make a living. Harrell made a career out of being in the Navy: "I was a hospital corpsman for eleven years and then I got commissioned to be a medical service corps officer for twenty-six years." He added, "I have a master's degree in management/ health care administration, which I got in the Navy, thanks to the GI Bill." When Harrell attended college, he had the intention of becoming a doctor: "I was in a pre-med curriculum for only one semester. I was probably better suited to be an administrator anyway."

In 1998, Alton and Jimmy returned to Sun Records. Harrell expressed, "It was an unbelievable feeling to go back there. We stood in essentially the same spot as we stood in 1959. In a way, it seemed like yesterday." Two years later, they recorded at Phillips International where Roland Janes engineered. The song, "Who Put the Rock in Roll?" was released soon after on the CD, *Rockabilly Hall of Fame #5*. Lott hadn't had anything to do with music since 1977. Interest had been renewed after his wife threw him a surprise birthday party, and he and The Faux Pas reunited on stage.

Alton and Jimmy would have reunited for shows sooner, but Harrell couldn't participate because of family commitments. Therefore, Lott did a few solo gigs. On May 18, 2007, at the Rockin' '50's Fest III in Green Bay, Wisconsin, Deke Dickerson assisted with vocals on the Alton and Jimmy tunes. Prior to the performance, fans mistook Lott for Sonny Burgess since they resemble one another. These days, Harrell has returned to the music, and he and Lott have participated in several festivals. Harrell declared, "It's so easy to slip back into the mood and feeling. I don't think you ever really lose it." On a semi-regular basis, Lott also performs with Andy Anderson.

The Paladins, The Planet Rockers, The Dave and Deke Combo, and The Vargas Brothers have all recorded songs by Alton and Jimmy. Harrell stated, "[At one of the festivals], Alton was in an area where disc jockey Del Villarreal was set-up, and he heard 'No More Crying the Blues.' Alton walked up to him and asked, 'Who is that?' Del replied, 'Oh, that's The Vargas Brothers. Who are you?' Alton said, 'Alton Lott.' Del then said, 'Oh my goodness, that's your song.' Alton told him, 'They do a great job.'" They still receive royalty checks from Sun. Harrell remarked, "I think we are lucky."

Sleepy LaBeef

Sleepy LaBeef switched from gospel to rockabilly once Elvis Presley gave the genre mainstream appeal. In May 1957, Starday Records released LaBeef's first single, "I'm Through" b/w "All Alone." He appeared on the *Houston Jamboree, Louisiana Hayride*, and

Grand Ole Opry and played regularly in Las Vegas. Glen Campbell or Kenny Rogers sometimes played in his band. LaBeef is notorious for mixing different genres of songs into a medley. Even though, foot stomping, hand clapping Southern gospel music is his favorite to sing. In 1979, LaBeef was one of the first rockabilly artists to perform in Europe, at the Wembley Festival in England.

Sleepy LaBeef was born on July 20, 1935, in Smackover, Arkansas. Thomas LaBoeuf is his real name, but he revealed, "I've been called Sleepy all my life."[4] Only his mother ever called him Thomas. LaBeef received the nickname Sleepy because he always looked half-awake. One release on Wayside, "Tore Up" b/w "Lonely," was issued as Tommy LaBeff. Beginning in 1965, his last name was changed from LaBeff to LaBeef on recordings. LaBeef's family was farmers, and he was the youngest of ten children. At fourteen, LaBeef traded his .22 rifle for a guitar. He taught himself how to play by watching Deacon Vernon McGee, who preached at his local Pentecostal church. LaBeef started with rhythm patterns but quickly learned lead licks. A year later, he began singing in church. The first tune he sang was "I Saw the Light." Gospel music was very inspirational to the young musician, but he heard blues and country too, thanks to KWKH and the *Louisiana Hayride* in Shreveport, the *Grand Ole Opry* in Nashville, and radio programs that broadcasted from Chicago, Little Rock, and New Orleans. He recalled, "Country, old Southern gospel, western swing, and boogie woogie were all mixed together, and they called it rockabilly." In 1951, he had his first public performance at a church in El Dorado, Arkansas. The McGee Brothers were also on the bill. Local fairs then hired LaBeef. He didn't graduate from high school, only went to the eighth grade. Instead, the teenager got a job working in an oil field and then driving truck.

At eighteen years old, LaBeef moved to Beaumont, Texas where he performed live every Friday night on radio station KTRM. Three months later, the city of Houston beckoned. He got a job with L.C. Loper and Company, where his duties included digging a foundation for the Houston Astrodome. LaBeef also disc jockeyed at KRCT and played on their Saturday evening program, the *Houston Jamboree*. There he sang gospel with his first wife, Louise, and

In 1957, Sleepy LaBeef's first single, "I'm Through" b/w "All Alone," was released on Starday Records (courtesy Sleepy LaBeef).

sometimes teamed with George Jones and Sonny Burns. In 1955, LaBeef signed with Starday Records. At his initial session, he auditioned some gospel tunes. Those remained unreleased; however, it wasn't long before he made the transition to rockabilly. A year later, he formed his first band with Wendall Clayton and Dee Knipe. At Gold Star Studios in Houston, they cut "Baby Let's Play House" and "Don't Make Me Go." Soon after, he recorded two songs ("All Alone" and "I'm Through") for Starday, which generated his first single. The A side of his second release, "All the Time," was co-written with Hal Harris and is his favorite: "Pappy Daily [co-owner of Starday] had said, 'We need you to write songs, so we can run them through our publishing company. That way, we keep the money.'" LaBeef commented, "I still draw royalties from them. They were honest."

Elvis Presley and Johnny Cash had already left the *Louisiana Hayride* when LaBeef appeared on the radio program. However, Bob Luman, Werly Fairburn, and Carl Belew were still regulars. Another alumnus of the *Louisiana Hayride* was Tommy Sands. He, George Jones, Roy Orbison, and LaBeef had taken turns opening for Presley on his tours of South Texas, primarily Galveston and Houston. LaBeef recollected, "Hal Harris was my manager, and he booked Elvis. One of us local boys would kill an hour or so and then the main show would be Elvis, Scotty [Moore], and Bill [Black]. I was definitely impressed by Elvis. He was a great talent. I think anybody would have to be blind and deaf not to know that." LaBeef also shared stages with Chuck Berry, Fats Domino, Little Richard, Buddy Holly, and John Lee Hooker. He commented, "I probably did learn something from working with those guys. I hope I did anyway." LaBeef didn't perform solo until 1965. At that same time, he gave up his day job to concentrate on his music career.

LaBeef cited several musical influences: Sister Rosetta Tharpe, Martha Carson, Red Foley, Tennessee Ernie Ford, Ernest Tubb, Lefty Frizzell, Jimmie Skinner, Roy Acuff, Hank Thompson, Bob Wills, Jimmy Heap, Big Joe Turner, Howlin' Wolf, and Muddy Waters. George Jones, Sister Rosetta Tharpe, and Bill Monroe are his favorite singers.

There were several independent label releases before LaBeef signed with Columbia Records in 1964. Don Law, who was head of their country music division, had called him personally with the offer. His first release on the label was "You Can't Catch Me" b/w "Everybody's Got to Have Somebody (to Love)." In early 1968, another Columbia track, "Everyday" peaked at number seventy-three on the country charts. Unfortunately, Columbia wasn't sure what to do with LaBeef and even told him, "'We don't know how to market you; we don't know what to call you.'"[5] With those remarks, his contract was not renewed. LaBeef was with them for four years and saw the issuance of six singles. Then, Shelby Singleton approached him about recording for his labels, first Plantation and then Sun International. Throughout the 1970s, he had releases on the revived Sun label.

On January 1, 1977, while on the Maine turnpike, fire destroyed the inside of LaBeef's tour bus, which was a 1948 Greyhound Silverado. His clothing, tapes, and record collection all went up in flames. It had been prepared to be his transportation for shows in thirty-nine states. That incident halted the tour, and for the next nine months, he took up musical residency at Alan's Fifth Wheel Lounge in Amesbury, Massachusetts. During this stint, author Peter Guarlnick frequently caught his act. At the time, George Thorogood was playing a blues club nearby, so Bob Bartaluci of Barren Records brought him to see LaBeef's show: "He sat in the audience the whole night. When George came out with his albums, he included many of the songs we had done in the first set [such as 'Move it on Over' and 'Ride on Josephine']." Before and after the accidental fire, LaBeef toured constantly: "We didn't get rich, but we had a lot of fun and met a lot of good people."

LaBeef is referred to as the "Human Jukebox," thanks to his ability to retain lyrics to six thousand songs: "I don't know why, but I used to just listen to a song twice, and I'd have it."[6] When LaBeef was younger, he performed five or six nights a week with a set list that always varied. Even today, his backing musicians are kept on their toes because he quickly changes from one song to another without any warning, and there is no rehearsal. LaBeef disclosed, "I'm more or less an interpreter of songs. I have to do a mixture, some old blues, classic country, gospel, and western swing—a variety to please the audience. I get adventurous and go in different directions. It's about having fun, not necessarily about teaching my backing band a lesson. They'll learn as they go, on the job training." Many times, he opens his show with Big Joe Turner's "Honey Hush," while "Amazing Grace" is one of his favorites to sing because everyone can join in.

After his contract with Sun International expired, he teamed up with Rounder Records in 1980: "Starting with the album *It Ain't What You Eat, It's the Way How You Chew It*, LaBeef followed with a string of powerful discs that drew upon his phenomenal repertoire of songs."[7] That was his longest relationship with any recording label—twenty years. He acknowledged, "I loved the people at Rounder, especially Ken Irwin. They are good people."

When deciding upon new material for a CD, LaBeef usually makes the song choices, picking those he feels most confident in singing: "Writers sometimes present me with different songs. I listen to them and whatever strikes me I choose or the record company decides and then I don't know what the songs are until I get into the studio." Two songs that he rejected were "We Split the Blanket" and "My Baby Thinks He's a Train." In regard to the latter tune, it was a number one song on the country charts for Rosanne Cash, but even then, LaBeef didn't care for it. In 2000, his new label, MC released the single "Detour" and the CD *Tomorrow Never Comes*. Critics applauded both efforts. Three years later, LaBeef underwent heart bypass surgery. Since then, his schedule is not as hectic as it once was.

Today, the rockabilly legend continues to perform in the United States and overseas, primarily at roots festivals. Once at a show in Spain, he shared a stage with Julio Iglesias, who hadn't learned English yet and had to have a translator. There were 80,000 people in attendance. Even though, LaBeef was well received, he is most content when playing to smaller crowds. "Sometimes it's more fun with less people. You can look them in the eye." After over fifty years as a performer, LaBeef is more popular now than he ever was: "Success is nice, but if you have it in your heart, then you don't get into [this business] to make a bunch of money. You do it because you love the music. That love keeps me going, and I thank the Lord for the strength to do it. I never had a number one record, but I am glad to be performing."

Eddie Bond

During his career, Eddie Bond recorded over three hundred songs. He was a regular member of the *Louisiana Hayride* and worked show dates with Charlie Feathers and Johnny

Horton. Besides singing, Bond was a shrewd businessman who invested in several areas of media, including television, radio, and nightclubs. For seventeen years, he was a disc jockey at KWEM in Memphis. While there, he promoted various artists by playing their records but also conducted live shows where special guests such as Webb Pierce, The Wilburn Brothers, Marty Robbins, Faron Young, or Bill Anderson would perform their latest and greatest hits. Journalist Bob Mehr noted "that Bond's musical reputation would come to rest on the dozen or so blazing rockabilly sides he cut for Mercury between 1956 and 1958, among them genre classics like 'Rockin' Daddy,' 'Slip, Slip, Slippin' In' and 'Boppin' Bonnie.'"[8]

Eddie Bond was born on July 1, 1933, in Memphis, Tennessee. His father was a Pentecostal minister, so Bond grew up singing gospel music. The rockabilly legend was the oldest of three as he had two younger sisters. At eight years old, Bond took an interest in music. He entered a competition where whoever sold the most garden seed won a Gene Autry guitar. With his new prize, Bond played night and day until his fingers bled, primarily practicing Hank Williams, Sr.'s "They'll Never Take Her Love from Me" and "Lovesick Blues." At thirteen, he entered the local nightclub circuit: "I played beer joints, just me and my guitar. I had a little microphone that I plugged in and hooked up to the radio [to amplify my voice]. I then tuned into a station. For pay, I just opened my guitar case, and they threw money in. I was making thirty dollars a night, which was pretty good for a little poor boy going to school and shining shoes for a living. They called me the 'Brown-Eyed Hillbilly' and that was a nickname I had for a long time."[9]

In 1950, Bond quit high school and took odd jobs before enlisting in the U.S. Navy. For the next eighteen months, he served in Hawaii. Upon discharge from the Navy, he created his band, The Stompers. Reggie Young was only sixteen years old when he joined Bond: "I advertised in the paper that I needed a guitar player. [At the time], Reggie played in a western swing band, Bob Williams and the Mid-South Playboys. I went to a show of theirs and hired Reggie. I just had to have him because he played so well, like Chet Atkins." Besides Young, The Stompers featured Johnny Fine on drums, Jimmy Smith, who was blind, on saxophone and piano, and John Hughey on steel guitar. Bond credited the band members with giving him experience and knowledge that he otherwise didn't have. Since Young was underage, Bond took him under his wing and became his guardian. They played regularly, but Bond also sometimes performed with Clyde Leoppard and His Snearly Ranch Boys at the Cotton Club in West Memphis, Arkansas. At first, Bond's father disapproved of his son's desire to be a singer: "It took a little selling, but when my dad quit preaching, he really got involved in my career. He was very supportive." His father was then a traveling salesman, who sold industrial paint for M.C. Campbell and Company: "He gave me a job. I was actually working there when I got married, and I always went through Nashville before I came home. The stars of the *Grand Ole Opry* had a softball team that played on Wednesdays, so I always tried to be in town then. [While at the ballpark] I visited with Faron Young, Webb Pierce, Little Jimmy Dickens, Marty Robbins, and Ernest Tubb. The games were strictly for fun, and there weren't any fans." Bond wanted to be close to country music, and he felt that was the best way, by hobnobbing with its artists. His concentration wasn't on paint, so the job didn't last long: "I had music on my mind so bad. It was like a fire burning, this desire I had for country music. I just had to do it."

In 1954, Elvis Presley auditioned to be a singer in Bond's band: "Neither of us had any

In 1956, Eddie Bond recorded Sonny Fisher's "Rockin' Daddy" for Mercury Records. Eddie Bond and the Stompers, clockwise from left: Ronald Smith (lead guitar), Enlow Hoskin (bass), Johnny Fine (drums), Curtis Alderson (vocalist/dancer), Jody Chastain (steel), and Eddie Bond (rhythm guitar) (courtesy Eddie Bond).

records out at the time. He came down to the Hi-Hat Club [in Memphis], which was a real sophisticated place. We played western swing with saxophone, piano, and drums. Elvis sang pop, and I sang old country. [Bond hired him to entertain the dancing crowd.] He was poor as could be, had slimy looking hair and wore old dirty black britches with a pink stripe down the side of them. This lady who was on the board of directors told me, 'You get that slimy looking snake out of here, or I'm gonna fire all of y'all.' I then had to run around and see if I could find Elvis another job. I did, and about two weeks later Sam Phillips released Elvis' first single, 'That's All Right' b/w 'Blue Moon of Kentucky.' That record went over big. The board of directors then came to me and said, 'Can you get him to come back?' I said, 'It'll cost you about five thousand now.' It just really did me good to tell them that." This version is different from the story that is more often told, in which Bond rejects Presley and tells him to "stick to driving a truck."

A year later, Bond ventured to Sun Studio in the hopes that he would be offered a contract. He recalled, "Sam Phillips was recording everybody, so naturally I went down and auditioned. He told me that my voice was just a little bit too mediocre. I don't know if he was complimenting me or not, but I wouldn't have been put down for anything." The tapes were quickly erased, so there is no log of which songs he recorded. California based Ekko Records then took an interest in the young singer and offered him a contract: "I had one session for them in Nashville where I cut four songs: 'Talking Off the Wall,' 'Love Makes a Fool (Every Day),' 'Your Eyes,' and 'Double Duty Lovin'.' [The tunes featured Hank Garland, Jerry Byrd, and Eddie Hill on guitar, Lightnin' Chance on bass, Buddy Harman on drums, and Marvin Hughes on piano.] I liked 'Love Makes a Fool (Every Day)' and 'Your Eyes' because they were country." Ekko issued two singles: "Talking Off the Wall" b/w "Double Duty Lovin'," which was issued in August, and "Love Makes a Fool (Every Day)" b/w "Your Eyes," which hit store shelves a month later. Unfortunately, neither platter sold enough copies for a call-back. Later that year, Bond signed with Bob Neal and was recruited to join his booking agency, Stars Incorporated: "Elvis Presley, Johnny Cash, Carl Perkins, Roy Orbison, and Warren Smith all traveled under that banner. For a year, I traveled with Carl and Johnny. One night, Reggie [Young] wasn't there, so Carl played lead guitar for me. We couldn't let him come out though because he was a star in his own right. Therefore, he played behind the curtain."

Eventually, Bond teamed up with Mercury Records: "Disc jockey Sleepy Eyed John had played my songs over the phone to the label's A&R director, [William David] 'D.' Kilpatrick. I couldn't make a living doing those country songs, so I was just lucky that I could do rockabilly. I signed a contract with Mercury [which ensured the release of] four records a year for three years." On March 17, 1956, the 45 rpm single "Rockin' Daddy" b/w "I've Got a Woman" hit store shelves. "Rockin' Daddy" peaked at number fifty-six on the *Billboard* charts. As it turned out, Bond was better off with Mercury since Sam Phillips was notorious for not paying royalties: "My feelings were hurt because I wasn't with the rest of them [at Sun]. I felt like an outcast until the checks starting coming in." In Little Rock, Arkansas alone, 6500 copies of the record were sold. Bond revealed, "'Rockin' Daddy' is more country. I really liked that one."

Due to constant touring, Bond accumulated 150,000 miles on his 1955 pink and white Oldsmobile 88. He admitted, "It just wore out, so I decided I'd be better off if I could get into radio. I went to KWEM in Memphis, and I told them that I had a lot of experience. I had never ran a board, didn't know anything about it. Even though, I had cut a really good audition tape, and they liked it. I was hired. [This allowed him to give promotion to the records that he wanted.] [W.S. Holland once said that] between me and Dewey Phillips, we could make a hit out of anything in Memphis. We really could too. One song in particular that I really got behind was 'Ballad of a Teenage Queen.' Jack Clement had brought it to me, saying he had written it and would I jump on it and push it for him? He was a good buddy of mine." Bond also continually played Elvis Presley's records and Johnny Cash's singles, especially "Cry, Cry, Cry." He added, "I could say my name and play my records all I wanted. Every record I had after that would be a [local] hit. [Incidentally, he had five other releases on Mercury before his contract was not renewed.] They didn't want me to record for them if I wasn't going to go on the road." Bond was still performing but usually for only two weeks at a time, such as at the Air Force base in Biloxi, Mississippi.

The six Mercury singles are now considered iconic, but at the time Bond's true ambition was to be a country singing star: "I never would have done rockabilly, but that's what got me on Mercury. If I hadn't done 'Rockin' Daddy,' 'Flip Flop Mama,' and the rest, then they wouldn't have signed me. There wasn't anybody doing country. We actually did better on the *Louisiana Hayride* than we did at the *Grand Ole Opry* because they had a crowd that really loved rockabilly. I got standing ovations and encores at the *Big D Jamboree* and the *Louisiana Hayride*. Later on, when I was able, I started singing country."

Bond cited his musical influences as Marty Robbins and Carl Smith. His favorite singers were Marty Robbins, Carl Smith, Webb Pierce, Roger Miller, Mel Tillis, and Elvis Presley. He also noted friendships with Johnny Cash, Carl Perkins, Roy Orbison, Mel Tillis, Webb Pierce, and Roger Miller. In regard to Pierce, "One of my favorite people in the business was Webb. He and I had more fun and did more things together."

During the 1960s, Bond owned five different nightclubs in Memphis and the surrounding area. One of them, The Diplomat, was home to such performers as Sun recording artist Gene Simmons and Sam the Sham. Bond recollected, "I also had a club called The Eddie Bond Ranch, and it held about six hundred people. It was located on a forty acre strip with three fishing ponds. [The Stompers served as house band and backed every major country act of the era.] It was just a real neat place that I had for about six years." Another one he owned was The Little Black Book: "I had been singing there on weekends. One night, the owner says, 'Why don't you buy in with me? You can be my partner.' The first week I had the club I didn't make any money. In fact, I had to put money into it, but then it did real well." Reggie Young played The Little Black Book with Bond: "Boy, I really had a knocked out good band then. I think we were number four across the nation. I wanted to be boss, so I could sing as long as I wanted." Every band that came into town had to deal with Bond in order to play and get promoted since he had a monopoly on Memphis. Everyone referred to him as "Mr. Memphis Country."

By the late 1960s, "I had discovered Sheriff Buford Pusser, who was the toughest lawman in Tennessee. [He tried to rid the area of moonshiners and gamblers.] I worked about nine years with him." The songs that Bond penned about Pusser's life were released on Stax Records in conjunction with his biopic, *Walking Tall*, being shown at theaters.

Throughout the 1970s, Bond continued to work on the radio, record, and perform. In 1982, his rockabilly career was revived when he traveled to England for the first time. Dave Travis was his booking agent. Bond disclosed, "I started Stomper Time Records after I lost my contract with Mercury." In 1958, he had purchased the label to record new material and have releases. Eventually, Bond got busier and lost interest: "I didn't really want to stay in the record business. Dave [Travis] made me a real good offer on it [so he bought it outright]."

Over twenty times, Bond traveled to various countries in Europe, including France, England, Sweden, Italy, and Germany. Once, he stayed overseas for forty days, performing at thirty-two different shows. He mentioned, "London and Europe have been real, real good to me. When I go there, I have to sing strictly the rockabilly stuff. If I don't do 'Slip, Slip, Slippin' In,' boy they start hollering. You got to sing your lungs out, so I hate that song, but everybody else likes it."

In later years, Bond slowed down his own career in order to promote his son Eddie Bond, Jr., who was also a singer: "I was really training and pushing him, even had two CDs out. He was well on his way. They'd start clapping when he walked in the door." Unfortunately, in 2002, he tragically passed away from lupus at the young age of thirty-four. Bond commented, "It liked to kill us all, knocked us to our knees." Bond lost interest in performing, although he participated in the Center for Southern Folklore Memphis and Music Heritage Festival as well as the Rockin' '50's Fest in Green Bay, Wisconsin, and the Viva Las Vegas Weekender. By 2006, he had sold all of his radio stations and nightclubs. Seven years later, on March 20, fans were saddened to hear of his passing from Alzheimer's disease.

Andy Anderson

Andy Anderson's signature tunes are "Tough, Tough, Tough" and "Johnny Valentine." The latter tune was number one in San Antonio, Texas. He commented, "Disc jockey Dewey Phillips first broke 'Johnny Valentine' on WHBQ in Memphis. He was a crazy guy, and so was I. We got along real well."[10] Anderson added, 'Johnny Valentine' worked because it had a Spanish beat, weird chords, and unusual lyrics."[11] He appeared on *American Bandstand* and *Wink Martindale's Dance Party*. His single, "You Shake Me Up," was extremely popular in the state of New York. In 2010, Anderson wrote his biography, *Memoirs of the Original Rolling Stone*, with assistance from Erika Celeste. Today, he enjoys recording his original material, which can be classified as contemporary Southern rock music, and participating in reunions with members of both The Rolling Stones and The Dawnbreakers. In fact, one of Anderson's compositions, "I'm a Rolling Stone, Dawnbreaker Too" reflects his career. His greatest honor came when he was inducted into the Mississippi Musicians' Hall of Fame.

Andy Anderson was born on May 15, 1935, in Memphis, Tennessee. His family owned a 15,000 acre cotton plantation: "Over four hundred families lived on that plantation. On Saturday afternoons in the 1940s, in order to get paid, all the workers would come to the main commissary/office. Most came in wagons pulled by mules; some came in pickup trucks or cars, while others walked. Saturday was kind of a party day. Times were really tough, and it was too far to go to Clarksdale, so the workers and their families would sit behind the commissary and have lunch." Elmore James, Mississippi Slim, B.B. King, Muddy Waters, Howlin' Wolf, and John Lee Hooker were traveling musicians, who would team up and circulate from one plantation to the next. Anderson's family's plantation was one of their stops. They would break out their instruments and start playing. Later in the day, the audience would chime in and participate too: "It wasn't anything booked or organized. [For pay, the musicians at least got fed and received tips from a hat that was passed.] The bigger the plantation, the more people they had to play for, [which increased their] chance of making money. Those performances were my first musical influences." Anderson worked on the farm too: "I pulled a cotton sack many a mile when I was a kid for twenty cents a pound. That's the way I made my spending money."

Anderson started singing when he was fifteen years old, and the first song he sang was "I'm Movin' On." At that same time, he picked up the guitar. For a Christmas present in 1951, his parents bought him a Harmony guitar for $37.50 at the O.K. Houck's Music Company in Memphis: "It was O.K. himself who sold and tuned the guitar, explained some chords and pickin' styles and suggested the Mel Bay Ten Easy Lessons."[12] Anderson listened to the *Randy Record High Life Show* to hear blues and rhythm and blues and the *Grand Ole Opry* for country music. In fact, that's where he first heard Hank Snow and learned some of his songs.

Hanging out in Memphis was one of his hobbies, and he would sometimes run into Elvis Presley: "I knew Elvis before I knew he could even sing. On Friday nights, my buddies and I would get in my 1951 Chevrolet station wagon and drive to Memphis. We'd go to a movie and then we'd go to the local hangout on Union Avenue, which was about a half a mile from Sun Studio. It was a place called The Jungle, a drive-in that sold soda, hamburgers, and fries. The eatery had trees with lights and real monkeys all over it. The cool thing, because of James Dean, was to wear black engineer boots, Levi's, and T-shirts, and every guy had long sideburns. We'd hang out by our car and try to look tough. That's where the lines in 'Johnny Valentine' come from. There was one verse in the song about that attire. The inspiration for 'Johnny Valentine' came from a song by The Mills Brothers called 'The Naughty Lady of Shady Lane.' It talks about this chick and how suave and cute she is and then in the last verse it is revealed that she is only nine days old. I thought well, ain't that slick. Let's write a song about a sexy young man and then reveal in the last verse that he's only ten years old. Well, that was my first blow-out with London Records. The last verse infuriated the label, 'Hey,

Andy Anderson had a group called the Rolling Stones and recorded for Sun Records eight years before the British Invasion (courtesy Andy Anderson).

that's not cool. We want this guy to be suave and debonair.' They made me change the words. The guy ended up not being the answer to the naughty lady of Shady Lane. London Records had changed the conjecture of the entire song. They made it a hit; selling about 750,000 copies, but they were all wrong." The Sun Records version contains the original lyrics.

Anderson revealed, "I first met Elvis at The Jungle in 1951/1952. I knew one of his friends, Cliff Greaves, better than Elvis, but we all just hung out, leaned on car fenders, and talked." One of the reasons Anderson had his station wagon was because he raced boats, which he continued doing in college. Anderson added, "The next time I saw Elvis was at my voice lesson. My mother had wanted me to take lessons. She was musically inclined—wrote beautiful poetry and played the piano. My mother took me to Memphis and enrolled me in classes with Zelma Lee Whitfield. At one of the lessons, I walked in as Elvis was walking out. I recognized him, and he recognized me. I said, 'What are you doing here?' and he replied, 'Well, what are you doing here?' I said, 'I'm learning to sing.' He said, 'Me too. Sam Phillips sent me here.' She taught us both to sing the same way, so ironically we sound an awful lot alike. Ms. Whitfield was very tough and made us sing the scales and sustain the notes. If you took voice lessons from her, and you paid attention, you came out qualified to sing. I have a hell of a range, and I'm sure Elvis did too."

Anderson's mother was supportive of his musical aspirations: "She died in 1953, so she never got to see The Rolling Stones. She saw me play at some high school functions with my first band, which included classmate Jimmy Giles on drums and my cousin Billy Anderson on piano." In 1954, Billy "Cuz" Covington and Joe Tubb invited Anderson to join their band after witnessing him win a talent contest by playing piano in Lee Hall at Mississippi State: "My mother had enrolled me in piano lessons when I was small with the dream that I might one day become a classical concert pianist."[13] Anderson conveyed, "I don't like the term rockabilly or to be categorized as such. We were and have always been a rock and roll band. The music that we played was so much more hard driven. We felt like we were the founders of rock and roll. The first thing we did when we started playing was hire a drummer." The Rolling Stones were Roy Estes on piano, Joe Tubb on lead guitar, Billy "Cuz" Covington on bass, Roger "Bobby" Lyon on drums, James Aldridge on rhythm guitar, and Anderson on vocals and rhythm guitar. In 1956, at Jimmy Ammons Studio in Mississippi, they cut five songs: "I Got a Woman," "I Love You," "Johnny Valentine," "Roll Over Beethoven," and a medley of "Rip It Up"/"Ready Teddy"/"Long Tall Sally." Ammons and Mabel McQueen had become their managers, but only for a year.

After the release of Elvis Presley's "That's All Right" b/w "Blue Moon of Kentucky," everyone within a 500 mile radius wanted to record at Sun Studio. Anderson recalled, "We knew everybody there. That was the natural place for us to go. We decided we were good enough and wanted to cut a record, so I just called and booked the studio. In November 1957, I recorded 'Tough, Tough, Tough' and 'Johnny Valentine' with The Rolling Stones (Tubb, Covington, Estes, and Lyon). Jack Clement was the engineer. I already knew Jack was good because I liked all the songs he cut. I didn't really learn anything from him because we weren't there long enough. While we were in the studio practicing, Jerry Lee Lewis came in. We sat there and jammed, taught him our version of Roy Orbison's 'Go, Go, Go,' which we actually wrote most of. Jerry Lee released it later as 'Down the Line.' We also cut 'Go, Go, Go' at the session, so three songs total. However, it has never surfaced; don't know what happened to it. I wanted to get on Sun with Sam [Phillips]. He had more people than he knew what to do with, but he was the only one who had the foresight and liked our music. Sam couldn't afford to put my songs out because he was in financial dire straits. I was impatient to get a record out, so the next thing we did was win a talent contest in Memphis. The prize was a recording contract. This agent from Murray Nash Associates in Nashville came down and said London Records wants a rock and roll group, so in January 1958, we went to Nashville to record. The producer asked us for union cards. Nobody belonged to the union. We didn't need to belong to one; we had more gigs than we could play. I was the only one who could [participate]. You didn't have to be in the union to be a lead singer, although I couldn't play rhythm guitar. I recorded 'Johnny Valentine' with Hank Garland, Grady Martin, Buddy Harman, Bob Moore, and The Jordanaires. They wouldn't let my band play, so that's why there are two versions. They wanted a slow song for the back side, so we cut 'I-I-I Love You,' which was a song I wrote."

Once Anderson returned from the recording session, he reconnected with his band. They did a few Sun package shows. He remembered one specifically with Roy Orbison and Billy Lee Riley and the Little Green Men that occurred in Memphis. He added, "We also played a couple of shows at a summer resort outside of Memphis with Elvis [Presley], Scotty [Moore], and Bill [Black]. I think the first show we ever played with Elvis was in a little town called Walnut Grove, Mississippi. It was a high school benefit show. Elvis, Scotty, and Bill showed up in Elvis' 1953 pink Cadillac with the bass [strapped to the top of it]. I ended up knowing Scotty and Bill very well. In fact, Bill played on a couple of songs that I recorded at Hi Studio in Memphis in June 1964. One of those songs was 'Mustang Kid.'" Anderson added, "My group and I were in college while all of these other guys were out of school. We tried to play as often as we could but couldn't go out and tour. I was registered to play football and golf at Mississippi State. My bass man was a track star and enrolled in civil engineering, and my piano man was an aero-nautical engineer. We weren't frivolous playboys but instead pretty tied down. It was extremely difficult [to balance music and college]. Rock and roll was a hell of a distraction, but we managed and all graduated with honors." His piano player, Roy Estes, eventually held high-ranking positions at NASA.

Anderson's major was in agricultural engineering, and he graduated in 1957: "We had a sizable cotton plantation up in the Mississippi Delta, and I was going to go back and run that. I wanted to gain as much technical knowledge as I possibly could. I was on the original team that helped develop the diet and studies on catfish farming before they ever really started doing it commercially." Anderson attended for an extra year upon receiving his diploma because he wanted to be with the band.

Often times, Anderson's group was confused with The Rolling Stones from England: "Joe Tubb came up with the name for The Rolling Stones because we were on the road all the time. Almost every night, we were partying, playing music, or doing something. We thought of rolling stones because a rolling stone gathers no moss. We decided to use the name because of our lifestyle at the time, not because Muddy Waters had a song ['Rollin' Stone']." To try and keep down the confusion, promoters booked them as The Original Rolling Stones. London Records had us on records as Andy Anderson and the Rolling Stones. We were the first rock group to record for the label. We just didn't like the personnel there. They didn't know a thing about rock and roll. The worst thing that they could have done was gone through an agent in Nashville, which in 1957 was as country [oriented] as you could get. Even the agent didn't know anything about rock and roll. It was a mess."

While in Nashville, Anderson and Willie Nelson became pretty good friends: "I left about the time Willie did. I threw my hands up and said, 'These cats don't know what they're doing. If you're not Roy Acuff and dyed in the wool country, you know you're in trouble. You're in the wrong place.' We did cut two hit records, but it wasn't for anybody but ourselves. We booked a studio one night for four hours in May 1958 and cut 'You Shake Me Up' and 'The Way She Smiled.' We also produced the session. I gave the songs to a friend who marketed them to Apollo Records. They said, 'We love it.' They released the single; we got a big hit in *Billboard*, *Cashbox* ['Pick of the Week'], and *Music Reporter*, all [three magazine charts] in the same week." The two sides featured Tubb, Covington, Estes, and Jimmy Whitehead on drums.

Anderson may not have found success in Nashville, but he and his group were a popular nightclub act: "We played rock and roll with an attitude. When we went into a place, we went in not to entertain but to create a riot. We played for two and a half hours straight with a thirty minute break and then used the last hour for encores. We created so much excitement when we played that people always booked us back. Promoters and club owners used to say, 'You want a wild band, you get The Rolling Stones.'" They played a lot of Chuck Berry, Elvis Presley, Carl Perkins, Jerry Lee Lewis, Johnny Cash, and Bo Diddley songs besides their own material.

In 1959, his dad asked him to come back and run the plantation: "My rightful place was to come back home. Before college, I could have run the plantation, but I wanted to get more engineering and irrigation background. I gave The Rolling Stones my notice that I was hanging it up, but then when I went up there, my dad said, 'You know the more I think about it you and [your step-mother] Mary would never get along, so I think the best thing for you to do would be to go back to Jackson and continue doing what you're doing.' Well, I had already given my notice, and the band had replaced me with a guy named Howard 'B.B.' Boone." In 1960, Anderson then had no other choice but to start another band, which was The Dawnbreakers. Its members were Lane Cameron on guitar, Buddy Meyers on drums, Lee Graham on bass, and Chuck Stapleton on piano. The name for The Dawnbreakers came about because "we'd go out and play a gig and if we were booked somewhere close the second night we'd come back home. We're talking about 200, 300, 400 miles every night. Many times when we were coming home, the sun would be coming up." He acknowledged, "We've always been known as the Mississippi Mafia. We dress in black pants and black shirts." "Tough, Tough, Tough" b/w "Gimme a Lock o' Your Hair" was their first release, issued by Century Ltd. in May 1960.

In 1965, Anderson made a career transition when he moved to California to become an actor under the guidance of the William Morris Agency and Aaron Spelling. Murray Kellum took over his vocal duties with The Dawnbreakers. Anderson disclosed, "I had done enough television shows that I felt like there was nothing to it; I can do this. I had a manager named Carl Brent, who was a buddy of mine from Mississippi State. Carl was also managing Judy Garland at the time. I had gotten transferred from the Chicago office of the William Morris Agency to Beverly Hills, and they assigned me an agent by the name of Skip Taylor. Skip, Carl, and I became very good friends. Skip had many groups come to him since he was in charge of rock and roll artists. Well, Skip couldn't handle all of them, and the agency wouldn't sign them, so Skip asked Carl and me to set up our own management company." The William Morris Agency passed on several artists, including Canned Heat, Jefferson Airplane, and P.J. Proby. Anderson and his team (Brent and Walter Williams) signed them instead. They leased and remodeled venues in Orange County, California, Dallas, Texas, and Jackson, Mississippi, to keep the groups playing regularly: "We'd circulate them. Canned Heat would play two weeks in Orange County then go to Dallas for two, then come back to Jackson for another two and finally turn around and go back to L.A. We had our own groups following each other into each one of these clubs across the country." He added, "Carl [Brent] later became good friends with Aaron Spelling. After about a year, I became Aaron's protégé. He was teaching me to act and putting me in bit roles when he was at Four Star Productions. That was going great, and I probably would have had the lead in *Mod Squad*." Unfortunately, fate stepped in and changed his destiny. Anderson's younger brother was diagnosed with terminal cancer: "I came back to Jackson [Mississippi] to be with him. When I left, I was working on a movie with Aaron, Steve McQueen, and Angie Dickinson. I had it made, but I couldn't get in the mood to go back."

During the 1970s, Anderson's music was rediscovered: "Sun didn't really own those masters because we paid for them. We just never got them back in the hope that Sam would get his act together and put the songs out, but he never did. Shelby Singleton got a hold of the Sun catalog and started going through all the masters and boxes that he had in the attic. They found 'Johnny Valentine' and 'Tough, Tough, Tough' and released them on Charly Records in England. That's how we actually got released on Sun, but they still pay us. I have an agent, Dave Travis, in London, and he collects our royalties. He's the one responsible for putting all the compilation deals together." From 1974 to 1976, Anderson had a musical act with J.J. Hettinger called The Eagle and the Hawk. They performed driving folk blues.

Nineteen eighty-three was the year in which Anderson became aware that his music was still popular in Europe: "Bison Bop Records, from Germany, tracked me down. They wanted to release all my stuff. I didn't have a clue that anybody over there even knew who I was. I came back to Mississippi and went in the studio with one of my engineering buddies. We took all my records that I have on the wall in my studio and made masters off the 45s, cleaned them up with Dolby, and gave them a master tape." An album was released with the material that same year, and it was called *The Bop That Never Stopped, Volume 28*.

In 2005, Anderson played the Hemsby Rock 'n' Roll Weekender: "I rehearsed my own music for three weeks before I went over there, so I would remember exactly how we recorded the songs back then. We played them as close as you could get to the original versions. [Incidentally, the tunes he sang were chosen for him by promoter Willie Jeffery. When Anderson performs them with his own band here in the States, he doesn't try to make them sound like the records.] The band I had was from Wales, and they were a good bunch of boys. They had learned my stuff, and we played good, but the stage was so small that we couldn't jump around and put on a show. I just had to stand there." In recent years, Anderson has played frequently with fellow Sun artist Alton Lott. In 2013, he participated in a set with Lott and Jimmy Harrell at the Viva Las Vegas Weekender. Anderson feels that music is therapeutic and will often give concerts for just him and his wife: "I don't just sit and strum but play like I'm in front of five thousand people."

Vernon Taylor

In the 1950s, Vernon Taylor recorded for both Dot Records and Sun Records. He toured with Patsy Cline, appeared on *American Bandstand*, and had his own radio show. Having retired from the music business in 1968, Taylor felt that his time in the limelight was over. He didn't realize that his music was still popular in Europe. In 1995, he made a triumphant return to the stage with an appearance at the Hemsby Rock 'n' Roll Weekender. Even though he doesn't have time to sing nowadays, he was able to return to his Sun Records roots recently: "We got involved with Lonely Street Productions. They were doing the [stage play] *Good Rockin' Live: A Tribute to Sun Records*. We went to see them at a prominent dinner theater in Lancaster, Pennsylvania. Somehow they knew I was there, so they turned up the lights and paid me tribute. They sang 'Mystery Train' in my honor. When I got home, Robert Shaw of Lonely Street Productions called and asked me to do a voice-over for the Sun show. The lights go down and I say, 'Hello ladies and gentlemen, this is Vernon Taylor. I'm here to invite you to join us this evening to celebrate Sun Records and the birth of rock and roll. Kindly turn off your cell phones. We guarantee you're going to be in for a great time. Now let's welcome *Good Rockin' Live*. Let's rock and roll.'"[14] Thanks to his legendary recordings and now the voice-over, Taylor has ensured his place in rockabilly history.

Vernon Taylor was born on November 9, 1937, in Layhill, Maryland. There were three other children in the family, two boys and a girl. Tragically, his sister died at age three. Taylor and his brothers grew up in the country: "My dad had a farm, but it wasn't big enough to make a good living, so he rented it out. I was six years old when we moved to Warrenton, Virginia to live on a cattle farm, which was close to 3,000 acres. My dad was basically a truck farmer, raising everything we needed. We didn't have to buy much from the store other than salt and sugar. He was a good teamster, loved to plow with a team of Belgian horses. My uncle and older brothers [helped out on the farm]. I didn't really help because I was rather young. [Besides farming], my dad loved to sing gospel music around the house and in church, [which provided early inspiration to me]. Daddy and his brothers went to a music school. In those days, music teachers would travel around to various communities and meet in local schools, and they would teach people how to sing. My mom had a beautiful voice, but she never would sing [in public]." Taylor remembered, "We hadn't been in Warrenton too long when Bill Monroe had a tent show. I believe Lester [Flatt] and Earl [Scruggs] were still with him. I remember that [concert] as being something that really influenced me."

Taylor acknowledged, "My brother, Robert, liked to play the guitar and sing a little bit. My brother forbade me to touch his Gene Autry guitar, but of course I'd mess with it when he wasn't in the house. I was in the third grade when I saw him at a high school assembly, and it shocked the heck out of me because I never heard him practice. They announced that he would sing a couple of songs. Man that got my attention. He came out, dragging a straight back chair and his guitar, sat down to the mike, pulled the mike down, shut his eyes, and started wailing on a couple of songs: 'When You Wore a Tulip (and I Wore a Big Red Rose)' and 'Just Because.' Robert rocked that place, and I was really influenced by that."

As a pre-teen, "I listened to [various radio stations] on Saturday night, including WSM-Nashville, WCKW-Cincinnati, Ohio, WWDA-Wheeling, West Virginia, and WRVA-

Richmond, Virginia. [The *Grand Ole Opry* was one of the programs he heard.] I'd lie in bed listening to these radio stations and absorbing all the music that I heard. We didn't have any money, but my dad and I would go to live shows. People like Roy Acuff and Happy Johnny and the Hoosier Hotshots were quite an influence as far as live entertainment. As I got older, we saw Clyde Moody and The Carter Family. Bill Carlisle and the Carlisles had a hot jumpin' record, 'No Help Wanted.' I didn't know what rockabilly was in those days, but that was a rockin' song. I was influenced by the very simple guitar playing on it. Then I have to say that the first Elvis Presley record I heard was 'Blue Moon of Kentucky.' That song kind of awakened us all to the fact that there was something out there besides just plain hillbilly music or country. That made us realize what was going on, and we were interested in finding out all we could. [A little later] when 'Mystery Train' came out, nobody ever heard anything like that before. There was nothing in comparison that was kickin' like that. I was aware of all kinds of music: big band, jazz, Dixieland jazz, and classical."

In 1954, while still attending Sherwood High School in Sandy Spring, Maryland, Taylor started singing and formed his first band: "I had a schoolmate named Denny Pilgrim. I have to credit him with getting me started in a band because he had a friend named Jack Quaintance. Jack was an aspiring guitar player, and he was pretty good. We started practicing about once a week, sometimes twice a week. We did that for quite a while. When we got to where we could work up a little repertoire, we did some performing: small time NCO shows, gigs on the backs of flatbed pickup trucks, carnivals, and talent contests. We did pretty well in [the latter] because we were doing rockabilly, and it always went over real big. The crowd seemed to like what we were doing, and we were [up against some tough competition, including a bluegrass group]. In fact, we won all four talent contests; although we didn't win a prize, we got a little notoriety in a local newspaper. Denny, Jack, Roger [Prease], and I would go around the D.C. area and see guitar greats like Charlie Byrd. We'd go to Georgetown in Washington, D.C. and see Wild Bill Whelan and the Dixieland Jazz Cats." Incidentally, Taylor loves Dixieland jazz and is a big fan of gospel. Also in '54, Taylor became serious about playing the guitar. Prior to that, at the age of

Vernon Taylor was the last of three artists, the other two being Elvis Presley and Junior Parker's Blue Flames, to record "Mystery Train" for Sun Records (courtesy Vernon Taylor).

eight, he tried his hand at playing the ukulele and harmonica: "I never was very good at either one of them." At seventeen, he started songwriting and wrote two tunes: "Why Must You Leave Me" and "Your Lovin' Man." The latter became his signature song even though it wasn't released until 1973. Taylor declared, "I wrote 'Why Must You Leave Me' about an old girlfriend. She moved away. I used to have some fun with her. I sure missed her and her horse."

His first band, The Nighthawks, featured Roger Prease on piano, Jack Quaintance on lead guitar, Denny Pilgrim on bass, and Taylor on vocals and rhythm guitar. They'd practice at Quaintance's house. Taylor remembered, "We would be out somewhere late at night driving home listening to [disc jockey Lee Moore] in Wheeling, West Virginia. He'd call himself the coffee drinking nighthawk." That's how they came up with the name for the group. They were called that until Don Owens came on board: "He chose to change the name to The Southerners."

All the band members dropped out of school because they were having too much fun playing music. Taylor was just starting the eleventh grade: "Well, it turned out that we ultimately had to go back to school. We all wound up going to Emerson Institute to take some summer courses and make up the year that we lost. That turned into a lot of fun because we decided to skip school and be mildly mischievous." It was threatened that the school wasn't going to allow Taylor to graduate until he made up the time: "The principal was very kind and gracious [though] and possibly saw some potential. Don Owens talked to him; they let me off the hook, and I graduated." School hadn't been top priority for Taylor. His sole concentration was music.

Taylor's parents were very encouraging of their son's musical endeavors: "When I was young, my daddy bought me a handful of guitars. I couldn't have asked for more supportive parents, and I'm grateful for that. I think they did that in the hopes of keeping me out of trouble. If it hadn't been for music, I think I would definitely have been in trouble, like a lot of kids that age. My parents were just poor down to Earth farmers, and they definitely wanted to see their children have a better way of life. They worked hard, sixteen hours a day."

The Nighthawks played lawn parties and attempted to perform at a high school dance: "We didn't do a lot of clubs." In late 1954, Quaintance, Pilgrim, and Taylor met fiddle player Curley Smith, who was playing with the Blue Mountain Boys: "During the break, we got up and sang three songs: one rockabilly number, an upbeat country tune, and a ballad. The tunes brought the house down. We were absolutely amazed. Curley Smith, the bandleader said, "Boys, I'm letting my regular band go. You're starting with me here next Saturday, and practice is Wednesday night at my house.' [In fact, he fired his band on the spot]. Fire house dance halls were big things around this part of the country in those days." Saturday night dances made money for the fire department because kids from the local high schools would attend. Taylor recollected, "We played with Curley at the Beltsville Fire Hall in Prince Georges County, Maryland. We also had an early morning radio show with him on Saturday mornings. Jack Quaintance had to go to college in Florida, so he was only with us at the fire hall for six months. We tried to decide on who we were going to get to play guitar, so Curley said, 'Well, we could get Roy Clark.' At the time, he was pretty busy, and he didn't always show up on time for the gig. We went with Joe Carroll." Carroll was playing with the group when Taylor originally met them. Taylor added, "After about a year, Curley was offered a job from Connie B. Gay, who had a radio station in Little Rock, Arkansas. He left us with the band [which they had for another two years]. Denny and I would sing. He had a good tenor voice. I think I did some of my best singing in that old fire hall. We performed a mixture of rockabilly, country, and hillbilly music. We had fun with an old Roy Acuff tune called 'I Like Mountain Music.' Jack sang with us too, but then when Joe Carroll came along, Joe was an excellent singer and guitar player. He was a seasoned performer. After a couple of years, Danny Pendleton came in one night. We were aware of him, but we didn't really know who he was because he had played steel guitar. He came up and asked if he could sit in. We said, 'Well sure, so he lugged his big ole Gibson triple neck steel guitar [up to the stage].' He gave us a full sound. We hired Danny on the spot. We also acquired a drummer by that time. Frank Gosman was our drummer for about a year." Incidentally, Pendleton had played guitar on some of Don Owens' Starday recordings. He introduced Taylor to Owens in early 1957. By then, they were no longer playing at the fire hall. Taylor revealed, "Don Owens was looking for a teenage heartthrob, and he thought he'd found it in me. That's what he was promoting. Soon after, he used us on a few things, which included a public event in D.C., playing for all the dignitaries at a theater. The DuPont Network was there, and they were looking for a Saturday night show. Don pitched them the idea [of a show featuring us], and according to Don they hired us on the spot." For three years, The *Don Owens TV Jamboree* ran on WTTG, channel 5: "I was the featured singer, and my band was the house band. Denny Pilgrim eventually quit the TV show and went to work with Patsy Cline. Terry and the Pirates had broken up, so Steve Foster came to play bass. Duke Maddox also came in to play drums." Patsy Cline and Roy Clark were both regulars on the TV show, while Grandpa Jones, Les Paul and Mary Ford, and Jerry Lee Lewis all made appearances. Owens then became Taylor's manager, found him bookings, and got him his contract on Dot Records: "Don and Dot Records' executive producer Mac Wiseman had been friends for years. Mac was headlining a show at the Glen Echo Ballroom [in Glen Echo Park, Maryland], and we opened for him. Mac told Don, 'I like the way that boy sings. Bring him to Nashville next Tuesday; I want to record him.' We got on a plane and were there a day or two ahead of time."

In late July 1957, Taylor recorded at RCA Studio A in Nashville with Hank Garland, Buddy Harman, Floyd Cramer, Roy Husky, Charlie McCoy, Millie Kirkham, and The Jordanaires. Four songs were recorded at that session: "Losing Game," "Satisfaction Guaranteed" (which was a song penned by Owens), "Why Must You Leave Me" and "I've Got the Blues" (which was originally Hank Snow's "I'm Gonna Bid the Blues Goodbye"). They had changed the title and shortened the song, but "Hank seemed to like it, so that was good." Two thumbtack laden pianos were used on the track "Satisfaction Guaranteed," which were played by McCoy and Cramer. Taylor remembered, "I was a nervous wreck, scared to death. I didn't perform as well as I could have." The Nighthawks understood that Dot Records was only interested in Taylor and not the whole band. They all had day jobs: "We were doing this as a hobby." During his visit to Nashville, Taylor attended a gospel show and a disc jockey convention with Don Owens: "That's where I met a lot of people [including Johnny Cash]."

That same year, he played a TV sock hop with Dale Hawkins in Richmond, Virginia: "He was a very nice guy. We had some fun talking. I sure liked his song 'Susie-Q.' It was one of my favorites." Taylor played several different TV sock hops all throughout the Midwest and up and down the East Coast. On September 9, 1957, Dot issued the 45 rpm single, "I've Got the Blues" b/w "Losing Game." On February 10, 1958, "Why Must You Leave Me" b/w "Satisfaction Guaranteed" was released. Even with extensive touring, Taylor failed to score a hit record: "You get two shots, and if you don't make enough noise you don't get a renewed contract. That's how it works. I didn't make quite enough noise."

Although Taylor didn't win over the executives at Dot, he gained a lot of road experience. He and The Nighthawks/Southerners worked with a variety of artists, which included Wanda Jackson ("It was at the Glen Echo Ballroom. She used my band, and I just stood there in the back by the drummer and played rhythm. I didn't want to miss any of that."), Patsy Cline ("Don would use my band the Southerners with Patsy, and I had to use a rock and roll group called Terry and the Pirates. One time Patsy and I shared equal billing. She had what it took. I knew she was going to be a star."), and George Jones. Taylor received top billing over Jones at the Glen Echo Ballroom.

In 1958, Owens was managing Cline, Taylor, and Roy Clark all at the same time. Owens booked Taylor and Cline on the same bill at the Villa Theater in Rockville, Missouri. He did it even though he knew there wouldn't be a backing band. Terry and the Pirates had a gig, and The Southerners were out of town. Owens had to rush to find a replacement. At the last minute, The Three of Us, a black rhythm and blues group, was hired and backed both artists: "I made out fine with them as I did some Coasters and rock and roll. Patsy had a little more difficulty." They didn't know about the band until they hit the stage, so there was no rehearsal. That's what made it so hard for Cline, and the fact that there was a saxophone in the combo. Both Taylor and Cline explained to the audience that The Three of Us was not his/her usual band: "The audience response wasn't quite as strong at the beginning but got better as the night went on."

After Dot Records decided not to renew his contract, Taylor moved onto Sun Records. Taylor disclosed, "The story goes that Sam Phillips saw me on *American Bandstand* with 'Losing Game.' He told Jack Clement, 'There might be some potential in that boy.' By the next year, Jack and Don [Owens] were talking. Jack said, 'I haven't been out that way in a while. I need a few days off. How about I just drive up, and we sit and talk a while?' When he came, he brought a copy of 'Ballad of a Teenage Queen,' that he had written for Johnny Cash. It was recorded, but not yet released."

Between 1958 and 1959, Taylor recorded several sides for Sun, but most of them were not released: "There were a lot of my records sitting around in the storage room, and I wish I had purchased a box. That would have been a pretty good investment." Sam Phillips enlisted a who's who to accompany Taylor, which included JM Van Eaton and Billy Lee Riley, and had Jack Clement produce. Charlie Rich played piano on "Blue Day Tomorrow": "Charlie hung out at Sun a lot. He was a very accomplished pianist, who was certainly schooled in jazz." He originally met Rich at Fernwood Studio: "He gave me the song 'Donna Lee,' but I sang it as 'Dinah Lee.' I think I loosened up more on that song. It took me quite a while to get loosened up even though Sun was a very relaxed atmosphere. I loved Jack's approach to things. He was the kind who believed in letting the tape roll."

Taylor, Roland Janes, Jimmy Wilson, Billy Lee Riley and JM Van Eaton all traveled to Nashville to record at the Quonset Hut Studio. Producer Jack Clement wanted stereo tape, and they didn't have that at Sun. At that session, "Today Is a Blue Day" and "Breeze" were cut. The tunes had been recorded a few days prior at Sun Studio, but the Nashville versions were the ones ultimately released. On November 24, 1958, Sun released "Today is a Blue Day" b/w "Breeze." "Today Is a Blue Day" was the most successful, at least locally, and Taylor feels that "Breeze" should have been the A side.

Even though, "Mystery Train" had already been recorded twice at Sun—first by Junior Parker and the Blue Flames and then by Elvis Presley and the Blue Moon Boys—Sam Phillips insisted that Taylor cut it as well. In fact, Phillips acted as producer. Taylor recalled, "I didn't want to record it because I didn't think I was worthy. Then, I didn't want to do it the same way. [Taylor's version is indeed different with saxophone accompaniment by Martin Willis]. I had just completed recording 'Mystery Train' when Scotty [Moore] walked in. Truthfully, I never liked listening to my version." On August 17, 1959, "Mystery Train" b/w "Sweet and Easy to Love" was issued. Incidentally, Roy Orbison wrote "Sweet and Easy to Love." Taylor acknowledged, "I never got the opportunity to meet him. Sam had pitched the song to me. I like it, but I think I could have sung it better."

Thanks to his exposure on Sun Records, Taylor made TV appearances on *Wink Martindale's Dance Party* in Memphis, Tennessee, *The Milt Grant Show* in Washington, D.C., and *The Buddy Deane Show* in Baltimore, Maryland.

Throughout the 1960s, Taylor continued to play with different bands: "I worked with my friend Duke Maddox, playing bass. I also played bass in a '60s rock and roll band, sometimes six nights a week. However, by 1968, I was done [beyond] the occasional sit-in." In 1973, "Your Lovin' Man" was released on a compilation called *Sun Rockabillies, Volume One*. It was one of the first issued by Shelby Singleton. However, it wasn't until 1988 that a reporter from *The Washington Post* informed Taylor of the news: "I had forgotten all about recording it. I don't know why Sam didn't release 'Your Lovin' Man' as it turned out to be my signature song."

Billy Poore convinced Taylor to play a benefit for Charlie Feathers, which occurred on August 12, 1989: "Billy was pretty persistent about it, and I didn't really want to do it, but am glad I did. I hadn't met Charlie before as I never saw him at Sun." Narvel Felts also performed: "We've become the best of friends."

Dave Travis first contacted Taylor about playing a gig overseas: "I was real leery about going over there because Billy [Poore] had told me so many horror stories. I was pretty hard on Dave when he called and turned it down. Then he called back a year or so later. They had asked Narvel if I still had all that hair, and he said, 'Yes,' so I guess that was part of the attraction." The Hemsby Rock 'n' Roll Weekender welcomed Taylor to its stage in 1995.

In 2001, Taylor performed, with backing provided by drummer WS Holland, at the groundbreaking ceremony for the Rockabilly Hall of Fame in Jackson, Tennessee. A year later, Taylor talked so much to adoring fans at the Rockin' '50's Fest in Green Bay, Wisconsin that he got hoarse. A lot of the same parks and carnivals that Taylor played when he was young hired him again.

Today, Taylor still works an eight hour a day job. The printing industry has kept him busy since 1960: "I'm employed by a world class book manufacturer, and I'm in the quality control [department]." Unfortunately, Taylor no longer sings: "I just don't have time for that. I'd love to as it's always in your blood." His last professional appearance was at a Patsy Cline memorial weekend in Winchester, West Virginia, in 2002.

Ace Cannon

Ace Cannon has the distinction of recording sixty-seven albums and forty-six singles. His biggest solo hit, "Tuff," scored a number seventeen spot on the *Billboard* charts, while his instrumental recording of "Blue Eyes Crying in the Rain" was nominated for a Grammy. Cannon made guest appearances, either as a member of the Bill Black Combo or alone, on several television shows, including *American Bandstand*, *The Ed Sullivan Show*, *The Merv Griffith Show*, *The Buddy Deane Show*, *Nashville Now*, and *Hee Haw*. Today, he continues to perform fifty dates a year and record albums for his label, RMD Music, Inc. Cannon has been bestowed with the honor of being inducted into the Smithsonian Rock and Soul Hall of Fame, the International Rockabilly Hall of Fame, the Memphis Music Hall of Fame, and the Mississippi Musicians' Hall of Fame. The versatile saxophonist "can honk out leering, hard driving rock and roll and ooze sensual romantic ballads without losing an ounce of his superior intonation."[15] Sun Records' founder Sam Phillips called him "the greatest saxophone player who ever lived."[16]

John "Ace" Cannon was born on May 5, 1934, in Grenada, Mississippi. When he was four years old, he and his family relocated to Memphis, Tennessee. Incidentally, he received his nickname Ace from Joe Cuoghi, the owner of Poplar Tunes in Memphis. At ten years old, Cannon picked up the saxophone: "My daddy told me to go in the band room at school and whatever instrument I wanted, he'd buy me one. I was always small for my age, and the only horn they had was a baritone sax. It was twice as tall as I was. In fact, it was so big that I couldn't handle it. I found out that they made different sizes, so I picked the alto sax. My daddy went and bought me one at a music store in uptown Memphis. I couldn't wait to get home to play it, so I took the sax in the backseat of the car and played 'Beer Barrel Polka.' It wasn't perfect, but you could tell what the tune was. I started playing by ear and learned how to read music."[17] He's not entirely certain why he was drawn to the instrument, but he did remember "I used to sit around and blow on a comb with a piece of paper behind it."[18] Cannon added, "I was in the school band and played the school song at all the pep rallies." Normally, school officials didn't allow someone in the fifth grade to join the band, but Cannon was so exceptional at playing by ear, they couldn't refuse his entry.

As a teenager, he had his own band and then teamed up with Buck 'Stuffy' Turner and his Buckaroos and Clyde Leoppard and his Snearly Ranch Boys: "They had to act as parent and guardian when I went out with them. They were hot back in those days. I used to do all my singing and copied everything Hank Thompson did. I learned every song he put out on record." As a singer, he was well known in the Memphis area nightclubs and also participated in a lot of talent contests. Those were held by disc jockey Dick Stuart (a.k.a. Poor Richard) where the prize was a transistor radio: "I finally won so many that they wouldn't let me be in the contest anymore."[19] Even though, he no longer participated in the contests, his relationship with Stuart didn't end. The disc jockey befriended the young singer and gifted him promotional copies of every Hank Thompson single that was issued. Later, Cannon enrolled at Memphis State College with the intention of majoring in music. He was also in the band. Cannon acknowledged, "I didn't go but two semesters, and then I quit and joined the Army Reserves. I played in that band for eight years." At nineteen, he got married and took a job working first as a file clerk then personnel manager for a company that manufactured Layne Pumps. That was the only day job he ever had, and it lasted six years.

Cannon cited his father, Earl Bostic, King Curtis, Cannonball Adderley, and Paul Desmond as his musical influences. Cannon recalled, "My daddy played guitar, fiddle, and sang. To show you how musically inclined he was, when I started bringing the horn home from school, he'd mess around with it and learned how to play it. I had to take the sax to school because I wouldn't leave it anywhere. It was just a God given musical gift we both had." As a youngster, Cannon performed with his father at beer joints, nightclubs, gymnasiums, and family functions. Country music was popular at the time, so that was what they played. Even though he was not an influence, fellow sax player Boots Randolph was a good friend: "We played two different styles. His [forte] was Dixieland/ragtime while I'm just a ballad player. I'd rather play ballads than fast rock and roll. I played at Boots' club in Printer's Alley in Nashville. I recorded his song 'Yakety Sax,' and he cut 'Tuff.'"

Ace Cannon enjoyed success with the Bill Black Combo before scoring a #17 hit with "Tuff" (courtesy Ace Cannon).

Elvis Presley and Cannon shared the stage only once: "I was playing the Eagle's Nest in Memphis when a disc jockey named Sleepy Eyed John brought Elvis [up to the bandstand] and asked if he could sing a song or two. We let him even though we had never heard of him. I think he had one record out. They were just trying to showcase him a little bit by letting him get some experience."

Cannon appeared on numerous recordings, but many of them he doesn't remember: "You'd go in and do a session, which lasted three hours. Then you walked out and just more or less forgot about it, unless it was some big artist." The first rockabilly performer that he ever worked with was Kenny Parchman, and that stint lasted for a year and a half. He also cut tracks with Jerry Lee Lewis and Warren Smith. He disclosed, "I played sax with Billy Lee Riley as one of the Little Green Men, before Martin Willis took my place." Cannon's distinctive playing can be heard on Riley's "Pearly Lee" and "Red Hot."

In 1959, Cannon joined the Bill Black Combo: "When Colonel Parker fired Bill Black and Scotty Moore, Bill decided to form his own group. I wasn't in it originally. Marty Willis was playing with him, but that was just around town. He had appeared on 'Smokie' and 'White Silver Sands,' and was set to play with them on New Year's Eve at Ellis Auditorium in Memphis. Marty didn't want to go on the road, so Bill just let him go and hired me. I was on the road with him for three years." Cannon added, "We booked dances on our own, and most of the jobs were at black nightclubs. Everybody thought that the Bill Black Combo was black."[20] The Bill Black Combo's versions of "Smokie" and "White Silver Sands" both peaked at number one on the rhythm and blues charts in 1959.

Another member, pianist Carl McVoy, didn't travel with the band: "Carl and his brother owned a construction company, so he couldn't leave." Bobby Emmons replaced McVoy on the road. Black traveled with the group, playing bass. Cannon added, "Being in the front, I did all the emceeing, and so many people thought I was Bill Black. He was way in the back and hardly ever talked. The piano player (Bobby Emmons), guitar player (Reggie Young), and I took all the leads. In fact, Reggie was really playing that Bill Black beat. He had an original sound. Instead of using a guitar pick, he used a fountain pen and slapped the strings with it. Then Reggie got called into the Army, and we used Hank Angus."

Several various techniques were used to capture different sounds on the records. For example, the studio's basement was used as an echo chamber. On "Sunday Blues," "I had to put taps on my shoes and walk down there on that concrete and act like I was somebody who would be just walking down the street and whistling."[21] Later, singers Gene Simmons and Bill Boyd joined the group. Simmons was a Sun recording artist and had a number eleven hit with the Halloween classic "Haunted House."

Besides working with McVoy in the Bill Black Combo, Cannon played sax for him on "Tootsie," "Little John's Gone," "Daydreamin'," and "You Are My Sunshine." The songs were cut in Nashville and also featured guitarist Chet Atkins, bassist Ernie Newton, and drummer Johnny Bernero. Incidentally, McVoy was one of Jerry Lee Lewis' cousins. Cannon remembered, "Carl was a lot more reserved than Jerry Lee."

In 1960, General Artists Corporation booked the Bill Black Combo on a Show of Stars package tour. For a month and a half, they traveled by Greyhound bus all over the United States with twenty-five other recording artists. Brenda Lee, Duane Eddy, Fabian, Jimmy Clanton, and Chubby Checker were a few of the other acts. The only time the Bill Black Combo went overseas was for gigs in Canada and the Caribbean—the Bahamas, Montego Bay, Nassau, and Freeport. The latter was a tour with The Drifters.

While Cannon was a member, the Bill Black Combo secured several spots on the *Billboard* charts, most notably with their renditions of "Josephine," which rounded out at number eighteen, and "Don't Be Cruel," which peaked at number eleven.

In 1961, due to a suggestion from Hi Records, Cannon made the transition from band leader to solo artist: "All my hits with the Bill Black Combo were on the same label, so they had seen my potential. [By that time, he had been dismissed from the group]. When Hi Records put out 'Tuff,' it didn't do anything for the first four or five months. Then all of a sudden, they called me in one day and said, 'We've got a hit on our hands.' Before 1962 was over, I had three records on the *Billboard* Hot 100." "Sugar Blues" was issued on Santo Records, and it secured the number ninety-two position. "Tuff" peaked at number seventeen, while the third was "Blues (Stay Away from Me)," which scored a number thirty-six hit. In regard to "Tuff," Cannon disclosed, "It's the most requested tune I got, and it's what made me."

Cannon wound up recording sixty albums and forty singles for Hi Records. His favorite album to record was *The Misty Sax of Ace Cannon*: "We turned the studio into a nightclub by setting up tables and inviting about fifty people. You can hear applause, hollering, and glasses tinging. I had more fun cutting that album than any of them." Cannon disclosed, "They were putting out two to three singles a year on me."[22] Incidentally, Carl McVoy was part owner of Hi Records along with Bill Black, Ray Harris, Joe Cuoghi, Bill Cantrell, Quinton Claunch, and Nick Pesce.

Cannon proved to audiences that he was quite the showman by sliding around on dance floors and jumping off bandstands. In the 1960s, he appeared on package shows with Roy Orbison and Charlie Rich. When fans weren't lucky enough to capture his high energy solo performances, they were treated to guest spots, such as appearances with Fats Domino.

In 1986, Cannon opened for Carl Perkins. They performed at various venues across the United States and toured Norway, Sweden, and Denmark: "It was terrific working with Carl. He was such a great guy—religious, fun, and easy going—the nicest guy you'd ever want to work for." A year earlier, Cannon had participated in the session with Perkins, Johnny Cash, Roy Orbison, and Jerry Lee Lewis that resulted in the *Class of '55* album.

The 1997 album *All the King's Men*, which was recorded by Scotty Moore and D.J. Fontana with special guests Ronnie McDowell, Keith Richards, Ron Wood, Jeff Beck, Steve Earl, and the Bill Black Combo, garnered Cannon another Grammy nomination.

In 2004, Cannon, Percy Sledge, Peaches and Herb, and James Ingram headlined tours in Barbados and Trinidad: "I've been over there twenty-five times since 1975. I'm very popular down in the Caribbean. In fact, I cut two albums, *The Saxy Sounds of Ace* and *The Golden Sax of Ace*, for West Indies Records in Barbados. They like the soul ballad type songs." Cannon revealed, "The style I just created myself. All my music comes from the heart."[23] Also in 2004, he shared stages with Narvel Felts and Sonny Burgess and the Pacers. Cannon commented, "I started doing shows with the Pacers way back in the late '50's/early '60's. We even had softball teams together, over in Newport and Batesville, Arkansas. The Pacers and I played against local guys. I was the pitcher and fastest runner on the team, and we usually won."

Nowadays, Cannon plays fifty show dates a year, mostly on weekends: "I don't go to any job without my manager, Carl Griffin, because he's my drummer, booking agent, business agent, and my bodyguard. He's 6'6" and weighs about 250." Music keeps Cannon busy, but he has allotted time for golf: "When I took up golf, I dropped everything else. [Before the Women's PGA and the Make-A-Wish Foundation golf tournaments, Cannon has played concerts.] I don't do anything but play the horn and play golf. I like the mind game golf plays on you and the challenge. I play it every single day. I'm addicted; there's no doubt about it."

Chapter Four

Country Hit Makers

Conway Twitty

In 1946, Conway Twitty recorded his first song, "Cry Baby Heart," at radio station KFFA in Helena, Arkansas. Ten years later, while stationed in Japan, he cut Chuck Berry's "Maybellene." Upon discharge from the Army, he heard Elvis Presley on the radio. This inspired Twitty to start his own band, The Rockhousers. Even though Sun Records neglected to add him to their roster, Twitty recorded a few tracks for Mercury Records before switching to MGM. In 1958, he scored his first number one song with "It's Only Make Believe." It went on to sell eight million copies and be a chart topper in twenty-two different countries. Twitty found success in Canada but also played the Steel Pier in Atlantic City, New Jersey, and various supper clubs across the United States. He remained for eight years in the pop field before transitioning to country music. Twitty enjoyed a remarkable thirty year career in that industry: "Starting with an arsenal of warmed-over Elvis mannerisms, he worked tirelessly at his music and his image until he became one of the biggest recording stars of the '70s."[1] Today, he is listed as one of the top five country music artists of all-time.

Harold Jenkins was born on September 1, 1933, in Friars Point, Mississippi. His stage name, Conway Twitty, was embraced once he signed with Mercury Records. He claimed that his manager Don Seat gave him the persona because Twitty wanted his records to stand out to disk jockeys. He chose Conway as in Conway, Arkansas, and Twitty as in Twitty, Texas. Seat disagreed and said his girlfriend came up with the name long before Jenkins ever became one of his clients. He said that Jenkins had wanted to be called Harold Lloyd. As a kid, Twitty's father taught him his first chords on the guitar. At ten years old, Twitty joined the Phillips Country Ramblers and performed on a local radio program: "He cited two important influences from his earliest years: the playing of the jukebox at the local honky-tonk and the singing at the 'little Negro church' across the cotton fields from his home."[2] He'd listen and sing along for hours. His neighbor Uncle Fred, who sang and played harmonica and guitar, introduced him to the blues. Twitty then heard country music when he tuned into the *Grand Ole Opry*.

As a teenager, music was on the backburner as far as a profession since Twitty had aspirations of becoming a professional baseball player. The Philadelphia Phillies had even shown interest, asking him to report to their training camp. There were also ideas of preaching as a vocation. In fact, "I tried that for a couple of years. I preached at youth revivals, and I worked with young people a lot, [even though] it wasn't really what I wanted to do."[3] In 1954, he was drafted into the Army. Twitty spent two years in Yokohama before being discharged on March 14, 1956. He then heard Elvis Presley on the radio: "I still had thoughts of baseball, but Elvis Presley stirred me up."[4] Incidentally, Presley was one of his biggest influences. Allen Harris conveyed, "Conway played some baseball in the Army but also got interested in music and formed a little band in Japan. When he got out, Elvis had a couple of hit records, and Conway said, 'Hmm, I can do that.' He could too, sound like Elvis when he wanted to."[5]

In early 1956, Bill Harris heard Twitty play guitar and joined forces with him to form The Rockhousers. The lineup featured Bill Harris on bass, Jimmy Ray Paulman on lead guitar, Billy Weir on drums, and Twitty on rhythm guitar and vocals. Weir recollected, "Harold [Conway] had played in the Army, but he had no regular musicians. He used a guitar player over in Memphis named W.H. Yarbrough, Sr. and said to him, 'I need a drummer. We just can't cut it anymore without one.' W.H. told him, 'Well, a drummer lives right down the street from me. You might want to check him out.' I actually had seen Harold [Conway] drive past my house as I was sitting on the front porch. I thought it was Elvis in that '55 red Mercury hardtop with a continental kit. I had told my parents, 'Man, Elvis just drove by.' It wasn't five minutes until I got a phone call from W.H. saying that this guy from Arkansas wanted to talk to me about playing some gigs with him."[6] Yarbrough Sr. was never a member of The Rockhousers since he didn't play with Twitty for long. He had chosen to become a minister. Jimmy Ray Paulman replaced him. Incidentally, Paulman acted as guardian to Weir since he was underage.

In 1960, after conquering audiences in the States and Canada, Conway Twitty played to sold-out crowds in the United Kingdom (courtesy Steve Bonner).

Twitty wrote a song paying homage to the band entitled "Rockhouse." In the summer of 1956, they auditioned at Sun Studio. Besides "Rockhouse," Twitty also sang "Lawdy Miss Clawdy," "Jim Dandy," "Long Black Train," and "Baby Let's Play House." Unfortunately, only "Rockhouse" has survived. The remaining tunes were probably taped over for re-use. Twitty's version of "Rockhouse" was not released at the time. However, Sam Phillips obtained publishing for the song and passed it on to Roy Orbison. On October 20, 1956, Sun issued Orbison's second release, "Rockhouse" b/w "You're My Baby." Weir disclosed, "There have been stories that there was a real cordial bargaining over 'Rockhouse.' That wasn't the case because Sam stole it. He knew it; Harold [Conway] knew it; we all did. We were in the car the day we heard it on the radio, and Harold [Conway] was not happy about that."

Twitty yearned to be on the little yellow label and traveled to Sun three more times—November and December 1956 and then January 1957. At the November session, Sam Phillips engineered while Twitty recorded "Crazy Dreams," "Give Me Some Love," and "I Need Your Lovin' Kiss." Paulman declared, "I remember we went in the morning, and we came out late that night. 'Crazy Dreams' was a song Conway had written. We played that over and over again. I never got so tired of a song. It just wasn't right for him."[7] The following month, Twitty cut "Just in Time" and "Born to Sing the Blues." The latter song was recorded again in January 1957. None of these efforts led to a contract. Weir commented, "We had done some demo stuff with Jack Clement, and that's how we got to audition for Sun. Harold [Conway] sounded too much like Elvis. Sam was looking for something different, so he just wouldn't fool with him." Paulman acknowledged, "Conway was a big fan of Elvis', so he tried to sing like him." Undaunted, Twitty's manager, Don Seat, shopped a demo tape to various record labels. Mercury Records was the only one who took an interest in the fledgling young singer.

Mercury signed Twitty to a contract, and his first session took place in Nashville on March 13, 1957, where he recorded "Maybe Baby," "Shake it Up," "I Need Your Lovin'," and "Born to Sing the Blues." By this time, Harris had quit the band and was replaced by Jimmy Evans. Martin Willis was also added on saxophone. According to Weir, "That was a totally different sound. We cut songs that were capable of airplay." On April 20, Mercury released the 45 rpm single, "I Need Your Lovin'" b/w "Born to Sing the Blues." Unfortunately, Twitty's plans for stardom fell by the wayside when "I Need Your Lovin'" only reached number ninety-three. Incidentally, Paulman wrote the tune, although not specifically for Twitty. On July 15, 1957, a second single was issued, "Shake It Up" b/w "Maybe Baby." Mercury was disenchanted that their new artist hadn't secured a Top Ten song but scheduled another session anyway. In October, three songs were cut: "Golly Gosh Oh Gee," "Double Talk Baby," and "Why Can't I Get Through to You." None of the tracks were issued at the time, and Mercury decided not to renew his contract.

In the 1950s, Twitty and the Rockhousers toured the upper part of Missouri as well as Mississippi, Arkansas, and Tennessee on weekends. Thanks to the fraternities, they also played after Ole Miss football games. The Silver Moon Club in Newport, Arkansas, the Delta Supper Club in West Helena, Arkansas, and the Trio Club in Pine Bluff, Arkansas were all regular bookings for them. Paulman conveyed, "We played a lot of dances without a drummer. I carried the band with my guitar playing. I was the one that gave the sound to The Rockhousers. We worked with Conway on some shows in Fayetteville, Arkansas. That's where I met Ron Hawkins. Conway would let him come up and sing a few songs. Ron was a great showman, but he wasn't too good a singer. I taught him to come in on meter."

Weir recalled, "We played with The Browns and got to know them real well. They even asked us to go on a European tour." According to Weir, "[In regard to his stage act], Harold [Conway] didn't move a lot. [Even though, the girls screamed]. He actually performed with his legs apart, didn't stand up straight like a country singer."

Paulman acknowledged, "Conway could dance. That guy could move when he wanted to, but he didn't do anything onstage. He just stood there, played the guitar and sang." The band tried to make their act exciting; Weir played while standing on top of his drums.

Weir stated, "I knew Harold [Conway] was on his way because he had the potential and the drive. He was developing his voice. [His signature vocal growl was present but wasn't dominant until he signed with MGM.] In those rockabilly days, he sang more of the Little Richard, Fats Domino, Brook Benton, and Al Hibbler material. [Twitty also sang Chuck Berry's "Maybellene" and a lot of Elvis Presley.] If we heard something on the radio that we liked, we would try to find a restaurant with a jukebox that had the song, so we could learn it. Then more than likely, we would play it that night. Harold [Conway] was writing country songs at the time, and we would sneak one in every once in a while."

Paulman's observations were different: "He hated country music and would not sing it."

Weir also disclosed, "In 1956, we played a sock hop at Humes High School in Memphis. Downstairs, the football team was having their award ceremony, and Elvis was with them. We were in the gym, and when we did 'Don't Be Cruel,' we noticed Elvis was watching us in the doorway. We stopped playing and did the stripper type ending on it. The next time we saw Elvis, he did the exact same thing."

Weir added, "Harold [Conway] was just like a brother. He treated us great." Paulman revealed similar comments, "I was with Conway probably about seven years. We were very close. I always admired him and liked his singing. Conway had a lot of talent."

Without a record label, Twitty and his band traveled to Hamilton, Ontario, Canada, to play a two week stint at the Flamingo Lounge in late 1957. Weir's parents wouldn't allow him to quit school, so JM Van Eaton was called upon to play drums. On opening night, everyone in the club walked out. The Flamingo Lounge was strictly a jazz club, so the audience didn't embrace their act, which featured rock and roll music and hepcat clothes. The owner even threatened to fire them. However, one of the guys who booked Twitty reminded the owner that even if he dismissed them, he would still have to pay for the two weeks. Reluctantly, he let them remain. Thankfully, by the end of the week, the band had won the acceptance of the crowd. When Twitty returned home, he lost three of his band members: Paulman, Van Eaton, and Willis. They all went to work for Billy Lee Riley. That fall, Twitty was re-hired to play the Flamingo Lounge. The band then had three new members: Blackie Preston, Jack Nance, and Joe Lewis. The latter two were recruits from Sonny Burgess' group, The Pacers. Twitty had pioneered the club circuit for American artists in Canada. He recommended fellow rockabilly performers Narvel Felts and Ronnie Hawkins.

Twitty's signature tune, "It's Only Make Believe," was written by Jack Nance. While sitting at a piano between sets at the Flamingo Lounge, the tune was penned. Twitty assisted with the finishing touches. A demo of the song along with "I'll Try" was sent to Don Seat. MGM Records showed interest in the tunes and set up a Nashville recording session for May 7, 1958. That day, four tracks were cut: "It's Only Make Believe," "I'll Try," "I Vibrate," and "Will You Love Me Then as You Love Me Now." MGM arranged for Grady Martin,

Lightnin' Chance, Floyd Cramer, and The Jordanaires to play on the songs. The producer, Jim Vienneau, had suggested that he keep the growl in his vocals. On July 14, the 45 rpm single "I'll Try" b/w "It's Only Make Believe" hit store shelves. Disc jockeys kept plugging "I'll Try" even though Tommy Sands had said that they should flip the record. During this time, Twitty actually quit and went home to toil on the family farm. It wasn't until disc jockey Doctor Bop in Columbus, Ohio, took notice of "It's Only Make Believe" that people started to pay attention to that side. To promote the record, Twitty and his band traveled to Columbus to make a special appearance on Doctor Bop's radio broadcast, which took place atop a drive-in restaurant. Due to crowd hysteria, Twitty had to be lifted over the audience in order to lip-sync his latest platter. That evening, "It's Only Make Believe" was played ten times in a row. By September 1958, "It's Only Make Believe" hit nationally and became number one on the *Billboard* charts. Since the song was very similar to another, "All of a Sudden My Heart Sings," a lawsuit was filed. It was settled out of court with the condition that Twitty would record songs from the Leeds Music songbook. Thanks to "It's Only Make Believe," MGM Records increased his royalties in a new contract.

In 1959, Carl Mann reworked Nat King Cole's version of "Mona Lisa" into an up-tempo tune. Mann remembered, "One night, we were playing at the Triple Club [in Puryear, Tennessee]; we started out doing 'Mona Lisa,' but I was doing it slow. The college kids started hollering that they wanted something fast to dance to, so we stopped and after about the first eight bars started on it fast. We had eight or ten requests to do it again, so we figured that was a pretty good indication that might be what we were looking for."[8] W.S. Holland then arranged an audition for Mann with Sun Records. Mann recalled, "We did three takes on 'Mona Lisa,' and then we did a backside, which was called 'Foolish Love.' While we were doing 'Mona Lisa,' Conway Twitty came into the studio. He shook hands with me and said, 'Man I think you've got a hit record.' When we left, Jack [Clement] said, 'Well I'll play it for Sam and see what he thinks.'"[9]

At this point, Mann had not been offered a contract with Sun, and he was getting anxious. While playing a club date in Canada with Carl Perkins, Holland found out some news that would change Sam Phillips' mind about releasing the song. Mann disclosed, "After the show, Ronnie Hawkins [who had been playing at the club next door] and W.S. bumped into each other. Ronnie told W.S. that he had talked to his old buddy Conway Twitty. Ronnie then said, 'Guess what Conway's next record is gonna be? You'll never guess; it's that old Nat King Cole song, "Mona Lisa."' Conway had gone to Nashville and had cut it as close to our style as he could. They told me he was gonna put it on an album."[10] On January 12, 1959, Twitty's version was released on an EP (extended play) 45 rpm record. In April, Phillips International, a subsidiary of Sun Records, released Mann's track. In July, Twitty saw the song issued as a single. It received quite a bit of airplay once disc jockeys latched onto it. Mann's version peaked at number twenty-five while Twitty's secured the number twenty-nine spot.

Nineteen fifty-nine was a pivotal year because Twitty scored two other songs on the charts. In September, "Danny Boy" peaked at number ten, while in December, "Lonely Blue Boy" reached number six. Twitty also attempted an acting career and appeared in three films: *Platinum High School*, *College Confidential*, and *Sex Kittens Go to College*.

In 1960, Sonny Burgess joined Twitty for a brief stint until Joe Lewis returned to the lineup. Burgess played electric bass in the Twitty Birds. Jack Nance had already quit a year earlier and was replaced by Porkchop Markham, who remained with Twitty for thirty years. In 1963, Twitty's contract with MGM expired. Two years later, he moved to Oklahoma City, switched to country music, and signed with Decca Records. Songwriter Harlan Howard had been instrumental in convincing Twitty to make the change from pop to country and also in persuading Owen Bradley to take a chance on Twitty.

In the late 1960s, Twitty saw the top of the charts again with "Next in Line," "I Love You More Today," and "To See My Angel Cry." In 1970, he scored two number one hits: "Hello Darlin'" and "Fifteen Years Ago." In regard to "Hello Darlin'," "Twitty had written it over a decade before he recorded it. The song, like scores of others, had been conceived, composed, and then filed in a big box. At the time, there was no market for country in his repertoire, so the singer had simply forgotten about it."[11] He actually had no intentions of recording the tune, but Owen Bradley requested one more song to complete the session. After a few run-throughs, Bradley added an electric piano to the track but also suggested that the first two words be spoken rather than sung. The technique paid off. For an entire month, the song remained at the top of the charts.

During this time, Twitty teamed up with Loretta Lynn: "Their duets included sexually suggestive numbers that initially upset mainstream country deejays."[12] It was a natural pairing since both were fans of one another's and shared the same record label. Early on, they did a three week tour of Europe together, which included a gig at Wembley Festival. Allen Harris played piano for both. He reflected, "In 1973, I was playing with Leroy Van Dyke, and we were doing a lot of package shows with Nat Stuckey. I found out through one of his musicians that he was fixing to go on tour with Conway and Loretta for three months [September to December]. Nat and I had kinda been knocking around ideas of me coming to work for him, so when I found that out, I went in and told him, 'If the opportunity's still open, I'll take it.' I sat and watched Loretta and Conway and memorized their show. Finally one night, Nat was through, and Conway was fixing to come on next when Joe Lewis says to me, 'Why don't you step in and play with us?' I said, 'Okay.' I was waiting for the opportunity. I had learned every lick on all of Conway's songs, and I played them just like the records. I saw Conway glance over at me two or three times, and I could tell he was pleased. I had been doing some singing with Nat, so when Conway would have harmony parts I'd sing the third part. I could tell that pleased him too. I thought I was getting along really well. Meanwhile, Mooney Lynn and I got to be drinking buddies. Conway didn't allow any drinking in his band or even around him. He was a teetotaler, and he insisted that if you were going to do it, to not do it in his presence. One night, Mooney asked if I wanted to come and work for Loretta. She needed a piano player. I really wanted a job with Conway, and Loretta's management was squirrely. It didn't look like Conway was gonna make a move, so I told Mooney that I'd go to work for Loretta. About a week later, Mooney came to me and said, 'Loretta and I had dinner with Nat and his wife, and we were talking about your band.' Nat said, 'You know, this is about the best group of people that I've ever had. It's a shame too, because every time I get a good group, somebody comes along and hires them up from under me.' Mooney then said, 'Al, I can't hire you now.' Even with all my scheming and planning, I still wound up without a job offer. The tour was over, and everybody went home. I stayed on with Nat, and we played the Carousel Club in Augusta, Georgia on New Year's Eve. I got a call from my wife saying, 'Joe Lewis has been trying to reach you. He wants you to call him.' I called Joe, and he said, 'Conway wants to know if you wanna go to work for him.' I said, 'Hell, yeah, I wanna go to work for him.' Joe then said, 'Well, how much notice you gotta give Nat?' I replied, 'Well, I can give Nat a two week notice.' Joe then said, 'That works out well because we're going to Atlanta on January 5th. Conway is hiring a guitar player to work a club for a week. That'll give us a chance to practice every day and get you guys into our arrangements. We booked the club for that purpose.' That day, when I told Nat I was leaving, it turned out he had the next two weeks off, so he said, 'Well, if you're leaving anyway, you can go ahead and leave now if you want to.' I called Joe back and told him, 'Nat turned me loose, so I can start early.' He said, 'Well, you go on the payroll tomorrow.' I went to work for Conway on January 1, 1974, and I worked with him for exactly ten years."

Twitty was not a member of the *Grand Ole Opry*. According to Harris, "He appeared on it, but Conway wouldn't join because he could make anywhere from fifteen to forty thousand dollars playing a concert on a Saturday night, and the *Grand Ole Opry* insisted that you play twenty-six shows of theirs a year at union scale. Conway was offered the opportunity, but he turned it down. He was a better businessman than that."

During the ten years that Harris was in Twitty's band, he also played with Lynn. They always did a fall tour together but also sometimes played in the spring. Harris remembered, "Loretta would follow the opening act. Then we'd have a little intermission. Conway would do his show. Finally, he'd call upon Loretta, and she'd come out to do duets." The following night, it would be vice versa. He added, "Conway didn't like rock and roll. Even though, 'It's Only Make Believe' was a monster pop hit, it was a country song. Conway told me that he had been telling his managers that he wanted to get out of rock and go into country. They said, 'Why in the world would you do that? There's much more money to be made in rock and roll.' Conway said, 'I'm just not happy doing it.' He said he was onstage one night and about halfway through the show he made up his mind. Conway finished the show but cancelled the rest of the tour. His managers liked to have a fit."

Every night, Twitty had basically the same set list. According to Harris, "When a new record came out, we'd add it and drop another that wasn't getting as much crowd response. If Conway got a request for 'Danny Boy' or one of the others he had back in the early days, he'd gladly do the song because it fit right into a country show. Every night, he sang 'It's Only Make Believe.' We played everything he ever recorded at one time or another. I know sometimes he took vocal shortcuts, instead of having to strain to hit the high notes. We stayed close to the original arrangement, and the audience didn't know the difference." Twitty acknowledged: "I've never recorded a song I didn't like, and when I reach the point when I get tired of a song, I take it out of the show."[13]

As far as meeting and greeting the fans, Harris had this to say, "Loretta would stay and talk to you as long as it was interesting. She's good hearted. I genuinely like her because she's a real person, what you see is what you get. A lot of people thought Conway was stuck up, but he wasn't. He just wasn't interested in telling you where he was last night and where he would be tomorrow. Those were the main questions. If you wanted Conway to be friends with ya, you had to walk up to him and say something about baseball. He would talk all day about that or tell him you got five new songs you want to pitch to him. He'd also listen to that. Conway came out every night after the concert with me and his brother, Howard. Conway would sit on the stage. Then I'd reach into the audience to take whatever they had to get signed. Conway would sit there for as many hours as it took for everybody who wanted an autograph to get one. [He posed for photos too]."

Besides live appearances, Harris played on many of Twitty's recordings: "We were listed on a lot of songs that we didn't actually play on, but Conway still paid us. A certain percentage of every recording session, television show, and anything else besides your salary went to the musicians' union, and they put it in a retirement fund. If you got enough points, when you retired, you would get a check from the union equivalent to a percentage of what you paid in. A lot of musicians [like the A-Team in Nashville] retired with $500,000. Conway also had a retirement program where he put a certain amount of money into an account. It started maybe five years before I left, and by the time I did, I had $36,000."

Between 1971 and 1975, Twitty and Lynn's duets topped the charts five times: "After the Fire Is Gone," "Lead Me On," "As Soon as I Hang Up the Phone," "Louisiana Woman, Mississippi Man," and "Feelins." In 1972, "After the Fire Is Gone" won them a Grammy for Best Country Vocal Performance by a Duo or Group. They were also awarded Vocal Duo of the Year for four years in a row (1972–1975) by the Country Music Association. Their collaboration is the most successful and most awarded in country music history.

Harris recollected a 1976 European tour he did with Twitty and Lynn. Other artists, such as Freddy Fender, were also on the package shows. Harris stated, "We were stationed in London but flew in and out of Poland, Sweden, and Germany. It was exhausting." Music kept Twitty and Lynn busy, but they also sought after entrepreneurial enterprises, including a booking agency called United Talent. Harris remarked, "When somebody came out with a new record that was a hit, Conway and Loretta's booking agent would call and say, 'Hey, how would you like to be the opening act for Conway Twitty and Loretta Lynn?' They were two of the biggest names out there, so everybody jumped." Kenny Rogers and Reba McEntire were two such artists.

As a solo artist, Twitty's hits continued throughout the 1970s and 1980s. Several peaked at number one: "How Much More Can She Stand," "I Can't Stop Loving You," "(Lost Her Love) on Our Last Date," "She Needs Someone to Hold Her," "You've Never Been This Far Before," "I See the Want in Your Eyes," "There's a Honky Tonk Angel (Who'll Take Me Back In)," "Touch the Hand," "Linda on My Mind," "I'd Love to Lay You Down," "Tight Fittin' Jeans," "Slow Hand," and "Desperado Love." Author Alanna Nash recognized, "His lyrics manage to do what most other country songs don't, which is to acknowledge a woman's sensuality and her desire to be treated with respect."[14]

In the 1980s and early 1990s, Twitty continued to perform for his legions of fans and invited them to visit his nine-acre theme park, Twitty City in Hendersonville, Tennessee. On May 3, 1993, Twitty cut his last recording with Sam Moore of R&B duo Sam and Dave. It was a cover of "Rainy Night in Georgia." Shortly after, on the way home from a gig in Branson, Missouri, Twitty pulled over to a truck stop as he had suddenly taken ill. On June 5, 1993, he died of an abdominal aortic aneurysm. Harris mentioned, "One of his daughters called and asked if I was planning on coming to the funeral? I said, 'Yeah, I've already bought tickets.' She said, 'Well, we would like for you and the rest of the band to sit with the family.' I was glad they felt that way about me. I couldn't have gotten into the church otherwise, as it was so crowded."

Unlike many of his contemporaries, Elvis Presley in particular, Twitty was able to separate the public persona from his real self. He commented, "Anytime that I'm not actually on the stage performing, I'm Harold Jenkins."[15] Harris expressed, "Conway did as little talking as he could possibly get away with. He said, 'People don't come to hear me talk or tell jokes. They're not interested in my religion or my political philosophy. They come to hear me sing, and that's what I'm gonna do. That's what I'm selling, an image. I don't have the right to destroy it or take it away.'" That philosophy kept him grounded and provided him with longevity in the music business.

Billy Swan

At the age of seventeen, Billy Swan penned the lyrics to "Lover Please." In 1962, it was a number seven hit on the *Billboard* rhythm and blues charts for Clyde McPhatter: "I never met Clyde, although I knew who he was. It was one in the morning and snowing when I heard the song for the first time on WLAC-Nashville. It made me feel so good that I did a spin with my 1949 Dodge Coupe in the middle of an intersection."[16] Instead of following up on its success, Swan continued to play in local bands. Later, he played rhythm guitar and sang harmony with Kris Kristofferson on a semi-regular basis. However, Swan is probably most well-known for his number one crossover hit, "I Can Help." It peaked at the top of the charts on both the *Billboard* Hot 100 and Hot Country Singles. As far as his career, he acknowledged, "I've been really, really lucky in a lot of ways for somebody who hasn't pushed it. I wasn't out to be a recording star or anything like that."[17]

Billy Swan was born on May 12, 1942, in Cape Girardeau, Missouri. As a kid, he enjoyed the tunes that cowboy Gene Autry sang in the movies. At ten years old, Swan sang his first song, "She'll Be Coming 'Round the Mountain." Country music was his earliest influence. His sister's records introduced him to Hank Williams, Sr.

At fifteen, he became interested in playing the piano: "My aunt had one, and every time I'd go over to visit my cousin, I'd sit and try to get that Jerry Lee Lewis rhythm going. I never took any lessons."[18] Swan added, "Even so, I don't pump the piano like Jerry Lee. To my way of thinking, no one can do that. He's a phenomenon." A year later, Swan started writing poems in school: "I had a teacher that inspired me."

At that same time, he began playing a little rhythm guitar. As a teenager, he appeared with a few different bands. In his first one, he played the drums. Then he sang with Mirt Mirley and the Rhythm Steppers for two years: "We did Top 40 songs of the time, like 'What'd I Say,' 'Whole Lotta Shakin' Goin' On,' Link Wray's 'Rumble,' 'Rawhide,' and 'Raunchy.' I heard rockabilly artists, like Elvis Presley, Jerry Lee Lewis, Charlie Rich, Billy Lee Riley, Carl Mann, and Bill Justis, on the radio." Swan hung out at the Hollenbeck Company of Cape Girardeau, Missouri, where they serviced jukebox and pinball machines. When the newest music arrived, the young singer was the first to hear it because he befriended the owner, Bill Hollenbeck. Their sales department ordered the records that would go onto jukeboxes. Swan commented, "I didn't have a record player."

Some of Swan's favorite artists include Presley, Johnny Cash, Bill Haley, Buddy Holly, Hank Williams, Sr., Johnnie and Jack, Webb Pierce, Faron Young, and Carl Perkins. In fact,

Swan recorded "Your True Love" with Perkins on guitar, and he told him, 'Thanks for making a bad song so good.' Swan remarked, "Carl was just a kind and humble man." Although he has many musical influences, Swan cited Gene Autry, Hank Williams, Sr., Johnnie and Jack, Webb Pierce, Elvis Presley, Buddy Holly, Carl Perkins, Chuck Berry, Jimmy Reed, Fats Domino, The Everly Brothers, Dion and the Belmonts, Jerry Lee Lewis, Carl Mann, and Narvel Felts. One of Swan's favorite memories is having met Pierce, Johnnie and Jack, and Lewis when he was a teenager. Working as assistant music director on Lewis' bio flick, *Great Balls of Fire*, was also a thrill: "I enjoyed the music part of it, but I think the movie could have been a lot better. Jerry Lee's a character but a good guy. I first met him in Cape Girardeau in 1959. He was so nice to me then and still is. I think a lot of Jerry Lee."

"Lover Please" was one of Swan's penned songs that had originally started as a poem. He had traveled to Memphis with Mirley and the Rhythm Steppers. They were scheduled for a session at Satellite Studios, per request

Billy Swan takes a break from his set at the Airline Club in Cape Girardeau, Missouri (courtesy Billy Swan).

by Bill Black. They only recorded one song, "Little Miss Heartbreak." Jimmy Boyer, their lead singer, commented to Black that Swan wrote songs. He then requested to hear one, so Swan sang three, including "Lover Please." Mirley and the Rhythm Steppers ended up recording the tune, and it was issued on Black's label, Louis Records. Then a little later, Dennis Turner recorded the song. Shelby Singleton became interested in that version and even wanted to release it on Smash; however, Black declined the offer to sell him the rights. Eventually, the tune made its way to New York City and Clyde McPhatter. Swan recalled, "Clyde wasn't crazy about the song."[19] However, Singleton convinced McPhatter by telling him he could cut a few of his own next time. In 1962, Mercury distributed the 45 rpm single, "Lover Please" b/w "Let's Forget the Past." Swan didn't capitalize on the song's success as he continued to work with Mirley and the Rhythm Steppers and another group, The Four Notes.

However, the singer/songwriter had intentions of working again with Black: "I wrote a few songs for his publishing company. I went to Memphis [Tennessee] a couple of times and recorded them, just me and the piano in his little demo studio." In January 1963, Swan moved to Memphis but only saw Black a couple of more times before his death. He commented, "Bill never talked about his time with Elvis, and I don't think I ever asked." According to Swan, Black had a framed 78 rpm copy of Presley's "Mystery Train" hanging on his wall. Black pointed to it and said, 'Now, there was a record.' He felt that it was the best track they [he and guitarist Scotty Moore] ever cut with Presley." Swan added, "Around 1966, I met Scotty in Nashville. We have been friends since. He's one of my rock and roll heroes. Bill was a warm, friendly, easy going and fun person to be around as is Scotty."

In August 1963, Swan arrived in Nashville and soon started work at CBS Studio. He hobnobbed with musicians by attending their sessions and playing ping-pong with them. Through these acquaintances, Swan got hired as an engineer's assistant. When Kris Kristofferson came to the Music City a year later, he and Swan briefly met: "At that time, I lived at the Tally Ho Tavern, which he mentions in his song 'Silver Tongued Devil.'" They ran into each other periodically, but Swan was surprised when Kristofferson showed up at his workplace. Swan remembered, "I had just given my two week notice to the general manager at CBS. As I was leaving, Kris walked in. He says, 'Do you know where I can get a job?' I said, 'Yeah, I just quit mine. C'mon.' We went back inside, and he got the job, replacing me. [Being the engineer's assistant] consisted of erasing tape, getting food for the engineer, and cleaning up between sessions. I had done that for a year. They had said, 'If you know anybody looking for the job, tell them to come in.'" While on Music Row, Swan wrote songs for Conway Twitty, Mel Tillis, Loretta Lynn, and Waylon Jennings.

In 1969, Tony Joe White had a number eight hit with "Polk Salad Annie," a session that Swan produced: "When I was at Monument Records, Bob [Beckham] would play these demos of Tony's, just him and his guitar. I'd tell Bob if I was ever to produce anybody, that'd be the guy. This went on for a while and finally he asked if I'd like to do it. Tony is a great songwriter and stylist." Swan added, "He got the sound [on the record]. All I really did was put some horns on it."[20]

That same year, Kristofferson, Swan, and Dennis Linde had a trio that worked The Troubadour in Los Angeles for two weeks: "It was the first time that Kris really went out and performed. The audience loved his songs so much, but I was a paranoid bass player. I had learned to play in only two or three days. Dennis was supposed to play while someone else was gonna be on guitar, but they backed out at the last minute. I had helped Kris demo a lot of his songs in the studio, so I knew 'em. I said, 'Dennis plays guitar; I'll play the bass, and we'll do it.'" During the first week, they opened for Linda Ronstadt and the Stone Ponys. By week two, the roles were reversed. Swan continued to work with Kristofferson off and on throughout the 1970s.

As a solo artist, "I Can Help" put Swan at the forefront of country music: "Writing the song on my organ was really easy; first the three verses then the bridge. It was then recorded live in only two takes. I was as surprised as anyone when it hit number one on both the country and pop charts [in 1974]. [In fact, it was Bob Luman who had originally made him aware that the song was climbing the charts]. I wasn't even listening to the radio at that time." In 1975, the Music Operators of America Jukebox Awards bestowed Swan with the honor of Record of the Year for "I Can Help." In his acceptance, Swan acknowledged, "I believe I've played enough jukeboxes to earn this." Both Jerry Lee Lewis and Elvis Presley recorded versions of it: "I love Jerry Lee's, but it was a thrill to have Elvis do it. I'm grateful that they both liked 'I Can Help' enough to record it." His connection with Presley didn't end there. Swan remembered, "Felton Jarvis was at my publisher, Combine Music, talking with Bob Beckham about Elvis and the things he had given people. For some reason, I said, 'Get me a pair of his socks.' A few months later, Felton walked into Combine and presented me with a pair saying, 'Elvis wore these when he recorded 'I Can Help.'"

Swan continued to cut sides for Monument as well as other record labels. He enjoyed a few more *Billboard* country charted hits, including "Everything's the Same (Ain't Nothing Changed)," which scored at number seventeen, "Do I Have to Draw a Picture," which secured the number eighteen spot, "With Their Kind of Money and Our Kind of Love," which placed at number thirty-two, and "I'm Into Lovin' You," which peaked at number eighteen. Unfortunately, none of the releases equaled the success of "I Can Help." However, he remains content with the fact that he had popularity with that song.

Both rockabilly and Presley fans embrace Swan's music. Swan conveyed, "I don't believe rockabilly music will become mainstreamed, but it will always have its fans. They love it with a passion. A good rockabilly record could still break through as there are some people who really do it well. As far as Elvis, I think he was just an unbelievable icon and charismatic person. He had it all and everything about his music was just perfect. We'll never see anything like him again." Swan paid tribute to his hero with the 2000 album, *Songs Like Elvis Used to Do*. He revealed, "Some Elvis fans hated it, while others loved it. When I did the *I Can Help* album, I recorded a slow version of 'Don't Be Cruel.' A lot of people commented and said, 'Boy, that's really a cool version.' I then talked to the people at Sun Studio about the idea of doing an album of Elvis' songs but re-arranging them."

Frank Sinatra hated rock and roll, so he may have scoffed at Swan's album, *SUNatra*. As the title suggests, it was a collection of Sinatra's songs performed in the Sun Records' style: "I had this idea after we did the Elvis album because I like Sinatra too. I took some of his songs and kind of re-arranged them, and again the people at Sun Studio liked the idea. Two or three might have had a rockabilly feel. 'I Love Paris' and 'Birth of the Blues' sound like Jerry Lee. I think Frank probably wouldn't have been too crazy about it though." Besides recording, Swan still performs when the opportunity presents itself. He declared, "I feel like a blessed man; I'm a happy grandfather, and I'm still doing music." He also occasionally puts pen to paper—and Swan admits that he wishes he could write another hit like "I Can Help."

Leroy Van Dyke

"Auctioneer" and "Walk On By" may be Leroy Van Dyke's signature tunes, but the country crooner should be recognized for a long list of accolades. In the 1960s and 1970s, he was the first to showcase a self-contained, staged, produced, and choreographed country show on the Las Vegas strip and was the only artist who was able to sell traditional country music on Bourbon Street in New Orleans. Van Dyke also enjoyed success with his television program and co-hosted country music's biggest syndicated radio show of all time. In 1953, he opened for Marilyn Monroe in Korea. Today, he still auctioneers and performs at state fairs, rodeos, supper clubs, festivals, and conventions around the world.

Leroy Van Dyke was born on October 4, 1929, in rural Pettis County, Missouri. Van Dyke has two brothers and two sisters and comes from a musical family: "My dad sang in church and at funerals. He was the best bass singer in our part of the country."[21] His dad was a musical influence. As far as others, "My earliest influence was the transcriptions on local radio stations. Gene Autry was one of them." He also cited Johnnie Lee Wills, Red Foley, and Hank Snow. Van Dyke conveyed, "I have been singing [since] I was three years old—in school and church, for funerals and weddings. Later, I sang in the high school mixed chorus and in the University of Missouri Mens' Glee Club. As a senior at the university, he started playing guitar: "I never wanted to play lead, but I got pretty good as a rhythm guitarist. From the time I was thirteen, I wanted to be a singer. My dad asked me what I wanted to do for a living. I was afraid to tell him what I really wanted to do so I said, 'Well, I guess I'll farm for a living like you do.' Then he waited for a few seconds and said, 'Well, you might want to get that out of your mind.' I said, 'Why?' He said, 'Well, there might be some things that you could do that other people can't, that might be better for you, and that you'd like better.' He waited a little while and asked me again, 'If you could do anything you wanted to, what would you do for a living?' I said, 'I'd like to sing for a living.' His words were, and I'm quoting him directly, 'You can do it.' I've had him right at my left shoulder all my life, telling me I can do it. [My parents] were fully supportive in everything that I've done. It took fifteen years before [I became a singer]. In the meantime, I finished high school, stayed home, and helped my dad on the ranch for a year."

Fair performances enabled Leroy Van Dyke to combine his two passions: auctioneering and music (courtesy Leroy Van Dyke).

In 1948, Van Dyke enrolled at the University of Missouri in Columbia. He double majored in animal husbandry and journalism: "It's not unusual because the livestock industry in this country is a huge business: farmers, ranchers, meat packing companies, and all aspects of livestock agriculture. There are many breeds of livestock and many newspapers and newsletters. Many of those newsletters and breed publications had to have people to represent them at the livestock shows and auctions. Journalism and animal science mix together very well." Upon graduation, Van Dyke did a semester of graduate work.

In 1951, Van Dyke developed another interest, auctioneering. He explained, "I had about four major interests in my life: singing, auctioneering, writing, and raising livestock and I have done all of them. I've done a lot of guest spots at charity auctions. However, I do mix auctioneering and entertaining at a lot of the state, county, and regional fairs and exhibitions that I play. I'll go in, and they'll have the junior livestock sale on the day that I work the grandstand. Then I go up and act as guest auctioneer, to help the 4-H Club and the FFA kids get more money for their livestock. Auctioneering is an interesting job, and it's a lot of fun." In 1996, he was inducted into the National Auctioneers Association Hall of Fame.

In 1952, Van Dyke was drafted into the Army and stationed at Fort Holabird, Maryland: "The first time I ever stood in front of a crowd, sang a song, and played my own accompaniment was at a talent contest in Baltimore [Maryland]. I won with 'Poor Boy.' [Elvis Presley sang the same song in his first motion picture, *Love Me Tender*.] My prize was a wristwatch and some cufflinks." A year later, he was sent to Korea: "I was a special agent in counterintelligence." Two years he served his country: "I didn't do much singing the first year because I was busy attending basic training and special agent school. There was no extra time until I got to Korea. I lived in a tent and spent a lot of time with my guitar."

Nineteen fifty-three was a banner year for Van Dyke. He opened for Marilyn Monroe in Korea: "One day the Colonel came down to my tent, and he said, 'I want you to do me a favor.' I said, 'Yes, I will if I can. What do you want?' He said, 'We have a USO show coming in, and I'd like for you to do an opening spot, fifteen minutes ahead of the entertainer.' I said, 'Who's coming in?' He said, 'Marilyn Monroe.' I said, 'You got to be kidding me. You want me to go out there in front of thirty thousand sex starved G.I.s and entertain them while they're waiting to see Marilyn Monroe?' He laughed, and then I laughed. I probably was the only country entertainer to ever open for Marilyn Monroe. She and I were backstage at the same time, but I just said hello. I would have liked to have gotten a picture with her, but she was on a real tight schedule, and she had security around her. They came and escorted her to the stage. As soon as she got done with her show, she left. You know when you're making history, you don't realize it." There are newsreels of her arrival on a tank. That was Van Dyke's unit, the 160th Infantry Regiment 40th Infantry Division, in the background.

Besides the appearance with Monroe, Van Dyke wrote "Auctioneer" while stationed overseas. The tune was penned as a tribute to his cousin Ray Sims. In 1954, after a two year stint in the Army, Van Dyke went to work for a livestock newspaper: "It was a chain of livestock newspapers called the Cornbelt Farm Dailies. They were headquartered in Chicago but also had outlets in St. Louis, Missouri, Kansas City, Missouri, and Omaha, Nebraska. I sold advertising and then I would attend the major livestock shows like the state fairs and the Chicago International Livestock Show and the Kansas City American Royal Livestock Show. I'd go into the office periodically on special projects but most of the time I was travelling in my car. I put on about fifty thousand miles a year." Van Dyke ventured all over the country, but his main territory was Wisconsin, Indiana, and Illinois.

Early in his career, Buddy Black was his manager, but only for a few weeks. Van Dyke explained, "I was doing a talent show in Chicago and sang 'Auctioneer.' I did not win, think I was third. Before I got out of the studio, a representative from Dot Records called the switchboard and left a message for me to call. At the same time, there was a guy named Buddy Black, who was an announcer for WGN Radio and TV. He was getting ready to go to work that day, and he saw me on television. He hurried down to the station, went to the switchboard, and said, 'Have there been any calls for that young guy, Van Dyke, that sang?' They said, 'Yes.' He said, 'Let me have it.' Buddy took the note, called, and talked me into a contract. I didn't know what was in it. He added his name on 'Auctioneer' as co-writer but had nothing to do with writing it. I had written the song two years before I ever met him. I found out he was an opportunist, so I just dissolved the contract. Buddy Black got all the performance royalties on that song for twenty-five years. He cheated me out of probably at least half a million dollars. I never did trust management again after that. A few years ago, we got it changed so that it was jointly published. We never did get his name off of it though, so his estate is still getting half of my money."

In 1956, Dot Records issued the 45 rpm single "Auctioneer" b/w "I Fell in Love with a Pony-Tail." He was still employed at the newspaper when "Auctioneer" was released. Van Dyke added, "I was crossing the Illinois River at Peoria when it came on the air. I almost ran off the road. I had to pull over to the shoulder, sit there and listen. It was just a total surprise to me as I didn't know the record was released yet. It [quickly] sold three million copies." Even though he had a number nine song on the *Billboard* country charts, Van Dyke continued to work for the newspaper: "I stayed for about nine months because it was a very busy time of the year. I didn't want to leave my employer with that job unfilled because it would be a major problem to replace me on short notice."

The record label signed him to a four year contract: "Dot didn't have any idea what to do with me because they didn't know whether 'Auctioneer' was a country, story, pop, or novelty song. [Four more singles were issued] but they didn't sell because they didn't promote them. I asked them to release me from my contract [before the four years was up]. They did, and then I was without a recording contract for about a year."

Van Dyke's next move was to join Red Foley on the *Ozark Jubilee*: "The show was on the air for five years, and I was there for the last three. I never was a co-host. If Red had to be gone on personal appearances, then most of the time Bobby Lord would take over for him. Then later on when they changed the format and the name, they had various artists that took turns doing the emcee work." *Ozark Jubilee* became *Country Music Jubilee* and then *Jubilee U.S.A.* Van Dyke added, "[One day at rehearsal] I sang my song and went back out into the theater [to watch]. Somebody tapped me on the shoulder. I turned and looked at him. He said, 'Who are you recording for?' I said, 'Nobody, I'm looking.' He said, 'I'll record you.' [It turned out that the guy was Shelby Singleton from Mercury Records.] During that period of time, I probably got turned down by more major labels than any other person you know. Nobody wanted to sign me. The only one I didn't ask was the one who asked me."

Van Dyke enjoyed the five year partnership with Mercury Records: "It was sort of a co-operative effort. They weren't tremendously dictatorial. We got along very well as far as subject material." It was with his second release on the label, which occurred in August 1961, that he scored a number one song on the *Billboard* country charts: "Kendall Hayes wrote 'Walk On By.' When we got the demo, it was very bad and incomplete. There was only a verse and a chorus. I changed a few of the words in the verse, rearranged the chorus, and then Gary Walker took it home and wrote the second verse. That's the version that everyone hears. I never believed in taking somebody else's credit. There are dozens and dozens of performers that wind up with their names on records that never have anything to do with the writing. I think that's unfair. I never wanted to cheat anybody. The only name on it is Kendall Hayes, but in the paperwork Gary Walker gets twenty-five percent credit, so he gets that share in royalties."

"Walk On By" featured Pig Robbins on piano, Buddy Killen on bass, Willie Ackerman on drums, and Harold Bradley, Jerry Kennedy, and Hank Garland on guitar: "They were one of the A-Teams." On other records, Van Dyke worked with the more famous A-Team, which included Hank Garland, Bob Moore, Grady Martin, and Buddy Harman: "I always had studio musicians on recordings. I learned just from experience of being in the studio. Nobody ever told me what to do, and I never studied what the musicians were doing. I wasn't a musician, just a vocalist." In regard to "Walk On By," Van Dyke commented, "I had a classic split record. I knew in my mind that 'Walk On By' was the best side, but Mercury was pushing the other side. It was just sitting there not doing much of anything. One radio station might have had 'Walk On By' on their playlist while another would have the other side of the record ['My World Is Caving In']. Once Mercury pulled their promotion off the A side and pushed 'Walk On By,' it went straight to the top." The tune stayed in the number one position for an unprecedented nineteen weeks and, in all, forty-two weeks in the charts. In 1994, Van Dyke acknowledged, "*Billboard* named 'Walk On By' the biggest country single of all-time: based on sales, number of plays, and the number of weeks on the charts."

Van Dyke made two guest appearances on the *Grand Ole Opry*. He recalled, "On my first appearance, I sang 'Auctioneer' and 'Walk On By.'" By 1962, he was regularly featured as a member. The *Grand Ole Opry* moved from the Ryman Auditorium to the new Grand Ole Opry house, and about once a month they would televise the show. Van Dyke guested on the televised shows as well. There is a colorized clip of him singing "Walk On By," which is available for purchase on the Time-Life DVD, *Opry Video Classics: Songs That Topped the Charts*.

For thirteen episodes, *The Leroy Van Dyke Show* was produced in Toronto, Canada: "I was the main performer as well as the host." It was a syndicated program and featured guests such as Skeeter Davis, Bill Anderson, George Hamilton IV, Margie Singleton, Stringbean, Roy Drusky, and Ferlin Husky ("We were very, very close friends. Ferlin was one of the best entertainers that the country music business ever saw.")

In 1967, Van Dyke had the lead role in the motion picture *What Am I Bid?* He conveyed, "My manager, Gene Nash, choreographed, wrote the screenplay, and also directed the movie. We had complete control over the storyline, production, and filming. We took that opportunity to pay back those people who were nice to me during my career." Country legend Faron Young was one of those people: "In 1954, I met Faron. I was traveling with the Drovers' Journal in Northern Illinois and heard about a country music show [featuring Faron Young] that was coming to the Beloit College field house [in Beloit, Wisconsin]. I went and got acquainted with him. He said, 'Hey, do you sing?' I said, 'Yeah.' He said, 'You got a guitar?' I said, 'Yeah.' He said, 'Go get it.' He put me on his show. He was a nice guy, who was very generous. Faron was a good act, a fine singer, and a good showman. The reason we put him in the movie was because there were a lot of people that were good to me along the way. Faron Young treated me very, very well. We also put Tex Ritter in the film. In 1957, he had put me on my first tour of county fairs. My cousin Ray Sims was also one of the featured guests."

Thanks to the Hubert Long Talent Agency, Van Dyke was kept busy touring: "He was a very reputable fella. Everybody liked him and knew he was honest. I was proud to be with him." Long contacted Van Dyke with an opportunity to co-host a syndicated radio program: "He said that the Southern Baptist Radio/Television Commission in Fort Worth, Texas was thinking about starting a show featuring country music called *Country Crossroads*. They wanted somebody with a pretty decent voice, that had some hit records, and that the people would know. They offered it to me, and I said, 'Yeah, I'll do it but don't ask me to get up there and preach because I won't do it. I'll read your copy, but I'm not creative enough to do any more than that.' The first episode was done live from the Country Music Hall of Fame in Nashville and was heard on thirty-five radio stations. Bill [Mack] and I were the emcees, but we never saw each other or the guests, [with the exception of the first show]. It was produced one piece at a time. I was on the road about three hundred days a year then, so I didn't have time to write any copy or go anyplace to film it. They would fly an engineer, the writer, and somebody with recording equipment [into the city where I was doing a show]. It was scripted with no ad-lib. I'd record the lines then they would splice the music in later. Bill did the same thing where he was. They had to conform to our schedules because we were busy. By the time I left in 1979, after ten years, *Country Crossroads* was being heard by thirty-two million people a week, and it was the biggest syndicated country music show in history."

Throughout the 1960s and 1970s, Van Dyke regularly showcased his talent in Las Vegas: "We were the first to put together a self-contained, staged, produced, choreographed country show for the strip. I played the Sahara, the Mint, the Freemont Hotel, and the Landmark." Van Dyke was able to witness one of the Sahara's main acts, Louis Prima, in action: "He had them jumping. His show was a sight to behold."

Besides transforming the music scene in Las Vegas, Van Dyke altered the landscape in New Orleans: "It was a shock to a lot of the patrons at Al Hirt's club on Bourbon Street because it was known for jazz music. I had a real slick professional show that had been designed and built for Las Vegas casinos. We got some strange looks since we were dressed in tuxedos and had a four piece band with three girl singers. Some of the people would just stare at us when we started the music, but then pretty soon they'd start patting their feet and clapping their hands. One lady, wearing a lot of diamonds and a fur coat, came up to me after the show. She said, 'I don't know what this is, but whatever it is, I like it.' We surprised a lot of people. They didn't know country music could be done that way. Traditional country music would not sell on Bourbon Street, but our show worked. The first time we played the club; we went in for two weeks but stayed for five." Van Dyke added, "Al is one of the greatest people and one of the best musicians I ever met. He was really, really nice to me." [Incidentally, Al Hirt also appeared in *What Am I Bid?*]

In recent years, Van Dyke performs seventy-five to one hundred shows a year: "Some years we're busier than others. One of the things that take up a lot of our entertainment activity is the Country Gold Tour, which is a package show made up of country music recording artists who have had million selling records, number one records, or massive television exposure, so that everybody knows his/her name. It's my wife Gladys' idea to put those together. She's been doing those shows for over twenty years. We've had the tour in twenty-four states and four foreign countries." State fairs provide the backdrop for a majority of the venues: "On the Country Gold tours, I carry a seven piece band. My son Ben plays in it. He started working with me when he was fifteen years old, playing trombone. He has since switched to guitar. He's recognized as one of the best backup guitar players in this business. I open the show as the host then do the emceeing. Narvel Felts has worked the tours with us. He always does a great job. I've never heard anybody like him. The first time we had him on one of our shows, he only had time to do four songs because [eight others needed to perform yet]. He got a standing ovation after every song. In fact, we don't allow encores on our shows, but he was so good I made him come back and do another song. The audience loved it. I didn't care [that it interfered with the schedule]."

Fifty-eight years of non-stop performing, and Van Dyke has never missed a show for any reason: "I just don't get sick. There were a couple of times when I really couldn't perform well because I had laryngitis. One time I lost my voice in Denver, Colorado; I could talk but couldn't sing. I did about forty minutes of comedy, and I got by with it." In his spare time, on a thousand acre ranch, Van Dyke raises horses and mules, which he eventually sells. Currently, he owns thirty-five Arabian horses, and the premium quality mules are bred from the Arabian mares.

Buck Owens and the Buckaroos

Buck Owens started his career as a session guitarist at Capitol Records. There he backed Wanda Jackson, Sonny James, Faron Young, Gene Vincent, Tommy Sands, and several others. Owens then took on the pseudonym Corky Jones and recorded a couple of rockabilly sides, which included "Hot Dog." In 1958, he met Don Rich, who then played fiddle. The next year, Owens saw chart action with "Second Fiddle," which peaked at number twenty-four and "Under Your Spell Again," which reached the number four position. In December 1960, Rich permanently joined Owens. By the time, Owens recorded "Act Naturally" three years later, he had formed the Buckaroos. Besides their success with Owens, the Buckaroos scored a number one instrumental album with *Buckaroo*. The Academy of Country Music gave them the award for Band of the Year four times, from 1965 to 1968. They also won the Country Music Award for Instrumental Group of the Year in 1967 and 1968. In 2005, CMT bestowed the Buckaroos with the number two spot on its list of the 20 Greatest Country Music Bands. Drummer Willie Cantu reflected, "I didn't realize that I was in a very unique situation and that we would be having the effect that we did."[22] During his career, Owens had twenty-one number one songs. According to Cantu, Owens created the Bakersfield Sound: "It was the way he sang and the way he played guitar. Merle Haggard and anyone else that's been credited with the creation really have nothing to do with the actual Bakersfield Sound. There's only one Bakersfield Sound, and that's Buck Owens."

On November 22, 1963, the day of President John F. Kennedy's assassination, Willie Cantu saw Buck Owens and the Buckaroos play at the Maverick Club in Corpus Christi, Texas. Cantu recalled, "That's the first time I had heard Buck Owens—on the jukebox with 'Act Naturally.' The country music that I was used to hearing was very nasally, old style country, not the current stuff like Ray Price, Jim Reeves, or Buck Owens. I had never heard such modern sounds. The band that I was playing with was more a Bob Wills' type of band—

Buck Owens and the Buckaroos created the Bakersfield Sound, which heavily influenced Merle Haggard, the Byrds, and the Flying Burrito Brothers. From left: Don Rich, Willie Cantu, Buck Owens, Doyle Holly, and Tom Brumley (courtesy Willie Cantu).

very stompy western swing. I was supposed to play that night. My band was going to alternate sets with Buck, but he got there and said, 'No, we'll do the whole night. It might make it go by quicker if we just stay up there and play.' Hearing Buck, even though the club was pretty empty (no more than fifty people showed up), was a great experience for me because I did not know that country music could sound that good. Don Rich and Doyle Holly heard me play the night before. They had come to town early and hung out at the club. Doyle got my phone number. He asked if I'd be interested in coming out to California if an opening came up with a band, not necessarily the Buckaroos. I thought sure, why not? I was able to move anywhere I wanted to since I had quit high school. It was my dream to go to New York City within a year because I wanted to be a jazz drummer. I was already a professional, but only really worked on the weekends. As impressed as I was that night, I never thought about becoming a Buckaroo."

Cantu added, "In the first week of February 1964, Buck called on the recommendation from Don Rich that I should be their next drummer. He asked if I would like to join the band although he had never heard me, and there was no audition." Owens had called Cantu personally because he didn't have a manager yet. According to Cantu, "Buck was just starting to break big. He already had 'Act Naturally' and 'Love's Gonna Live Here.' [Both tunes had reached the number one position on the country charts in 1963.] 'Together Again' is really the song that broke through for him. [It too was a number one song, but in 1964.] Buck always wanted to have a hand in what was going on, so it kind of made sense that he would call me. Even though, I never really expected to hear from him or even Doyle. I only worked at the Maverick Club for two months, and it was my first experience playing country music. It was handed down to me by a drummer friend who had gotten it from another friend of ours. Nobody could stand it, but I ended up trying. They fired me because they wanted to hire another drummer, who was married to one of the waitresses." However, the club owner gave Cantu a high recommendation when Owens called to inquire about him.

Owens' previous drummer had been dismissed: "They were doing a big show in a school auditorium in Albuquerque, New Mexico. Mel King wanted to set up his drums in front of the amplifiers rather than behind, which is the normal practice. He was very insistent upon having his drums up front. Don Rich was the bandleader, and he would not do anything that Don asked him to do. Don went backstage and told Buck what was going on. Buck came onstage, picked up his drums and threw them off the stage without saying anything. I'm thinking that perhaps there might have been a drummer with another band that sat in with them or maybe they played the whole performance without a drummer. Either way, that was the end of Mel King."

Cantu then replaced King: "I had to ask my parents' permission to leave home and go to Bakersfield, California. The day that I arrived was the day that Buck and the guys, using a studio drummer, were in Hollywood recording 'Together Again' and 'My Heart Skips a Beat.' Buck's wife, Phyllis, who had picked me up at the airport, said, 'Buck doesn't know how familiar you are with his music, so here is a collection of his albums so far.' I remember spending that Saturday afternoon listening to the LPs. I didn't meet Buck until that Monday. We were still a week or so away from our first gig, and I kept waiting for him to say, 'Well, we're gonna get together and rehearse tomorrow,' but it never happened. He did say, 'I want you to go to Las Vegas with me,' so we went for a couple of days. We talked and got to know each other a little bit. Nothing was mentioned about a rehearsal. I might have asked, and he said, 'We never rehearse.' Buck was just reliant on me being familiar with the music and thinking from what Don and Doyle had told him that I wouldn't have any problem playing."

A week after Cantu's arrival, their first performance took place in Redding, California. Cantu recalled, "Don and I ended up rooming together. They handed me my uniform, but I was still nervous because we hadn't talked about anything and had no rehearsal. Buck came into our motel room, just to see that we were okay and that I was dressed properly. I asked him, 'Is there anything I should know before we play?' He said, 'Yes, there are two things. First, we play on top of the beat. The other thing is if I don't like what you're doing, I will tell you.' I did not understand what he meant by playing on top of the beat. I just knew that you play on the beat; that's how I learned. I asked Don, 'What does he mean?' Don's response was, 'You'll hear it.' That was the last anything was ever said because once we started playing

I forgot about it and just played the music. There was never a problem with me dragging or rushing the beat. I had heard the records, so I basically knew what to do. It was simple enough. I had been playing professionally for about three years, so I was pretty confident in what I could do. You can really hear the jazz influence in my playing. They were so strong as a group that I just fell in and got swept away. I gained an understanding of what Buck was talking about by just doing it."

That first year, Cantu played over three hundred days out of the calendar year, thanks in part to Owens' manager Jack McFadden: "When I joined, Buck was still doing a lot of club dates. We were doing a few package shows, auditoriums, and arenas, but not many. The more popular Buck got the fewer clubs we played because they couldn't afford him, and we could play for a lot larger crowd. It became less fun as years went by because we were only getting to play for an hour as opposed to playing for four hours in a club. Even though, it was great going onstage with the band. A lot of times I'd get chills just hearing Buck and Don sing 'Together Again.' That in itself was a great experience."

At seventeen, Cantu had joined Buck Owens and the Buckaroos, which made him the youngest member. Lead guitarist Don Rich was twenty-two; bassist Doyle Holly and steel guitar player Tom Brumley were both twenty-seven; and vocalist Buck Owens was thirty-four. Cantu recalled, "They treated me as an adult but joked that I was the kid in the group. I behaved in such a manner that there was no need for them to really treat me any other way. I was definitely always an equal partner in the band. I did my part, and there were never any problems." Brumley and Holly hadn't been in the band too long before Cantu's arrival. In fact, Brumley had only been a Buckaroo for a couple of weeks, and he was already in the studio recording with Owens. Rich was the only remaining original member. Kenny Pierce was also one of the originals but had only stayed for a year. By the time Cantu joined, he had been replaced by Holly. Merle Haggard was a Buckaroo for a short time and came up with the name. Cantu disclosed that his contract with Owens was exclusive: "Merle had wanted me and Don to record with him, but Buck wouldn't allow it. In the long run, it was a good thing because it made Merle really focus on getting his own sound together. Our pay with Buck was adequate for the time."

During Cantu's tenure, Owens recorded numerous sessions. Ken Nelson produced the recordings at Capitol Records' Studio B. Cantu added, "I never heard the songs until we actually got to the session." The first singles that Cantu appeared on were "I've Got a Tiger by the Tail" b/w "Crying Time" and "I Don't Care" b/w "Don't Let Her Know," both released in 1964. "Crying Time," "I Don't Care," and "I've Got a Tiger by the Tail" were all number one songs on the country charts.

The Buckaroos recorded two instrumental albums while Cantu was a member. The first was released in July 1965: "Buck encouraged those albums. It could have been his idea even. The Buckaroos became as popular as Buck. That's really what he pushed for, for the band to have equal billing. Although, I don't know that he would have liked the idea of Don going off on his own. I had thought about the Buckaroos becoming a separate entity because wouldn't it be cool to have a band that could play all these different styles of music. That was my dream, and it became a topic that Don and I used to discuss a lot. In the end, Don would always say, 'Well I don't know if I could ever leave Buck.' I had wanted us to play more than just country, but it never went beyond Don and me."

In January 1966, "Waiting in Your Welfare Line" peaked at number one. Cantu conveyed, "I think that song took the longest, at least ten takes. That tune was kind of a departure from anything else Buck had ever done, and the set up was different. We never really had to do a lot of takes on a song, usually just one or two, and we had it."

An album that was recorded live at Carnegie Hall in New York City was issued in March 1966. On the cover, they are wearing their famous bedazzled Turk tailored outfits. Incidentally, the uniforms were bought and kept by Owens. Cantu recalled, "We were the first modern country act to play Carnegie Hall. Only the best people played there. The place was packed because there were a lot of fans in the area. I was in total awe of the experience." That album reflected their live act. Cantu mentioned, "Fans wanted to hear the songs, so Buck didn't stand up there and try to make jokes and kill time. Basically we were there to take care of business. There was no set list, and I don't know how we did it. Some of the older songs ended up in a medley because there was only so much time. If a new song of ours had become a hit, then that was added to the show. It might be one of the few songs that would get the full treatment from beginning to end." Part of their appeal was the close harmonization between Rich and Owens: "Don and Buck had been singing together for so long that their harmonizing was a natural fit. It was something that just happened. When Don hooked up with Buck, he was just hired as a fiddle player. Don wanted to play guitar like Chuck Berry. He learned how to play from Buck. Don was a direct copy of Buck until he developed his own style. [During this time] Buck discovered that they sounded good together when they sang."

In April 1966, James Burton and Richie Frost joined Owens in the studio. Cantu revealed, "Buck decided that he wanted to try and add a different flavor to his sound and hopefully spur Don and I with some different ideas. He had James and Richie come in to record 'Where Does the Good Times Go' and 'Open Up Your Heart.' Don and I then went in and did our take on the same songs. The released versions are our interpretation of the way James and Richie had played. That session was a departure from the usual freight train rhythm that Buck was known for. It kind of brought about a different phase in the Buckaroos' sound." In February 1967, Owens saw another tune hit the top of the country charts with "Where Does the Good Times Go."

The television program, *Buck Owens' Ranch Show*, was filmed at WKY-TV studio in Oklahoma City: "There was no audience, so we just performed for the cameras. We would go in for a week or two and just do a marathon of taping. I don't know how many shows we knocked out in one day, but I do know they were pretty long days, and I didn't look forward to it. I did it for a year or two, but the show continued after I left the Buckaroos." According to the Video Beat website, "It was a nationally syndicated half-hour show that ran from 1966–1972. Four times a year, Buck and the Buckaroos would film a dozen or more shows that would then be broadcast weekly. The show featured Buck Owens in his prime and showcased the famous 'Bakersfield Sound.'"[23] In the first season, many of Owens' hits were performed, including "Act Naturally," "Love's Gonna Live Here," "I've Got a Tiger by the Tail," "I Don't Care," "Crying Time," "Waitin' in Your Welfare Line," "Together Again," and "My Heart Skips a Beat." Two volumes with four episodes each are available for sale at http://www.videobeat.com.

Cantu remembered that during his stint with the group that Doyle Holly quit a couple of times: "There were two different bass players that replaced Doyle. The first, Ray Saltan, only lasted for a week or two. I think Buck called Doyle to ask him back because we were getting ready to do *The Jimmy Dean Show*. I don't know what kind of deal he worked out, but he somehow talked him into coming back. The other, Wayne Wilson, was with us for a whole year, and he also recorded with the band. He was on the *In Japan* album, which was released in 1967."

After several hits, including many number ones, Buck Owens and the Buckaroos were in high demand by promoters. However, Cantu recollected playing only once at the *Grand Ole Opry*: "All they allowed a drummer to play with was either a brush and a stick or two brushes and a snare drum on a stand, so all the drummers played standing up. When we were at the Opry, I was in the back setting up my full set of drums. Mind you, I didn't know the story; all I knew was the way we played. The other drummers were coming up to me and saying, 'No, you can't do that. They won't let you play. You have to do what we're doing.' I then went and talked to Buck about it. He said, 'Well, we're not playing if you can't get your full set of drums out there.' I don't know who Buck talked to or what was said, but we were there, and the audience was waiting for us to play, so I guess they had no choice other than to let me go out there with my full set of drums." One of their regular gigs was the Golden Nugget in Las Vegas, where they would play week long stints a couple of times a year. Cantu revealed, "We never practiced, just got on the bandstand and played. Buck might have an idea for a song, and he'd get together with Don and his guitar, and they'd work it out. There was nothing for the rest of us to figure out, with Tom possibly being the exception."

They were always billed and marketed as Buck Owens and the Buckaroos: "He never separated the two." It even read that way on the side of their tour bus, which was actually a Dodge motorhome. The vehicle was custom made: "Don and Tom had it designed for us." Each band member took turns driving: "We didn't trust a bus driver. [Most of them had issues with alcoholism]. We decided it would be easier if we just counted on ourselves. Buck wasn't around since a lot of times he would fly, and we would just meet him there. We also did all the setup; we were our own roadies. Buck did not get involved with the loading and unloading because he was busy doing other things. It really wasn't his job, but I know Buck wouldn't have hesitated helping us if we needed it because he was as strong as an ox."

Owens and the group always signed autographs for their fans: "That was one of the things that Buck insisted upon. Since we were going to sign autographs, I guess he felt that perhaps it would be a good time for us to sell albums and songbooks. We'd all get behind the tables with our boxes of merchandise. We'd sign autographs for at least an hour after the show. The fans loved that, and he did too. Buck loved the attention where I was the total opposite. I did it because I had to. It was Buck's idea to put himself out there for the people. That's how he kept his fans."

In September 1967, Cantu quit Owens, and Jerry Wiggins replaced him. Cantu disclosed, "I was married at the time and had a daughter. My wife had chosen to live in Canada. I had gotten a call from the draft board asking me to come take a physical. I passed and was just waiting to be called [to duty]. When my wife found out about it, she called the draft board and had me reclassified. I then had to be with them. That's when I quit the band and moved to Canada. [Anyway] I really didn't see a future as a Buckaroo. It was time for me to move on and do something else." Cantu then played drums in a Dixieland jazz combo.

In 1969, Owens joined forces with Roy Clark to co-host *Hee Haw*, a variety show that combined country music and comedy skits. Many of the biggest names in country music performed on the program: Conway Twitty, Loretta Lynn, George Jones, Mickey Gilley, Sonny James, David Houston, and Waylon Jennings. The Buckaroos were the house band. Cantu commented, "*Hee Haw* gave Buck the national exposure that he was looking for." It originally ran for two years and then syndication picked it up for another twenty-one. However, Owens left in 1986.

As for the other members of the Buckaroos, Tom Brumley quit in 1969 and was soon recruited by Rick Nelson to become a member of his Stone Canyon Band. Doyle Holly moved to Nashville in 1971 and had a couple of minor hit songs: "He managed to chisel out a little musical career for himself." In 1973, "Queen of the Silver Dollar" peaked at number thirty-seven, and "Lila" scored a number twelve position. Don Rich remained in the band until he was killed in a motorcycle accident in 1974. According to Cantu, Rich and Owens were very, very close, and Owens was devastated by the news.

Owens forged ahead with new members of the Buckaroos. He continued to record and score number one tunes, which included "Tall Dark Stranger," "Who's Gonna Mow Your Grass," "Made in Japan," and "Johnny B. Goode." He also recorded and toured with his son Buddy Alan. Owens then purchased several radio stations, including KNIX-AM and KNIX-FM in Phoenix and KUZZ-FM in Bakersfield. That entrepreneurial expertise secured his financial future. In 1988, Dwight Yoakam rediscovered Owens and brought him into the studio to record a duet of "Streets of Bakersfield." It became Owens' first number one single in sixteen years. Eight years later, Owens was inducted into The Country Music Hall of Fame. In August 1999, the remaining original members (Holly, Brumley, and Cantu) reunited for a concert at Owens' nightclub, the Crystal Palace, in Bakersfield.

On March 25, 2006, shortly after a performance at the Crystal Palace, Owens passed away from a heart attack. Upon his tomb, the inscription reads "Buck's Place." Owens influenced many artists, including The Beatles, Yoakam, and The Mavericks. They have all paid tribute to him by recording his songs.

Chapter Five

Pop Sensations

Dodie Stevens

Nineteen fifty-nine was a banner year for Dodie Stevens. She had a number three hit, "Pink Shoelaces," on the *Billboard* Hot 100 chart. The teenager also starred in the movie *Hound Dog Man* with Fabian, graced the pages of fan magazines, and appeared on *American Bandstand*. Brenda Lee and Shelley Fabares were her friends, and she talked on the phone with them on a regular basis. Stevens also toured with fellow teen idols: Fabian, Ricky Nelson, Bobby Rydell, and Frankie Avalon. For three years, she enjoyed fame and popularity. At sixteen, Stevens left her singing career behind and got married. In 1966, she re-emerged as Geraldine Stevens. Ten years later, she became a background singer for Mac Davis. Today, Stevens is a vocal coach and continues to perform at rock and roll oldies concerts across the United States.

Dodie Stevens was born on February 17, 1946, in Chicago, Illinois. Her real name is Geraldine Ann Pasquale. Stevens explained, "In 1959, everybody changed their name, including Frankie Avalon. It was the thing to do, to have a stage name. [My real name] could hardly fit on a 45. I wanted to use the name Geri because that was my nickname, and I was fine about changing the last name. It was going to be Stevens, which I liked, but Carl Burns, the president of Crystalette Records, didn't like me using Geri because if a disc jockey just said, 'This is Geri Stevens,' people would automatically think the song was by a guy. He said, 'That's not good. Let's change everything.'"[1] Burns and Johnny Grant, who was a disk jockey and later became the mayor of Hollywood, gave her the stage alias Dodie Stevens: "They were sitting at a bar one night, and Carl was telling him about this new artist he had on the label and how he needed to come up with a new name. The two of them started kicking around a few names, and these were the three that came up: Carmen Stevens, Carol Stevens, and Dodie Stevens. I liked Carol Stevens, but one already existed. I didn't like Carmen as that sounded too ethnic. I also didn't like Dodie, but that was their decision."

Some people never got used to the alteration as close friends and family continued to call her Geri or Geraldine: "My sister never stopped, but at one point my parents started to call me Dodie. I think it was just whenever they were with me in a professional situation. It made more sense, but then they would continue doing that at home. That's when I said, 'Please don't do that.' Now, I've kind of grown into the name, and I've gotten over the things that I didn't like about it as a kid. I look at it as something to be proud of, something that brought me my success, and something that continues to work for me."

Both of Stevens' parents were artistically gifted: "My father could have been an opera singer while my mother was a wonderful dancer. [Unfortunately] neither one of them had the opportunity to do anything with their talents." She acknowledged, "[As for me] I began taking voice lessons at the age of five. I have a sister, who is a year older, and my parents offered lessons to both of us. They never wanted to show any kind of partiality. My sister hadn't shown any kind of interest in singing even though I had started from the age of two. I was singing all the time, whereas my sister was more of a tomboy. She played baseball in the neighborhood with other kids and climbed trees. My parents saw very early on that she [didn't really care about the lessons] and asked if she wanted to continue. She said no that she didn't really like it, so they didn't force her. My sister didn't take more than a few months of lessons."

At the age of seven, Stevens made her first television appearance on *Art Linkletter's House Party*, where she sang "Merry-Go Merry-Go Round." That tune was recorded in 1954 and issued on Gold Star as a 78 rpm single under the name Geri Pace. Stevens recalled, "It was a small studio in Hollywood. We went into the bathroom for acoustics because they didn't have an echo chamber."

As a preteen, she listened to a lot of vocal groups and then a little later The Shirelles: "I liked the female groups." Stevens added, "There wasn't any one artist that I thought was the best, or I wanted to sing like. [Therefore, she didn't name any musical influences.] I really loved Aretha Franklin, but that was a little bit later in my career." Stevens then cited Franklin, Melissa Manchester, Stevie Wonder, Peter Gabriel, and Kenny Loggins as her favorite singers.

Stevens was on a Los Angeles television show, *Strictly Informal*, when she caught the attention of Crystalette Records owner Carl Burns. He had tuned in to see another artist who was on the label. She reported, "The owner liked my voice very much and got in touch with someone at the television station to see if he could talk with me or my parents. He divulged that he was interested in recording me, but because I was so young, only eleven at the time; he said it was important to find a song that was age appropriate."[2] Burns wrote down her contact information and said he would record her as soon as he found the ideal song. Stevens didn't hear anything for a year and a half, but then Burns called with "Pink Shoelaces."

Dodie Stevens was only thirteen when she recorded her million-selling hit "Pink Shoelaces" (courtesy Dodie Stevens).

Her signature tune was cut live in only two or three takes: "I was given the name 'One Take Dodie.' Back then, that was a really good thing because everybody recorded at the same time. If you could do it all in one take without any mistakes that saved the record company a lot of money." Her reaction to hearing "Pink Shoelaces" on the radio for the first time was 'That's me! Listen to that.' It's kind of hard to put into words what that meant. I remember being in the car, riding in the backseat with my sister. I never thought it would be [such a big hit] because it wasn't like anything else." Eventually, "Pink Shoelaces" peaked at number three, sold over a million copies, and was awarded a gold disc.

She originally wasn't a fan of the tune: "It wasn't the kind of song that I liked on the radio. I was listening to Frankie Avalon, Fabian, and girl groups, such as The Shirelles. They were singing love songs whereas 'Pink Shoelaces' was a novelty song. It had lyrics that were kind of silly and stupid. I found out about ten years ago that the writer, Mickie Grant, wrote the song on a bet from her friends. [At the time] she was writing lyrically meaningful heavy songs, songs about being in love and things that took a lot of thought to write. She was very prolific, so her friends said, 'I bet you couldn't write a song that had no meaning.' Mickie then wrote 'Pink Shoelaces' to prove them wrong." Grant had sent the tune to the record company: "Mr. Burns immediately thought of me, said it was just perfect."[3]

Stevens remembered, "Crystalette was a very small independent label. The office couldn't have been larger than a bedroom. 'Pink Shoelaces' was their first hit record and because it took off so fast, they weren't prepared. That's when they went to Dot Records and signed a distribution contract with them." Besides Stevens' version, a group in Mexico sang "Pink Shoelaces" in Spanish and a female artist in England recorded it. The tune was also used as a theme for a Mexican soap opera. In late 1959, after only two releases on Crystalette, Stevens moved onto Dot Records.

Living life as a normal teenager was next to impossible once Stevens became popular. She disclosed, "My freshman year was when I recorded 'Pink Shoelaces.' Before you knew it, everybody knew that Dodie Stevens went to Temple City High School. [Kids then ridiculed and bullied her.] I'd leave two/three weeks at a time to go on tour, and the teachers had to know why. Some of them were very understanding, helpful, and let me make up the work when I got back or gave me work to take on the road. Others, I don't know if it was jealousy or them being mean, would just give me a F. I tried to do normal things at school as I didn't like anybody treating me differently. I auditioned to be a pom pom girl, so I could go to football games and sing our high school theme song. I got picked because I was good, not because I was Dodie. There were some parents and a few girls on the cheerleading pom pom squad who didn't think that was fair since I already had such a wonderful life. They didn't think that I should be doing that too." Those critics weren't aware that juggling school with a music career proved to be very challenging. Stevens disclosed, "Earlier in the day or after school, I was learning a new song for an album and then I would study for a test until midnight or one o'clock in the morning. I wasn't like my sister, who had a photographic memory. She could read something once, remember it, and then get all A's. I had to read something over and over again. I remember getting headaches as it was an overload on my brain. Once it got to be a physical problem, that's when my parents were very open to not forcing it upon me anymore. They said, 'We see it is taking a toll, so we will allow you to quit school. We'll get you a tutor.' In the second semester of her junior year, Stevens dropped out: "My career was flourishing, so I said, 'I want to put all my focus into that.' My concentration and passion were in music."

Incidentally, Stevens never got a tutor: "There just wasn't time for it, and I didn't want to do anything, but sing, so I continued with my voice lessons. My teacher's name was Helen Bishop, and she had me singing a lot of Judy Garland songs. I think it was something that she wanted me to do because I don't think I would have even been interested if she hadn't introduced me to her songs." Stevens grew to love Garland and her music: "She was extraordinary. Judy Garland always gave me goose bumps when I heard and watched her sing. I have never seen or heard any artist that could compare." Stevens added, "In fact, my second album, *Over the Rainbow*, contained all songs that Judy had recorded. Before I recorded 'Pink Shoelaces,' I did an USO show at a venue in Hollywood and benefit shows for the City of Hope. Ms. Bishop was very instrumental in [setting those up for me]." Stevens added, "[Besides voice lessons] I also took dance classes." In her younger years, it was tap and ballet and then as a teenager, she took up jazz: "I did that for about ten years and loved it. Jazz really helped me when I went to work for Mac Davis because they weren't hiring just a singer; they needed somebody that also danced."

Stevens was one of the teen idols of her time, so thanks to Dot Records and her management team, she was often booked on package tours with male heartthrobs. She remembered, "I had a major crush on Ricky Nelson. He was cute and sweet. I worked a lot with him, Fabian, Frankie Avalon, Bobby Rydell, and Chubby Checker. I got to go to parties with most of them." There were no paparazzi then, so to get photos, cocktail parties were arranged where all the celebrities and photographers from the different magazines were invited: "That's when they would interview you or take pictures of you with somebody that was there. Then the caption would read, 'Dodie and Fabian are seen at Hollywood party.' Well we didn't go there together. We just both happened to be invited. Sometimes photo shoots were also set up, like Bobby Rydell and I did one at the beach." Surprisingly, Stevens acknowledged that "I could basically go anywhere I wanted to and not be bothered. [Sometimes] I would go shopping with my friends and have people come and ask for my autograph."

Besides touring with Fabian, she also starred in the movie *Hound Dog Man* with him. Stevens revealed, "He was my idol, plus I had the biggest crush on him, but you have to keep in mind I was thirteen, and he was sixteen. Fabian have eyes for Dodie? Are you kidding me? He treated me like a sister and had eyes for girls his own age like Annette [Funicello], whom he was dating. I wanted to be one of those girls, so when I was asked to be in the movie and play his girlfriend [I jumped at the chance]. I always tried to look and act older in the hopes he would like or notice me, but it never worked." Director Don Siegel was impressed with both youngsters, even commenting to Stevens' parents that she had natural ability. To promote the film, a magazine photo shoot was set up at an Italian restaurant in Lake Arrowhead, California.

After her initial success, Dot Records wasn't sure what to do with Stevens. They had pigeonholed her as a novelty artist and weren't sure which direction to set her career in. She even recorded some country material, including Patsy Cline's "I Fall to Pieces," although she wasn't a fan: "I was thirteen/fourteen years old, and Dot would say, 'Record this; record that.' I didn't like it when I was recording a lot of ballads. My self-titled debut album was comprised of old standards and songs from the 1940s. I wanted to be doing rock and roll, like Elvis. I was a teenager, so I wanted to sing songs that I could dance to."

From 1959 to 1960, Stevens had a few more songs enter the top 100: "Yes-Sir-Ee," "Five Pennies," "Miss Lonely Hearts," "No," and "Yes, I'm Lonely Tonight." The latter tune was an answer song to Elvis Presley's "Are You Lonesome Tonight?" The arrangement was also very similar to his.

At sixteen, she got married and later gave birth to a daughter. For four years, she didn't sing as her religiously zealous husband insisted she stay home to be a housewife and mother. In fact, his Pentecostal faith had preached against being in show business because it was of the devil: "They really convinced me that I did the right thing by leaving music and that I had to obey my husband." In 1966, she left the marriage because of physical abuse and mental corruption. Besides the torment afflicted upon her, Stevens has other regrets of marrying so young. Career opportunities were lost, such as Dr. Pepper, who had wanted her to be a spokesperson and do commercials for them, and a Broadway play, that was being written specifically for her to star in. Although, she remarked, "If I had to choose one or the other, I would definitely choose my daughter. I would do it all over again."

Once Stevens returned home and was safe, she made the declaration, "'I don't know how to do anything else but sing, and that's what I want to do.' I continued using the name Dodie Stevens but found that it was working against me, in two ways: if I was going to people who had remembered me from my early years, then they couldn't get away from the fact that I was a novelty singer, or if it was people who were younger, they didn't know Dodie Stevens, and therefore they really weren't that interested." She returned to her former manager, who assisted her in any way he could. Ultimately, Stevens embraced adulthood and changed her name to Geraldine Stevens, eventually shortening it to Geri Stevens: "For quite a few years, I worked a lot of dinner houses and clubs throughout the country and Canada. I also recorded a couple of songs for World Pacific Records. One of the tunes was an answer to 'Ruby, Don't Take Your Love to Town' and was titled 'Billy, I've Got to Go to Town.' Then, in 1972, I auditioned for Sergio Mendez. I was with him for a year, during that time we recorded three albums and toured Japan, Hong Kong, Mexico, and the U.S." Mendez played piano and was leader of the band, Brasil '77. He always had two female singers, who stood on either side of him, sing all of the songs." Stevens left the group because Mendez and the group were going back to Brazil.

Beginning in 1973, she was hired as background vocalist for various artists, including Raquel Welch. Stevens revealed, "Raquel wasn't and isn't a singer. It was because she was so famous and beautiful that her management wanted to extend her celebrity beyond movies. People would come just to see her. They worked up a show where she did some singing and dancing, but because she wasn't a good singer and not necessarily a good dancer, they hired backup singers to kind of cover her. I was like a stand-in for her, in the sense that I would be doing backup vocals with the other three singers, but if she forgot lyrics or couldn't sing a particular part because it was too high, then I stopped background singing and went right into singing her part. I worked with her for a year. In fact, she was the first one I did background for." Word got around that Stevens was a good singer, and calls began to come her way. Loretta Lynn then employed her, for two years: "It wasn't an exclusive contract. I only had one of those, with Mac Davis, where I couldn't work for anybody else." With Lynn, she only sang on stage with her, no recordings. Stevens remarked, "Loretta was wonderful and very easy going. She never made you feel like she was the star and you were one of the peons. It was like working for your girlfriend."

In 1976, Stevens began singing background for Mac Davis. Besides live appearances, she also recorded with Davis and was featured with him on the TV shows *The Midnight Special* and *Solid Gold*. It's a gig that lasted twelve years until Davis retired from touring. Stevens recalled, "I was doing a performance with Loretta in Reno, Nevada, and her former musical director came to see the show. He also happened to be the musical director for Mac. They needed to find another girl to do backup. The musical director heard me sing, liked it, and said 'I want to hire you for this position, but you have to be able to dance. You'll have to go through an audition, and if you pass, then you got the gig.'" Davis attended the audition to judge for himself, and she was hired on the spot. Stevens disclosed, "Mac was great—nice, down to Earth, and humble. He's another good ol' boy. If he wasn't the kind of guy that he is, I wouldn't have lasted twelve years."

Upon Davis' retirement, Stevens left the background circuit and returned to her own music: "I co-produced a 1950s/1960s musical revue called *Bop*, and we did that for about three years."

In the early 1990s, Stevens and her daughter recorded a country CD, *Outlaw of the Heart*, under the name a.k.a. Stevens. It contained all original songs, co-written by Stevens and Peter Newman. Then they did some performances and sold the CD off the stage since it hadn't been issued on a label. Stevens mentioned, "There wasn't as much popularity as we hoped there would be. It was because we were being likened to The Judds. We would pitch the CD to record companies or management, and we'd get, 'Oh, you're just like The Judds. We've already got them, so we're not really interested.' We were nothing like The Judds because we did country with a rock and roll edge and both of us always sang lead." Once the country stint didn't pan out, Stevens moved on to record jingles for Dole Pineapple and Sprint.

Most recently, Stevens has been very active with songwriting. She conveyed, "I also recorded a children oriented CD with my daughter, Stephanie. On *Life Is a Song, Sing-Along*, I wrote songs for the purpose of children being able to sing along. I called them positive musical affirmations." She added, "I look at the world, in which we live, and it seems to be getting more violent and out of control. I know you don't just wake up one day, and you're this person who kills others or does criminal acts; it's learned behavior. I thought maybe there was a way that I could bring my writing and music to kids, to somehow make the world a better place. I then went on to record another album, *A Singing Healing Journey*, which was along the same lines, but for adults. In 2011, we sang the single 'I'm Not a Bully' at an elementary school assembly in La Jolla, California. That was a wonderful experience. Just to hear the children singing was quite a rush. The last song that I wrote, 'We the Children,' was in memory of the victims of the Sandy Hook, New Jersey, elementary school shooting. It was created for the purpose of comfort and healing, my way of expressing a broken heart. In a lot of the news reports, there was a link to a website where people could send cards of condolences. Rather than doing that, I wanted to make a CD of the song and send it to the families."

Recording keeps her busy, but she also teaches voice and performs across the country.

She has been a vocal coach for the past thirteen years: "Students typically sign up for four consecutive weekly lessons. I teach them that you can't just sing the notes well; you have to sing and act out the story of the song with hand gestures, facial expressions, and dance. It takes a lot of hard work and practice. You can't just do it once a week and expect to develop." Her pupils range from age seven to eighty: "It's very rewarding to see those who are very talented but also those who start out with not much talent and develop an extraordinary voice." In regard to touring, promoters usually book her on a bill with other oldies acts, such as Fabian. In fact, in 2003, they both participated in a PBS musical special, *At the Drive-In*. Stevens realizes that her fans come to the show to hear her sing "Pink Shoelaces": "Now, I'm able to actually perform the song. The lyrics come to life, and it becomes fun for me." After her performances, Stevens loves the meet and greet portion: "It gives me a chance to thank the fans for coming and for being so gracious. I give all the years of success that I've had to them. They get all the respect and glory for it because without them I wouldn't have an audience today. I love what I do, and I'm very grateful. It's kind of a mutual love affair and respectability that we have for each other."

Robin Luke

In the summer of 1958, Robin Luke's song "Susie Darlin'" peaked at number five on the *Billboard* charts. His popularity soared. Soon after, he appeared on *American Bandstand* and headlined tours with Fabian, Frankie Avalon, and Bobby Rydell. In August 1958, he was a featured guest on *The Perry Como Show*, where he sang "You Can't Stop Me from Dreaming." Luke had several more releases on Dot Records, but none of them were successful. On January 1, 2011, he retired after twenty-six years of chairing the marketing department at Missouri State University in Springfield. Today, he participates in oldies package shows. Luke commented, "I was never going to pursue [returning to music] while I was at the college with a full-time job."[4]

Robert Luke, Jr. was born on March 20, 1942, in Los Angeles, California. Since birth, he was called Robin, a nickname which was given to him by his mother: "She was born in Belfast, Ireland. There are many men who are named Robin there. My dad's nickname was Bob, so I became Robin."[5] Luke's mother was musically inclined, with the ability to play both violin and clarinet. He recalled, "She had me listen to music and bought me little Golden books with records that she let me play on the record player." Luke acknowledged, "My father worked for Douglas Aircraft as a service representative. We moved many, many times, and I was in many different schools before I ever entered high school. Between 1948 and 1953, I lived in College Park, Georgia because my dad went to work for the Atlanta airport. I listened to the radio, which played country and western. Before my folks would ever get into a house, they'd usually stay in a hotel for a period of weeks. We were fortunate to stay in the number one hotel, the Henry Grady Hotel, in Atlanta. They had a supper club in the hotel, and my parents and I ate there almost every night. They also had a stage where people would perform, [and one of the acts was Eddy Arnold and His Tennessee Plowboys]. I was about five years old, and my parents told me I was just totally in a trance, watching him play his guitar and sing songs like 'Bouquet of Roses' and 'Molly Darling.' The waiters allowed me to go backstage and watch from the side every night. [In two months, Luke saw Arnold fifty times.] My parents said that he would come over and talk and let me touch his guitar. He was kind."

Luke immediately was attracted to music. Shortly after seeing Arnold in concert, Luke's mother decided he should play a musical instrument. He remembered, "A piano was out of the question and a trumpet was a little loud in the hotels, so she decided upon a guitar. For Christmas, she had bought me a plastic Arthur Godfrey model ukulele, and within three months I had learned all the songs from the Little Golden Book plastic records. For some reason, I had also learned how to play proper chords without instruction. [Impressed by my talent] my mother asked around to find the very best guitar teacher in the Atlanta area. One name kept coming up, and it was Perry Bechtel. She found out where his studio was, went by herself on a bus to the music store, and then walked up to Perry's studio and informed him that she would like him to teach her son how to play guitar. At this time, Perry was one of the most celebrated guitarists in the world, having played in many major orchestras. He tried to explain to her that he only took students who were master performers, and they would come to Georgia for a week to learn the fineries of guitar playing. [However] she was insistent, so I think to get rid of her, he said, 'Well, I'll tell you what, why don't you have him practice and come back next week for an audition at this time?' [She had bragged about her son's expertise on the ukulele.] She came home and took me to Sears Roebuck and Co. and bought me my first suit, Glen plaid with a red bow tie. I practiced like crazy that week, and then she told me I had one chance. We went back to the music store, and she took me to the back of the studio. I played my ukulele for half an hour or so, and then Perry turned to my mother and shook his head, saying, 'I will teach him how to play the guitar, but he will have to have a Gibson.' [Weekly lessons were arranged, while his mother paid two dollars a week for an eighty-five dollar LG-2 Gibson.] My mother asked, 'What are you going to charge for the one hour lesson per week?' He smiled and said, 'Mrs. Luke, I have absolutely no idea. What can you afford?' She said, 'Well, I guess if I'm paying two

In 1958, Robin Luke secured a #5 hit on the Billboard charts with "Susie Darlin'," which turned him into an overnight pop sensation (courtesy Robin Luke).

dollars a week for the guitar, I could pay two dollars a lesson.' He said, 'That will be fine.' I never missed a week in five and a half years. I was the first beginning student and youngest he ever had. For a year, he never let me play a song. I ran scales and learned how to read music. When I finally could play three or four chords well and run the scales in different keys, he gave me sheet music with songs that he had written out. By the time I was seven years old; I could improvise and play just about anything." One of the first songs he learned was "The Third Man Theme."

By eight years old, the young protégé was a pretty accomplished player, so he was asked to sing and play at school functions. The invention of rock and roll changed his musical landscape. One incident in particular made him gravitate toward the genre, Luke disclosed, "I was at the Georgia Park swimming pool, on the high dive about to jump in. The radio was playing rhythm and blues through the speakers, when all of a sudden 'Work with Me Annie' by The Midnighters came on. That song knocked me out. I stood on the high dive listening. As soon as it was over, I went down the stairs, ran into the locker room, put on my clothes, ran three blocks to the music shop, and paid sixty-nine cents for that 45. I wore the grooves out on the record. To me, it's one of the greatest rhythm and blues songs of all-time." Once Luke became a teenager, he was popular at parties because he'd drag along his guitar and have sing-a-longs, everything from "Kumbaya" to "On Top of Old Smokey." Around that same time, rockabilly was becoming popular, and Luke practiced hard to learn all the hot guitar licks: "I listened to disc jockey Tom Moffatt's 'Uncle Tom's Gabbin'' every night. That's where I first heard Chuck Berry. He had incredible guitar licks like no one had ever played before. I was fourteen years old when Chuck came to town. I begged my mother to let me go; she finally said okay, and we went. I was totally mesmerized by his performance."

Luke cited his mother, Eddy Arnold, Perry Bechtel, and Buddy Holly as his musical influences. Luke disclosed, "I sang Eddy's 'Bouquet of Roses' and Molly Darling' throughout my youth." Holly and Chuck Berry are his two favorite performers: "I had the privilege of playing with both of them. I was on *The Dick Clark Saturday Night Beechnut Show*, which was filmed live at the Little Theater in New York City, with Buddy. We were bored backstage in the green room. Everybody else had left, so we sat there most of the day just copying each other's songs. We were both guitar players, so we were very interested in each other's chord structures and the way we each did phrasing, turnarounds, and fills. I know how to play 'Peggy Sue' because I watched every movement he made. It is now sort of a signature tune for me. At almost every concert, I play it, and the crowd goes wild."

In 1958, Luke performed at the Punahou High School's annual fair's talent show with best friend Dick Ednie on the gut bucket. The teenager was approached backstage by local disc jockey and television personality Kimo McVay, who asked if he would like to make a record. McVay then introduced him to Bob Bertrum, who owned Bertrum International Records: "It was a local company that made hula records for the tourists and some attempts at entering the rock and roll market." Luke recalled, "Soon after, Bob took me to his recording studio, which was an apartment with one bedroom. We played 'Susie Darlin'' through one microphone on a portable Ampex tape recorder that had what they called sound on sound. It took about a month and a half to record. I think we overdubbed seven times, and I played several instruments on the record, including the ukulele, guitar, and drums, which was actually a Capitol Records cardboard box that I used a set of brushes on. There's also percussion on the record, a clickety-click-click sound, which was a Sheaffer pen in the pocket of my trousers that I hit with two sticks. The echo chamber was the bathroom and to get that echo you had to flip a switch. There'd be a speaker at one end and a microphone at the other to pick up the echo. Pat Boone used to joke that I had the bedroom ballad. We became dear friends because we were both on Dot Records. Dot wanted me to re-record it, so I was brought over from Hawaii and taken to United Recording Studio in Hollywood. They tried to emulate the song and duplicate it for sound. That version was absolutely beautiful. In fact, I wish I had a copy, but it didn't have that hollow sound and all the overdubbing. If one listens to 'Susie Darlin', it's a very mushy recording, and that's because we overdubbed seven times with a rather inexpensive recorder." Therefore, on July 21, 1958, Dot issued the original recording as a 45 rpm single, "Susie Darlin'" b/w "Living's Loving You." In the spring of 1958, the same two sides had been released on the International label. In fact, that happened with a couple other singles, where they were pressed by both record labels.

Before success was bestowed upon the teenager, he was already headlining shows in Hawaii with The Everly Brothers and Sam Cooke. Luke mentioned, "Sam was an amazing entertainer. I can't think of anyone who was more professional and polished. He always wore a suit and tie. We really hit it off." In fact, Luke acquired an autographed photo from Cooke, which read 'To Robin, a swell guy.' Sam Cooke. Luke disclosed, "When I'd be backstage with other artists, sometimes we'd get bored and since we had 8x10's for fans, I'd say, 'Hey, sign one of your photos for me.' I have a collection of one hundred autographed photos, thanks to my mom who kept them for me. I had always sent them home to her."

"Susie Darlin'" did very well locally. In fact, while on vacation in Hawaii, Art Freeman, a distributor for Dot Records, heard the tune and presented it to the label. As soon as it was released nationally, "Susie Darlin'" shot straight up to the number six position in *Cashbox* magazine. Luke set the record straight concerning the origin of the song: "I wrote it on the beach as sort of a story about losing a girlfriend. [The original title was] 'All Night Long' because I have that line repeated over and over again. Then I found out there was another big hit [with the same name], so I retitled it 'Susie Darlin'.' It is not written about my sister, but rather named after her. At the time, she was five and a half years old. I just plugged in her name because it kept me out of trouble with all the other gals in my high school. If I had named it after one of them, I would have been doomed. " He added, "I surfed every day for five and a half years. After surfing, some beach boys and I would get out our guitars and start playing. Incidentally, Hawaiians are very melodious as a group; they can all sing and play a ukulele or guitar. If you listen to the beats and chord structure, I think there's a real Hawaiian influence to 'Susie Darlin'.'" Luke remembered feeling pretty good about hearing the tune on the radio, although he felt he sounded better in the studio than on the actual recording.

He was still living in Hawaii but traveled to Hollywood to record. While there, Luke dated a gal, who was friends with Ricky Nelson: "My father's best friend was very successful and had a seven acre [property] on Sunset Blvd. His daughter and I used to go out. She was a pretty good tennis player and said, 'C'mon over and play tennis.' She lived right next door to Jayne Mansfield. We used to peek through the fence to see Jayne and her husband in the swimming pool. We were playing tennis one day when she says, 'Oh, by the way, I've got a friend who'll be coming along in a minute.' All of a sudden, here comes Ricky; that's how we met. We played tennis and had a great time, but he was really good, so it was no contest. He cleaned my clock." After that encounter, they hung out a bit, which included going to the movies: "He was very shy, and so was I. That's probably what drew us together. Frankie Avalon was also very shy. I think he was the worst of all of us. People thought Frankie was rude because he was afraid to talk to anybody."

Luke's parents instilled in him the importance of a good education: "From the time I can remember them telling me things, they drummed into my head almost every week that they only wanted two things from me: one, to never embarrass them, and two, to get a good education." In 1959, Luke moved to California and attended Pepperdine University in Malibu. There, he received two degrees: one in psychology and the other in chemistry/biology.

On January 4, 1960, Dot issued the 45 rpm single, "Bad Boy" b/w "School Bus Love Affair." Luke disclosed, "I was at home, ready to go to class when the president of Dot, Randy Wood, called and said, 'There's a song in England that just went from nothing to number one in two weeks called 'Bad Boy.' I want you to get in the studio tonight.' I had heard the original since they had flown it over from England. Dot tried to duplicate the background to as close to Marty Wilde's version as possible. At about one in the morning, we recorded 'Bad Boy.' Two days later, it was on the shelves at Wallich's Music City in Hollywood."

That same year, Luke went on tour in Sydney, Australia: "I was there with Johnny Cash, Bobby Day, and The Playmates." To promote the show, he participated in an on-air interview with radio station 2UE: "I was on the second floor of a large department store, and police were in the lobby [trying to contain a thousand kids]. There was a car waiting for me, but it went a lot longer than we thought, so I got carried down the stairs. As I got to the doors, I turned around because I had heard this enormous noise. The kids had broken through the police line and were running after me. I got through the doors and to the car but then got clobbered. I was scared to death. I had just bought a real nice sweater, Australian Angora wool, and they ripped it right off me. I was on my back, so I started sliding, trying to stand up. I then felt somebody grab my pants, and that's when I got a little vicious. I finally got in the car, but that was a very frightening experience, and frankly I don't think I dated a gal for about two months."

In 1962, Luke's contract with Dot ran out. The singer switched vocations when he returned to college and took up teaching: "I went to the University of Missouri-Columbia and received my M.B.A. degree and my Ph.D. in business marketing. From 1972 to 1977, I was an assistant professor at Old Dominion University [in Norfolk, Virginia]. Then I accepted a position as associate professor at the University of the Virgin Islands. I had raced sailboats most of my life, and that was a wonderful place to do that. [In 1979, he represented the Virgin Islands in the Pan American games and was invited to try out for the '84 Olympic team.] [Also] in 1984, I was nominated to come to Missouri State University and start the marketing department."

In 1995, Carl Perkins requested Luke's presence for his book signing at Sun Studio in Memphis: "I walked up to him; he put his arms around me and said, 'Man, it's been a long time.' He then said to one of his assistants, 'Go over and get my briefcase.' He told me, 'I got something for you.' Carl then reached into the briefcase and said, 'I wanted you to have this, and I didn't know if I'd be here personally to give it to you.' [Three years earlier, Perkins had battled throat cancer.] Carl had signed an 8x10 of one of his oldest pictures. It reads, 'To Robin—I'll always love 'Susie Darlin'.' Carl Perkins." That day, Luke had Perkins and co-writer David McGee autograph a copy of their book, *Go, Cat, Go: The Life and Times of Carl Perkins*.

A year later, Chuck Berry invited Luke to his seventh birthday party at the Blueberry Hill in St. Louis, Missouri. Both he and his wife attended as they loved Berry: "We sat at the table with him. His son, daughter, CPA, and attorney also sat with us. They had finished a business meeting that day, and he said, 'C'mon over to my birthday party.' Chuck had just gotten back all of the rights to his songs. [At one time, he was selling his song royalties for as little as two hundred dollars apiece.] We performed that night. He got up and sang about three songs then I went up and sang four. When I sang 'Peggy Sue,' people literally jumped onto the tables and started dancing. I felt really embarrassed because I was getting a bigger response than he was. He had gone into the green room while I performed but then came back for my last song, which was "Susie Darlin'." When I finished, Chuck hugged me and said, 'Man that was a great song.' That was a very emotional moment for me. Then he hung around, took pictures with me and my wife and signed his biography for me."

At least thirty other versions of "Susie Darlin'" exist. In 1962, Tommy Roe covered the tune, and it peaked at number thirty-five. Even though Luke's career was short lived, fans remember him, and he has no regrets: "Either things came to me too easily or I knew all along I didn't want to make singing a career, so I didn't feel that pressure some other people did. I was smart to go the direction I did."[6]

Carl Dobkins, Jr.

In 1958, country singer Jimmy Dean recorded "My Heart Is an Open Book." Columbia Records released the tune, but it failed to chart. A short time later, Decca producer Owen Bradley suggested to Carl Dobkins, Jr., that he lend his vocals to it. He obliged even though he wasn't too thrilled about the song. In December 1958, Decca issued the 45 rpm single, "My Heart Is an Open Book" b/w "My Pledge to You." Dobkins' pop infused version peaked at number three on the *Billboard* Hot 100 charts and remained there for twenty-four weeks. Besides touring constantly within the United States and Canada, he paid fourteen visits total to Dick Clark's afternoon and evening television programs. During his popularity, Dobkins had ninety fan clubs and was featured in several fan magazines. In 1962, he quit touring on a regular basis and recorded only periodically. Today, Dobkins performs at rock and roll oldies shows.

Carl Dobkins, Jr. was born on January 13, 1941, in Cincinnati, Ohio. All of his Kentuckian relatives, including his parents, were musically inclined. The singer joked, "I think there's a gene in every other baby born in Kentucky that gives them the gift of playing a guitar."[7] When he was nine years old, he developed an interest in the ukulele, which was bought at Willis Music in Cincinnati for nine dollars. It had an Arthur Godfrey attachment, which "was a plastic push button device that went onto the neck of the uke and pressed on the strings to play chords. I took it off and looked to see where the buttons were hitting the strings and started using my fingers. After that, I applied it to the first four strings on a guitar until my hands were big enough to make a full six string chord." The first songs he played were simple with only two or three chords, such as "You Are My Sunshine." Dobkins started singing publicly at sixteen although he stated, "I've sung for as long as I can remember." At the same age, he began songwriting: "Like most teenagers, I wrote about feelings and my girlfriends."

Dobkins cited Elvis Presley, Gene Vincent, Bill Haley, and Patti Page as his musical influences. He admired "Page's method of phrasing and later copied some vocal tricks from Presley and Buddy Holly."[8] He listened to those artists as well as Teresa Brewer and Dean Martin on WCIN-Cincinnati.

Gil Sheppard was a disc jockey before he became Dobkins' manager: "My [high school] buddies took me to meet him at a remote DJ show that he was broadcasting from, onboard a Volkswagen bus. I had a ten dollar demo of two of my songs, and he played the record on the air. [By working in a bakery after school, Dobkins had earned the money to record.] It became my first and only release on Fraternity. [In January 1958, Fraternity issued the 45 rpm single "Take Hold of My Hand" b/w "That's Why I'm Asking."] I was with them for only a few months. [The label's president] Harry Carlson, let me out of the contract, so we could sell 'If You Don't Want My Lovin'' to Decca." On Sunday afternoons, Sheppard held teen dances at a nightclub called Castle Farms in Cincinnati to give Dobkins some experience. Eventually, A&R director Harry Silverstein convinced Decca to sign Dobkins.

On May 26, 1958, Decca issued the 45 rpm single, "If You Don't Want My Lovin'" b/w "Love is Everything." The songs were recorded at King Records in Cincinnati with backing provided by The Orbits and vocal accompaniment by The Seniors (Keith Ross, Paul Powers, and Harry Clifton). Sheppard also had the trio as clients. Dobkins stated, "They started out as a church group, but I didn't go to their church." Incidentally, "If You Don't Want My Lovin'" peaked at number one in Charleston, West Virginia. In 1959, it was re-released and scored a national hit, number sixty-seven on the *Billboard* charts.

Carl Dobkins, Jr., appeared on Dick Clark's two shows fourteen times, thanks in part to his #3 hit, "My Heart Is an Open Book" (courtesy Carl Dobkins, Jr.).

With the first single, Decca saw promise in their newly signed teen idol but hadn't fulfilled their vision for him quite yet. Owen Bradley then offered "My Heart Is an Open Book" to Dobkins. He recorded the tune at the Quonset Hut Studio in Nashville with the A Team: Bob Moore, Buddy Harman, and Hank Garland along with members of the Anita Kerr Singers: Anita Kerr and Dorothy Ann Dillard. Dobkins remembered, "Hank taught me the opening guitar riff to Elvis' 'A Fool Such as I.'" Bradley produced the session: "He was a real pro, but made you feel at home in the studio. We would go through a stack of dubs that he thought was my style, and we'd pick them together." Even though "My Heart Is an Open Book" was released in December 1958, Decca had difficulty getting airplay, so therefore it didn't chart until April 1959. Two months later, upon graduation from Mt. Healthy High School in Mt. Healthy, Ohio, Dobkins set out on tour, which included record hops and an appearance on *American Bandstand*. Dobkins explained, "As an artist, you would go out to these record hops for free to promote your record. Dick Clark, he was a super nice guy who would always come by the dressing room after the show and thank you for playing."[9] "My Heart Is an Open Book" went up and down on the charts before finally peaking at number three. Dobkins recalled, "I was thrilled to death. Most radio stations thought of Decca releases as hillbilly music and not teen tunes, so they threw the first promo copies in the trash before listening to it."

In August 1959, Dobkins enlisted in the U.S. Army Reserves. Before departing for six months of active duty, he recorded in Nashville. His next hit came with "Lucky Devil," scoring a number twenty-five position on the *Billboard* charts. After his initial servitude was finished, the 'Teenage Rage' went back to recording. On April 18, 1960, Decca released the 45 rpm single, "One Little Girl" b/w "Exclusively Yours." The latter song reached number sixty-two on the charts. Dobkins had married his high school sweetheart in September 1960 but kept it a secret because he felt it would hurt his mass appeal.

Two years later, his contract with Decca expired. At that same time, Dobkins removed himself from the circuit: "If you wanted to make your living in the business, you had to live on the road. I didn't want that."[10] Touring extensively had been his mantra for three years. Four or five times a year, he would spend a whole month on the road with other acts in a bus that may or may not be air conditioned.

In 1969, Dobkins went to work for a trucking company. Later, he was employed as a productions control engineer by General Electric in Evendale, Ohio. Nowadays, Dobkins periodically returns to the stage to perform. Even though he is considered by most to be a pop singer, a few have given him a rockabilly distinction: "Evidently some of my recordings were rockabilly." Dobkins once played a show in Vienna, Austria with Buddy Knox and is a member of the Rockabilly Hall of Fame. He summed up his career by saying, "God has been very good to me over the years. I have a lovely wife of fifty-three years, two beautiful daughters, and five terrific grandkids. I've had good health, a loving family, friends, and fans from all around the world that still remember my music and send me nice emails."

Chapter Six

Roots Revivalists

The Four Charms

In 1998, The Four Charms were created by Jimmy Sutton and Joel Paterson, who shared vocal duties. Jonathan Doyle and Jim Barclay rounded out the quartet. Their first show took place on December 31, 1998. As a band, they were heavily influenced by rhythm and blues, jump blues, and artists such as Slim Gaillard, Bill Jennings, Tiny Grimes, Roy Milton, Louis Jordan, and Wynonie Harris. According to Sutton, "I would play with Joel once in a while and just because I needed to do something, we started The Four Charms. I kept it very small and manageable. I knew the saxophone player [Jonathan Doyle] because he was a replacement in The Mighty Blue Kings. I met the drummer [Jim Barclay] at a jam session in Chicago."[1] Paterson stated, "I think Jimmy and I met in Milwaukee. I was playing a gig with a blues band. In Madison, for years, I had the Joel Paterson Trio. That was a blues band mixed with rockabilly. Jimmy would come and play gigs with us. We did that a lot and kind of worked on material. I finally moved to Chicago in 1998 to start The Four Charms with Jimmy. He knew Jon Doyle from The Mighty Blue Kings, and we found Jim Barclay at a club. We tried Jim out, and he was real good."[2] Roots music was fairly new territory to Barclay until he teamed up with Sutton and Paterson: "I met Jimmy and Joel at the Beat Kitchen in Chicago. I was there to sit in with another jump blues band. That was 1998, and I had been playing professionally since I was sixteen. Drumming [in The Four Charms] was pretty natural since the early roots/blues/rockabilly/western swing drummers were all coming from a jazz background like me. The swing element was the same."[3] Doyle had a similar introduction to roots music, through Sutton. He remembered, "I met Jimmy through The Mighty Blue Kings and didn't really get to know Joel until The Four Charms. I met Barclay when The Four Charms started."[4]

One of the regular bookings for The Four Charms was the Green Mill in Chicago, where they played every Tuesday night for five years. Sutton revealed, "From vaudeville variety club to a jazz club to a hillbilly honky-tonk, the Green Mill has been there since 1907. Then it turned back into a jazz club. I call the Green Mill the classiest dive in the world. It was always just standing room only [when we played] even though we were probably the most non-jazz there." Nick Willett frequently attended their shows. Sutton conveyed, "Nick had a specific corner he would hang out in. Once in a while, we'd have him sing a song or two."

On April 15, 2005, at the Rockin' 50's Fest in Green Bay, Wisconsin, Jimmy Sutton's Four Charms captivated audiences with their mix of jump blues and swing. From left: Jonathan Doyle, Jimmy Sutton, and Joel Paterson (author's collection).

In 1999, The Four Charms played their first festival gig, the Viva Las Vegas Weekender. Barclay recalled, "It was my first time at anything like that, so I was doing a lot of people watching." Barclay's favorite gig with The Four Charms occurred in Barcelona, Spain in 2002: "Due to a scheduling mix-up, we got no sleep the night before and had to fly all day. We were all exhausted and didn't start playing until 2 a.m. I was knocking down café con leche, hoping I'd be awake when it was time to hit. However, the crowd was super excited, and we just killed it. We reached a whole different level that night—musicality, energy, and showmanship."

Besides their own bookings, The Four Charms backed numerous legends and contemporary acts. Barclay commented, "I always did my homework, by listening to the original stuff, but also didn't assume that was the way they wanted it to sound. I think it's a mistake to assume the older acts want to play like they did in the '50s. They are artists after all, and many want to move forward. I just try to listen to their cues and provide them with what they need to have a great show. Hands down, my favorite was playing with Wanda Jackson. She is such a sweetheart and still sounds amazing." Doyle commented, "My favorite gig is one in which the rhythm section is locked in, and the band is all listening to each other. I'm honored to have gotten the opportunity to play with some legendary folks. There have been some that I was unfamiliar with, that I had to go listen to, so it's always a learning experience." Paterson mentioned, "When we back someone, I usually have to do some last minute brushing up on the songs. I'm always kind of learning them at the last second and then playing them. Sometimes, the artist will give you a CD to learn the original versions, and then if you're lucky you get to practice once with him/her. I started a song once in the wrong key with Wanda Jackson. She got through it but gave me a dirty look. I felt bad about that." Usually artists will have a set list that they follow. The exception to that rule is Sleepy LaBeef.

Paterson acknowledged, "You don't know what he's going to play. It's fun for a little while, but then your head starts spinning. He definitely keeps you on your toes [by switching songs quickly]. I don't know how he keeps all those songs in his head."

Bassist Jimmy Sutton was born on June 16, 1966, in Chicago, Illinois. He is the youngest of three boys: "My brothers had a big impact on me because they had guitars and amplifiers. You want to do what your older brothers are doing." Sutton revealed, "The first concert I ever attended was Count Basie and his Orchestra performing at my church sometime around 1976. The second time he came to play, I made him a cartoon flip book of him playing piano. [In the last image, Count Basie is looking at a bust on top of the piano with a balloon above his head saying, 'Hey, that's me.'] I remember giving that flip book to him, and he gave me this great big sweaty hug. Count Basie came and played these benefit concerts and I just thought that was really hip." Sutton's first rock concert was The Ramones, who performed at the University of Chicago's Ida Noyes gymnasium in 1979: "I was a Ramones freak." A rockabilly revival was also happening then, so he heard The Blasters, The Stray Cats, and The Shakin' Pyramids: "That introduced me to the original rockabilly artists, then rhythm and blues, jump blues, jazz, blues, country blues, country, hillbilly, and honky-tonk. It just kind of exploded from there. When I was younger, I had heard Top 40 hits from the '50s and saw movies like *The Lords of Flatbush*, *American Graffiti*, and *American Hot Wax*. Those were definitely more rock and roll, but there were hints of rockabilly. I was taught that Elvis and his Sun sessions were the beginning of rockabilly, that hybrid of black rhythm and blues and white honky-tonk."

At fourteen, Sutton started playing bass. He is completely self-taught: "Unfortunately, I didn't really take any lessons." Prior to that, he had been strumming the guitar: "One of my brothers told me that he was gonna play guitar and that I should play bass instead." At the same time that he picked up the bass, Sutton also began singing: "I really wouldn't call it singing. For the longest time, I was horrible. I don't consider myself a singer; I just say I sing. I also started my first rockabilly band, The Rockin' Blue Notes, with Slink Moss." Years later, they teamed up again, along with Joel Paterson, in a group called Slink Moss Explosion: "My stage name in that band is Mr. Bones. Joel's is Mr. X, and the guy who sings, writes the songs, and plays the drums when he sings is Slink. It started as a joke to take on other names."

Art was his main interest before performing became his top priority. Sutton remarked, "I went to art school [Columbia College and then the American Academy of Art, both in Chicago.] I was a free-lance illustrator. I used to do jobs for the *Wall Street Journal*, Disney, and a bunch of other corporate companies. Things really started to look up for me as far as clients." Pieces of his artwork were also sold.

In 1991, Sutton and his then wife Gabrielle created a free admission event called the *Big C Jamboree*, which was held the first Thursday of every month: "We'd have a host band, which was usually an out of town act." That band would play a couple of half hour sets. Then the evening would be rounded out by singers who had signed up via a list where each one performed three songs apiece. Even though Sutton is no longer involved with the monthly showcase, it continues to pack in the crowds. Schedules for the *Big C Jamboree* and notifications for all other artists coming to Chicago and the surrounding area can be viewed at http://bigcjam.com/.

A few years after the formation of the *Big C Jamboree*, Sutton's group, The Mighty

Blue Kings, started to get popular: "I knew that you couldn't tour and be successful when you're older. I mean you can, but it's just harder physically. I chose music because who doesn't want to be a rock star? I dropped art like a hot potato and started playing music full-time in 1995."

Sutton confirmed that his main bass influence is Willie Dixon: "I especially love his work in The Big Three Trio." He added, "I like to play it all: jump blues, rockabilly, rock and roll, country, and honky-tonk. I definitely enjoy playing songs where I get to do some slap solos."

Sutton joined forces with Ronnie Dawson in 1993, doing a few shows together in Chicago before a tour of Europe. Sutton acknowledged, "I used to have this band from 1988 until 1995 called The Moondogs, and we did a bunch of shows with the Reverend Horton Heat at a club called Wild Jack's in Chicago. Nobody knew who he was then. I remember Jim Heath said, 'Man, you know who you guys got to play with? Ronnie Dawson.' It was pretty exciting because I had just picked up an album by Ronnie, one of his first on No Hit Records. It was a recent recording, and I was really happy to hear one of the '50s artists who sounded like he still had it going on. Ronnie didn't sound like he was resting on his laurels; he was still rocking. Jim also told me, 'Man, I'm gonna hook you guys up. He's gotta come up here to do some shows.' I remember picking Ronnie up from the airport. It was just me and him, and we hit it off right away." Working with Dawson was a career highlight: "I just loved every moment of it. We'd get onstage and just go nuts. We became good friends and stayed in touch. Ronnie never really made you feel like you were the young guy that didn't know anything. He was a great inspiration and influence. There were other times when Ronnie asked me to do tours, but it was during the time of The Mighty Blue Kings, and I just couldn't because we were doing so well on our own. [Once in a while], I was out in the audience, and he called me up to sit in. He did that at his last show, and I kind of felt like it was saying goodbye."

In 2004, Deke Dickerson invited Sutton to join him on tour: "Both Deke and his drummer Chris 'Sugarballs' Sprague are great musicians and very easy to play with." One of their stops included the Ponderosa Stomp in New Orleans where they backed numerous rockabilly legends, including Dale Hawkins and Sonny Burgess. Sutton recalled, "From the beginning of the night, Dale was very eager to get onstage. He wasn't scheduled to go on for another couple of hours, but he stood on the side of the stage with his guitar and said, 'Let me know when you want me to play.' He was one of my favorites to back. Ray Sharpe was another of my favorites. I really thought his set was great, and that he had things together musically." The festival was a marathon of playing for Dickerson, Sprague, and Sutton. They went in to rehearse at noon and then played from five o'clock in the afternoon until four thirty in the morning. Sutton admitted, "That was the longest I've ever played non-stop."

Saxophonist Jonathan Doyle was born on January 30, 1976, in Palos Hills, Illinois. At eleven, he took up the saxophone: "I learned tenor sax first. It was a horn that my uncle had and loaned to me." The first songs he played were from musical exercise books. Besides being proficient on sax, Doyle can also play clarinet, jug, ukulele, and piano. He added, "I play most of the saxophones now: soprano, alto, C-melody, tenor, baritone, and bass."

Doyle cited Lester Young, Coleman Hawkins, Maxwell Davis, Don Wilkerson, Johnny Hodges, Sidney Bechet, and Edmond Hall as his musical influences; however, he stated that his peers have had the biggest impact, and they include Rebecca Michalak, Josh Berman, Jason Adasiewicz, Jimmy Sutton, Joel Paterson, Ryan Gould, J.D. Pendely, Westen Borghesi, David Jellema, Albanie Falletta, and Erik Hokkanen.

Along with Sutton, Doyle was a member of The Mighty Blue Kings: "I dropped out of DuPaul University [in Chicago] to join the band. It was a pretty high energy gig. I believe I was with them for a year and nine months." The Mighty Blue Kings were formed in the summer of 1994, and they played traditional rhythm and blues and jump blues. Two years later, they issued their first album, *Meet Me in Uptown*. Sutton acknowledged, "It was all self-done. The guy that was booking us at the time helped put together a show for our record release at the Green Mill. They gave us all the original lights, and it just looked beautiful in the club. We had all our friends volunteering to help us. We were praying for a thousand people, just to break even from all the money we put into it. We ended up with three thousand people. That was a pretty amazing night, where we sold close to eight hundred CDs and around two hundred and fifty T-shirts. After that, we bought a van and a trailer and started touring, [which included a stop at Summerfest in Milwaukee]."

Guitarist Joel Paterson was born on December 2, 1970, in Boston, Massachusetts. As a youngster, he and his family moved to Madison, Wisconsin. Paterson remembered, "My mom was a big music fan. She always had a lot of cool records: Robert Johnson, Muddy Waters, Lightnin' Hopkins, and Jimi Hendrix. I wanted to play like Jimi Hendrix, but I soon got into the blues, and then that's all I wanted to play." At thirteen, Paterson had taken up the guitar: "The first licks I ever learned were by Lightnin' Hopkins. I had a record, and I just played that stuff by ear. Probably the first song I learned on slide guitar was 'I Can't Be Satisfied' by Muddy Waters. I used to play that over and over, along with country blues and Robert Johnson type stuff on State Street in Madison for spare change. I always tried to sing, but I was pretty bad back then. [He figured that the first song he sang was either by Robert Johnson or Muddy Waters.] I mainly think of myself as a guitar player. I am pretty much self-taught. [He said he's always learning and plays the guitar daily.] I sang more when I started the Joel Paterson Trio. Then with The Four Charms, I sang about half the songs." While in Madison, he played many gigs with his combo, the Joel Paterson Trio. He admitted, "I was kind of in my own world as there wasn't any rockabilly scene. I was playing blues and was into '50's music, but I really had no idea that there was anybody else who was into that. It wasn't until I met Jimmy and moved to Chicago that I discovered a whole new world." He and Sutton suggested different records to one another.

Besides guitar, Paterson can also play electric bass: "When I record stuff at home, I always put down a bass part. I don't play it in public too much. I used to play a little bit of standup bass in a blues band, but when I met Jimmy Sutton I stopped that right away." He also dabbles in playing drums and harmonica. Both Marcel Riesco and Nick Willett have sung renditions of Roy Orbison's "Candy Man" with Paterson accompanying them on harmonica.

Paterson cited Les Paul, Freddie King, Charlie Christian, Tiny Grimes, Scotty Moore, Merle Travis, and Arthur 'Blind' Blake as his musical influences. In regard to Blake, Paterson mentioned, "I was obsessed with him when I started playing. He was my first guitar hero. I learned how to fingerpick because of him. My main guitar is a Gibson 295. It's like the gold one that Scotty played on Elvis' Sun sessions. It has a hollow body, and it's a great all around guitar. I can play rockabilly, jazz, blues, everything on it."

Music isn't the only talent that Paterson and Sutton share since Paterson was also an artist: "I went to art school in Madison, and I did some self-portraits in oil paint. Then I got too busy with music, so I haven't really done that in years. These days, I do the graphic design for The Modern Sounds' CD covers. That's how I get my artistic side out."

Drummer Jim Barclay was born on March 1, 1973, in Dayton, Ohio. At fifteen, he started playing drums: "I don't remember the exact first song I played along to, but it was probably off *Pyromania* by Def Leppard. I was in love with that record." While still in high school, Barclay had his first club booking with a cover band. He continued to play in various bands throughout college. Besides drums, he has studied all types of percussion instruments: "I have a marimba and xylophone that I mess around with from time to time. I especially like early twentieth century ragtime music for the xylophone."

Barclay attended the University of North Texas in Denton, Texas where he received a Bachelor's degree in music: "I was a jazz studies major, so I had a lot of improvisational classes and jazz history. I also had the opportunity to play in the ethnic ensembles and study West African drumming, Brazilian Samba music, and Javanese Gamelan. Of course, I studied everything having to do with percussion. It was very rigorous, and while my focus was on a drum set, I had pretty intense lessons on timpani, snare drum, and mallet instruments. Most importantly, I was able to meet some wonderful people. Some of the guys I went to school with are now playing at the highest level with the likes of Sting, Steely Dan, Melissa Etheridge, Alanis Morissette, and Miranda Lambert, and the faculty there is world renowned. In the early 1990s, it was the largest music school in the country."

Barclay gives credit to Led Zeppelin's drummer John Bonham and jazz drummer Philly Joe Jones as being his two biggest influences. He added, "My mom played violin when she was younger, and my dad played some drums in high school. They were always very supportive, but I probably got my main inspiration from other friends and just wanting to play the drums. When I got it in my head that I wanted to be a drummer, a lot of other things fell by the wayside. I spent a lot of my formative years playing jazz, but I also love rock: Led Zeppelin, The Beatles, Elvis Costello, and Joe Jackson, to name a few. More than any particular type of music, I just love to play the drums. I love to add my voice to the mix and create something. My favorite is simply music that is performed well, with honesty and integrity."

Barclay, Sutton, and Paterson have all backed Nick Willett on numerous occasions. Barclay acknowledged, "Nick is a great guy. We met him back at a *Big C Jamboree* [in Chicago] in 1999. He stuck around the whole night without saying much, and if I recall, they worked him in as the very last act. Nobody knew him, and there wasn't much audience left, but as soon as he started singing you could feel the attention immediately shift. Jimmy and Joel both recognized the raw talent he had." Paterson recollected, "I remember meeting Nick vividly because he was this guy I had never heard of before. He had his name on the list, but it got too late, and he didn't get to play. Nick then came up to me and Jimmy, and he started singing this Sun era Elvis stuff. We couldn't believe he could sing it so well. Nick, Jimmy, and I used to play as a trio where we did Sun material, but that was way back in the day. We jammed together on songs like 'Just Because.'" Barclay added, "We played many gigs together throughout the years. Some of my favorites were at the Oneida Casino in Green Bay. They loved Nick there." On one occasion during a week long stint in July 2006, they just kept playing: "The sound guy loved it, and we had some musician friends, Scott Ligon and Joel Paterson, who sat in. By the time the night was done, we had played almost four and a half hours straight. It was only supposed to have been a ninety minute set. The crowd never left, and no one from the casino minded because the music was so good and pure. I think Nick is at his best when he has a nice, tight, well-rehearsed set that leaves the audience wanting more." Paterson conveyed, "I'm always ready for longer sets with Nick because he likes to play. He gets excited, and the audience does too, and he doesn't know when to stop. It's a high energy show, so time flies by. Nick rehearses because he likes to have the set tight."

In the summer of 2008, Barclay was asked to audition for the role of W.S. 'Fluke' Holland in the musical *Million Dollar Quartet*: "Unfortunately, I was playing a different show during their [initial] run and couldn't do it. As the *Million Dollar Quartet* continued, they knew they would need a sub, and I was available to do that. I continued to sub until 2011. I did several shows with the original cast: Eddie Clendening, Levi Kreis, Lance Guest, Robert Lyons, and Kelly Lamont. They were great to play with and totally appreciative of the job a sub has to do, which is come in, often on short notice, and kill it."

Nowadays, Barclay plays in The Possum Hollow Boys along with Marc Edelstein, Casey McDonough, and Dennis Leise. He explained, "We are billed as a honky tonk/rockabilly band, but we stretch things a bit—giving ourselves the moniker of 'stream of consciousness country music.' Casey and Dennis play guitar and sing. I joined them in 2008, while Marc, who plays upright bass, came onboard in 2010. They have a great CD that was recorded before my time with the band. We have been playing less lately, mostly due to all our other musical commitments, but I'm sure when the time is right we will pick it up again." Barclay acknowledged, "I perform fairly regularly with a handful of different bands. I play in a really talented pop project called The Lincoln Squares. It's made up of guys I met through the theater community. The songs are all original. We just put out our first EP on digital download [which is available for purchase at http://thelincolnsquares.com/]. Another group I'm really proud of is Balkano. Billed as a 'Klezmer band with a Baltic twist,' we play a fusion of music from all over the Middle East as well as some original material inspired by Bulgarian and Turkish influences. The music is really challenging but very organic too. Some of the melodies date back thousands of years. However, right now, I'm actually cutting back on gigs a bit to pursue another hobby, cycling. It's something I did as a kid before I picked up the drums and a few years back I got bitten by the bug again. I'm getting ready for a full season of racing, so I'm trying to limit the number of nights I'm out until 2 a.m." Barclay also has a regular day job, which is residential consulting in a real estate firm.

As for Sutton, he keeps busy touring with rising star JD McPherson. Sutton founded his own record label, Hi-Style Records, and has a recording studio, which he built from 2005 to 2010. It's one of only a few in the country that has vintage microphones and analog equipment. McPherson's debut solo release, *Signs and Signifiers*, was recorded there and released on Hi-Style. Doyle was also one of the featured musicians: "I just happened to be in Chicago when they were recording the album." In 2012, *Signs and Signifiers* secured the top spot on the Americana Airplay Charts. These days Doyle plays in swing and hot jazz combos in Austin and New Orleans, such as Albanie and her Fellas, Tuba Skinny, and Thrift Set Orchestra. From 2006 to 2013, he was regularly featured in the group White Ghost Shivers. Doyle declared, "I was also very pleased to work with Willie Nelson on two different two week tours and to play clarinet for him on *Austin City Limits*. I appeared on his 2009 album, *Willie and the Wheel*."

Paterson is active in several different bands, but primarily The Modern Sounds. It is a trio consisting of Paterson on guitar and vocals, Alex Hall on drums, and Beau Sample on upright bass and vocals: "I knew about Beau when he was with Cave Catt Sammy. I think I must have met him at a Viva Las Vegas Weekender way back in the day when The Four Charms played. We talked on the phone and said, 'Man, we should be playing together.' Then he finally moved here. I knew Alex from playing some jazz gigs with him. I thought those guys would be a natural fit together, and they were." Paterson recalled, "We formed the band in 2007 and do everything from '30's jazz to '50's rockabilly. We change our style for the venue, so sometimes we'll play Buddy Guy and obviously do more blues. We try to mix it up and keep it interesting. We'll rehearse a little bit, but we're pretty good at working stuff out onstage. We like to improvise because it keeps things fresh."

The Modern Sounds play pretty regularly at the Green Mill: "When we play there, we play more '30s and '40s jazz." Incidentally, The Modern Sounds were voted 'Best Chicago Jazz Band' in a 2009 *Chicago Reader* poll. In April 2011, they (Paterson, Sample, and Barclay, who was subbing for Hall) opened for Jeff Beck with Imelda May and Darrel Higham at the Cadillac Palace in Chicago: "It was Imelda and Jeff doing their Les Paul Tribute." That December, The Modern Sounds revved up the crowd before Jerry Lee Lewis hit the stage at the Congress Theater in Chicago. In 2012, The Modern Sounds issued a double CD, *Hold It Fellas/Stomp Stomp*: "I think that was probably my favorite recording session because we got together and played live. We recorded the album in about three days. There's a lot of mistakes, but you have to try to live with it. They never sound perfect to you. You try to get through the song, but if there's an obvious mistake then you start over. My guitar solos are always better about the second take. If they go any longer than that, then they start to go stale."

Before The Modern Sounds, Paterson played in Devil in a Woodpile: "For six years, we played every Tuesday at the Hideout in Chicago. That was my main band. I also played with Kelly Hogan, and then I started The Western Elstons with Jimmy [Sutton], Casey [McDonough], and Scott Ligon. I was learning to play pedal steel, so I wanted to have a country band. I had already played with Jimmy and Scott in a little rockabilly trio, so we added Casey on drums. Alex [Hall] came along later. Scott loves The Everly Brothers, so he sings a lot of their songs and a lot of early Hank Williams, Sr., and George Jones. We also do a few Buck Owens tunes. In fact when I was learning to play pedal steel that was all I played along with. [The Buck Owens' songbook] is the bible for pedal steel licks." Paterson still plays with the latter group as well as the Cash Box Kings and Nick Willett.

In 2013, Paterson released another solo album, *Handful of Strings*, on his Ventrella label: "I played all the instruments, overdubbing the parts one at a time. That's how Les Paul did it in the early '50s. A band can record an album in a day, but it took me forever. I have a room turned into a home studio where I can record guitar, but I don't have the space for a full band. Even though, it's definitely better with other musicians." Previously, Paterson issued solo projects—*Down at the Depot* and *Go Lightnin'*. He remembered, "At the time, I wanted to make a record that documented my early years—a definitive blues record. I learned playing solo acoustic blues, and I don't get to do it live very often because it's a hard thing to play in a bar. For *Go Lightnin',* I had a full blues band back me [which included Sutton, Barclay, Mark Haines, and Rick Sherry]. *Down at the Depot* was solo guitar. I've thought about reprinting that record because people still ask for it. I sold out of copies a long time ago."

As far as The Four Charms, they released two albums, *Flatland Boogie* and *Triskaidekaphobia*. From the first album, Sutton stated that "Sherry Flip," "My Mumblin' Baby," and "You Came a Long Way from St. Louis" were the most requested songs. He penned the tune "Flatland Boogie" while on tour with The Mighty Blue Kings: "For a year and nine months straight, we played the Green Mill in Chicago every Tuesday night. We thought that was a great way to get an audience, so instead of just going out West and doing one string of shows, we thought we'd set up a tour where we based ourselves out of a hotel in West Hollywood." Every night of the week, The Mighty Blue Kings played in a different California town: San Francisco, Los Angeles, Long Beach, Sacramento, and San Diego. Sutton disclosed, "We had been on tour for six weeks. The song was about me just dying to get back to Chicago." Another track on The Four Charms' first album, "Midnight at the Mill" was referencing their gig at the Green Mill. Paterson related, "After a show there, we sat in a booth and scribbled down some lyrics." Barclay reflected, "In my opinion, *Triskaidekaphobia* is The Four Charms fully realized. We had been together for several years and were really gelling. More importantly though, you can hear all of our various influences: my jazz, Joel's blues, Jonathan's artsy free jazz and traditional jazz, and Jimmy's rockabilly. We weren't trying to create a period piece, just playing naturally. I challenge you to find another record that sounds just like it." Sutton added, "I really enjoyed recording *Triskaidekaphobia*. It wasn't as tense."

In 2007, The Four Charms performed their final concert at the Rockin' '50's Fest III in Green Bay, Wisconsin. Paterson stated, "We worked a lot [in our time together]. I don't know how many gigs we played total, but for years, we played two, three, four nights a week." He added, "I miss playing with Jon Doyle a lot. He was so great, and I'm sad that he moved to Austin. He just needed a change of pace." The Four Charms may reunite one day, but for now, each individual member is busy with other projects.

Ronnie Mack

Ronnie Mack grew up listening to a wide variety of music: classical, rock and roll, country, and pop. In the late 1970s, he moved to Los Angeles to pursue his dreams of becoming a singer. In 1981, he teamed up with Ronny Weiser and Rollin' Rock Records. The Los Angeles rockabilly scene was thriving then, and bookings were plentiful. Club 88 in Los Angeles was particularly popular. James Intveld and the Rockin' Shadows, The Blasters, The Go-Go's, and The Motels all played there. In fact, he shared stages with all of them. Mack conveyed, "The first time James, his brother Ricky, and I met, we all hung out backstage. We got to talking about Ricky Nelson, and then James started playing the solo to 'Travelin' Man.' He knew it note for note, and I thought, 'Wow, that's really cool. They are young guys who know this stuff.' We became close friends."[5] James Intveld played a lot of gigs with Mack and was later part of the house band for his popular barn dance. Even though Mack played frequently, he is probably most well known for producing his barn dance for twenty-five years.

Ronnie Mack was born on April 18, 1954, in Baltimore, Maryland. At four years old, his grandfather began buying him various toy instruments: guitar, drums, saxophone, and accordion: "They weren't very good, but I learned the basic chords. He bought me a little better guitar when I was six. He then gave me a chord book, and I learned songs by Ricky Nelson. When I was in the second grade, I sang 'Hello Mary Lou' in front of my seventy classmates at a Valentine's Day party. The song had six chords, but I didn't know all of them. I only knew about three, but I got through it, and nobody knew the difference." After that, the school asked him to bring his guitar and sing for other special occasions: "I always did one of Rick's songs, like 'Lonesome Town.'"

In June 1976, Mack moved to Los Angeles, California. Two years later, he met Ray Campi and Ronny Weiser: "I somehow got ahold of some of Ray's records. Then I met him when he and the Rockabilly Rebels played one Sunday night at the Palomino Club." In 1979, Mack formed his band, the Black Slacks, which featured Greg Loeb on guitar, Ted Merkel on drums, and Marcy Rae on electric bass: "'Black Slacks' was a song by Joe Bennett and the Sparkletones, but the reason I chose that name was because Robert Gordon had that song out, and it was getting a lot of local airplay. We were gonna play The Playtime in North Hollywood, and I called Ronny to ask if he would come see us because I wanted to try and get on Rollin' Rock Records. He came and brought Art Fein with him. I had Marcy on electric bass, but she wasn't in the band for very long. I then got Howard Weisbrot. Ronny told me that he would sign me to the label, but I had to have an upright bass in the band. He said that he wasn't gonna sign any more bands that had electric basses. Howard got an upright bass and learned how to play it pretty quickly. In 1981, Ronny signed us. We went down to his studio garage, and we recorded a whole bunch of songs." Out of a five year partnership, only two singles were released. Weiser had sent a bunch of bands to Europe, and they didn't get paid. He then had to recoup the losses, which caused him to go broke. The two 45 rpm singles were "I Wanna Dance with You" b/w "You Make Me Wanna Rock" and "Hold Me Tight" b/w "The Usual Thing." Mack conveyed, "Ron didn't go for 'The Usual Thing' because it wasn't pure rockabilly. I thought it was real commercial, and I was still young, wanting to get played on the radio. I recorded the real traditional stuff and then I tried to record some pop-a-billy."

During the late 1970s and early 1980s, Mack was a regular on the Los Angeles rockabilly scene. He had a very high pompadour at that time: "My hair is pretty fine, so I really had to put on a lot of spray to hold it up. I walked around like that all the time and used to get such looks. I'd be waiting in line at the bank and could hear people snickering behind me." For his gigs at Club 88, Mack hung flyers around town and handed out stacks of discount tickets at record stores. He stated that it was really tough trying to convince an audience to come see you, and promoters made you work hard to secure a prime weekend slot. You had to perform at midnight on a Monday and then other odd hours throughout the week. Even then there was no guarantee that you would open for a bigger name. Mack recalled, "At the time, The Blasters were a new band, and I would play clubs with them where only twenty people showed up." In 1980, Mack played before Billy Burnette's set at Blackie's in Santa Monica. A year later, he played the same venue: "I always incorporated some of Rick [Nelson's] songs into my sets, such as 'Believe What You Say,' and 'Fools Rush In.'" At the end of the evening, he sang "Mystery Train" while jumping off the stage and sliding across the floor on his knees.

Dennis Wilson of The Beach Boys approached him with a compliment on his routine: "That was really great." In 1982, Mack played with Gene Vincent's guitar player, Johnny Meeks, at the Landmark in Glendale, California. When Meeks had a disagreement with the owner, Mack, James Intveld, Ricky Intveld, and Patrick Woodward took over the gig.

K-Tel then contacted Ronny Weiser about releasing an album. Originally, Weiser wanted all of the artists from Rollin' Rock Records to be represented, such as Ray Campi, Rip Masters, Jackie Lee Cochran, and Tony Conn. However, the label owners weren't interested in the older acts, so ultimately a group from Seattle, Washington, called The Alley Gators and Mack were chosen. Each recorded six songs for inclusion. Mack recollected that the album was entitled *The Alley Gators*, issued in 1983, and featured his vocals on "Marie, Marie," "Julie," "I Wanna Dance with You," "Recipe for Love," "You Make Me Wanna Rock," and "Waitin' in School." He added, "I don't think it did very well because I never saw it anywhere or saw anyone who had it. I only made $600, but it was nice to have been on a K-Tel album. That was the closest I ever came to a big label."

A different version of "Waitin' in School" is available on Campi's CD, *Ray Campi—With Friends Along the Way, Austin to L.A.* Mack acknowledged, "Ray has always been great that way, helping out the younger people." Besides his own bookings, Mack played in Campi's band for more than ten years. He disclosed, "When I got on Rollin' Rock Records, Ray put me on his shows right away. At the very beginning, he would just have me come up and do two or three songs with him and the Rockabilly Rebels. Then I played rhythm guitar in his band. Finally, he featured me on some songs. We played the punk and new wave scene, and Ray had a good following." In 1983, Mack and Campi ran into Bonnie Raitt at The Alley, which was a rehearsal studio in North Hollywood. Mack remembered, "Bonnie said to Ray, 'Oh, I'm a big fan of yours.' She had seen him at the Palomino Club. Ray had been trying for a long time to get on *Austin City Limits* [but to no avail]. Bonnie was gonna do the show in December, so she got him, Sleepy LaBeef, myself, and The LeRoi Brothers on there too. She is the sweetest person." On December 31, 1983, Mack

Besides rockabilly performers, legendary acts like Bruce Springsteen and the Mavericks have guested on *Ronnie Mack's Barn Dance*, a show that ran for twenty-five years (courtesy Ronnie Mack).

played a show with Campi, Jackie Lee Cochran, and Jimmie Lee Maslon at a punk rock club called On Broadway in San Francisco: "When Ray came onstage, he said, 'I feel dizzy.' He did the show but felt bad for a long time after, several years. As it turned out, he had Meniere's disease. It must have cleared up for him because he doesn't talk about it anymore."

In January 1984, Mack opened for Los Lobos at The Country Club in Reseda, California. For twelve years (1986–1998), Mack sat in with piano player Bobby "Fats" Mizzell at the Tam O'Shanter in Los Angeles. Periodically, Intveld would play drums on their sets. Phil and Dave Alvin showed up to watch on occasion, and Kay Starr stopped by one evening. Mizzell asked if she wanted to sing a song or two, but she politely declined, saying she didn't know if she still could. Mack declared, "Bobby was a great piano player, especially for boogie woogie and rock and roll. He knew every Fats Domino song, note for note. Bobby was a good singer too, but people sat around the bar just to watch his left hand pound the keys. We did some rock and roll, but we mostly had to play old pop standards by Frank Sinatra, Tony Bennett, Nat King Cole, and Doris Day. [Two of the tunes Mack sang were "Again" and "I Left My Heart in San Francisco."] Rick [Nelson] had done a lot of those, and I had sung along with the recordings. It wasn't hard for me to sing them, and I really did like it. Through that gig, we got to play other places like private parties." Mack was even offered a gig to play guitar with Sha Na Na on a cruise ship. He auditioned, thanks to some prodding from Intveld but didn't get the job since it entailed choreographed dance moves while playing. He stated, "I'm really not that great of a guitar player. I'm just average. [Their piano player] Screamin' Scott [Simon] liked the way I played, so that's why he asked me."

Mack cited Rick Nelson as his biggest musical influence: "I was about four years old when I started liking him. I grew up in Baltimore, and we didn't get *American Bandstand*. You had to have a special antenna to get the Washington, D.C., station that carried it. [Therefore], I didn't get to see the artists that were being played on the radio. I constantly listened to the radio though and was a big fan of Elvis Presley, Buddy Holly, and The Everly Brothers. I also liked country music. I remember when I was six years old; my mother walked into a department store and bought me a greatest hits album by Hank Williams, Sr. I played that over and over. I also had an album by Flatt and Scruggs that I really liked."

To pay homage to his favorite singer, Rick Nelson, and his leather covered guitar, Mack had one made to look similar: "I couldn't afford to have a real one, so I had a guy paint something that looked just like it on my Yamaha guitar. He painted my name in pink and black. It looked wonderful." Later, in 1988, someone stole the guitar out of his locked van. Mack had stopped at a newsstand to check out *Billboard Magazine* as he had wanted to know how high on the charts Rosie Flores' "Cryin' Over You" had climbed.

Mack briefly spoke with his hero on a couple of occasions: "Rick was always very, very nice to me." In 1977, he had been videotaped for the television special, *Rick Nelson at the Fair*, but was ultimately replaced by The Sweet Inspirations. He had sung "My Best Friend," a tune he had written, to some fan club members in Nelson's hotel room. The unused clip showed a close-up of Mack with Nelson saying, "I'm really honored that somebody would consider me their best friend. I hope I never do anything to disappoint him."[6] A few years later, their mutual friend Alan Bush gave Nelson a tape of Mack's songs. Mack revealed, "He had [my 1982 Rollin' Rock 45 rpm single] 'I Wanna Dance with You' b/w 'You Make Me Wanna Rock' right next to his record player. With a pen, he had put a star next to each title.

I guess that meant he liked my songs and might consider recording them. Rick once said in an interview that he just couldn't find any of those kinds of songs around anymore, so I guess he was looking for rockabilly material. The tape included tunes that I had recorded for Rollin' Rock, including 'You'll Never Know What You're Missin'' and 'Milk Cow Blues.' Alan told me that Rick put the tape in his pocket and said he would listen to it in the car on the way to Laguna Beach."[7]

In July 1985, Nelson returned to the studio to record a second version of "Do You Know What I Mean." Mack conveyed, "I was at Ronny Weiser's studio because Ricky Intveld was playing drums on a session with Ray Campi. At some point, Ricky said, 'I got to leave as I got a session with Rick Nelson. Why don't you come with me, Ronnie? Come on and hang out.' I went, and it was Greg McDonald who said, 'Why don't you sing scratch vocals for "Do You Know What I Mean?"' I wasn't sure of all the words but somehow I got through six takes. The band had wanted to run through the song a couple of times as a rehearsal. Producer Jimmie Haskell and the engineer were in the control room trying to get all the settings just right. I think I sang it a little more rockabilly by adding a couple of Buddy Holly hiccups. Rick showed up late, as always, so he quickly sang his vocal and put his acoustic guitar on it. I remember him standing in front of me and saying, 'Did it sound rockin' enough?' I said, 'Yeah,' but actually I wasn't real crazy about the guitar solo. He and the band had to catch a plane right after the session because they were going back East to do one of Richard Nader's rock and roll shows."[8]

Also, in 1985, Fats Domino and his band toured for three weeks with Nelson. One of those dates occurred in August at the Sacramento Civic Center. Mack recounted, "At the sound check, The Coasters and I were just watching when Greg McDonald yelled out, 'Hey Ronnie, go get your guitar.' I went to the dressing room, got it, and then went on stage. He said, 'You know 'Lonesome Town,' 'I Got a Feeling,' and 'It's Up to You,' don't ya?' I said, 'I've never done 'I've Got a Feeling,' and it's been a while since I've done 'It's Up to You,' but I know them.' He said, 'Well, we need you to do them because Rick's not gonna be here.' I got to do all the songs with The Jordanaires and Rick's band. I remember some of the guys didn't feel well because the ride in from Ohio had been a rocky one. It took eleven hours to get to Sacramento on the old beat up plane they had. The concert started with the Jordanaires. Rick went on right after that, and then there was an intermission. I went on, did my two songs, introduced The Coasters, and backed them. Fats closed the show."[9]

Between 1986 and 1989, Lonesome Town Records issued three Mack singles: "My Best Friend" b/w "Kentucky Means Paradise," "It Won't Take Much" b/w "My Heart Is Achin' for You," and "Lonesome Town" b/w "Brand New Heartache." All those releases got airplay on KFOX in Torrance, California. Disc jockey Paul Bowman played "The Usual Thing" too: "It was number one on KFOX for six weeks straight." On the radio station's charts, "It Won't Take Much" scored a number one for two weeks; "Kentucky Means Paradise" hit the number two position, while "My Heart Is Achin' for You" peaked at number four. Mack also appeared on five television episodes of *Paul Bowman's Million Dollar Country Music Show*. Mack reflected, "[In regard to] 'Brand New Heartache,' it was originally an Everly Brothers song. In the early '70's, Gram Parsons and Emmylou Harris did it. I always liked the song, so Rosie Flores and I recorded it."

Mack soon realized that he wasn't going to become a big star. He grew tired of playing for just the soundman and bartender and of hearing hecklers in the crowd saying, 'Go home,' 'Shut up. We're listening to the jukebox.' He then switched to promoting shows. In January 1988, the first *Ronnie Mack's Barn Dance* took place at Little Nashville in North Hollywood. During the evening, thirteen different bands sang three songs each. There was a house band that included a lead guitarist, bass player, drummer, and steel guitarist: "Steve Duncan played drums in it for quite a while before he moved back East." Marty Rifkin played steel. James Intveld also played electric bass, and Dale Watson played lead guitar for a few years. Besides emceeing, Mack originally played rhythm guitar in the house band but later only sang one tune at the beginning of the night and one at the end. Most of the barn dances paid tribute to a particular artist, such as Eddie Cochran, Gene Vincent, Patsy Cline, Buddy Holly, and Hank Williams, Sr. At the first birthday tribute to Ricky Nelson, James Burton showed up to play guitar, and Rose Maddox was there too. Burton played his signature guitar riffs on "Fools Rush In" and "Hello Mary Lou," while Mack provided the vocals. He recalled, "On 'Hello Mary Lou,' James says to me, 'I don't remember the solos to that.' He played it note for note." Sharon Sheeley always came to the Nelson birthday tributes: "I got to be real good friends with Sharon." [She constantly spoke of Eddie Cochran and her love for him and had a painting of him on a wall in her home.] On one occasion, Nelson's children Tracy, Matthew, and Gunnar made an appearance. In fact, Matthew and Gunnar sang a couple of their father's songs. In the 1950's, Ray Campi had recorded "I Got a Feeling," so he sang that and also "Good Rockin' Tonight" and "Milkcow Blues Boogie." For two years, KCSN (California State University-Northridge) broadcast two hours live.

After Little Nashville closed its doors, the barn dance relocated to the Palomino Club in North Hollywood. In 1990, they had an hour long version, which served as opening act for Buck Owens. Del Shannon sat at the front table. Brooke Shields with her date David Keith were also in attendance. On another occasion, Bruce Springsteen was a member of the audience. That evening, Big Sandy, Lucinda Williams, Rosie Flores, James Intveld, and Dave Alvin took the stage to remember Hank Williams, Sr.'s birthday. Mack recalled, "The place was just packed; there was a line outside to get in. Bruce showed up with his wife, Patti, who was five months pregnant. They stayed for about an hour and then left." Mack realized that the Palomino Club was going broke, so he moved to another venue. The barn dance's home then became Jack's Sugar Shack in Hollywood: "One night, Bruce [Springsteen] showed up with a friend. When the barn dance was over, I had something called the *Hillbilly/Rockabilly Party*, which was basically a jam [session] for any working singers and musicians. [Incidentally, Marty Stuart and Marshall Crenshaw participated in those as well. Crenshaw sang a Gene Vincent tune and his song, "The Usual Thing."] I asked Bruce if he wanted to come up. He said, 'Yeah.' I said, 'Do you want to sing?' He replied, 'No, you sing. I'll just play and sing behind you.' I gave him a whole bunch of solos though, so he could show off. They stayed for three hours." The barn dance was once again broadcasted on the radio, every Thursday at midnight. Disc jockey Robert Douglas at KXLU (Loyola Marymount University in Los Angeles) allowed Mack airtime: "It was a lot of work. I would have the show taped and then I would have to edit it down to an hour." When the barn dance moved to Crazy Jack's in Burbank, it was taken off the air: "They had no way of taping, so I just had to stop." Eventually, the event was held at Joe's Great American Bar and Grill in Burbank. In August 2009, the barn dance switched from Tuesday nights to Mondays.

On January 7, 2013, after its twenty-fifth anniversary, Mack halted production on the barn dance. A few other club promoters had begun doing the same thing with equal or better success, and Mack found the competition to be a little bit too stiff. His event was free to the public, with the rare exception. In the early 1990s, Mack recruited Janis Martin to play the Palomino Club. In 1992, he had charged $15 when The Collins Kids, with backing provided by The Dave and Deke Combo, played the same venue. Mack revealed, "It was just wonderful. Larry [Collins] played just like he did when he was a little kid, duck walking across the stage with his double neck guitar." With a usual no admission fee, he wasn't making any money to pay the artists. Mack knew that local rockabilly acts wouldn't keep attracting the crowds. Only a legend would keep the interest of the audience, unfortunately, his regular day job at a cigar shop didn't allow him the privilege of continually hiring one. Mack disclosed, "The scene now just isn't what it used to be. It hasn't been that good for quite a while." During its tenure, the barn dance received rave reviews. Mack recollected, "At its peak, it was really a big thing. We got tons of press. The *L.A. Times* did several articles and reviews of shows. Even *Variety Magazine* did a couple of reviews." Jay Leno filmed some footage for a segment he did on country music. In 2007, Jim Hollander directed a DVD, which is entitled *First Tuesdays at Ronnie Mack's Barn Dance*. James Intveld, Rosie Flores, Dave Alvin, Big Sandy are all featured performers, and Dwight Yoakam is interviewed. In fact, Yoakam was a big fan of both Mack and Ray Campi because they kept the music scene alive. In an issue of *Music Connection* magazine, Yoakam listed Mack as his favorite Los Angeles artist. He also frequently played the shows that Mack and Art Fein assembled in honor of Elvis Presley's birthday. There were forty-five different artists on the bill, and each sang two Presley tunes.

Mack eventually stepped away from recording and performing. He didn't feel like he had the voice to succeed: "I was always a light weight, like Frankie Avalon singing rockabilly. To people, I wasn't the real deal." Rip Masters had once commented that Mack wasn't any good and that he shouldn't even bother. Mack returned to the rockabilly scene in 2015 with *Ronnie Mack's Salute to the Music of America's Legends*, held the first Saturday of every month at Viva Cantina, a nightclub in Burbank. These events have an admission fee. The premier artist honored was Big Jay McNeely. Future tributes are set for Linda Ronstadt, Cliffie Stone, Glen Campbell, and Rick Nelson.

James Intveld

Most rockabilly fans will recognize John Waters for writing and directing two cult classic films: *Hairspray* and *Cry-Baby*. The latter film starred Johnny Depp. On August 18, 2013, some of the cast reunited at the Hollywood Forever Cemetery to commemorate the Ninth Annual Johnny Ramone Tribute. In attendance were Traci Lords, Ricki Lake, Johnny Depp, John Waters, Joe Dallesandro, and James Intveld. Intveld did not appear in the movie, but he provided vocals for the soundtrack. In the film, Depp lip-synched to "King Cry-Baby," "Doin' Time for Bein' Young," "Teardrops Are Falling," "Please Mister Jailer" and "High School Hellcats." Intveld was personally chosen by Waters to sing the songs. The movie was released in 1990, but Intveld had already been a mainstay on the rockabilly scene for ten years.

James Intveld was born on November 12, 1959, in Venlo, the Netherlands. His parents and older sister Jayne (born June 21, 1958) moved to California when Intveld was a year old. His younger brother Ricky was born on December 30, 1962. Incidentally, contrary to popular belief, Ricky Intveld was not named after Ricky Nelson but rather actor Rick Jason, who at the time was a star of the TV series *Combat*. Besides a sister and a brother, Intveld's family also includes a half-brother Ronald, who lives in Holland.

At an early age, Intveld and his two siblings received an education in rock and roll from their parents. In fact, Intveld's father relocated the family to California in the hopes that he would become a singer. He does occasionally sing these days. If he is at one of his son's shows, he may be called up to sing an Elvis song or two. James Intveld remembered, "I must have been five or six when we started singing for my parents. We'd put on little shows in the living room, where we'd make our parents sit on the coach, and we would mime to records. [Some of those artists included Hank Williams, Sr., Elvis Presley, Dean Martin, and Lefty Frizzell.] The first song that I ever sang was a song called 'Room Full of Roses.' I taped myself [singing it] on my dad's tape recorder in the bedroom. I got a drum set when I was five. It was sort of a half toy/half real drum set. My uncle and my parents got that for me. I [then] got a guitar when I was eight. We went to this little cake shop to get a cake for somebody's birthday, and they had guitars on the wall. I saw a Kent ¾ nylon string acoustic guitar, and I said, 'I want to play guitar.' My parents put the guitar on layaway. It cost fifteen dollars, and they paid a dollar a week. After fifteen weeks, I had my guitar. Then I took my first guitar lesson from the lady who owned the little cake shop in Compton [California]. She wanted to make some extra money, so she gave guitar lessons out of the back room for a dollar a lesson."[10] The first song he played on guitar was "She'll Be Coming 'Round the Mountain": "That's the one they taught me."

Intveld added, "I had my first band, Freedom, when I was ten years old. It was a bunch of guys from my school who got together and started a little band. We had a guitar mass at our church, and that's how I originally met those guys. When I was thirteen, I played in jazz band at school. I learned how to play upright bass. They wanted me to play electric bass on one of the songs, so I got one from my cousins. I went to public school in Compton, California, but school started getting pretty rough, so my parents pulled me out. I was getting into too many fights. They [then] put me in Catholic school for about three years. All through high school, I played guitar and some bass. Then I went to Santa Ana College for a couple of years, and I studied music theory. It was a prerequisite that you had to take a piano class, so I learned how to play piano during that time. When I did a movie about Art Pepper, I had to learn how to play saxophone. In between all of that, I learned how to play steel guitar and banjo. I'm not really that great on all of them, but I've done it all over the years. When I go in the studio, I record a lot of stuff by myself. I played every instrument on my first album [the 1996 release *James Intveld*]." Incidentally, "that was named the best studio recording project and the best country or roots CD of 1996 by California's *Music Connection* Magazine."[11]

Balancing college with playing music was a challenge for both Intveld and his parents: "My parents were supportive of me doing music when I was a kid but once I graduated from high school they wanted me to get serious about getting a real job. They were both factory workers and wanted me to have a better life than they had. I think they weren't all that excited about me and my brother playing clubs because they wanted us to either go to school or to learn a good trade. Then maybe we could play music on the weekends. I totally understand, but we just couldn't help ourselves. I tried to go to college for a little while, but then I dropped out. I said, 'Man this is not what I want to do. I'm not gonna spend all my time going to college. I'm gonna go out and start playing music in the clubs because that's all I want to do.' My mind was only thinking about music. I was only going to college at that point for my parents. I quit when I was twenty and have played music full-time ever since." Today, his parents attend every show of his that they can: "They're proud of me now."

Intveld cited Lefty Frizzell, Elvis Presley, Fats Domino, and Hank Williams, Sr. as his musical influences. Even though he has played many rockabilly shows and festivals, Intveld doesn't consider himself to be a rockabilly singer: "When I first started out, I was a country singer. I think of myself a little bit more like how Conway Twitty was a country singer and then he did a bunch of rockabilly but then he was still a country singer. I think most rockabilly singers, the ones from the '50's, never considered themselves [as such] but instead country singers that rocked up music. There's a difference to me. I love rockabilly music, and I like to sing some of it. I don't consider myself a rockabilly because I do a lot of hard core country. To me, I'm a country singer that plays some rockabilly. [However] I got interested in rockabilly because my dad brought home an album of Elvis' Sun sessions and a Gene Vincent album. The movie *The Buddy Holly Story* came out when I was seventeen. I saw it, and I really got into Buddy Holly. My dad had a Buddy Holly album, and I went out and bought the Buddy Holly box set. I learned all the songs, and just thought this is great it only takes three guys to make music. I thought I can do this; I don't need a fourteen piece band. I learned I could actually play the songs, and it sounded good. Right after the Gene Vincent stuff, I started reading liner notes and knew about Eddie Cochran and then Warren Smith, Billy Lee Riley, and Roy Orbison and his Sun recordings. I just got into all of them."

Even though Johnny Depp landed the lead role in John Waters' *Cry-Baby*, it was James Intveld who provided the vocals for the movie's soundtrack (courtesy Joel Aparicio).

In 1980, Intveld's musical aspirations came to the forefront when he and his younger brother formed The Rockin' Shadows along with bassist David Harrington. Bill Black replaced Harrington after only a few months and then eventually Patrick Woodward became the permanent bassist. Intveld recalled, "Bill was replaced with Patrick because we wanted an upright bass player. Ricky saw Patrick playing in the Billy Zoom Band at the Whiskey a Go-Go [in Hollywood, California]. After the show, he walked up to Pat and said, 'Hey man, you're a great rockabilly bass player.' I think he had given him my card or something, and said, 'My brother has a band and maybe you want to play with us?' I think Pat kind of shrugged it off like whatever kid. My brother came home and told me about this guy and said, 'There's this really cool bass player. He plays upright bass, does all the slapping, and knows how to play this style.' Back then, there wasn't anybody around that was doing that. [However] my brother also said, 'Ah he doesn't seem too interested.' Then one night [in 1982], Patrick came to see us open for The Blasters at Club 88 in Santa Monica. After our show, Patrick walked up to my brother and said to him, 'Y'all still looking for a bass player? Here's my number.' He liked what we were doing. Pat joined us right after that gig. He said that he made up his mind when he heard me sing: 'I heard you sing and I went oh this guy can really sing. This is the guy I want to play with.' He said there were a lot of people that tried to play rockabilly back then, but he didn't think they were very good singers."

That same year, Intveld and The Rockin' Shadows (with Steve Grindle on bass) released a 45 rpm record, "My Heart is Achin' for You" b/w "You're My Baby." Intveld penned "My Heart is Achin' for You" while the B side was a cover version of Roy Orbison's 1956 Sun recording. Intveld explained, "I started to write little songs when I was ten years old, not even being conscious of it, but the first song I wrote that was a real legitimate song was 'My Heart Is Achin' for You.' [Those others were either discarded or stuffed away in a box.] [As for the flip side of the single], I chose 'You're My Baby' because we thought it was more obscure than other songs we covered, and I wanted a two beat type of groove since 'My Heart Is Achin' for You' was a shuffle." The band had wanted to record with Woodward: "We were trying to get into some studio to record, but it never really came together."

In the early 1980s, the Los Angeles rockabilly music scene was thriving with acts, such as The Blasters, X, Levi Dexter and the Rockats, and The Paladins. Intveld and his band The Rockin' Shadows were also a popular crowd pleaser: "It was such a good place to play music, and there were so many different types of artists. We all played shows together and there were good crowds because there was a scene that was pretty healthy." The trio garnered a lot of attention and had loyal followers, including a group of gals who named themselves the Shadowettes. Intveld remarked, "They came to most of our gigs, and one night they decided to make shirts and wear them to the shows."

In 1983, The Rockin' Shadows opened for Rick Nelson at the Rumble Seat Garage in Long Beach, California: "It was not like Rick to get to a gig early for any reason, but this time he did, and he liked what he saw."[12] Nelson invited Ricky Intveld and Patrick Woodward to join his band. James Intveld admitted, "I was excited to play a gig with Rick. The fact that he wanted to hire the band, on one side what a great opportunity, but I was also horrified at the same time because this is my band. At the time, my brother was like, 'No way am I gonna not play with my brother,' so he turned it down. Patrick said to me, 'I ain't getting any younger man. I got a good opportunity to play with Rick; I should probably do it.' I said, 'Yeah I agree with you. Go ahead and do that.'"[13] Woodward latched onto Nelson's offer while Intveld remained for a while with his brother.

Ricky Intveld eventually accepted Nelson's invitation. James Intveld remembered, "We were at the Forum seeing a Richard Nader show with Rick, Jerry Lee Lewis, and a bunch of other artists when I started to feel kind of guilty. I said to my brother, 'Man, you know right now we're sitting out here in the audience, and we ain't got two nickels to rub together. You could be out there making money by playing these big concerts with Rick Nelson. Maybe you oughta go do that.' He said, 'Are you sure you want me to?' I said, 'Yeah man, go ahead and do it; get some experience. I'll be okay.' Right after the gig we went backstage, and we said to Patrick, 'Ricky's gonna do the gig.' Patrick said, 'Okay' and told Rick Nelson. It was decided then it was gonna happen."[14]

With the arrival of Intveld and Woodward, Nelson's rockabilly aspirations were now complete: "I've gone back to trying to get the best parts of the beginning of rock and roll, which is what I know the most about."[15] On November 12, 1983, Nelson participated in a recreation of the 1971 Madison Square Garden concert. [The 1971 version had been inspiration for his hit song, "Garden Party."] Fortunately, this time around, he was accepted. Nelson commented, "I knew that I had a band behind me that was as good as anything that had come out of the 1950s. The New York press built the whole thing up, they were calling it 'Rick Nelson's comeback,' but I've been 'coming back' all my life so really it was nothing new to me."[16] Gene Taylor from The Blasters, who had played a few dates with Nelson previously, provided piano accompaniment. Nelson added, "I think there'll always be a market for '50s rock and roll, but it still surprises me when I see kids of sixteen or seventeen singing along with me. That's a great feeling."[17] According to James Intveld, "That was my brother's first gig with Rick, never rehearsed, just showed up and played. I think he was nervous, but we had run down all Ricky Nelson's stuff back at the house with Patrick."[18] Incidentally, Intveld had taught his younger brother how to play the drums.

After Ricky Intveld's and Patrick Woodward's departures from The Rockin' Shadows, the name was no longer used, and James Intveld forged ahead with a new lineup: Jerry Angel on drums and Steve Grindle on bass, who was already in the band since he had replaced Woodward when he went to join Nelson's band. In 1985, *Roadhouse 66* starring Willem Dafoe hit theaters. In the film, Intveld and his brother perform "My Heart Is Achin' for You" and back Dafoe on "Marie, Marie." James Intveld conveyed, "Originally the role was written for Charlie Sexton, but for some reason he wasn't able to do it. The director Mark Robinson saw me playing at the Palomino [Club] one night and thought to use me. I had thought about changing my name to James Fury professionally but then changed my mind since it really pissed off my whole family." Instead, that was used as his moniker in the movie.

On December 31, 1985, Intveld's life changed forever. His younger brother Ricky and former bassist Patrick Woodward were tragically killed along with Rick Nelson, his fiancée Helen Blair, road manager Clark Russell, pianist Andy Chapin, and guitarist Bobby Neal. Their 1944 DC-3 had encountered problems with the heater, which caused a cabin fire. The plane made an emergency landing, but it was too late as it burst into flames. Nelson and his entourage had been en route to Dallas, Texas, to play a New Year's Eve gig at the Park Suite Hotel. Ricky Intveld had turned twenty-three years old the day before the incident. Upon hearing the news, his brother and family were inconsolably grief stricken. Intveld confessed, "That was a huge loss for me. It completely changed my life. It just seemed impossible to me that he was gone. It was like living with something that couldn't have happened."[19] Intveld's greatest memories of playing in the music business have been the times he shared the stage with his brother: "We were such a force, and the music was everything to us." All three of Intveld's album releases have been dedicated to his brother.

In 1988, Ronnie Mack recruited his friend James Intveld to play his weekly barn dance, which was then held at a club called Little Nashville. Intveld declared, "It got so big that we moved it to the Palomino. Ronnie and I were always hanging out, and he asked me if I could play with him. Sometimes I'd play guitar, and sometimes I'd play bass. I ended up being the bass player in the house band for years until I got hired by The Blasters. When I did that, Jeff Steele replaced me."

By 1990, Intveld had switched gears and had ventured into the world of cinema, first as a vocalist for a movie soundtrack then as an actor. John Waters wrote the screenplay and directed *Cry-Baby*, and he ended up personally choosing Intveld to sing the songs for his campy 1950's style musical. Intveld recalled, "Well, originally I think they had tried to get Johnny Depp to do the singing for it, and then they weren't completely convinced that he could actually do it. Even though I had heard the tapes, and they were pretty good. I think they were just looking for somebody who was a little bit more of a professional. I didn't know that they had put out a search for [a vocalist], but I had gotten a call one day from the production company saying, 'Hey can you call us back? We're making this movie, and we need somebody to do the singing. We want to speak to you.' By the time I called, I had found out that they had done a search all over the country for a guy to do the voice. They kind of narrowed it down to a bunch of different professionals then it came down to basically three guys that they decided could be potentially the right guy: Colin Winski (a rockabilly singer from Arizona), Billy Burnette, and me. They took all three of us into the studio with Al Kooper and had us record two songs as sort of an audition. One song was 'Teardrops Are Falling' and the other was 'Red Hot.' They wanted us to sing a ballad and also kind of a hard rocker. Then they sat John Waters down and said, 'We're gonna play you these tracks, and we're not gonna tell you who they are. You tell us who you think the voice of Cry-Baby is.' They played all three voices, and he picked me. I was on set with Johnny [Depp] in Baltimore, [Maryland]. Originally when I heard that they were making this film, another friend of mine was up for the job of musical composer. He called and said, 'Hey man, there's this script for this character who's exactly who you are. Do this.' He sent me the script, and I read it. I thought, 'Wow this is great,' so we kind of submitted [information] to go in and then I never heard about it after that. I never auditioned, never heard about the project anymore until they called me about [providing] the vocals. I walked in the room, and John Waters was like, 'Oh my God, you're Cry-Baby.' He thought, 'Well, it'd be great to have you be in this movie,' but the problem with it was Johnny Depp had just come off a TV show, *21 Jump Street*, and he was already a well-known personality. He had box office [appeal], and they were looking for that because John Waters had only done obscure films up to that [point]. John said, 'Maybe I can put you in the movie as Johnny's sidekick,' but I couldn't be in the movie because we were too similar. There was no way I could play his sidekick."

A year later, Intveld joined forces with Dwight Yoakam, playing bass on his unplugged gigs: "We were both playing shows and were friends. On the weekends, we'd go motorcycle riding. He wanted to go out and do some acoustic tours without the full band and electric bass. The guy that was playing bass with him didn't play upright. Dwight just called and said, 'Hey man, how'd you feel about coming out, maybe playing some of these acoustic shows with me because I need an upright player?' I was like 'Yeah cool, I'll come out and do it.' I did two tours with him. I also did a TV show, played on some songs for a movie soundtrack, and did a commercial with him. He would call me when he wanted someone that played upright."

Intveld then worked with River Phoenix on the movie *The Thing Called Love*: "It was kind of an odd situation. I had gotten a phone call from Steven Soles, who was doing the music. He goes, 'Hey, I got a session for a movie. Can you come in and play bass?' I say, 'Okay.' I'm in the studio with a bunch of other musicians when here comes Steven Soles, and he brings River Phoenix over to meet me. He says, 'Hey River, this is James Intveld. This guy that you're meeting is this character, so you need to hang out with him.' I find out a little while later that this movie is about a country singer who drives an old pickup truck. He's a little bit on the edge of country and rock. We're in the booth talking about it, and I find out that it's the same movie that they had called me about two years before. The movie was originally written for Randy Travis. They had taken a meeting with me to maybe have me star in the movie, but I wasn't famous enough. They offered it to River a while later. They had rewritten the script, and he decided to do it." Intveld added, "River and I became real good pals. We hung out for months together. He'd come see me play; we'd work in the studio together and in the hotel room on songs. He really knew how to sing and play guitar, but he was playing this character that was sorta based on someone like me. River was a very, very talented person and a very generous and cool guy. It was a huge shock to me when he died. That was pretty tragic."

From 1992 to 1995, Intveld played lead guitar in The Blasters: "Dave Alvin had quit earlier [in 1986], and they had a few other guys that played guitar: Hollywood Fats and Smokey Hormel. They had both moved on to do other things. Well, actually Hollywood Fats had passed away. I jammed with those guys then we decided that we'd all work together. They had asked me years before if I wanted to join The Blasters, and I turned it down because I was doing my own thing. For about five years, I had gone through a series of trying to get a record deal, and I wasn't having any luck with anything major."

Rockabilly legend Ray Campi helped Intveld secure a record label: "I was in The Blasters when that happened. Ray said, 'Hey I want you to be on this album for Bear Family. Can you write a song and record it for these guys?' After I made that recording, the owner Richard Weize called and said, 'Hey I really like your track. I'd be interested in having you make an album for me, but I want you to make it the same way.' I had played all the instruments myself on ['Barely Hangin' On'], that I did for the Bear Family 20th Anniversary Box Set. Originally what had happened was I didn't have any money to hire a band to come in and record the tracks. I did it when The Blasters weren't on tour, but once I got the record finished they wanted me to tour. I had to quit, so I could do my solo act. The record came out on Bear Family Records. They never had an artist that could tour, but I toured in the little cargo van that they used to deliver records."

One of the songs on his self-titled 1996 release was "Cryin' Over You," which Intveld originally wrote for Rosie Flores: "I went to see her play at a club in Pasadena, [California]. I'd seen her play a few times before that but that was the first time I saw [her sing] a whole set. During the break, she came and sat with me. I said, 'I just really, really love what you're doing, but you need to have more original songs. You should write some more songs.' She said, 'Well, I'm writing; I got some originals.' I said, 'I'm gonna write a song for you.' I left that night and on the way home I wrote 'Cryin' Over You.' I wrote it specifically for Rosie. I got up in the morning and got my tape recorder. I sang the song [and played acoustic guitar]. I had gotten her number, called, and said, 'I wrote a song and I want to see if you like it.' I then brought the tape to her next gig. About a week later, I got a call from somebody in her band saying, 'Hey, I think Rosie's gonna sing your song tonight at the Club Lingerie.' After playing a few songs, she introduced 'Cryin' Over You.' She had a singles deal on Warner Bros. and was about to get an album deal. I went with her to Nashville to do this showcase for Warner Bros. We played 'Cryin' Over You,' and I sang the harmony with her. Warner Bros. decided that was the hit and cut it as the single for the album." "Cryin' Over You" b/w "Midnight to Moonlight" was issued as a 45 rpm record, and both tracks were also featured on Flores' 1987 self-titled release. Her version of "Cryin' Over You" peaked at number fifty-one on the *Billboard* charts. Over the years, Intveld has played many gigs with Flores and has appeared on several of her albums.

Also, in 1996, Intveld began working with The Mavericks' lead guitarist Eddie Perez: "I met him when I used Russell Scott's band on a tour of Germany." After that tour, Perez joined Intveld.

Intveld assisted Joaquin Phoenix and Reese Witherspoon with their portrayals of Johnny Cash and June Carter Cash in the 2005 biopic *Walk the Line*. He helped them hone their vocals and learn their instruments since neither had musical training. Intveld also sang Carl Smith's tune "Time's a Wastin'," although it went uncredited: "The scene where the guys [Johnny Cash and the Tennessee Two] are all learning to play together on the porch ends with me and Reese Witherspoon singing it on a little radio. T-Bone Burnett forgot to give me credit."

In 2007, Intveld was recruited to play upright bass for Trisha Yearwood in the music video for her song "Heaven, Heartache, and the Power of Love": "I was the assistant director on that video. They had guys sidelining for the day, which means guys that are in the background playing instruments, and the bass player didn't show up. The director said, 'Hey, we know you play upright bass. Is there any way you could do it?' I said, 'Well, I'll do it, but I'm not going through make-up, and I'm not gonna do a wardrobe change.' All I did was put a shirt on. Basically I assisted directed with a megaphone, calling, 'Cut, action, and roll camera.' Then I'd put the megaphone behind the drums and pick up the bass. I had been in a bunch of other videos too." Two years previously, he appeared in the music video for "The Seashores of Old Mexico" by George Strait: "In that one, I was originally supposed to be playing a young Merle Haggard, and Merle was supposed to be playing the old fella. That video opens with me lying in bed, and George is calling. I tell him to come out to Mexico. Merle didn't make it to Cancun, Mexico where we were shooting, so we just got an older man to play me as an older James."

Intveld was also given the opportunity to convert a letter James Dean had written into a short film: "I was approached by Joshua Triligy to participate in a project called *Letters of the Underground*. It was a movie that consisted of thirteen short films about letters that were written by famous people. He asked if I would direct one of the short films for a competition that was part of the Silverlake Film Festival. The winner was going to get a personal meeting with some big production company and a chance to show them a script of their own. He asked if I would be interested in doing the short film on a letter Hank Williams, Sr. had written. We tried to make the film from the letter and cast Hank Williams III, but it never came together. Then they approached me with this other letter that James Dean had written, and they had Jake LaBotz in mind [to play him]. I agreed to do this film and use Jake, but then Jake got cast in *Rambo IV* and had to go to Thailand for three months. Since he was not available, I put out a casting call for a James Dean. I cast Rafael Killyan. We shot the movie on favors and with Jeff Cunningham, a very talented cinematographer. The film ended up winning. I never saw the finished film, so I don't know what happened to it." According to the Internet Movie Database, the short was renamed *West to Eden* and released in 2007.

In 2008, Intveld's third album, *Have Faith*, was issued: "I was really down when I was making that album, and needed to hear that, to try to turn myself around. My whole life has been rough, with a lot of sadness and bad things in it."[20] Incidentally, The Jordanaires provided backing vocals on the album: "I've known The Jordanaires since the mid '80s when they were working with Ricky Nelson, and my brother was in the band. We were all friends back then. In 1985, we had done some demos together. Bill Rowe was a songwriter, and he wanted Rick to cut a bunch of his stuff [which included 'Rock and Roll Fool']. Rick Nelson was supposed to be there to sing, but he was about eight hours late for the session. We were all just sitting around when my brother said, 'Why don't you just get James to sing?' I then did a couple of tracks. Whenever I would go to Nashville to do a show of my own, I'd call Gordon [Stoker] or Ray [Walker], and they'd come see me play. We all kept in touch."

April 2010 marked the beginning of a three year tenure playing guitar for John Fogerty: "In November 2009, I got a call from Billy Burnette to see if I could cover for him with John on *The Tonight Show with Conan O'Brien*. The following year Billy left. They [then] called and offered me the gig." Intveld also appeared with Fogerty on *The View*, *Late Show with David Letterman*, and the *American Idol* finale, in which Fogerty sang a duet with that season's winner Phillip Phillips. Intveld, Fogerty, and the band served as musical guests at the Kremlin in Russia for New Year's Eve 2010. He quit working with Fogerty to concentrate on his own career and finish his fourth album: "I'm really careful about my records. I want them to be really, really good. I don't make quick records: three days in the studio, mix it, and then throw it out there for people to consume."

September 23, 2010, marked Intveld's *Grand Ole Opry* debut, in which he sang "Step Aside" and "Sing a Sad Song." Two other times he appeared on that historic stage: December 24, 2010, in which he sang "A Woman's Touch" and "Walk with Me," and April 21, 2011, in which he performed three songs: "Sea of Heartbreak," "Softly and Tenderly," and "Pretty World." Even though he got to appear on the *Grand Ole Opry* and Ernest Tubb's *Midnight Jamboree*, he ultimately decided that Nashville wasn't right for him and went back to California. He had moved to Nashville in 2005, but Intveld discovered that the town and its music scene weren't all that he hoped they would be.

Nowadays, Intveld is kept busy performing at clubs and festivals around the world. His regular band consists of Kip Dabbs, Storm Rhode IV, and Lorne Rall. Intveld commented, "I met Kip nineteen years ago when he was playing in The Rhythm Lords. He played with me for a couple of years then he moved to Hawaii to pursue a career in graphic arts. He moved back to Los Angeles and then hooked back up with me and has been with me ever since. Lorne played with me nineteen years ago, but we lost touch when I stopped touring. He's been back with me [off and on]. [On occasion, Bob Gothar has played bass for Intveld.] I met Storm in Austin, Texas about fourteen years ago. We did a few gigs together but then he went on to play for this girl singer who was supposed to have a big career. When she quit the business, he moved out to Los Angeles to be closer to his kids, and we reconnected." Besides his country band, Intveld fronts an eight piece dance band called James Intveld and the Swing Sinners. They cover tunes by Louis Prima, Louis Jordan, Big Joe Turner, and Frank Sinatra. Intveld is no longer concerned with hitting the big time but rather content with playing for those who want to hear him: "I didn't dream about the music business. I dreamt about music."[21]

Rosie Flores

For five decades, Rosie Flores has been on the music scene. She's appeared on the *Grand Ole Opry* and *Austin City Limits*, made guest spots on Ralph Emery's television program *Nashville Now*, and has had singles on the *Billboard* country charts. Throughout the years, numerous bands and record labels helped hone her talents. Being criticized for not being country enough, superstardom eluded her. Rockabilly has always been at the core of her being, and she continues to entertain fans at clubs and festivals today. In 2014, she was bestowed with the honor of winning two Ameripolitan awards, one for Best Rockabilly Female and the other for Best Honky Tonk Female.

Rosie Flores was born on September 10, 1950, in San Antonio, Texas. Flores grew up surrounded by music: "My parents were huge music fans. My father liked jazzy stuff, like The Mills Brothers and Peggy Lee and country artists such as Ernest Tubb. They also really liked Dean Martin, Frank Sinatra, and Ella Fitzgerald. My parents took me to see all the Rogers and Hammerstein musicals, and we would go see live plays. We always used to watch any kind of music variety show."[22] She remembered watching *American Bandstand* and *The Ed Sullivan Show*. When she was seven years old, Flores began singing: "My father used to buy *Hit Parader*. [She picked tunes out of the magazine that she wanted to learn.] When he realized my brother and I could sing, he started recording us. That's my earliest memories of actually singing, and we still have some of those recordings. In fact, on my *Rockabilly Filly* CD, there's a piece of one of them—'I'm Gonna Sit Right Down and Write Myself a Letter.' It's like a bonus track. When I was in Catholic school, I can remember singing 'Ave Maria' [on pitch and including all the high notes.] I sang it for my mother, and then she made me sing it in front of my aunts and cousins."[23] Flores added, "Once I started listening to myself on different recordings, it kind of gave me confidence to keep singing. I decided to get into the school choruses. By the time the '60s came, I started singing everything from Motown to girl groups to The Beatles to The Rolling Stones."

At fourteen, Flores took an interest in the guitar: "My brother, Roger, who was about two years older, was already a guitar player. He was hanging out with his high school friends, and they started a band. I asked if he would teach me a few chords on the guitar because I'd love to learn. [He did], and I picked it up really quickly. He said, 'Boy, you got that fast,' and

I said, 'Well, why shouldn't I? It's easy.' I'd knock on his bedroom door and say, 'Show me a few more, show me a few more,' until I knew my way around chord changes. The first little lick I ever played was the theme to the *Twilight Zone* TV show. After that, I bought my own acoustic guitar and started practicing with different folk artists like Bob Dylan, Joan Baez, and Lead Belly. At that time, I wanted to be a folk singer. If I had had a manager, I probably would have been signed. I was really cranking out the songs and performing in the living room."

Flores continued, "When The Yardbirds, The Rolling Stones, and Led Zeppelin came out, they made me want to play electric guitar. My brother also played electric, and I wanted to follow in his footsteps. He showed me how to play, get certain sounds, bend and sustain notes. He kind of showed me the ropes and then I became enamored with guitar players like Jeff Beck, Jimmy Page, and B.B. King. The first real lead guitar part I ever learned was the intro to 'Johnny B. Goode.'" Blues guitar patterns and trying to play like Buddy Holly urged the teenager forward: "I had a lot of the Chuck Berry and Keith Richards influence. When I was sixteen, I formed my first band in high school. We were called Penelope's Children. I had the first all-girl rock and roll band that I know of. My father came to a show at school that I had put the band together for. We had borrowed the gear from my brother's band. My father was so excited by how good we sounded that he took us down to the music store and signed for $5,000 worth of gear: drums, a PA system, guitars, amplifiers, microphones, microphone cords, guitar straps, and picks. We were overwhelmed with pure happiness because we were so into our band and really wanted to continue. It kind of gave us some seriousness, and the fact that an adult was behind us meant a whole lot. It was so encouraging. Both my bass player and drummer's parents were so moved by the gesture that they helped pay for the stuff. I remember one of the first times we were practicing in the garage, and my dad came out to listen. He said, 'Well, you better start getting your bookings because the payments are eighty dollars a month.'

Rosie Flores convinced her musical heroes Wanda Jackson and Janis Martin to participate on her 1995 album *Rockabilly Filly* (author's collection).

We were like, 'Cool, we're gonna get to work. We got a reason to play now.' We would make payments but when we couldn't, he'd make them for us." At eighteen, she and the band opened for Creedence Clearwater Revival and The Turtles: "We had to join the musicians' union in order to play but that ensured we got paid when the promoter had wanted us for free. The members of CCR were really nice to us. They let us use their amps and drums since ours were too small sounding. The Turtles didn't say much. CCR even hung out with us after the show."

Flores had transitioned from folk to The Beatles to The Stones to country to rockabilly then to hard rock: "I kind of tasted a little bit of all of them." Flores' list of musical influences is lengthy because so many genres have inspired her style. However, she named Elvis Presley, Buddy Holly, Jerry Lee Lewis, Brenda Lee, The Ronettes, The Supremes, The Beach Boys, Dick Dale, B.B. King, Muddy Waters, The Rolling Stones, The Yardbirds, Led Zeppelin, Gram Parsons, The Flying Burrito Brothers, The Byrds, Neil Young, Poco, Tammy Wynette, George Jones, Waylon Jennings, Gary Stewart, Bob Dylan, and Tom Petty.

In 1976, Flores created Rosie and the Screamers. Three years later, she started a rockabilly band in San Diego, California, called The Reboppin' Screamers: "When I was a kid, I loved Buddy Holly and Elvis. I didn't really realize I still loved rockabilly until 1979. It was so difficult to find players who understood the genre, the sound, and the style. I then moved to Los Angeles and started searching out others who were in the scene. I found Levi Dexter and the Rockats, Ray Campi, and James Intveld. They opened my eyes to rockabilly again. Their excitement made me want to sing and play it. Rockabilly's got that beat and cool groove. I loved the energy onstage and how the guys from the '50's used to roll on the floor and kick their legs up and stand on top of their basses. The level of showmanship that goes along with those rockabilly bands is really pretty high. They don't just stand there singing like a folk band. They're moving and shaking it. You're looking at something up there that's rebellious, raw, and in your face. I was all over that, so I spend a lot of time shaking onstage and really moving. I still have a lot of energy. It just comes out of me because I play the kind of music I love. I just loved the look that goes with it too. I think a wonderful thing about rock and roll is how fashion follows it, and that was one of the reasons I loved rockabilly so much."

Flores first heard and fell in love with the music of Elvis Presley, Jerry Lee Lewis, Johnny Cash, Buddy Holly, Johnny and Dorsey Burnette (The Rock and Roll Trio), Gene Vincent, and Eddie Cochran: "I discovered Wanda Jackson and Sonny Burgess at the same time. I didn't find out about Janis Martin until 1979. I was at a Levi and the Rockats show, and I was telling this girl in the audience that I was in a rockabilly band, called Rosie and the Reboppin' Screamers. She goes, 'What do you do?' I said, 'Well, I do some covers by Wanda Jackson, Gene Vincent, and Eddie Cochran.' She goes, 'Well, do you do any Janis Martin?' I said, 'Who?' She looked at me kind of funny and said, 'If you don't know who Janis Martin is, then you don't know anything about rockabilly.' I drove back to LA, went to the nearest record store and found her Bear Family recordings. Right away, I latched onto what she was doing and became a big fan of all her music. The Palomino Club became my home and after being influenced by honky tonk singer Gary Stewart, I discovered my voice somewhere between Tanya Tucker and Gene Vincent."

Flores also began songwriting on a regular basis in 1979: "When I was five years old, I wrote a song on the piano called 'Candy Yummy for My Tummy.' At sixteen, I wrote one of my most requested songs, 'Bandera Highway.'"

By 1983, Flores had teamed up with the all-female punk band, The Screamin' Sirens, whose lead singer was Pleasant Gehmen. She started out playing bass but quickly switched to lead guitar. Flores conveyed, "After five years together, I made the movie *The Runnin' Kind* with them." She left the group to go solo: "I started doing country shows around Los Angeles with Dwight Yoakam. The scene was very strong at the time, and I fit in quite well because I was a country singer before The Screamin' Sirens. After the movie *Urban Cowboy* hit, it got too corporate country, and that's when I switched to punk." She quickly became a fan of X, The Blasters, Los Lobos, Social Distortion, and Fear.

In 1986, Warner Bros./Reprise signed Flores to a recording contract. That same year, she was nominated for Best New Female Vocalist by the Academy of Country Music. Her self-titled debut featured the James Intveld penned tune "Cryin' Over You." He had written the song after seeing her in concert and commenting that she should have more original material. Intveld harmonized with her on the recorded version. It peaked at number fifty-one on the *Billboard* Country charts. Flores remembered, "Warner Bros. tried to restrict me from doing rockabilly or recording my own songs. They told me that 'rockabilly was the kiss of death.' I recorded Wanda Jackson's 'I Gotta Know' and Carl Perkins' 'Turn Around,' which paid tribute to my influences without stirring up too much trouble. Other than that, they were a great label. I learned a lot from them and am grateful for the fact that they helped to put me on the map. I was the first Latina to be on the *Billboard* country charts. I was dropped from the label [after only two years]. They had other people like k.d. Lang and Randy Travis that they were more interested in developing." In 1992, Flores moved onto HighTone Records: "They were very allowing on the creative end. They trusted me one hundred percent, and I had a great time making records and videos for them."

Janis Martin and Wanda Jackson were both recruited by Flores to sing duets on her 1995 release, *Rockabilly Filly*. In fact, that session reignited the spark within Jackson to tour again: "It wasn't hard [convincing Wanda to come out of retirement]. I asked her to record with me, and she went ahead and did it. [Incidentally], my recording process is to record live and then do overdubs when needed. After the record came out, I just called and said, 'I'm gonna tour behind this record, and I'd love to bring you along to help me promote it. Let them see that you're still out there, and you're still as wonderful as you ever were. People would flip to see you again. You have so many fans out there.' She was like, 'Really?' She just jumped at the chance. She and her husband were real excited about the idea." Jackson recollected, "I told Rosie I would be happy to help her publicize her album any way I could."[24]

Opening night was at Bimbo's 365 Club in San Francisco, California. A friend of Flores', Dick Montana of The Beat Farmers, had passed away that morning, but Jackson told her that the show must go on and that he would want her to perform: "She really helped me through it. That was when I realized that I could learn a lot from her, not only from the vocal standpoint but just how to be in the business. I produced the show in a way that I would start out doing about five songs from *Rockabilly Filly* and then I would bring her up to do the two duets that we sang together on my record and then we would back her on a bunch of her songs." An acoustic set would follow where Flores and Jackson would sing together. One of the tunes they would always do was Jackson's favorite Presley tune, "Trying to Get to You." The band would then return for more tracks off the album. Finally, Jackson would return to close the show. Flores commented, "A lot of people remember that opening night. I've gotten a lot of compliments on it. It was a fairly successful six week tour across America. The only problem I had, I ended up getting ripped off by the booking agent." He had put the monies earned into his personal account and then the IRS put a lien against it for not paying his taxes. A judgment was reached in court with an attorney's help from the musicians' union. She then had to find another lawyer to help her collect the money. That action prompted the booking agent to pay back most of what was owed. Unfortunately, Flores still lost around $4,000. It took her four years to pay back the musicians. Flores added, "I feel really proud that I had a hand in helping Wanda come back out. I felt like I was kind of rediscovering Janis and Wanda at the same time in 1995." Jackson commented, "Rosie has been very important to me."[25] While promoting *Rockabilly Filly*, Flores also toured a lot with Sun recording artist Sonny Burgess: "I met him through his manager who thought we'd be great on the road together. I think they were impressed with what I had done for Wanda and Janis, plus they knew I loved the older Sun rockabilly guys. He's an amazing guitar player, writer, and singer." In 1996, they appeared together on *Late Night with Conan O'Brien*, in which Flores sang "You Tear Me Up" and Burgess performed his signature tune "Red Headed Woman." Flores conveyed, "A lot of people love 'You Tear Me Up.' It was and still is really, really popular."

As far as playing other instruments, Flores admitted, "I have a piano and a set of drums, but I'm not somebody that would be hirable. My two instruments are voice and guitar." Although for several years she concentrated solely on being a singer: "I would always have really great lead guitar players in my band. As I got older, I picked up the guitar again in a more serious way to where I could be thought of as a bonafide lead player." By the time, she was in her 40's; she was the only lead guitarist in the band.

National Public Radio enlisted Flores to narrate their ten part documentary series on rockabilly music, which was called *Whole Lotta Shakin'*. The archives can be accessed at www.rockabillyradio.org. In 2008, she won a Peabody Award for her participation.

In 2012, Flores released *Working Girl's Guitar* as well as Janis Martin's *The Blanco Sessions*, which she produced. The latter took a long time to be issued because Flores couldn't find a record label that was interested. She ended up raising money for the production and manufacturing costs from fan donations via Kickstarter. After raising the money, she realized it still wasn't enough, but luckily found Cow Island Music to back the rest of the project, which included manufacturing, mixing, mastering, and distribution. Upon its debut, Flores quickly went to work on setting up a tour with fellow rockabilly songstress Martí Brom. The series of dates was called "A Tribute to Janis Martin," and it featured a sold-out show at the Rock and Roll Hall of Fame in Cleveland, Ohio: "We got really good response. We had sixty-four photographs showing on a screen behind us while we told her life story. We sang her songs, and the band sounded great. It was the first time we ever did anything like that."

Flores remains active with songwriting and showcasing her talent around the country: "I have a band in Austin that I've been playing off and on with called Rosie Flores and the Rivetors. I wish that I'd have had the same band for twenty years because it's hard to keep changing, but financially it makes more sense to fly in and hire musicians in the area that I've worked with before or that come highly recommended." Most recently, she's been busy writing a nonfiction book about a woman who spent her life in rock and roll. Flores hopes to have it released in 2015. The singer/songwriter has also been participating in shows with her friend James Intveld. On June 21, 2014, he hosted the *Midnight Jamboree* in Nashville with Flores as his special guest.

Eddie Angel

Eddie Angel has enjoyed the most success with Los Straightjackets, but rockabilly enthusiasts would probably recognize him for his work with The Planet Rockers. The band was formed in 1989 and two years later they opened for Morrissey. Recently, they have reunited to play festivals, both here in the States and overseas. When he's not in a band, he backs others like Linda Gail Lewis and Sue Moreno. His guitar playing is one of the most sought after in the industry. In 1996, he was nominated for a Nashville Nammy in the category of Best Guitarist and inducted into the Albany, New York, Musicians' Hall of Fame.

Eddie Heeran was born on March 12, 1953, in Albany, New York. Eddie Angel is a stage name, given to him by Tex Rubinowitz: "I don't know where it came from or why. He had names for everybody."[26] Angel comes from a family with three older sisters and one brother: "Two of my sisters, whom I grew up with, were Elvis and '50s rock and roll fanatics. That stuff and music that was on the radio was what I heard growing up. When I was eleven, The Beatles came out, and I [became] totally taken in by them. I remember arguing with my sisters about who was better: Elvis or The Beatles. I loved early Elvis. 'Don't Be Cruel' is a great record. I love 'Young and Beautiful.' [He's also a fan of "Don't," "Mystery Train," and "One Sided Love Affair."] A lot of rockabilly guys hate The Beatles, and I understand because nothing they do is as great as a cool rockabilly record. I get as excited now hearing a great record as I did when I was fifteen. There's always something I haven't heard. I think my brain was kind of wired to play '50s rock and roll because that's what I grew up on."

At age twelve, Angel started playing guitar: "My brother's friend showed me how to play 'Peter Gunn.' In my very first band, the Kreases, we would do songs like 'Hang on Sloopy' and 'Louie Louie.' I was pretty shy then about singing. I didn't really start singing until I was in my twenties. Now I think I have a pretty good voice." Even though he's most famous for being a guitarist, Angel played clarinet in his fifth grade band and can now accompany himself on piano.

Angel added, "In the '70s, I was in a jug band in Albany, [New York] called The Star Spangled Washboard Band, and we toured a lot on the East Coast. We played colleges, bluegrass festivals, and Disney World. We were pretty popular. I was just one of the side musicians. There were four guys up front that were the main guys. I did that for two years." He played in other bands before being offered an opportunity to join Tex Rubinowitz: "That really was the thing that put me on the trajectory, to where I'm at now. Tex put out a couple of rockabilly 45's on Ripsaw Records. One of the records, 'Hot Rod Man' b/w 'Ain't It Wrong,' came out right before I joined." Rubinowitz stated, "Bryan Smith was the stand-up bass player in The Tennessee Rockets and had played in The Star Spangled Washboard Band. Scotty Flowers was the drummer and introduced me to Eddie. Eddie loved rockabilly music and when I played him the tape of my songs, he got excited and said that was the kind of music he wanted to play."[27] Six months later, Angel became a member of Rubinowitz's band, The Bad Boys. Without prior rehearsal, their first gig was on January 3, 1980. Angel remembered, "All of a sudden we were the most popular band in Washington, D.C. Every place we played was sold-out, everybody from punk rockers to truck drivers. We'd go to New York City to play, and people like The Cramps would come backstage because they were big fans of Tex's. [Also in New York City], I remember opening for The Stray Cats before they were anybody. I know they had Tex's records because he talked to them. It was a real exciting [time]." Angel added, "I learned a lot from Tex. He was like a rock and roll philosopher. His philosophy was rock and roll was the first music that was non-exclusive, which meant it was for everybody [while jazz and classical music was directed toward a specific audience]. Tex really brought into focus what rock and roll was and what it meant. The talent that I had with him was always in me; he just brought it out. His favorite guitar player was Link Wray. Through Tex, I became a total devotee of Link. Before our shows, Tex would always play a tape of Link Wray, and then we worked up a bunch of his instrumentals. We used to do 'Rawhide,' 'Run Chicken Run,' and 'Jack the Ripper.'" They played together until Rubinowitz quit the music business in 1986.

In 1980, Eddie Angel joined Tex Rubinowitz's band. They soon became the hottest act in Washington, D.C. (author's collection).

Wray and Rubinowitz were named as Angel's musical influences, along with Chuck Berry, The Beatles, Gene Vincent's original guitarist Cliff Gallup, and Elvis Presley's first guitar player Scotty Moore. Angel remarked, "I've gotten to meet Scotty. I made it a point to go down to where he had a [tape duplicating service]. I went there and was just hanging around. When he walked in, that's when I flipped out. [I got tongue tied]. It was like the next thing to meeting Elvis. The music that they [Elvis Presley and the Blue Moon Boys] are responsible for just blows my mind. Scotty's paid me some very nice compliments. I played on Marshall Chapman's *Dirty Linens*, and she gave a copy to Scotty. He said something [to the effect] other guys try to sound like him, but I am him." Years later, on October 15, 1999, Nick Willett opened for Kid Rock and Hank Williams III at the Bluegrass Inn in Nashville. Willett's band featured Angel on guitar, Brad Ber on bass, and Jimmy Lester on drums. That evening, their set list consisted entirely of early Presley tunes, which included "Too Much." That particular song is one in which Scotty Moore has commented that he could never again duplicate its guitar solo. Due to the fact that they had done so many takes, he couldn't remember what he had played. Incidentally, Willett sent Moore a copy of the recording, which was available on his CD, *Off the Record*. Moore mentioned to him that the live show reminded him of Elvis Presley's shows at the Eagle's Nest in Memphis. He and bassist Bill Black had backed him on those dates.

In 1989, vocalist Sonny George and guitarist Angel formed The Planet Rockers in Nashville. Bassist Mark Winchester and drummer Phil Swartz were added later. Angel explained, "I had moved to Nashville in 1986 with Jeannie and the Hurricanes, who had gotten a record deal with CBS. [Their lead singer was a gal who sounded like Wanda Jackson.] We all got day jobs to pay our way and were here a year before we got an offer [to record]. Then another year [went by]. It seemed like all we ever did was sit in offices and talk to lawyers, managers, or record company people. We never played. All of a sudden, I went from playing all the time to once every two months. We were [signed] but then unceremoniously dropped. I was kind of at a crossroads. I thought if this is the music business then I don't want any part of it. I then made friends with a guy named Mike Smyth. He was a record collector and dealer, originally from London, who was looking to open a record store. He was my best friend, and he was telling me not to quit. Mike said, 'There's this guy that comes into the store a lot who's looking to start a band. His name is Sonny.'" Introductions were then made. Angel added, "Sonny and I got together and learned some songs. We needed a bass player and drummer and didn't know who to get. At the time, there was nobody in Nashville who even knew what rockabilly was. I met Bill Swartz through Jimmy Lester, another drummer [who eventually played for Los Straightjackets]. I met Mark [Winchester] by coincidence. We were doing a video shoot with Becky Hobbs. He had just moved from North Carolina and was looking for something new. We ended up all rehearsing at Mike's store, [then the gigs started rolling in]. Basically, Mike shaped the repertoire [because all of our songs came from his record collection]. He's probably got the best rockabilly record collection in the world. He had a big influence on us."

Paul Kennerley, a successful country music songwriter, quickly became a fan of The Planet Rockers: "He flipped over us. He thought we were the greatest thing since sliced bread. He was like, 'I want to record you guys.' We went into his home studio, and he produced the first record. [We then needed a label], so Paul brought the head of MCA Records to one of our gigs in Franklin [Tennessee]. The guy said, 'Look Paul, I can't sign these guys. They're not country.'" Angel added, "We met Barney Koumis, and he put our album out on No Hit Records." 1991's *Coming in Person* is Angel's favorite: "That's the one that I think has the best songs and the best sound."

From 1990 to 1992, The Planet Rockers frequently played around Nashville and traveled to England a few times, which included a gig at the Hemsby Rock 'n' Roll Weekender. Angel commented, "In 1990, we went to London and played the Town and Country Club with Ronnie Dawson and Mac Curtis. That was pretty cool and an introduction to the English rockabilly scene. We were amazed, had never seen anything like it. Every night of the week there was something going on, like a record hop where they played rockabilly. I think the English had a lot to do with finding out about Charlie Feathers, Sonny Burgess, [and all the rockabilly artists]. [They helped make rockabilly accessible to everyone]. The English are known for being anthropologists, studying other people's cultures. It took a while for them to warm up to us because they didn't know who we were. The first time we kind of got a cold reception, but now I think they consider us one of the best bands of that time." After three albums, The Planet Rockers called it quits. Winchester left to join Emmylou Harris. However, in recent years, the original lineup has reunited a few times. The group even recorded a new album, *The Return of The Planet Rockers*, at Phillips International Recording Studio in Memphis. The German record label, Witchcraft Records, will issue the latest CD.

In 1994, Angel started his own label, Spinout Records. He originally issued 45 rpm singles on The Planet Rockers and The Neanderthals. Later, he released CDs, including *Hunkerdown* by The Legendary Shack Shakers.

In regard to Los Straightjackets, "We [Danny Amis and I] wanted to do an instrumental band. [The group had started in 1988 as a trio—Angel, Amis, and Jimmy Lester—but soon disbanded. They reunited six years later and added bassist E. Scott Esbeck.] Danny had the Mexican wrestling masks, and he just loves Mexican culture, so he came up with the whole shtick. [The group wears identical black clothing, gold Aztec medallions, and individualized Mexican masks.] My contribution was that I always loved playing instrumentals, and I had [written] a lot of songs. When we started Los Straightjackets, it was just for fun. I thought we would be a local average band that maybe played once a month. That's the irony because I thought The Planet Rockers would hit the big time. " Los Straightjackets have played numerous festivals, have appeared on *Late Night with Conan O'Brien*, and have released thirteen studio albums. In 2003, the band was nominated for a Grammy for their album *Rock 'n' Roll City*, which was a collaboration with Eddy Clearwater.

Even though Angel has enjoyed the most success with Los Straightjackets, he has worked with a who's who in the music industry. There used to be a gospel show that would be showcased right after the *Grand Ole Opry*, and on one Saturday night in the late 1980s, Angel played it with Martha Carson: "She was already a star on the *Grand Ole Opry*, but Elvis was on one of her early tours along with The Wilburn Brothers and Hank Snow. [Incidentally] Elvis recorded [her song] 'Satisfied,' but it has never been released." Angel has also backed Robert Gordon in the studio, on his 2004 CD, *Satisfied Mind*: "He's an amazing singer, probably has the greatest voice I ever heard." In 1994 and 1995, Angel toured with rockabilly legend Ronnie Dawson: "He was one of my closest and dearest friends in the music business. I wrote songs and recorded with him too." In 1997, Angel did a number of shows with Link Wray: "That was a thrill. Link would sit down and tell me stories. He was one of the sweetest people I ever met."

These days, Angel is kept quite busy, usually juggling two bands at once. However, he has also done several shows and recorded two albums, *Eddie Angel Meets The Beatles* and *Eddie Angel Plays Link Wray*, as a solo act. Angel admitted, "I'd rather be in a band. It's fun having other people around to take the pressure off. I was pretty nervous about [going solo] because I wasn't sure if I was gonna stink or not. All I ever wanted to do was be in a band; I didn't want to be the star. If you're in the music biz your whole life you realize it's such a financially unstable way to make a living that you have to keep busy. I got lucky with Los Straightjackets. They are the first band that allowed me to really make a living. I love playing music, so I guess that's what motivates me now."

Billy Hancock

In the late 1970s, the Washington, D.C., rockabilly scene was thriving with artists such as Danny Gatton, Robert Gordon, and Tex Rubinowitz. Billy Hancock has shared show dates with all three. He had this to say about Gordon: "He's a great guy. Robert's like my brother."[28] However, Rubinowitz and Hancock played together the most and appeared on one another's albums: "I met Tex back in the '70s at a place called the Cellar Door in Washington, D.C. We put rockabilly shows together for about a year." They would each sing a set with the same backing band. It was upon Hancock's recommendation that Ripsaw Records signed Rubinowitz. He recalled, "Tex was so different." When Rubinowitz formed his band, The Bad Boys, Hancock forged ahead with the Tennessee Rockets. In the liner notes for *Shakin' That Rockabilly Fever*, Tapio Väisänen stated, "From 1978 to 1980, the Tennessee Rockets nailed some of the best examples of pure authentic rockabilly music to be recorded in the USA at the time."[29]

Billy Hancock was born on November 4, 1946, in Washington, D.C. His father was a freight agent for the Southern Railway while his mother was a retail salesperson for various record stores, including Waxie Maxi. At five years old, Hancock was introduced to rhythm and blues, jump blues, and country through records that his mother brought home. Some of the artists that he heard were Roy Brown, Amos Milburn, Johnny Otis, Roy Milton, Louis Jordan, Hank Williams, Sr., Cowboy Copas, Hank Thompson, Hank Snow, Slim Whitman, Webb Pierce, and Lefty Frizzell. Hancock continued his musical education by tuning into radio stations— WARL in Arlington, Virginia, WPIK in Alexandria, Virginia, and WUST in Washington, D.C. He recalled, "As a little kid, my mother used to make me sing songs for my aunts and uncles. It embarrassed the hell out of me, but I did it."

Before enjoying a successful solo career, Billy Hancock played alongside guitar virtuoso Danny Gatton in Danny and the Fat Boys (courtesy Billy Hancock).

At twelve years old, he started taking guitar lessons: "My mother showed me all three chords that she knew—G, C, and D7. Then she said, 'Well, that's my extent of guitar knowledge. Now, I'm sending you off.' I can play guitar very well because I had a teacher, Frank Mullen, who was a contemporary of Charlie Byrd and Barney Kessel. When I started taking lessons, there was no such thing as rock and roll guitar players." His parents were very supportive: "They're the reason I got into it." In 1958, Hancock sang publicly for the first time: "When I was twelve, I played at the Whippoorwill Lake Festival in Warrenton, Virginia. There I sang Carl Perkins' 'Your True Love' in a talent contest." Four years later, Hancock began his singing career. He disclosed, "I started out playing beer joints in and around Washington, D.C., and Alexandria, Virginia. From there I went to Greenwich Village in New York City, and I played four nights a week at a place called Your Father's Mustache. On my nights off, I would hit all the bucket house clubs for kicks, such as The Gaslight, The Bitter End, and The Village Vanguard."

Hancock admitted that he has many musical influences, but Carl Perkins ranks high on the list. In the 1950s, he saw him appear on a local television program where Perkins sang "Blue Suede Shoes" and told his mother, 'That's what I want to do.' She said, 'You wanna do what?' I said, 'I want to learn how to play guitar and play with Carl Perkins.' She laughed and replied, 'Oh, all right.' Little did she know that in a couple of years I would be learning to play guitar and in another twenty I'd be playing with Carl. I probably played with him a hundred times. One time at the Bayou in Washington, D.C., he sent his son, Greg, to get the family Bible. Carl opened it and showed me all kinds of pictures from the March 22, 1956, automobile crash. He was sure the head injury that his brother Jay sustained in the accident led to the tumor on his brain. Jay was never right after the accident, had double vision." Buddy Holly, 1950s era Elvis Presley, and Charlie Feathers were also cited as influences: "Buddy was the biggest influence on my entire life. I thought I would die when he got killed."

At seventeen, Hancock took up the bass. He disclosed, "I was playing in a band, and we got fired because they got someone better. That used to happen a lot. I went down to see them, and they had a great guitar player, named Mike Boyd. I found out that they were looking for a bass player. I applied for the job, but I didn't have a bass. In fact, I had never held one in my life. They asked me to audition, so I got my dad to co-sign for a Fender Precision Bass and a brand new Fender Bassman amp. I stayed up all night long—listening to records, playing every line, and memorizing everything I could think of. I went down and made the audition. They thought that I had been playing for years. I never told them that I learned how to play overnight." Jimmy Edwards was the lead singer. Hancock played with him for six months before they left Edwards and went to New York City. There they changed their name to The Monarchs and signed with Kapp Records. Unfortunately, there was already a group with that name who had a hit, "This Old Heart": "They threatened to sue our record company if they didn't pull our record, 'Some Other Guy' b/w 'Behold.' The label conceded and changed our name back to The Stingers. After that, we lost momentum, and Kapp lost interest in us." Hancock returned to Washington, D.C., and teamed up with Danny Gatton, whom he had met through Boyd. Danny and the Fat Boys were popular locally: "We played together almost every day for seven years." Tragically, on October 4, 1994, Gatton killed himself with a self-inflicted gunshot wound: "I saw that coming as he had tried it twice before." In recent years, Turkey Mountain Records remembered his legacy by issuing a three-CD box set, entitled *Danny Gatton and the Fat Boys' Scrapbook*. On it, there are seventeen unreleased tracks.

Besides Gatton, the rockabilly revivalist has played with a who's who in the music industry: "I've played with just about everybody." In the late 1960s/early 1970s, Hancock backed Gene

Vincent on several different occasions. He recollected, "In the summer of 1968, I played with Big Joe Turner at the Peppermint Beach Club in Virginia Beach, Virginia. They needed a band to back him for a week. He was tremendous. In 1973, I opened for Bruce Springsteen at the Childe Harold in Washington, D.C. He just had one album out, *Greetings from Asbury Park*, and so the rest of the tunes he did that night were cover songs. Two of them were by Buddy Holly—'Listen to Me' and 'Rave On.' He adores Buddy. Bruce claims that before every performance he sits down, relaxes, and listens to Buddy Holly for at least fifteen minutes. He says, 'I always listen to that man. It keeps me honest.' Bob Dylan will say the very same thing. I love Bruce, and I think his music is honest. I really liked the guys in his band too. I became instant friends with his bass player, Garry Tallent. [Incidentally, Hancock taught Tallent how to slap on electric bass. He can make an electric bass sound like an upright.] In October 1974, I brought Amos Milburn to Washington, D.C., to play. On the bill, I added some of his old friends—The Clovers and Bull Moose Jackson. I played bass in his band, and it was a great night. On my first album, *American Music*, with Danny and the Fat Boys, I wrote [a song entitled] 'A Tribute to Amos Milburn.' Amos loved it as it was the first time that anybody really acknowledged him. He was just so glad. I also backed Charlie Feathers. He was a one of a kind guy. I worked with Roy Buchanan, and every time Dale Hawkins would come within a hundred miles of D.C., he would make sure that he dropped by. Roy would say, 'I got a call from Dale. He's coming down tonight.' I'd say, 'Oh great. We always have fun when he does.' I'd make Dale do my favorite song, 'La-Do-Dada,' which he always felt was such a stupid song. I met Dale on several occasions, and he was a super nice guy. In 1983, I worked with Rick Nelson at the Roosevelt Hotel in Hollywood, California. He was a really humble, nice guy. I saw him many times in concert, including the Steel Pier in Atlantic City in 1962."

In 1979, Hancock recorded an album with Fats Domino, which was released a year later as *Fats 1980*. "The guy who originally produced Lloyd Price gave me a call and said, 'I want you to play bass on this stuff.' I said, 'I'll be right there.' Mitch Collins was also on the sessions since he played piano along with Fats. Fats was one hell of a cook. He would always stay in a hotel suite and bring food to the sessions that he had made from his own recipes. I got him to write down his recipe for jambalaya."

Mitch Collins was one of the Tennessee Rockets and appeared on Hancock's album *Shakin' That Rockabilly Fever*. Jeff Lodsun and Evan Johns were also featured players. According to Hancock, "When Danny and the Fat Boys split up, I grabbed Lodsun and Collins. The first bass player was Don Mulkey, and he's on 'Rootie Tootie,' 'Do It If You Wanna,' 'I Can't Be Satisfied,' and 'You Pass Me By.' I found Bryan Smith, who was the second bassist, playing with a bluegrass group. As a matter of fact, I taught Bryan how to slap the bass. He was playing right next door to where I was, and when we were both on break, I said, 'Do you slap bass?' He said, 'No, I've seen it done, but I don't.' I just took his bass and showed him how." Hancock continues to use the name of the band even though there are different members now. One at a time, each member left Hancock—first Lodsun, then Smith, and finally Bob Newcaster left in 1983.

Ripsaw Records originally didn't want a Billy Hancock album: "They just wanted me to try a single. However, the first single did so well that it led into an album. They had seen me play with Danny and the Fat Boys and back then I was known as a producer." The band started recording the sessions in August 1978 and then the singles started appearing that December. A single was released every six months: "Rootie Tootie" b/w "I Can't Be Satisfied," "The Boogie Disease" b/w "Knock-Kneed Nellie," "Miss Jessie Lee" b/w "I'm Satisfied," and "Redskins Rock 'n' Roll" b/w "Lonely Blue Boy." The magazine *Melody Maker*, which was the British equivalent of *Billboard*, ranked "Rootie Tootie" at number one on the English charts. Four singles were released on Ripsaw, but not an album: "I believe they were looking for a company that had more money for tour support and promotion than they had, and they found it." In 1981, *Shakin' That Rockabilly Fever* was issued on Big Beat Records and then on Solid Smoke. That same year, Hancock made his first appearance overseas, at a string of rock and roll shows in France.

Eddie Bond recorded "I'm Satisfied" while both he and Buddy Knox cut "Knock-Kneed Nellie": "I think I like Buddy's version a little bit better." Hancock had always wanted to speak with him but never got the chance: "When I was a kid, I loved Buddy's music. I think 'Hula Love' and 'Whenever I'm Lonely' were my favorites." Hancock remembered writing "Knock-Kneed Nellie" and "Rockabilly Fever" both in one day: "'Knock-Kneed Nellie' came from listening to Charlie Feathers' 'Stutterin' Cindy' and 'Tongue Tied Jill.' It seemed like Charlie was forever writing songs about impaired young women. That's what I had in mind when I wrote 'Knock-Kneed Nellie.' Charlie was very proud to tell people that he influenced the song. Tex Rubinowitz came up with the title for 'Rockabilly Fever.' He said, 'Man, I can't wait to start this tour; I've got that rockabilly fever.' I said, 'There's a song there.' I wrote those two songs in the middle of a blizzard." The writer of "The Boogie Disease," Isaiah Ross, once performed the song with Hancock at Alvin's Finer Delicatessen and Twilight Bar in Detroit, Michigan: "I brought him onstage, and we traded verses."

On March 9, 2011, Sue Moreno joined the Chris Casello Trio onstage at the Mercy Lounge in Nashville. Eddie Angel also played guitar. Hancock came down to watch. He stated that Angel told him, "'You sing 'Bad Boy,' and I'll play the guitar solo that you played on the record.' We had a lot of fun." That December, Hancock reunited with the original members of the Tennessee Rockets for one show only.

Today, Hancock has his own local TV show, which began in 2002. It is a thirty minute program that combines interviews with musical sequences. His brother, Dale, is the executive producer and director while Hancock is host and conducts the interviews: "My brother took classes on how to become a cameraman. He asked me one day, 'Billy, how would you like to have a television show?' I said, 'Tell me about it.' He did, and I said, 'Okay let's do it.'" NRBQ, Thom Shepard, The British Walkers, and disk jockeys from the golden age of rock and roll have all been featured guests. Hancock also continues to entertain audiences: "I play practically every night, more now than ten/fifteen years ago." They are primarily acoustic shows—just him and his guitar. Hancock acknowledged, "I love to perform."

The Paladins

Dave Gonzalez and Thomas Yearsley formed The Paladins while still in high school. David "Whit" Broadley and Gus Griffin rounded out the quartet. For two years (1980–1982), Broadley was the lead singer. Sadly, he passed away from complications of diabetes on July 22, 2014.

The Paladins' first few gigs were rough because no one knew what to think of the young men with leather jackets and greasy pompadours. They were bullied and chastised based strictly upon how they looked. In those early days, The Paladins played a mix of jazz, rockabilly, blues, and country, along with tunes by Buddy Holly and Elvis Presley, as well as original material. Gonzalez conveyed, "We were trying to combine blues, country, swing, soul, jazz, rock and roll, and rhythm and blues; everything that we loved into our sound. After we did our first record, The Stray Cats came out. Then more rockabilly bands started popping up. Some got into being exactly like the records used to be, and others were like us. We had a rockabilly beat and feel to everything, but we were more country or more blues than a lot of those other bands were. I'm not saying we're better or worse. I admire a lot of the bands that came out that sounded so much like 1950's recordings. We tried to get that vintage sound, and we still do, but it's just because that's the way we play."[30] The Paladins toured frequently and acquired quite a large fan base. Since their formation, they have shared show dates with X, Los Lobos, Reverend Horton Heat, Wanda Jackson, and Stevie Ray Vaughn. Thousands of show dates and nine studio albums have cemented their roots' legacy. The *Los Angeles Times* called the group "One of the most powerful roots rocking groups in the nation!"[31]

Dave Gonzalez, who was born in 1961, in Los Angeles, California, started singing at twelve years old: "When I was just a little kid, my folks gave me a guitar; I'd stand next to the record player, strum and sing along. I was lucky to have a lot of really good rock and roll records around the house along with blues, jazz, and country. [Thanks to my parents] I heard

In the early 1980s, The Paladins shared many playbills with The Blasters, James Intveld and the Rockin' Shadows, and Levi Dexter and the Rockats. Left to right: David "Whit" Broadley, Dave Gonzalez, and Thomas Yearsley (courtesy Joel Aparicio).

The Rolling Stones, The Beatles, Chuck Berry, Elvis Presley, Roy Orbison, Carl Perkins, Buck Owens, Merle Haggard, B.B. King, and Count Basie—all the good stuff. I had an uncle who played guitar and knew every single Buck Owens and Merle Haggard song. My grandmother was married to a guy who was a horn player and arranger for Stan Kenton, so she was into jazz. I loved country music and jazz from the start. When I got into rockabilly, it made me realize that I could play the jazz chords, country licks, and blues riffs all at the same time. To me, the rockabilly that I love sounds like country dudes trying to play jazz and blues with the rock and roll/rhythm and blues backbeat." In regard to playing guitar, "I started strumming around 1965, but I couldn't really play a whole tune. It was in junior high school that I really started learning my chords. In 1974, my cousin gave me an electric guitar and a Freddie King record. He was about ten years older than I and was already playing in bands. Luckily, I had a lot of older people that I knew in the neighborhood and people from school. The word started getting out, and I got a chance to play with a lot of older cats." He figured that the first song that he learned how to play was either Chuck Berry's "Johnny B. Goode" or The Beatles' "Day Tripper." At the same time he picked up the guitar, he played the drums: "It seems like any time we had a little band going in the neighborhood, the drummer couldn't make it or wasn't good enough, so I'd always end up being the drummer. Then somewhere along the line they found out I could sing, and the next thing I knew I was singing." Gonzalez can also play the bass and a little piano.

The Paladins formed in 1980. According to Gonzalez, "When Thomas Yearsley and I first met we were both high school seniors, he was the guitar player, and I played bass. [Soon after, the talented youngsters switched instruments.] We had just moved to San Diego and were looking for a band. We jammed with a lot of people and went through a lot of drummers. We could never keep a solid drummer for a long time until we got Gus Griffin." David "Whit" Broadley, who was ten years older than Gonzalez, was also added to the lineup. In fact, he co-founded the group and was the group's original lead singer: "Whit played rhythm guitar, sang, and wrote with us from 1980 until the end of 1982. He was my great friend and mentor. We had met in 1979 when I was working in a lumber yard, and he was working for a general contractor. We hit it off right when we met as he was playing a Muddy Waters cassette in his work truck. I told him I was fortunate enough to see Muddy perform live in 1978 at the Golden Bear Club in Huntington Beach, California. Whit and I became good friends and blues records collectors. [He was also a big rockabilly fan and had a lot of its records in his collection.] Whit turned me onto Johnny Burnette and Gene Vincent, among others, and that completely blew my mind. He really changed the course of my guitar playing and the rest of my musical life from that point on." Gonzalez commented, "When we started out, we got hooked on the early Sun Records' sound, which then progressed musically into the other Memphis/Southern sounds, like Stax, Goldwax, Hit, etc."[32] Gonzalez added, "Whit named us The Paladins after that TV show, *Have Gun Will Travel*. The star of the show was Richard Boone, and his character's name was Paladin." In 1981, Tim Mays became The Paladins' manager: "Whit knew Tim. Tim booked us on a gig and said afterward, 'I'd be glad to be your manager. I think we can work together.' He went onto become one of the greatest concert promoters to ever work in San Diego. He brought everybody to town who was anybody. We got a lot of chances to open up for some big artists. Tim also helped to administer our recording contract."

Gonzalez had started writing songs in junior high school, but it was upon Mays' and Mark Neill's suggestions that he got serious about it. He remembered, "They said, 'Hey, you guys are cool but don't just be a '50s cover band. Don't just play all the rockabilly standards; write some songs.' We built kind of a mini demo recording studio. We'd be in there every night, banging away at it: writing songs, making demos, and getting ready to record the next album. I'm still in pursuit of the next song, every day. The way I write songs is a real reflection of what's in my mind and heart at the time."

By then, they were touring constantly: Los Angeles, San Francisco, Las Vegas, Phoenix, and Tucson, Arizona. A 1959 Cadillac Fleetwood was their mode of transportation. The Paladins also played a punk rock venue called the Zebra Club in San Diego: "Tim was a big punk rock promoter, so we played on a lot of punk shows. Somehow we slid into that scene. I guess rockabilly has somewhat of a punk rock attitude to it sometimes. In December 1982, we went out to Texas and played at Antone's and the Continental Club in Austin. Whit [Broadley] was still with us, but after we got back to California, he told us to go on without him because he wasn't cut out for any road work." [That same year, they appeared on the compilation album *Who's Listening San Diego?* with their version of The Rock and Roll Trio's "Lonesome Train (on a Lonesome Track)."] The Paladins treated audiences to a wild stage act that included acrobatics, such as backflips: "I've been very fortunate that I've never been real hurt, but our bass player has fallen off the stage a couple of times. He bounced back every time though. I know there are a lot of bands that are wilder than we are."

The band shared the same playbill many times with Rosie Flores, James Intveld, and Levi and the Rockats. Gonzalez remarked, "Rosie was already on the scene in San Diego. She was known as the best guitar player [in town]. We started playing shows together, and she became a friend of ours. The same goes for James and Ricky Intveld and their band The Rockin' Shadows. We even did quite a few gigs where it was James, Ricky, me, and Thomas. We were great friends. I met Levi Dexter when I first came to L.A. in 1980. I had met some people at a show who turned me onto him. Levi was then the big star because he was from England, was already on TV, *The Merv Griffin Show*, and had a couple of albums out. We loved him and still do. I think he's one of the greatest showmen, and he's been at the top of the scene forever." By late 1983, Griffin had quit the band. Scott Campbell replaced him on drums.

In 1987, Kim Wilson co-produced their self-titled debut album. They had made his acquaintance when they opened for The Fabulous Thunderbirds. Gonzalez stated, "We were big fans of The Fabulous Thunderbirds, and people were latching onto The Paladins. We were getting a lot of good gigs at the time, which included a whole bunch opening for them. We initially asked Jimmie [Vaughn] if he would do it, but he turned us down. Then we noticed just about every night when we played, Kim would hang out, stand on the side of the stage, or come back to talk to us. He said, 'Hey, if Jimmie doesn't want to do it, I'll do it.' I really felt having a great singer like him as our producer would be a good thing. Alongside him on that record was another great producer, Mark Neill. He's the guy we started with and who put us on the map. Mark really knew how to get the rockabilly sound. One of the good things about working with him was he'd catch the track when it was the right one, which kept you from overdoing or underdoing it." Neill had worked with The Paladins on their compilation contributions, which included 1983's *Best of L.A. Rockabilly*, and also recorded and produced their first 45 rpm single, "Slippin' In" b/w "Honky Tonk All Night." There were two producers on the first album because the group started to record with Neill in late 1985 and then went to Texas and got Wilson to do a session with them. Gonzalez revealed that there wasn't much overdubbing when recording with Neill: "Occasionally, we'd have to do a harmony vocal, an extra guitar part, add a rhythm guitar or extra special guest. We always approach everything with everybody playing at the same time to get the track and get the feel. We've never been big on overdubbing. We were always saying, 'Hey, we want all the mikes up, and we're gonna cut this all at the same time like our heroes did.'"

Nineteen eighty-seven also provided them with the chance to open for Stevie Ray Vaughn on New Year's. Gonzalez recounted, "He was a great guy. We exposed a lot of people to rockabilly music." They also worked with B.B. King: "He liked that we were kind of bluesy and gave us a big opportunity by playing with him many times."

Gonzalez acknowledged, "There's a certain magic to the first album as we were young and hungry. It was a fresh scene, and we wrote a bunch of songs. We were pulling a brand new sound out of the air while thinking about all of our heroes." Incidentally, that debut release was issued by Wrestler Records, and they never received a dime from sales. Thankfully, they weren't with the label for long. Alligator Records showed interest in The Paladins and bought out their contract. Two albums were released on Alligator: 1988's *Years Since Yesterday* and 1990's *Let's Buzz*. The latter CD featured Lee Allen on saxophone: "That was one of the highlights of my whole life. I still get chills when I hear Lee on that record."[33] By this time, Yearsley was no longer with the Paladins; Joe Jazdrewski had joined as bassist. Gonzalez remembered, "Alligator Records gave us a lot of freedom. They let us pick our own producer. [Founder] Bruce Iglauer really loved us but knew we weren't a blues band. He was really more into his Chicago blues band sound. He said, 'Hey, I gave you guys the best shot I could. You sold a lot of records for me. Everything's cool, but I think you guys should do your thing, and I should do mine.' That's what we did, and there were no hard feelings when we left."

In 1988, The Paladins received an invitation to play overseas: "The very first gig we played in Europe was in Oslo, Norway. Scandinavians loved Americana: blues, country, and rockabilly. The promoter brought us over and booked us for a couple of weeks. Then we flew down to Holland and played on a big blues show with Koko Taylor. Another promoter was at that show, loved us, and brought us back again." Since then, they have played fifty times in Europe.

The Paladins have had many drummers over the years: Gus Griffin, Scott Campbell, Brian Fahey, and Jeff Donovan. Gonzalez revealed, "Jeff was with us for five years, and for the first two years he played with both us and Dwight Yoakam at the same time. Dwight was red hot but decided to take a little time off, so that's when Jeff came with us. Then Jeff decided to get off the road, wanted to just stay at home with his wife and son. That's when Brian came back, and he's been with us ever since."

In 2002, The Paladins went their separate ways. Gonzalez stated, "I was in search of another sound and more work in the studio [instead of being on the road so much]. I had the chance to work with a great singer named Chris Gaffney, and it was an opportunity that I couldn't turn down. He had played accordion one time on a Paladins record, and we had played quite a few gigs together. I was a big fan of his. I really wanted to play more country music and have a bigger band, which would include steel guitar and piano. Finally, Chris and I started writing tunes and cutting demos. [Hacienda Brothers were born]. I then sent a song to Dan Penn. He came out to Tucson, recorded and produced our first record, 2005's *Hacienda Brothers*. As the Hacienda Brothers, we made four records in five years. We were in the studio a lot. Chris kicked my butt into being a better guitar player and harmony singer. If I did sing a lead vocal, it was very difficult to get up there after he did because he was so great." The other members of the group were Dave Berzansky on steel guitar, Hank Maninger on bass, and Dale Daniel on drums. In 2007, they were nominated for Group of the Year by the American Music Association and played the *Grand Ole Opry*. Unfortunately, tragedy struck the band when Gaffney passed away on April 17, 2008, from liver cancer.

The Stone River Boys were born out of the Hacienda Brothers. Gonzalez said, "Basically when Gaff got sick, we had a lot of bookings. People were starting to do benefits, to try and raise money for Gaff and his wife. [He had wanted to do those bookings and give the money to Gaffney, but the band agreed it wasn't the same without him.] I decided to go to Texas and recruit some of my friends who were big fans of The Paladins, Hacienda Brothers, and Gaffney. Mike Barfield knew Gaff as they were both on HighTone Records. He agreed to do it. Dave Biller, one of my favorites on steel, said yes. Kevin Smith came along on bass, and Tom Lewis played drums. We had an all-star lineup. We did that first tour to get money together for Gaff. Everybody pitched in, and we cut two songs in a studio in Nebraska. Then Gaff passed away. Mike and I were talking about it, and Mike just loved the way the recording came out, so I told him, 'Hey, let's make a new record.' We called it the Stone River Boys. We went out and finished that record and pounded the pavement pretty hard for three years." Smith was not a permanent member of The Stone River Boys but was rather replaced by Scott Esbeck.

These days, The Paladins reunite on occasion, although they were quite active in 2014. Its current lineup is Gonzalez, Fahey, and Yearsley. On January 4, 2014, The Paladins performed at The Rhythm Collision Music Fest and Car Show at the American Legion Club in Riverside, California. On June 13, 2014, they played the Observatory in Santa Ana, California. In July 2014, they participated in the Rock Baby, Rock It Weekender, which was held at the Continental Club in Houston, Texas. In October 2014, they played the Great Southern Blues Festival in Australia. Gonzalez declared, "It's fun to get back together and do it every once in a while. We had a real good run, and we're glad people still want to hear us play."

Jerry King and the Rivertown Ramblers

Jerry King and the Rivertown Ramblers were a five piece traditional rockabilly band based out of Cincinnati, Ohio. Having formed in early 2003, one of their greatest honors came when they shared the playbill with Sonny Burgess and the Pacers, Billy Lee Riley, Scotty Moore, Stan Perkins, Ace Cannon, Billy Swan, and D.J. Fontana at the Sun Studio 50th Anniversary Show. In 2012, the band went on hiatus. It's unclear whether or not they will reunite even though there is a strong desire to tour again. For now, fans will have to be content with their four released studio albums.

Lead singer Jerry King, whose real name is Jerry Girton, was born on October 13, 1975, in Madison, Indiana. He explained, "We came up with the stage name King because of Elvis

Presley and King Records."³⁴ King grew up listening to Presley's music since his mom is a huge fan. He first heard and enjoyed his '50s tracks: "[Then], on my own, I started looking for other '50s artists and thought, 'Wow I really like this stuff.' I found Carl Perkins, Jerry Lee Lewis, and all the main Sun [Records'] guys. Then I started getting more and more into obscure stuff." As far as singing, he began in a Pentecostal church at the age of eighteen. At that same time, he took up the guitar: "I always played an instrument. When I was twelve, I started playing the drums. I even played in church, [so naturally the music was more gospel influenced]. I can play a little piano but not well, and also upright bass." The Rivertown Ramblers' bassist, Jeremiah Brockman, would disagree with that assessment: "Jerry is one of those multi-talented and versatile people. You could hand him a tuba, and he'd be playing it in five minutes. It drives me up the wall. He can play piano; he plays guitar. He can play my bass, and he's an excellent drummer. Plus he just has a real nice set of pipes. Jerry's good at doing hiccups. I think he works on that. What a great musician he is."³⁵

Jeremiah Brockman was born on July 18, 1974, in Cincinnati, Ohio. At age twenty-three, he started playing bass: "I'm completely self-taught with some pointers from other bass players. I just watched other people and saw what they did. I also got a great video called *Slap Bass: The Ungentle Art* by Mark Rubin and Kevin Smith. That showed me a lot of techniques. I never took any formal music lessons. I wanted to play rockabilly music with the intention of getting an upright, but that was just a little bit out of my price range, so I got an electric bass first. I learned to play electric and played it for about six months before I was able to get a beat up old upright bass. I had to drive to Rhode Island in my little Geo Metro to pick it up because I couldn't find anybody to ship it. [I knocked the bass' neck off,

On April 11, 2005, at the Rockin' 50's Fest in Green Bay, Wisconsin, Jerry King and the Rivertown Ramblers sang Charlie Feathers' "Tongue Tied Jill" with assistance from his children Wanda and Bubba. From left: Bubba Feathers, Dave Johnson, Jerry King, Jeremiah Brockman and Wanda Feathers (author's collection).

which was hanging out the car window, when I hit a tree.] That was the end of that one." Of course, he later got another: "I'd like to get a lot more practice, but I live in an apartment. Right when I hit a note with the pegs sitting on the floor, it reverberates throughout the whole apartment. I shake the place. It's hard to do that if I want to keep the neighbors on my good side. I mess around with the guitar, but you don't wanna hear it. It's a hard instrument that I'd like to learn how to play."

Punk music was Brockman's passion before rockabilly changed his life: "I was just a kid trying to find something else to get into because I was sick of punk rock. I kind of stumbled into rockabilly through bands like The Cramps, Reverend Horton Heat, and The Stray Cats. I'll never leave the rockabilly scene. I love the music, the people, and the style." Before creating The Rivertown Ramblers, Brockman was in a band with Caroline Gnagy of The Casey Sisters, which was called Caroline and the Cowtown Playboys. In 1998 at a show in Lawrence, Kansas, he sold merchandise for their opening act, Kim Lenz. Shortly thereafter, Gnagy became Lenz's road manager. Brockman also played for a short time with another rockabilly group, The Stardevils.

The Rivertown Ramblers were King's first professional band. The combo formed in early 2003, but he didn't join until March. They didn't even have a name when King signed on to sing lead: "Bassist Jeremiah [Brockman] and guitarist Jason [Roeper] started the band. They had Jayson 'Chewy' Clarke as singer, but they decided that wasn't going to work. He ended up playing rhythm guitar. Then Scott Cheesebrew was going to front the band, but they never did any shows that I'm aware of, just rehearsal. For one reason or another that didn't work out. Jeremiah and I knew each other. [They were once brother-in-laws since Brockman was married to King's sister.] I mentioned to Jeremiah how I'd like to start a band. He's like, 'Well, basically I've already got something started. Would you like to come and try being the singer?' I started singing for them, and we picked up drummer Dave Willman. Within a month, we were out playing gigs."

King's parents and his sister were all supportive of his talent: "My mom tried to go to as many [shows] as she could. My dad lives in Tennessee, and he enjoyed our stuff too. Every time we recorded a new CD, I sent him a copy. When he came to visit, he definitely came with me to a gig."

The band enjoyed success around the country and regular bookings in the Midwest, which included Tavern on the Bend in Cincinnati, Ohio. Brockman recalled, "Our contract with them was for once a month, and we'd play for four hours. It's murder on your hands. I'd get blisters all over them." Another place they played was the Southgate House Revival in Newport, Kentucky. King declared, "The first rockabilly song I sang in the Rivertown Ramblers was [Roy Orbison's] 'Mean Little Mama.'" Their set always began with that particular tune. Brockman acknowledged, "We almost always closed with 'Money Honey.' It usually got pretty wild with us jumping on things and kicking stuff. 'Raging Sea' was another real fun song to do." The band might be the only one to have ever tackled "Suspicious Minds" in a rockabilly style. King conveyed, "Somebody came up and asked for it, so we gave it a shot. We were just fooling around as we had never done it before." Brockman disclosed, "Jerry could do a real nice Elvis tribute. We got a lot of requests around our area for Elvis, Buddy Holly, and Chuck Berry, but we did more obscure stuff." The Rivertown Ramblers' original tune "Go Fast" was one that audiences seemed to like.

Although King admitted that he was a little shy, one would never guess it by his most wild performance to date at the Rockin' '50's Fest II in Green Bay, Wisconsin. On April 11, 2005, The Rivertown Ramblers tore the roof off the place and was one of the highlights for many attendees. Charlie Feathers' children Bubba and Wanda were in the audience and were called onstage to sing their father's tune "Tongue Tied Jill." Incidentally, a studio version appears on the band's second album. As far as his stage antics are concerned, King commented, "Rock and roll was wild and crazy back then, and I tried to play it with the same enthusiasm." Presley had his gyrations and floor routines; Sonny Burgess formed human pyramids and jumped off three foot stages, and Billy Lee Riley sang on top of pianos. King showcased a lot of the same zeal in his performances by standing atop tables, hanging from rafters, and lying on the floor without missing a beat. Brockman commented, "I think we had more injuries than any other band." King fell off tables while Brockman lost his balance on the bass: "I'm gonna have to tone it down because I give myself whiplash when I'm playing. Most of the time that I'm rockin' my head back and forth, jumping around, and kicking things I hardly even know I'm doing it because I just get so excited about the music that I'm playing. I think that I kind of lose myself. When I'm around my house, I'm a pretty tame, calm guy. It's when I get up there playing the kind of music that I love to play, something just clicks in me, and I go a little crazy." King declared, "I fell down a lot and sometimes it hurt."

The band wanted everyone to have a good time, but on a rare occasion, the audience got a little too involved. Once at a show in Athens, Ohio, King remembered, "We were playing, and a guy had gotten naked [in front of the stage]. He didn't have a stitch of clothing on. I was laughing so hard that I couldn't keep singing. That was kind of embarrassing." King acknowledged, "I just love the music. There are other kinds out there that I guess I could play, but I never cared to play anything else. I really don't have a definition. I just know rockabilly when I hear it, but if I were to play two songs to tell someone what it was, they would be Elvis' 'Good Rockin' Tonight' and Charlie Feathers' 'One Hand Loose.' Those [tunes] embody rockabilly." Brockman commented, "Rockabilly is a big slappin' upright bass, minimalistic drums, a wild frantic singer, and a wild guitar man. There's a lot of Bill Haley stuff that I don't think is rockabilly, but somebody else might. It's real hard to pigeonhole it, and say this is rockabilly and that isn't."

King named Presley and Feathers as his musical influences along with Carl Perkins and Johnny Horton. Presley also tops his list for favorite singers along with Roy Orbison ("love to hear him sing a ballad") and Marty Robbins. King disclosed, "I wish I could have met Charlie Feathers. I would like to meet Gene Maltais. I think he recorded like six songs, but all of them are fabulous. I've never gotten to see Lew Williams. I know he played in Green Bay [Wisconsin], but it was a different night than us, and I had to go back to work. I'd like to meet or play with him because Lew had some crazy good stuff. His songs from the '50s are just phenomenal. I hear he's one of the best older guys still doing it." Brockman remarked that his musical influences were Charlie Feathers and former High Noon bassist Kevin Smith, while his favorite singers are Feathers, Gene Maltais, Sparkle Moore, Mac Curtis, and Benny Joy. Smith tops his list for someone he admires. Brockman also looks up to Pete Midtgard from the Twistin' Tarantulas ("Their stuff is a little heavy for me, but Pete blows me away."), Steve Buckel ("He's an excellent bass player, who took my spot in The Stardevils."), Bill and

Johnny Black, and Bob Moore. Brockman recollected, "I met Marshall Lytle [bassist for Bill Haley's Comets] briefly. I didn't get a chance to talk to him much. It seemed like whenever I went to see The Comets play, they'd just get mobbed afterward. I had wanted to get some ideas on bass playing from him because he was a pioneer, genius, and innovator."

Sun Studio and its recording artists also had a major impact on the group, so they decided to record their first two albums, 2003's *The Sun Sessions* and 2004's *Out of This World*, and part of their third, 2006's *A Date with Jerry King and the Rivertown Ramblers*, at the historic landmark. King admitted that standing in the same spot that Presley stood was awe-inspiring: "To go in, think about all the people who recorded there, and all the great music that was produced just gives you goose bumps." Brockman recollected, "We had a blast. The engineer, James Lott, really knew what he was doing and did an excellent job. We only had so much time to put down the tracks, so we really tried to get down to business. [However] every once in a while we'd have a couple of minutes in between songs to just kind of soak it all in. There's something about that place that's magical. It sends shivers down your spine [to record there]." They never intended on returning to Sun for their second album. Brockman mentioned, "We were going to record at Jewel Records but had equipment problems. They didn't have some stuff that we would have liked to have had. We went back to Sun because we were real happy with how our first CD turned out."

In regard to their first time in the studio, King revealed, "I liked *The Sun Sessions* because there was a lot of raw energy on it." Brockman added, "The first song we recorded was 'Mean Little Mama,' and I was still just a little bit nervous. I liked how it came out though. We did that in one take. I didn't feel like I was totally in the groove until somewhere in the middle of the session. That's when we recorded 'Crazy Woman,' which is my favorite. 'I Want Your Lovin'' rocked pretty good. We did that song on maybe two or three takes. By the end of the night, I might have been a little too loose. There was even some stuff that was left off the CD." King wrote three songs for *The Sun Sessions*: "Evelyna," "I Want Your Lovin'," and "Go Fast" and co-wrote "West, South" with Jayson 'Chewy' Clarke: "The band started in April, and we recorded in May; otherwise, I would have had more originals. I wrote those three songs real quick. [Brockman said he wrote them a week before the recording session]. We were in such a rush to put out product to sell." Upon issuance, there was an accidental error with the Canadian printers, in that the songwriters were not acknowledged. King penned more tunes for their second release, *Out of This World*. "Six Feet Deep" is a song about dying: "It's got an upbeat tempo, and I didn't even think anybody would catch that. I just thought it would be funny." "Cadillac Frame" compares a girl to a car, while "You're Swell" is an ode to a 1950's catchphrase. "2, 3, 4 Time'n Daddy" is a shout out to their bassist Jeremiah Brockman. As for their third album, King acknowledged, "We took a lot of time with *A Date with Jerry King and the Rivertown Ramblers*. I like to rock out, but I really enjoy recording ballads, like 'Price of Love.'"

Over the years, there were a few lineup changes. The band originally consisted of Jerry King on vocals and rhythm guitar, Jayson "Chewy" Clarke also on rhythm guitar, Jason Roeper on lead guitar, Jeremiah Brockman on upright bass, and Dave Willman on drums. Willman was replaced by Dave Johnson in 2004; guitarist Jon Pidgeon temporarily played from 2004 to 2005, and Kris Merritt took over bass playing duties, on and off from 2005 to 2009. Due to work commitments, Brockman wasn't able to participate in the 2005 Viva Las Vegas

Weekender, so Steve Buckel took his place. On occasion, pianist Blair Carman backed them on show dates. At the time, he was too busy with his own career to be made a permanent member.

The bandmates had side jobs as well. King sometimes played guitar for Carman and Ace Brown. In October 2003, Brockman backed Gene Summers and Glen Glenn at the Overton Park Shell in Memphis, Tennessee: "I loved playing with Glen. That was a real highlight." He has also played bass with Bill Watkins: "He's a super sweet man who's a lot of fun to work with." The house band at the former Hernando's Hideaway in Memphis, Tennessee was led by Bubba Feathers, and they sometimes invited Brockman onstage to sit in. He remembered, "When we [The Rivertown Ramblers] recorded our first album down there, we got up and did a set. I think of Bubba and Wanda as really good friends. I met Wanda at the Rockin' '50's Fest in Green Bay, Wisconsin in 2002 and then that same year I went to the International Rockabilly Festival in Jackson, Tennessee where I really got to hang out with her a lot. Charlie Feathers is my all-time rockabilly hero so being able to play with his children makes me feel good." Feathers' "One Hand Loose" is Brockman's favorite rockabilly song, which he owns on a scratchy 45 rpm record: "I'm a big record collector. I like to go to thrift stores, flea markets, and antique malls and hunt for old 45's. I find '50s rock and roll records, come home, and blast them on my record player. There's nothing like the sound of vinyl."

In September 2010, after a performance at the Shake the Shack Rockabilly Ball in Seattle, Washington, Jerry King and the Rivertown Ramblers stopped touring regularly. They reunited a couple of times for special occasions, including a wedding reception in 2012. However, that was the last time they shared a stage. King's involvement in law enforcement prevents him from such luxuries: "I didn't think I was giving up music when I left, but my job is remote and there are things about it that make playing inconvenient at best. If I can find a decent job back home, I'll go right back to it."[36] Even if The Rivertown Ramblers are never heard from again, King's talent and love for rockabilly has been passed down to his two sons. His oldest, Christopher, fronts his own three piece combo called the Chris Girton Band. In fact, on May 11, 2014, he teamed up with Brockman, Roeper, and Johnson to perform a reunion of sorts at the Southgate House Revival in Newport, Kentucky.

Jai Malano

For decades, Texas has been a hotbed for singers and musicians. This fact can be challenging for those who want to be discovered. Jai Malano is one of those singers who hope for superstardom. Unlike many of her contemporaries, she was a late bloomer, having started professionally showcasing her vocal talents at age twenty-nine. Since then, Malano has performed regularly with The Royal Rhythmaires, but now she is preparing for a solo endeavor. There are very few African American females on the roots music scene, so her talent and showmanship will more than likely stand out.

Jai Malano was born on May 12, 1981, in Tallahassee, Florida. Besides her presence in the family, Malano has a brother and two sisters: "We all played instruments coming up in school. I played the flute; one of my sisters played the clarinet, and my brother played the saxophone. My mother was a choir director, and my father sings. He has a beautiful voice but doesn't sing professionally. About six months ago, I purchased a keyboard, and I've just kind of been messing around with it. I'm nowhere near where I would like to be, but I have composed one song. I don't have any lyrics for it, but I've saved it in the [keyboard] memory."[37]

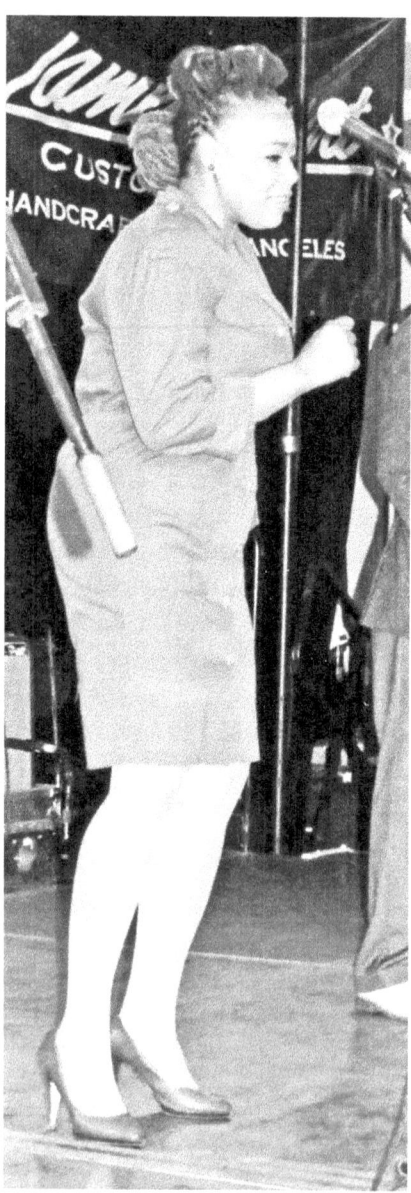

Even though fans might recognize Jai Malano as a rhythm and blues songstress, she cites a variety of influences, which include Elvis Presley, Ruth Brown, Amy Winehouse, and Beyoncé (courtesy Don Rieck).

A month before her thirtieth birthday is when Malano finally got the courage to share her vocal talent publicly. She didn't have any club or solo experience prior to that open mike opportunity. Malano revealed, "The friends I was with said, 'You can sing. You should show them and get up there.' I was like, 'Uh, I don't know. What if I hit a wrong note? Y'all think I can sing, but they might not think I can sing.' I asked the band if they could play [Etta James'] 'At Last,' and they said, 'Yeah, what pace, what rhythm, and what key do you want?' I said, 'I don't know where to start. You can start on E flat. Follow my cue, follow my rhythm; let's just be creative onstage.' It was just one song, but the audience loved it. That's kind of what prompted me to think I could really be successful at this. I applauded the band for their work and then we just went our separate ways. We didn't exchange information."

Malano added, "Two weeks later, I went onto the internet and found The Royal Rhythmaires on Craigslist." The band had posted an ad looking for a vocalist. She joined the group in 2010, three years after its formation by founders Douglas Brown and Ed Cannon. Malano admitted, "I don't think they had a permanent singer. They had a bunch of different people that would get up and do stuff with them occasionally. We just kind of found each other at the perfect time." Prior to Malano's arrival, The Royal Rhythmaires had backed various artists, including Gene Summers and Big Jay McNeely.

The Royal Rhythmaires are a five-piece rhythm and blues band that is comprised of Alex Hernandez on baritone saxophone, Douglas Brown on tenor saxophone, Daniel Porter on piano, and Ed Cannon on upright bass. For now, Jai Malano is their vocalist: "I sang in my high school choir for extra credit, but as far as singing, writing, being in the forefront, having a little bit more creative control, and doing it from a professional prospective, [this is my first experience]. I didn't really think it was something I could do and be successful at. I also didn't think that I was very talented vocally; I still have my doubts. [However], I try to cover male or female vocalists who I can compete with or who I can at least match. I love to do stuff by Aretha Franklin, Etta James, and Little Richard, but I try to stick with songs that will complement my vocal style."

Malano cited Etta James as one of her influences along with Tina Turner, Ruth Brown, LaVern Baker, Big Maybelle, Big Mama Thornton, Elvis Presley ("not for his musical or vocal capabilities but more for his ability to entertain the way that he does"), Elton John, and Rod Stewart. Beyoncé Knowles and her sister Solange would also be considered influences but "not for their vocals but rather for their ability to entertain and their ability to tap into a bunch of different markets and capitalize on them." Malano admires their business savvy. She acknowledged, "I have so many influences that it's hard to name them. I really, really love roots, rhythm and blues, and soul. Even though, I'm not a purist in any sense. I love artistry, and I love musicians. I just love anyone who can get up there and do something with passion and be good at it."

Every weekend, Malano meets with the other members of The Royal Rhythmaires for rehearsals and gigs in Fort Worth, Texas, which is over three hours away from her current city: "We average two to three shows a month. I never go onto any stage assuming that the sound is gonna be the same. A lot of times the sound guys are not at the sound board. They'll fix it but then something will happen, and they're not there for you. I have learned to count while I'm singing so that even if I can't hear myself or my band members, I know a certain word is on a certain number. You just adapt, to prevent yourself from becoming frustrated. We haven't toured overseas as much as we would like to, but we have done a lot of gigs." One of their regular bookings is at the Scat Jazz Lounge in Fort Worth: "We like to refer to it as home because we play there once a month. The crowd, the staff, and the club owner love us, and we love all of them in return. It's just a really good atmosphere."

Due to work constraints and family obligations, the male members of the combo are not able to tour much outside the state of Texas. Plus, dealing with promoters in regard to salary and travel expenses have proven challenging: "It seems like a small band when you're around these guys everyday but when it comes down to talking about money and travel, we're not a small band at all. It's easier for me to just pick up and go." However, the group enjoyed the opportunities to play the Viva Las Vegas Weekender in April 2012 and April 2014 and the Rhythm Riot in the United Kingdom in November 2013: "Going to England and seeing it just really solidified what everyone else had already told me. It was everything that I could have imagined and more. I loved the way that everyone was so welcoming and eager to hear us. It was like finally we're in a market where people really, really love and understand the music that we do." Since playing the Rhythm Riot, she's received other offers to play overseas.

Besides live appearances, Malano has also recorded two albums with The Royal Rhythmaires: 2013's *Shuck and Jive* and 2014's *Talk to Me*, which were recorded at Fort Horton Studio in Austin, Texas. With producer Billy Horton, each album took two days to record using vintage equipment: "We go through every song with no overdubbing. We try to do the best we can, not to make any mistakes. Two days of that is very exhausting, but Billy is really, really good at what he does. As far as recording and knowing how to use the equipment the way that they do, Jimmy Sutton and Billy Horton are the only two people that I can think of." She would love to record at Sutton's Hi-Style Studio: "If I go into his studio, I would like for him to have his hand in it because I've heard what he can do. He is pretty amazing."

Band members Cannon and Hernandez arranged a deal with Rhythm Bomb Records in Germany. Therefore, the studio tapes were sent to the record label for release. Incidentally, the band's contract is for one CD issuance at a time. That same label showed interest in Malano as a solo act. That effort will include all original songs. She explained, "I enjoy what I do with the band, but I had my own dreams before I joined. I was gonna get to Europe and work with Amy Winehouse. I just really was in love with her, her style and her talents. I would also love to work with Adele, Duffy, and Little Richard. The Royal Rhythmaires are totally supportive, and I appreciate that." Currently, she is choosing songs and picking a band for her solo release. Malano added, "I would love to record 'Night Time is the Right Time.' I just love [Ray Charles'] version of it. I've always wanted to do that song, but I can never find anybody to do it with me. I can't do both vocals. I would also love to do any song by Aretha Franklin." She also wouldn't mind adding tracks by Etta James, especially her ballads, and Amy Winehouse. On YouTube, Malano has posted her versions of Winehouse's "Valerie" and James' "I'd Rather Go Blind."

Original material is an integral component to a singer's development. Malano understands this concept: "I love music of the mid '50s and late '60s. I feel that was the time of real musicianship, real artistry. The lyrics during that time are amazing because they tell stories. That is what I try to do with my writing style. I don't think music should just be about the rhythm. I think every song needs to have a message; especially if it's going to be a song that I'm gonna sing. I started out writing poetry and writing for my campus newspaper, and somebody told me that I was a good writer. They said, 'Well, you know you can write music.' I said, 'I don't know how to write music because music has to have a rhythm, a melody, and a harmony. I don't know how to turn my words into a song.' Even though I started writing songs, the first ones were so stupid and corny that I was embarrassed to tell anyone that I had written them. Eventually, I got the hang of it. When I write songs, I've already gotten my melody. I'll record myself singing the songs. I write the lyrics down and send Alex [Hernandez] an email with the demo. He can then read it as he is listening. I can't arrange, so he's basically just transcribing the melody that's already in place. On the first album, I wrote a song called 'Johnston Brother.' It's about a man who constantly cheats on his wife. The song 'Party Time' is about prostitutes, but you would never guess that by listening to it. 'Cajun Boy' is about a naïve girl in the South who comes across a master manipulator. He pretty much destroys her life and finally she realizes that he never was a friend of hers. On the second album, I wrote 'Treat Me Like a Dog' because people treat their dogs better than they treat the average person. 'Talk to Me' is basically about how you don't have to do anything for me except hold a conversation and not try to get something out of the deal." She writes the originals while the band chooses which songs to cover by other artists. Etta James' "Tough Lover" was one of the cover tunes. She has sung onstage the following songs: Ruth Brown's "As Long as I'm Movin'," Big Mama Thornton's "Hound Dog," and LaVern Baker's "I'll Never Be Free."

If Malano's career continues to progress as she hopes, then she has no qualms about quitting her day job: "I work as a parent educator, working with families of small children. [Two hours a week, I go into the home to discuss health, safety, discipline, and schooling.] Unfortunately, there is no handbook on how to be a parent. I work for a company that kind of provides that service to people." Even though Malano loves her job, her main passion is music: "I don't want to sound or perform like anybody. I want to be an original, doing songs that sound good and that compliment my voice. I also want to give people what they want to listen to."

Chapter Seven

International Rockabilly Performers

Junior Marvel

Like many of his contemporizes, Junior Marvel's style, look, and sound were heavily influenced by Elvis Presley. In fact, his stage name is an ode to the hillbilly cat. Since 1988, Junior Marvel has been a staple on the rockabilly scene, playing to enthusiastic crowds at the Screamin' Rockabilly Weekender in Spain, the Rockabilly Rave in England, the Rockin' '50's Fest in Green Bay, Wisconsin, and Ubangi Stomp in Spain. Besides his own appearances, several of his fellow rockabillies, like James Intveld, Big Sandy, and High Noon, have called him onstage to sing at their gigs. The most difficult performance he ever had to play was an unusual request: "Patrick Ouchène and I played some songs while on the same stage as the coffin that contained our friend. When we stopped playing, he was taken for his last ride to the cemetery."[1]

Junior Marvel was born on June 10, 1965, in Venlo, the Netherlands. Incidentally, James Intveld lived across the street from where he was born. Frank Marquez is Junior Marvel's real name. His stage alter ego is an ode to Marvel comics: "When Elvis was a child, he used to read comics, especially the ones about Captain Marvel Junior. It was my idea because I always wanted to do something to honor Elvis." Junior Marvel has been singing for as long as he can remember: "My mother even wrote on the back of a photograph, when I was just a few months old, that I was always singing. Amongst the first songs I sang were Frank Sinatra's 'Strangers in the Night,' Guy Mitchell's 'Singing the Blues,' and Johnny Ray's 'Yes Tonight Josephine.' They were in my father's record collection, between the Spanish and Latin American vinyl. When I was seven years old, I sang 'Borriquito,' which played on the record player in my classroom. I was already a fan of Elvis Presley's, but I wanted to please my father." At fifteen, Junior Marvel attempted to play the guitar: "It didn't work out until some friends showed me how. Roger Corneille and his father taught me the basics. [Incidentally] Roger is the guitarist on my *Mess Around* CD. The first song I learned to play was Elvis' 'That's All Right.'" Junior Marvel added, "I played some other instruments for a while, including slap bass in The Bellhops and the blues harp, which was just for fun, but I never had the motivation or time for real practice. I was not the type who could sit for hours in my bedroom practicing. I was restless, so it was easiest for me just to learn the words to songs and find the right chords. I was satisfied banging out my three chords and belting a rockabilly song."

It's no surprise that he first learned how to strum a Presley tune since the hillbilly cat is his biggest musical influence: "I was six years old when I first heard 'Jailhouse Rock.' That song was the eye opener, and when I saw him on TV, I went berserk, especially when he sang '(You're So Square) Baby I Don't Care' by the swimming pool [from the movie *Jailhouse Rock*]. From that day forward, I drove my mother and father crazy. Although, she did make me the jersey he was wearing in the movie. The only thing they forbid me to do was comb my hair that way. [However] since I was thirteen, I have worn my hair in a fifties style. [He admits that] starting out it looked more like Count Dracula's hairdo. When I bought Elvis' records and saw the photographs, I started to roll up my jeans, and I tried to find clothing that looked like his. I [eventually] became a collector of '50s clothing." Junior Marvel acknowledged that he's also a huge fan of Gene Vincent, Eddie Cochran, Johnny Burnette, Bill Haley, Hank Williams, Sr., the complete Sun catalog, rhythm and blues, hillbilly, and country: "I have a lot of other influences, but I don't want to say any names because I'll forget important people, [but a few would be Johnny Cash, Johnny Horton, Louis Jordan, and Big Joe Turner]. I heard all of these musicians on the U.S. military radio shows that were broadcasted for GIs stationed in Germany. I used to tape these shows when I was very young [from sixth through ninth grade]."

Junior Marvel jammed with friends before his first official band, The Shaking Silhouettes. Then, in 1988, he went with The Bellhops. At that time, he began songwriting: "I wanted to stand out because most of the bands played the same songs in the same style. I always had pen and paper with me. If I had a good idea, I wrote it down immediately [whether that was on milk cartons or his clothing]. I kept all these ideas, and on a good day, I would try to piece them together. I wrote so much material that I'm still recording my own songs. I don't have any real stories behind any of them, except for 'Bop '56,' which is a tribute to Gene Vincent and 'Hi-Fly Bop,' which is dedicated to Elvis Presley." While with The Bellhops, he backed several legendary rockabillies, including Ray Campi, Johnny Powers, Eddie Bond, and Sonny

The critics have raved that Junior Marvel's albums sound so authentic that they find it hard to believe that the material wasn't recorded sixty years ago (courtesy Junior Marvel).

Burgess. In 1993, he started The Del Tones with Rolf Hartogs on guitar. In between bands, Junior Marvel played with Bugaboo Tang and Cat Rhythm.

In 1994, he formed The Hi-Flyers, which is still his regular band. Junior Marvel explained, "I knew Nils [Becker] and the guys when they played in The Bopstreet Boys. Sometimes I replaced their singer when he couldn't make it to a gig. I really loved Nils' guitar playing and said that if he ever needed a singer that he should call me. Well, a few years later, he did." The current members of The Hi-Flyers are Junior Marvel on vocals and rhythm guitar, Nils Becker on lead guitar, Maico Mastjoshusman on drums, and Bernd Scheffer on upright bass. In their twenty years together, there have been a few other members: Uwe Tenfelde, Huey Moor, and Alex Wolfruhm all took turns playing bass while Be Bop Joe played drums for a while. Junior Marvel added, "I never went solo. I only ask other bands to back me when The Hi-Flyers are not available. I always preferred the traditional route, especially when all the neo-bands came around in the '80s. I didn't like the new versions of rockabilly. I especially disliked psychobilly. In my eyes, they were turning beautiful songs into something ugly. I decided then, that if I had the chance to play in a band, it would sound like the originals, and I have always stayed true to that. I don't want to disappoint organizers, so if they book me, I'll give them a good show. You have to be different and bring variety to your set lists, so I like to mix rockabilly with some jazz, blues, and country." His favorite rockabilly cover tunes are The Rock and Roll Trio's "Train Kept a Rollin'" and Clint Miller's "Bertha Lou."

After a few tours in Spain, he was booked to play the Screamin' Rockabilly Weekender in June 1997. Junior Marvel acknowledged, "I became friends with Leo Castro, who has a very good radio show, and Carlos Diaz, the owner of El Toro Records and organizer for the festival. Carlos asked me to record some songs for El Toro, so I started to send outtakes for their compilations. Finally, I got the green light for my own album. I had planned for a long time to record my favorite rhythm and blues song, Ray Charles' 'Mess Around.' I also wanted it to be the name of the album. Glenn Corneille would have guested on pumpin' piano, but just two weeks before recording; he got killed in a car accident." On the sessions, Roger Corneille played guitar; Jaako Bucholtz played slap bass; JJ Slijk played rhythm guitar, and Maico Mastjoshusman played drums. K.C. Byrd engineered using vintage recording equipment. Junior Marvel added, "We recorded *Mess Around* live, and in only three sessions, without a decent rehearsal. I never had a contract with El Toro or any other label. I don't want any commitments or limitations."

Besides engineering the *Mess Around* sessions, K.C. Byrd played lead guitar for Junior Marvel and The Hi-Flyers when they backed Sun recording artist Jack Earls: "When I warmed up the show, the crowd went berserk. They went even wilder for Jack. Right after that wonderful concert, a real tragedy happened, our bass player Uwe's baby girl died in his arms. Years later, I met Jack in Green Bay [Wisconsin]. We spoke, and he asked how Uwe was doing. I was surprised that he remembered my name. Jack is the finest and most down to Earth person I've ever known in the rock and roll scene. He was my favorite artist to work with, and I will never forget him."

Music keeps him busy, but Junior Marvel finds time to enjoy his various collections. He conveyed, "I have lots of 78s, 45s, and LPs. The 45s and 78s are mostly U.S. pressings, and my Sun singles are my favorite. My record collection is huge and my pride and joy. I only have a few CDs, except for Elvis' that I can't find on vinyl. I want to have everything that Elvis recorded, especially from the '50s. 1950s clothing is also a big passion. I used to have one of the finest collections in Europe, but three years ago, I had to throw away sixty percent of it due to moth holes. That was one of the most painful experiences [I've ever had]. I'm buying [vintage] clothes again for appearances and daily use, but now I also buy reproduction. Thirty years ago, it was a piece of cake [to find vintage clothing] and for super low prices, but it's not so easy anymore. I also have many autographed photos, ninety percent of which were given to me. Before I divorced my second wife, I restored a house from 1935. It had a lot of artifacts, furniture, and collectibles, and I was very proud to have owned an original kitchen designed by Raymond Loewy."

In 2013, Junior Marvel joined forces with The Hi-Tombs, so currently he is juggling two groups at once. The Hi-Tombs are Fredo Minic on lead guitar, Mike van Lierop on upright bass and vocals, Henk van Lieshout on drums, and Junior Marvel on rhythm guitar and vocals. He revealed, "On some occasions, I play with pick-up bands, such as The Barnstompers or Little Boy Arnold and His Western Oakies, but that's more difficult because I have to focus on the band. [When that happens] I choose simpler songs and hardly play my own compositions. It's more mainstream material. With The Hi-Flyers, I only have to take care of my singing and playing; I can work more on my stage act."

Mars Attacks

Legendary Sun Records artist Sonny Burgess had a trumpet on his original 1950s recordings, so Jerry Chatabox, promoter of the Rockabilly Rave, thought that backing from Mars Attacks would be an ideal pairing. Guitarist Martin Telfser explained, "When he heard our *Dirty Tricks* CD, Jerry called and asked if we wanted to back Sonny. We said, 'Of course we want to!'"[2] They both were then booked for the 2004 festival. Many other bookings with Burgess followed, including gigs in England, France, and Germany. After the Rockin' '50's Fest II in Green Bay, Wisconsin, they did a short American tour together. Riedberger mentioned, "Sonny is very friendly and so easy to work with. He really is a very cool man. My favorite songs of his are 'We Wanna Boogie,' 'Ain't Got a Thing,' and 'Fannie Brown.'"[3] Incidentally, the songs Telfser enjoys performing with Burgess the most are "Red Headed Woman" and "Sadie's Back in Town." Besides their own bookings, they also have an act in which the lead singer Roland Riedberger and Barbara Clifford team up to do a Johnny Cash and June Carter Cash tribute. In fact, in 2007, an album was released to reflect that project.

Roland Riedberger was born on May 7, 1975, in Chur, Switzerland. As a youngster, he began singing, citing Elvis Presley as his biggest influence. In fact, when he started playing guitar at seventeen, the first song he learned was Presley's "Don't Be Cruel." Ten years earlier, Riedberger was already adept at playing trumpet.

Martin Telfser was born in 1974, in Austria. He first heard rock and roll thanks to his parents' records of Bill Haley, Elvis Presley, and Fats Domino. His mom and dad continue to be supportive of his musical endeavors. In 1985, Carl Perkins' television special, *Blue Suede Shoes: A Rockabilly Session* cemented Telfser's love for the genre. Soon after, he discovered

Some of Sonny Burgess' early Sun recordings prominently featured trumpet, and Mars Attacks has helped him recreate that sound today. From left: Oliver Pfanner (upright bass), Roland Riedberger (rhythm guitar), David Karlinger (drums), and Martin Telfser (lead guitar) (courtesy Martin Telfser).

the music of Johnny Burnette, Big Joe Turner, Slim Harpo, Muddy Waters, Elmore James, Hank Williams, Sr., and Johnny Cash. Compilations from Sun, Decca, Imperial, and Chess Records also expanded his musical horizon.

Telfser commented that Scotty Moore, Grady Martin, and Carl Perkins were his musical influences. At seventeen, he learned a few chords and became more serious about the guitar two years later: "The first song I wanted to play was 'Johnny B. Goode,' but of course I couldn't, so I started with a two chord seventies song."

He has written quite a few songs for the band, including "I'm Gonna Buy Me a Ticket," "Dirty Tricks," "You'll Never Break Me," "Deep Down in the Mud," "Tattoo Bop," and "Leavin' It All Behind." Telfser admitted, "I started writing when I was twenty years old. Most of my songs have a true story behind them." Riedberger acknowledged, "I began writing when I was twenty-four years old." Some of the songs he has penned for Mars Attacks are "She's the Girl," "Heartbreaking Man," "I Gave You My Life," "I Don't Know," and "Please Can You Say."

In February 1998, Mars Attacks was formed. Their traditional rockabilly sound differs from other bands because it features trumpet, which is a very rare addition. Telfser recollected, "All of us had other bands we played in, but we were looking for something exciting, new, and fresh—wild and authentic rockabilly."[4] They tour two to three times a month, but if they are working on new material they will book more frequently. Its current members are Roland Riedberger on vocals, rhythm guitar, and trumpet, Martin Telfser on lead guitar, Oliver Pfanner on upright bass, and David Karlinger on drums and harmonica. Riedberger lives in Switzerland while the rest of the band live in Austria, but thankfully they are only an hour apart from one another. Telfser commented, "Usually we practice once a week, but that depends on how often we play or if we are preparing new songs." As a band, their inspiration comes from many different artists, but mainly Johnny Burnette and Carl Perkins.

Armadillo Records issued their first two albums then they switched to Blue Lake Records. Telfser conveyed, "We were introduced to the studio owner, Juan Rodriguez, by Armadillo Records. Everything is recorded live onto vintage equipment (two track tape recorders in mono), and the sessions usually take place over one weekend." In April 2011, Part Records issued *Recaptured!*, which is a re-recorded compilation of Mars Attacks' out of print albums, *Run for Your Life* and *Dirty Tricks*. According to Telfser, "We took the songs that we liked most and added two bonus [tracks]. I think the songs are now really sounding the way we sound live."[5] In March 2013, Mars Attacks released their sixth studio album, *Blood and Thunder*. Even though most of their material is original, they occasionally record cover tunes. Telfser recollected, "When we cover a song, it's usually one that we can put our own stamp on and that works very well for us at live shows."

Mars Attacks have backed others besides Sonny Burgess, and they include Billy Lee Riley, Narvel Felts, Rosie Flores, and Roddy Jackson. Telfser commented, "We backed Narvel twice. The first time was at the Rockabilly Bombardment in Austria and then at the Good Rockin' Tonight Festival in France. He is a very nice guy and very professional. It was quite a challenge to learn his stuff because it's not the usual rock and roll progressions. I always love to play live. All over the world, we've had some great experiences. It's great to have played all the countries in Europe, the USA, and Australia."

Lil' Esther

The rockabilly scene in Holland is alive and thriving thanks to Lil' Esther, The Tinstars, Miss Mary Ann, The Barnstompers, Annita, Junior Marvel, and Sue Moreno. Lil' Esther revealed, "We've got rockin' clubs, like the Cruise Inn in Amsterdam, and festivals that happen every year."[6] Sometimes, if the gals are on the same show, they will sing a song or two together. In fact, both Miss Mary Ann and Lil' Esther participated in a tribute to Janis Martin at the Rockabilly Rave in 2010. It was later filmed and released as *Love Me to Pieces*.

Lil' Esther, whose real name is Esther van der Meer, was born on November 22, 1964, in Leiden, the Netherlands. The vocalist proclaimed, "My sister, Judith, and I started singing at a very young age [Esther at seven, Judith at eight] in a choir called The Mascottes. We did that for a couple of years until we moved to another town." Their parents liked country, Hawaiian music, and 1960s soul, so they heard a lot of that music growing up. At the age of fourteen, Lil' Esther discovered the more obscure rockabilly and rock and roll musicians through her own research: "I always liked the music my mother listened to, but when I got older I became more interested and curious about the roots and wanted to dig deeper."[7] She conveyed, "When I was nineteen, my sister, good friend, Marga, and I started The Bugaloos. We were the first close harmony girl group in Europe. After practicing for a while, we found some good musicians, which included my sister's husband Ed on drums, Errol on upright bass, and Rick on guitar. The first song I sang with them was The Fontane Sisters' 'Seventeen.'" A year later, they played their first gig in Holland. Lil' Esther added, "After playing all over Europe for a couple of years, Rick left the band and was replaced by Joe Sixpack. We played different musical styles from the '40s and '50s: rhythm and blues, jazz, western swing, hillbilly, and rockabilly. [Their set lists included material by Les Paul and Mary Ford, The Everly Brothers, The Davis Sisters, The Miller Sisters, and The Louvin Brothers.] We played together for seven years."

In May 1990, The Bugaloos shared the bill with headliners Andy Anderson, Larry Donn, and Nappy Brown at England's Hemsby Rock 'n' Roll Weekender: "We were the very first non–English/non–American band to be invited. It was a very good experience." They also released two albums, a self-titled debut in 1990 and then *In the Mood* a year later. On occasion, *The Big Bill Turner Show* featured The Bugaloos, and the episodes were filmed for release on VHS and DVD.

Lil' Esther started her career with the Bugaloos but is most recognized for her work with the Tinstars (photograph by Martine Eyzenga, courtesy Esther van der Meer [Lil' Esther]).

Upon the demise of The Bugaloos, Lil' Esther played with Jess 'n' Jill and the Sinners for two years. In that band, the vocal duties were divided first between Lil' Esther and Marga and then between Lil' Esther and Deanne. The other members included Jan van Leeuwen on drums, Tjarko Jeen on guitar, and Peter Crowfield on double bass. According to Lil' Esther, "We played '50s rock and roll. The girls dressed in leopard dresses and high heels while the guys wore vintage gabardine suits. We were quite popular and played all over Europe." She then joined The Ranch Girls for about a year: "Working with Miss Mary Ann was very nice. We had a lot of fun together." During that time, Lil' Esther was also travelling a lot with The Tinstars. She eventually chose to focus strictly on the latter band. With The Tinstars, she transferred her attention from harmony singing to a solo act: "One day, someone wanted to book me for some shows, so I used The Tinstars as backing."[8] That was the beginning of a twelve year partnership.

As far as musical influences, Lil' Esther cited Kay Starr, Ella Mae Morse, Patsy Cline, Ella Fitzgerald, Billie Holiday, Janis Martin, Wanda Jackson, and Barbara Pittman. The Everly Brothers and The Andrew Sisters also had a large impact on her style. Singing is her mainstay, but Lil' Esther plays a little rhythm guitar, mainly at home when she's practicing new songs or with friends at jam sessions.

She has never written any songs as her concentration and passion lie in singing; however, she has various songwriters contribute: Don Cavalli, who penned "The Garden of Love," "So Far from Me," "Gone Is My Mind," and "Arguments and Alibis"; John Lewis, who wrote "Small Change"; and Big Sandy, who gave her "Confusin' Love" and "Love That Man." She exclaimed, "I'm very proud that all these fantastic musicians have been willing to write me songs." In regard to Cavalli, Lil' Esther commented, "I met Don a long time ago at a show in Paris [France] with The Tinstars. We loved each other's music, started to talk, and quickly became friends. When I began to work on songs for my first album, *In the Garden of Love*, he sent me a tape [of tunes he had penned]. I picked out a few that fit best [stylized them], and then recorded the four songs on two albums. I have some more of his songs that I plan to record in the future."

Lil' Esther continues to tour and record regularly with The Tinstars. In fact, she was once married to their lead vocalist Rick de Bruijn. Recently, Lil' Esther started a new project, a band called The Bugalettes, which feature three female vocalists in close harmony: Dee-Ann, Deanne, and her. The group is a continuation of her old one, The Bugaloos, only with new members: "We still have some rehearsing to do, but it's working out very well." Even though she's sung in many different bands with various styles, she admitted, "I just love to sing them all, from rock and roll to big band to jive to everything in between. Each genre has its charms and a completely different [approach to singing]."

Jack Baymoore

In 1959, Sun artist Ray Smith recorded "Rockin' Bandit." Even though Jack Baymoore and the Bandits have performed that song in concert, the band's name is not paying homage to the tune. Since 1989, Baymoore has been on the rockabilly scene, and he continues to impress both fans and fellow artists. In fact, Jerry King's favorite younger artist is Baymoore: "The European guys are really ahead of the genre as far as rockabilly goes."[9]

Jack Baymoore was born on February 3, 1966, in Uddevalla, Sweden. Kent Vikmo is his real name: "Years before starting a band, I came up with the name (Jack Baymoore). [Then I just used it for those purposes.] My last name translated from Swedish to English is Vik=Bay and Mo=Moor. I added an e and suddenly had an English sounding last name. Kent is English too, but I wanted something else. I thought Jack sounded cool, and it's a name that you can say without knowing a person."[10] As a kid, he played his father's original 78 rpm records and 45 rpm singles, which included Little Richard's "Good Golly Miss Molly" and Elvis Presley's "Mean Woman Blues": "My dad had some great records but never played them." When Baymoore was twenty-three years old, he started singing publicly. The first tune that he sang was Eddie Cochran's "Twenty Flight Rock." Rockabilly music surrounded his youth: "While my friends were listening to Kiss, I listened to Elvis [Presley], Jerry Lee [Lewis], and all the 1950s music that was available to a ten-year-old kid in Sweden. In 1979, the movie *Grease* arrived here, which I liked, and then the big rockabilly revival with The Stray Cats and Robert Gordon, who played on Swedish national television." He was also familiar with Shakin' Stevens, who had major hits in the early 1980s. Baymoore added, "There has never been any other music for me."

Baymoore cited Elvis Presley, Hank Williams, Sr., Big Joe Turner, and Johnny Cash as his biggest influences although he admitted that there are hundreds of fantastic artists that inspire him. He picked up the guitar after learning how to sing: "I was very influenced by the television miniseries *Elvis: The Early Years*. It came to Sweden in 1993 [three years after its American debut]. The show starred Michael St. Gerard, and in the first episode he [as Elvis] recorded 'My Happiness' for his mom, Gladys. I bought a guitar and learned how to play and sing that song. Even though, I can only play chords. That's what happened in my first band, Blackout, I couldn't play an instrument, so I had to do the singing." Blackout's other members included Uno Eiving on bass, Olof Larsson on drums, and Urban Axelsson on electric guitar: "Uno and I were old pals from the biker scene in Sweden. [They both rode vintage Harleys.] The band was together from 1989–1996, and we played some festivals, but mostly rock and roll gigs at car clubs and night clubs. Our first gig was at a biker party in spring 1990." Three years later, Blackout's LP, *Stop That Clock*, was released: "The recordings were done here in Sweden. Then we went to Amsterdam to do a gig and deliver the material." Baymoore wrote some of the lyrics for four songs, which were included on the LP. The group disbanded when Eiving and Baymoore created the Bandits.

Baymoore is one of the artists that have recorded for Tail Records: "In 1995, owner Lars Strandheim asked if I wanted to sing on a recording project with some other very good Swedish rockabilly musicians. He liked my voice, but not the neo-rockabilly style of the band I was playing with. [The new musicians] and I got together and did a rehearsal with some songs that we liked. It sounded like we had been playing together for ten years, just on the first rehearsal, so we decided to do much more than just a few recordings. [The band formed in 1996.] Tail has some nice vintage equipment, and the first recordings were very authentic [sounding] with all the songs done live. There wasn't a single overdub, and the band and I were in a very small room. [The songs were recorded analog and then transferred directly to a master for vinyl pressings.] Those are my favorite recordings because the sound was a bit unique at the time, and we got such great response. Then in 1999, Lars got some newer [equipment] and [combined] it with all the old tube gear and vintage microphones.

[One of the reasons this happened was because Baymoore wanted the tunes transferred to CD.] We took our previous vinyl recordings and put them out on CD. For our albums, *Big Boys Rock* and *Diggin' Out*, we recorded them live but had the possibility of having a single track each for guitar, vocal, etc. Before that, we all recorded on just two tracks. Overdubbing saved a lot of time and energy." Each album only took three or four sessions to complete, prior to final mixing: "We all lived some distance from the studio, so we came midday and left for home late. We usually did about four songs in a day." Incidentally, he didn't have a contract with Tail, but rather an agreement for one album at a time.

The Bandits' lineup is the same today, with the exception of upright bassist Jan Larsson, who joined in 2001. The other band members are Jyrki "JJ" Juvonen on electric and steel guitar, Antti Pihkanen on electric guitar, and Tage Pihkanen on drums. Baymoore proclaimed, "The name Bandits sounded good with Jack Baymoore, and if anyone met these guys, they would know it's an obvious name for this bunch. Our first gig was Rockin' Night in April 1996 at a boat clubhouse in Jonkoping, Sweden. We still play maybe once a month since we all have more music projects than we can handle." As a band, they have backed legendary rockabilly artists Ersel Hickey, Rusty York, and Lew Williams. In August 2013, Atenzia Records released Baymoore and the Bandits' fourth CD, *Let's Drag*. It features five cover tunes: Glenn Barber's "Ice Water," Sleepy LaBeef's "Little Bit More," Jack Lane's "King Fool," Carl Mann's "Gonna Rock and Roll Tonight," and Charlie Feathers' "Too Much Alike." Baymoore added, "The cover songs were chosen by the band members, who came up with suggestions before our first session. The female vocalist on 'Walking the Line' was supposed to have been Eva Eastwood, but she changed her mind at the last minute, so I asked a friend of mine, Paula Nyman. Paula had backed me on other occasions. I also re-recorded three songs from earlier records: 'Move On,' 'Fireball Roberts,' and 'A-V8 Boogie.' [In regard to 'A-V8 Boogie'] I was very influenced by Lou Millet's song 'Shorty the Barber.' His style of intense singing, with the ability to do a whole verse without taking a breath, was very powerful. I hadn't heard anyone recording any newly written songs in that style. I had a hot rod at the time, still do, and it's a 1929 Ford Roadster with a flathead V8 engine. In the

Jack Baymoore, known for his blend of traditional rockabilly, rock and roll, and western swing, formed his band the Bandits in 1996 (courtesy Jack Baymoore).

1940's, the hot rodders called those cars A-V8s. The Model A's only had four cylinder engines, so they were modified with a V8 for higher speed and performance. I wrote 'A-V8 Boogie,' in the Lou Millet style, about my hot rod." He mentioned that "A-V8 Boogie" was a true story, but some of the others he has written are purely fiction. He works a lot with having the right lyrics and storylines to follow the specific style, whether that is hillbilly bop, rockabilly, or rock and roll.

Besides music, Baymoore had a small role as an extra in the movie *Dogville*, starring Lauren Bacall, James Caan, and Nicole Kidman: "The movie was done, only thirty minutes from my home, in the winter of 2002. I was first asked to help with all the vintage cars that were being used in the movie, but then they asked if I wanted to [audition for a bit part]. I was a 1930s gangster, dressed in perfect vintage clothing, and drove the boss' car, which was a 1932 Cadillac limo. [It was a non-speaking part.] [Off-camera], I only spoke briefly to Nicole but got a hug and a kiss."

In 2008, Baymoore became associated with a new project, entitled *Elvis Forever*: "I was contacted by Rival Management and Live Nation about a joint [endeavor] they were working on. Henrik Aberg, who is an Elvis performer, was also contacted. [They shared vocal duties. Baymoore lent his voice to the songs from the 1954 to 1962 era as well as the "1968 Comeback Special."] *Elvis Forever* was a well-produced musical journey through Elvis' life with his first recordings in 1954 up to his last in 1977. Forty-four songs were performed in two hours." In the fall of 2008, the show made stops at concert halls throughout Sweden. In total, sixteen thousand people witnessed the extravaganza. In Stockholm, Sweden, at the final concert of that year, the show was recorded and later released on DVD. In 2009, the musical made a triumphant return, went on hiatus the next year, and then in the fall/winter of 2011 took its final bow. *Elvis Forever* wasn't the last of his encounters with the king. Baymoore explained, "*Remember Elvis* is a very small [production] with just me and piano player Ingemar Thorell. He and I have been friends for many years. We do Elvis' music intertwined with stories about his life." "Good Luck Charm," "Peace in the Valley," and "In the Ghetto" are a few of the featured tunes.

Only occasionally, Baymoore plays with *Remember Elvis*, but regularly with his other group, Tennessee Drifters. Baymoore revealed, "The Tennessee Drifters' main style is the combined sound of Sun Records' Johnny Cash and the Tennessee Two and Hank Williams, Sr., and the Drifting Cowboys. Hank used the name Luke the Drifter as an alias to record religious folk music. Tennessee Drifters' members are the original ones—Anders Johansson on electric guitar, Michael Lith on upright bass, and I sing and play acoustic guitar. In 2003, our first gig was at a small packed café. I drove a 1954 Chevrolet with the bass strapped to the roof. Unfortunately, it fell off on the way home." On April 17, 2014, Atenzia Records issued the first Tennessee Drifters' album. Five years prior to that, the group was honored with a Swedish Country Award.

Baymoore may be passionate about music, but he's a classic car enthusiast. In 1993, he and one of his friends formed a vintage motorcycle and hot rod car club called A-Bombers: "There are about ten members, and the style is authentic and custom hot rods and motorcycles from the 1930s to mid–1950s. I have four cars: 1929 Roadster hot rod, 1928 Roadster hot rod, 1940 customized Mercury Coupe, and a 1940 LaSalle convertible. Currently, I am building a new Roadster with a 1928 body and a 1932 chassis. It'll run with a 200 HP 1946

Flathead." Unlike his contemporaries Deke Dickerson and Big Sandy, Baymoore is not a record collector: "I love this music and listen to it all the time, but I put all my money into vintage hot rods and custom cars."

Miss Mary Ann

In 1989, Miss Mary Ann made her first appearance with The Ragtime Wranglers. At that time, she shared vocal duties with Caroline in The Ranch Girls. In May 1998, she released her first solo effort, an EP with "Hey Little Dreamboat," "Flying Saucer Boogie," and "Hang on Folks, Here We Go." Later that same year, Caroline decided she no longer wanted to tour and was replaced by Lil' Esther for a year. Upon Lil' Esther's departure, Mary Lou then became a permanent member. Promoters have sometimes requested The Original Ranch Girls, and they have pleased fans by reuniting. One of their most memorable shows took place in 2005 at the Rockin' '50's Fest II in Green Bay, Wisconsin. Today, Raina Thompson-Brody harmonizes with Miss Mary Ann in the newest formation of The Ranch Girls.

Miss Mary Ann was born in Delft, Holland. She disclosed, "Both my parents were singers in a choir, and my sister played the violin. At the age of six, I was sent off to choir practice. The whole purpose of singing together in a group was lost on me, and I took it as a competition of who could sing the loudest. I was asked in a friendly way to leave and maybe find a way to sing solo. To be honest, I wasn't paying much attention to what the first song was that I sang as long as it was loud enough."[11] At nine years old, she wrote her first song, which was in Dutch: "I had seen a television program about very poor children having to fend for themselves, and it upset me. I was going to set things straight and tell the world about it. The English translation of its title would be 'Injustice.'" Miss Mary Ann added, "A funny incident, a sad experience, or loving memories will get me writing. The song, 'Can You Hear It,' which I recorded with The Ranch Girls, was written about my parents. When my mother's hearing became very poor, she was given a hearing aid. My dad would pretend to talk to my mother but would get quieter and quieter. She would keep cranking the volume up on her hearing aid, and then suddenly he would say loudly, 'Can you hear me?'"

Miss Mary Ann discovered rockabilly and rock and roll through her older sister's record collection: "With further investigation, I got interested in hillbilly and western swing as well." Patsy Cline is her biggest influence although she also cited Charline Arthur and Marty Robbins. Those three are also included on her favorite singer list along with Johnny Horton, The Collins Kids, The Louvin Brothers, Jimmy and Johnny, The Dinning Sisters, and The Boswell Sisters. Incidentally, one of her prized possessions is a Nudie stage outfit worn by Lorrie Collins. It's a green gabardine shirt and skirt suit with black leather fringe and bucking Palominos on it.

At eighteen, Miss Mary Ann moved to Rotterdam, the Netherlands. Later, she made London, England her home. In 1989, The Ragtime Wranglers played for the first time with The Ranch Girls at a gig in Oss, Holland. Miss Mary Ann recalled, "Joe [Sixpack], Sietse [Heslinga], and I go way back. We were friends before we started playing together. First, we formed a group called The Greyhounds with Joe on guitar and Sietse singing, and it existed for about three years. We tried to play rockabilly, but looking back it was probably closer to rock and roll. We played songs like 'Hot Rocket' and 'Black Slacks.' [After that group], Caroline and I created The Half Pint Pygmies with two other girls because at that time there were not any female harmony groups in Holland. We sang in a doo-wop style. [They rehearsed once a week even though they didn't have a band and weren't sure of their repertoire.] Caroline and I left the group to form The Ranch Girls. She organized the gig at the Cruise Inn's D-day festival, but we didn't have a band yet, so I asked our friends Joe, Sietse, and Errol Buwalda to help us out." They teamed up and became The Ranch Girls and The Drifting Texans. Two years they played together before musicians were added, on steel and rhythm guitar, and their name was changed to The Ranch Girls and The Ragtime Wranglers. More lineup changes occurred, and now Huey Moor plays bass in The Ragtime Wranglers.

With The Ranch Girls, Miss Mary Ann's favorite song to record was "My Adobe Hacienda." "It was a real challenge to get the harmonies right." She admitted, "We record everything live in one room except for when we do harmony singing. The Ragtime Wranglers prefer it that way. A singing partner and I can turn [the sessions] into a giggle fest and for some reason this doesn't seem to amuse the boys." In 1998, Lil' Esther became a Ranch Girl for about a year: "When Caroline no longer had time to travel, we [the guys and I] asked our friend Esther if she would like to be the new Ranch Girl. Joe had played together with Esther in her first band The Bugaloos, and Esther and I were friends. [She agreed], but then her other band, Lil' Esther and the Tinstars, got very busy, and we used to tour a lot too, so she had to make a choice. Although I was sad to see her go, I still believe she made the right decision. I think The Tinstars show off her abilities as a singer." Mary Lou then became the other half of the duo, in June 1999.

In June 2013, The New Ranch Girls, Miss Mary Ann and Raina Thompson-Brody, made their debut at the Rockabilly Rave. Miss Mary Ann revealed, "One thing about singing harmony is that it is addictive if you do it with the right partner, and Raina is just that. I think fans of The Ranch Girls will love her. People, who have heard us sing, say our voices blend very well together. We are looking forward to doing lots of gigs."

Miss Mary Ann reformed the Ranch Girls with Raina Thompson-Brody, and they made their debut at the Rockabilly Rave in June 2013 (courtesy Miss Mary Ann).

Selected Discography

Alton and Jimmy

CDs

Various Artists, *Rock Boppin' Baby: Sun Rockabilly—Vol. 5*, AVI, 1996, one track by Alton and Jimmy—"No More Crying the Blues"

Various Artists, *The Very Best of Sun Rockabilly* [2 CDs], Charly UK, 1997, one track by Alton and Jimmy—"Have Faith in My Love"

Various Artists, *The Sun Records Story* [3 CDs], Snapper UK, 2001, one track by Alton and Jimmy—"Have Faith in My Love"

Various Artists, *Sun Rockabilly Meltdown* [3 CDs], 101 Distribution, 2009, one track by Alton and Jimmy—"I Just Don't Know"

Various Artists, *Feel Like Rockin': Tennessee Rock 'n' Roll* [2 CDs], 101 Distribution, 2011, one track by Alton and Jimmy—"No More Crying the Blues"

Still Shakin', Wisteria Hill Music Publishing, 2013, tracks include "Got It Made in the Shade," "No More Crying the Blues," "I Just Don't Know," "Rockin' in the Shadow of Sun," and "Looking for Someone"

Vinyl

45 rpm Singles

"No More Crying the Blues" b/w "Have Faith in My Love," Sun Records, 1959

Andy Anderson

CDs

One Man's Rock and Roll, Union Pacific, 1988, tracks include "Johnny Valentine," "Chop Suey," "Tough Tough Tough," and "The Way She Smiled"

You Shake Me Up, Sunjay Records, 2003, tracks include "Tough Tough Tough," "Tall Oak Tree," "Please Forgive Me," "All by Myself," and "Sad Notes"

Tough Tough Tough, Buffalo Bop Records, 2003, tracks include "I Got Me a Woman," "Mustang Kid," "I'm Gonna Sit Right Down and Cry Over You," "I-I-I Love You," and "Johnny Valentine"

Vinyl

45 rpm Singles

"Beautiful Weekend" b/w "Sight Seeing," Kapp, 1957

"Johnny Valentine" b/w "I-I-I Love You," Felsted, 1958

"Tell Her Yourself" b/w "Double Mirror Wrap Around Shades," Cardon, 1958

"You Shake Me Up" b/w "The Way She Smiled," Apollo, 1959

"Deep in My Heart" b/w "Chop Suey," Century Ltd, 1960

"Gimme Lock a Yo Hair" b/w "Tough Tough Tough," Century Ltd, 1960

"Long Tall Texan" b/w "You Just Wait," 1960

"I'm Gonna Sit Right Down and Cry Over You" b/w "Promise Me," Century Ltd, 1960

"San Antonio Rose" b/w "Sunset Blues," Century Ltd, 1961

"All by Myself" b/w "Tall Oak Tree," Hermitage, 1962

"Say Goodbye to Donna" b/w "We Were Happy," Cougar, 1967

"So Long I'm Gone" b/w "Sad Notes," Cougar, 1967

"Long Way to Go" b/w "Rhonda," Aerie Records, 1975

"There Ain't Nothing in the World Like a Texas Woman" b/w "Dead End Canyon," Aerie Records, 1976

LPs

Various Artists, *The Bop That Never Stopped, Volume 28*, Buffalo Bop Records, 1984, six tracks by Anderson—"You Shake Me Up," "Gimme

Lock a Yo Hair," "I'm Gonna Sit Right Down and Cry Over You," "Deep in the Heart of Texas Rock," and "Promise Me"

Eddie Angel

CDs

Ronnie Dawson, *Rockinits*, Crystal Clear, 1989
The Planet Rockers, *Coming in Person*, No Hit, 1991
The Planet Rockers, *Invasion of the Planet Rockers*, Sunjay, 1992
Los Straitjackets, *The Utterly Fantastic and Totally Unbelievable Sound of Los Straitjackets*, Upstart/Umgd, 1995
Sonny George, *Country & Western Roundup*, Hermitage, 1995
Los Straitjackets, *Viva Los Straitjackets*, Upstart/Umgd, 1996
Ronnie Dawson, *Just Rockin' and Rollin'*, Upstart/Umgd, 1996
Eddie Angel's Guitar Party, Musick Recordings, 1997
The Planet Rockers, *26 Classic Tracks*, Spinout Records, 1997
The Planet Rockers, *A Night at the Twist and Shout*, Spinout Records, 1998
Various Artists, *Halloween Hootenanny*, Geffen Records, 1998, one track by Los Straitjackets—"The Munsters' Theme"
The Neanderthals, *Latest Menace to the Human Race*, Get Hip, 1998
Los Straitjackets, *The Velvet Touch of Los Straitjackets*, Yep Roc, 1999
The Neanderthals, *The Modern Stone-Age Family*, Sundazed, 1999
Bob E. Rock, *This Is Bob E. Rock*, No Club, 1999
The Planet Rockers, *Hillbilly Beat*, No Hit, 2000
The Planet Rockers, *Live—on the Rampage*, No Hit, 2000
Los Straitjackets, *Play Favorites*, Yep Roc, 2000
Los Straitjackets, *Sing Along with Los Straitjackets*, Yep Roc, 2001
Los Straitjackets, *Damas Y Caballeros*, Yep Roc, 2001
Los Straitjackets, *'Tis the Season for Los Straitjackets*, Yep Roc, 2002
Nick Willett, *Nick Willett*, Styleline, 2002
Various Artists, *Dressed in Black: A Tribute to Johnny Cash*, Dualtone Music Group, 2002, one track by Eddie Angel—"Straight A's in Love"
The Neanderthals, *Shutdown 2002 B.C.*, Spinout Records, 2002
Los Straitjackets, *Supersonic Guitars in 3-D*, Yep Roc, 2003
Eddy "the Chief" Clearwater featuring Los Straitjackets, *Rock 'N' Roll City*, Rounder Records, 2003
Los Straitjackets, *Encyclopedia of Sound Vol. 1*, Lovecat Music, 2004
Los Straitjackets, *Encyclopedia of Sound Vol. 2*, Lovecat Music, 2004
Robert Gordon, *Satisfied Mind*, Jungle Records, 2004
Nick Willett, *Off the Record*, Styleline, 2005
Eddie Angel Meets the Beatles, Spinout Records, 2005
Young at Heart, Spinout Records, 2005
The Neanderthals, *In Space*, Spinout Records, 2005
Eddie Angel Plays Link Wray, Spinout Records, 2006
Various Artists, *Cat'n Around, Volume Three*, Pink 'n' Black, 2006, one track by the Planet Rockers—"Rampage"
Los Straitjackets with the World Famous Pontani Sisters and Kaiser George, *Twist Party*, Yep Roc, 2006
Los Straitjackets, *Rock En Espanol Vol. 1*, Yep Roc, 2007
Los Straitjackets, *Smells Like Teen Spirit*, Yep Roc, 2008
Los Straitjackets, *Los Straitjackets in Concert*, Yep Roc, 2008
Los Straitjackets, *The Further Adventures of Los Straitjackets*, Yep Roc, 2009
Los Straitjackets, *Yuletide Beat*, Yep Roc, 2009
Los Straitjackets, *Jet Set*, Yep Roc, 2012

Vinyl

45 rpm Singles

Martha Hull, "Feelin' Right Tonight" b/w "Fujiyama Mama," Ripsaw, 1980
"Lynxtail" b/w "Rampage," Rebel Riot, 1981
Bob E. Rock, "Humes High" b/w "Do You Believe It," No Club, 1986
The Planet Rockers, "King Fool" b/w "Snap Jack," No Hit, 1992
Eddie Angel's Dinosaurs, "Jurassic Beat" b/w "Caveman," No Hit, 1993
The Neanderthals, "Twinkle Toes" b/w "2000 Lb. Werewolf," Norton Records, 1995
Ronnie Dawson, "Up Jumped the Devil" b/w "No Dice," No Hit, 1996
Los Straitjackets, "At the Drive-In" b/w "Theme from Magnificent Seven," Pennimann, 2000
Los Straitjackets, "Hark the Herald Angels Sing" b/w "Silver Bells," Yep Roc, 2011

LPs

Tex Rubinowitz, *Tex Rubinowitz*, No Club, 1985

Jack Baymoore

CDs

Blackout, *Stop That Clock*, Tombstone Records, 1993

Jack Baymoore and the Bandits, *A-V 8 Boogie*, Tail Records, 1999

Jack Baymoore and the Bandits, *Big Boys Rock*, Tail Records, 1999

Various Artists, *Real Rocking Music*, Sunjay, 2000, two tracks by Jack Baymoore and the Bandits—"A-V8 Boogie" and "Too Many Women"

Jack Baymoore and the Bandits, *Diggin' Out!*, Tail Records, 2003

Various Artists, *Mera Raggar Klassiker*, Capitol/EMI, 2004, one track by Jack Baymoore and the Bandits—"To Fall in Love"

Various Artists, *RaggarRock*, Mariann, 2004, one track by Jack Baymoore and the Bandits—"Pink Dress (and a Diamond Belt)"

Various Artists, *Rockabilly*, Warner, 2009, two tracks by Jack Baymoore and the Bandits—"Move On" and "To Fall in Love"

Various Artists, *Walldorf Rock 'n' Roll Weekender Soundtrack*, Rockin' Rollin' Products, 2009, one track by Jack Baymoore and the Bandits—"Bankrobbin' Rock 'n' Roll"

Jack Baymoore & Henrik Aberg, *Elvis Forever*, Darrow Records, 2011

Various Artists, *Viva Las Vegas Rockabilly Weekend #15*, Viva Las Vegas/Tom Ingram, 2012, one track by Jack Baymoore and the Bandits-"Bankrobbin' Rock 'n' Roll"

Jack Baymoore and the Bandits, *Let's Drag*, Atenzia Records, 2013

Vinyl

45 rpm Singles

Jack Baymoore and the Bandits, "A-V8 Boogie" b/w "Saturday Jump," Tail Records, 1997

LPs

Various Artists, *Rough Tough Rockabilly Vol. 2*, Tail Records, 1996, four tracks by Jack Baymoore and the Bandits—"A-V8 Boogie," "Tag Along," "I'm Not Crazy," and "Mobilin' Baby of Mine"

Jack Baymoore and the Bandits, *Roarin' Down the Track*, Tail Records, 1997

Eddie Bond

CDs

Rockin' Daddy [2 CDs], Bear Family Records, 1999, tracks include "Rockin' Daddy," "Flip Flop Mama," "You're Part of Me," "I Got a Woman," "Double Duty Lovin'," and "My Bucket's Got a Hole in It"

Various Artists, *As Good as It Gets: Rockabilly* [2 CDs], Disky, 2000, one track by Bond—"Here Comes That Train"

Various Artists, *Rockin' Bones: 1950s Punk and Rockabilly* [4 CDs], Rhino Records, 2006, one track by Bond—"Rockin' Daddy"

Various Artists, *From Boppin' Hillbilly to Red Hot Rockabilly* [4 CDs], Proper Box UK, 2006, one track by Bond—"Double Duty Lovin'"

Various Artists, *Great Rockabilly: Just About as Good as It Gets* [2 CDs], Smith & Co Holland, 2007, two tracks by Bond—"Boppin' Bonnie" and "Flip Flop Mama"

Memphis Rockabilly King, Stomper Time UK, 2007, tracks include "Boppin' Bonnie," "Rockin' Daddy," "Slip, Slip, Slippin'-In," "Juke Joint Johnnie," "Here Comes That Train," and "The Monkey and the Baboon"

Various Artists, *Rockin' Memphis* [4 CDs], Proper Records UK, 2008, three tracks by Bond—"Baby, Baby, Baby (What Am I Gonna Do)," "Flip Flop Mama," and "I've Got a Woman"

Various Artists, *Sun Rockabilly Meltdown* [3 CDs], 101 Distribution, 2009, one track by Bond—"This Old Heart of Mine"

Various Artists, *Sun Records: Whole Lotta Shakin' Going On* [2 CDs], 101 Distribution, 2011, one track by Bond—"Rockin' Daddy"

Various Artists, *Essential Rockabilly: The Mercury Story* [2 CD], One Day, 2012, four tracks by Bond—"Rockin' Daddy," "Flip Flop Mama," "Boppin' Bonnie," and "Slip, Slip, Slippin'-In"

Vinyl

45 rpm Singles

"Talking Off the Wall" b/w "Double Duty Lovin'," Ekko, 1955

"Love Makes a Fool (Every Day)" b/w "Your Eyes," Ekko, 1955

"Rockin' Daddy" b/w "I've Got a Woman," Mercury Records, 1956

"Slip, Slip, Slippin'-In" b/w "Flip Flop Mama," Mercury Records, 1956

"Boppin' Bonnie" b/w "Baby, Baby, Baby (What Am I Gonna Do)," Mercury Records, 1956

"They Say We're Too Young" b/w "You're Part of Me," Mercury-Starday, 1957

"Hershey Bar" b/w "Lovin' You, Lovin' You," Mercury-Starday, 1957

"Love, Love, Love" b/w "Backslidin'," Mercury-Starday, 1957

"The Blues Got Me" b/w "Standing in Your Window," D, 1958

"Can't Win for Losing" b/w "When the Juke Box Plays," Stomper Time, 1959

"Boo Bop Da Caa Caa" b/w "You'll Never Be a Stranger to Me," Stomper Time, 1959

"It's Been So Long Darling" b/w "Your Old Standby," Stomper Time, 1959

"The Little Black Book" b/w "Is My Ring on Your Finger," Coral Records, 1960

"Can't Win for Losing" b/w "You'll Never Be a Stranger to Me," Wildcat, 1960

"I Walk Alone" b/w "Only One Minute More," Spa, 1960

"This Ole Heart of Mine" b/w "Second Chance," United Southern Artists, 1961

"Tomorrow I Will Be Gone" b/w "(Let's) Make the Parting Sweet," Memphis, 1962

"As Long as I'll Forgive" b/w "I Guess I've Got the Blues," Pen, 1962

"Every Part of Me" b/w "In from Stepping Out," Diplomat, 1963

"Big Boss Man" b/w "Empire," Tagg, 1964

"Monkey and the Baboon" b/w "Short Honeymoon," Diplomat, 1964

"I Just Found Out" b/w "Back to Vietnam," Millionaire, 1965

"I Can't Fight This Much Longer" b/w "Now and Then," Goldwax, 1965

"Raunchy" b/w "Cold Dark Waters," Memphis, 1965

"Here Comes the Train" b/w "Someday I'll Sober Up," Memphis, 1965

"Running Drunk" b/w "We Live in Separate Worlds," XL, 1966

"Let the Good Times Roll" b/w "You Don't Miss Your Water," Villa, 1966

"Second Chance" b/w "Buford Pusser Goes Hunting with a Switch," Tab, 1966

"Dedicated to Dwana Pusser Christmas in Heaven" b/w "Christmas Time," Tab, 1970

"The Legend of Buford Pusser" b/w "Buford Pusser," Tab, 1971

"Winners Circle" b/w "Juke Joint Johnnie," Tab, 1973

"Rocking Daddy" b/w "That Glass," Tab, 1975

"Air Watch 79" [qm] b/w "Law Enforcing Man," Deccer, 1975

"Whatever Makes You Happy" b/w "The Love of My Life," Advance, 1976

LPs

Various Artists, *KWKH: A Night at the Louisiana Hayride*, Mercury Wing Records, 1960, one track by Bond—"One Step Closer to You"

Eddie Bond Sings Greatest Country Gospel Hits, Phillips International, 1962, tracks include "Just a Closer Walk with Thee," "I Saw the Light," "Satisfied," "Where Could I Go but to the Lord," and "If We Never Meet Again"

Favorite Country Hits from Down Home, Millionaire, 1967, tracks include "My Bucket's Got Hole in It," "Blue Blue Day," "I'll Step Aside," "Mr. Moon," and "You Can't Hurt Me Anymore"

Eddie Bond Sings Legend of Buford Pusser, Enterprise, 1973, tracks include "Buford Pusser's Child," "Christmas in Heaven," "Law Enforcing Man," and "200 LBS. O' Swingin' Hound"

Caution: Eddie Bond Music Is Contagious, Magnum Force, 1988, tracks include "Another Man's Shoes," "That Glass," "Before the Next Teardrop Falls," and "Somebody That Won't Lie"

Eddie Bond Sings Carl Smith, Balser, 1989, tracks include "Let's Live a Little," "Are You Teasing Me," "Just Dropped In," and "Doorstep to Heaven"

Ray Campi

CDs

The Eager Beaver Boy—Rockabilly Lives, Bear Family Records, 1990, tracks include "Hot Dog," "All the Time," "Let 'Er Roll," "Good Time Woman," "Pretty Mama," and "Play Anything"

Rockabilly Rocket, Magnum, 1996, tracks include "Don't Get Pushy," "Ruby Ann," "How Can I Get on Top," "Cravin'," and "Separate Ways"

Ray Campi: 1954–1968, Eagle Records, 1996, tracks include "City Lights," "O Sole Mio," "One Kiss Away from the Blues," "Do You Love Me," and "Always There's One"

Ray Campi: 1954–1968, Eagle Records, 1996, tracks include "Scrumptious Baby," "Trouble in Mind," "Parts Unknown," "Billie Jean," "Butterfly," and "Here Comes That Heartache Again"

Perpetual Stomp: 1951–1996, Bacchus, 1996, tracks include "Caterpillar," "Toe Tapping Rhythm," "Cat'n Around," "Wild Side of Life," and "Tore Up"

Rockabilly Rebellion, Rollin' Rock Records, 1997, tracks include "Rockabilly Music," "Don't Blame It on Me," "Love Me," "Rockin' at the Ritz," and "Quit Your Triflin'"

At the Thunderbird Rock 'n' Roll Venue, Rockstar, 2002, tracks include "Rattlin' Daddy," "Honky Tonk Man," "I'm Comin' Home," "Hungry Hill," and "My Heart's on Fire"

The Road to Rockabilly, Enviken, 2003, tracks include "Caterpillar," "Play It Cool," "It Ain't Me," "Give That Love to Me," and "Loretta"

Rockabilly Blues, St. George Records, 2006, tracks include "Sugar Cane Mama," "Got Love If You Want It," "Mystery Train," "Mona," and "Sugaree"

Vinyl

45 rpm Singles

"Play It Cool" b/w "Caterpillar," TNT Records, 1957

"It Ain't Me" b/w "Give That Love to Me," Dot Records, 1957

"My Screamin' Screamin' Mimi" b/w "With You," Domino, 1958

"The Man I Met (A Tribute to the Big Bopper)" b/w "Ballad of Donna and Peggy Sue," D Records, 1959

"French Fries" b/w "Hear What I Wanna Hear," Colpix, 1960

"Shenandoah" b/w "Billie Jean," Winsor Music, 1963

"Civil Disobedience" b/w "He's a Devil," Sonobeat, 1968

"Eager Boy" b/w "Dobroggie," Rollin' Rock Records, 1976

"Tore Up" b/w "If It's All the Same to You," Rollin' Rock Records, 1976

"Sixteen Chicks" b/w "Pan American Boogie," Rollin' Rock Records, 1977

"My Baby Left Me," b/w "Li'l Bit of Heartache," Rollin' Rock Records, 1977

"Booze It" b/w "Wrong, Wrong, Wrong," Rollin' Rock Records, 1977

"Scrumptious Baby" b/w "I Didn't Mean to Be Mean," Rollin' Rock Records, 1977

"Rockin' at the Ritz" b/w "Quit Your Triflin'," Rollin' Rock Records, 1977

"Rattlin' Daddy" b/w "Wild One," Rollin' Rock Records, 1977

"Texas Sands" b/w "How Low Can You Feel," Rollin' Rock Records, 1977

"Caterpillar" b/w "Play It Cool," Radar, 1979

"Teenage Boogie" b/w "Rockabilly Rebel," Radar, 1979

"The Newest Wave" b/w "Once Is Enough," Rondelet, 1981

"Rockabilly Man" b/w "Hollywood Cats," Rollin' Rock Records, 1981

"Chicken" b/w "Finlandia Is Grandia," Goofin' Records, 1992

LPs

Ray Campi Rockabilly, Rollin' Rock Records, 1973, tracks include "Caterpillar," "Play It Cool," "My Screamin' Screamin' Mimi," "Long Tall Sally," "You Can't Catch Me," and "It Ain't Me"

Rockabilly Rebel, Rollin' Rock Records, 1975, tracks include "Sack of Love," "Doin' My Time," "Don't Give Your Heart to a Rambler," "Jungle Fever," and "When I Saw Your Face in the Moon"

It Ain't Me: It's Ray Campi—the Eager Beaver Boy, Rollin' Rock Records, 1976, tracks include "Pretty Mama," "Wicked Wicked Woman," "Chug-a-Lug," and "Good Time Woman"

Born to Rock, Rollin' Rock Records, 1977, tracks include "I'm Coming Home," "Honky Tonk Man," "Get Rhythm," "Born to Rock," and "Hillbilly Cat"

Rockabilly Rocket, Rollin' Rock Records, 1977, tracks include "Chew Tobacco Rag," "Ruby Ann," "Jimmie Skins the Blues," "Running After Fools," and "Little Young Girl"

Gone, Gone, Gone, Rollin' Rock Records, 1979, tracks include "Don't Blame It on Me," "Mind Your Own Business," "All Night Express," "Don't Turn Me Down," and "I'm Coming Home"

Wildcat Shakeout, Radar, 1979, tracks include "Honey Bop," "Sack of Love," "Cat Clothes Shop," "It Ain't Me," and "Teenage Boogie"

Rockabilly Music, Rollin' Rock Records, 1981, tracks include "Lucky to Be in Love," "Rockabilly Music," "I've Been Around," "You Nearly Lose Your Mind," and "Boo Hoo"

Rockabilly Man, Rollin' Rock Records, 1981, tracks include "Don't Come Knockin'," "Hold That Train," "Hollywood Cats," and "Recipe for Love"

Give That Love to Ray Campi, Domino, 1987, tracks include "Ballad of Donna and Peggy Sue," "Caterpillar," "You Cheated, "How Low Can You Feel," and "Play It Cool"

Rockin' at the Ritz, Rounder Records, 1990, tracks include "Pan American Boogie," "Eager Boy," "Everybody's Movin'," "My Baby Left Me," and "Tore Up"

Ace Cannon

CDs

16 Greatest Hits, Deluxe, 1985, tracks include "Tuff," "Honky Tonk," "In the Mood," "White Silver Sands," and "Yakety Sax"

Golden Memories, Heartland, 1986, tracks include "Good Hearted Woman," "Paper Roses," "Blue Eyes Crying in the Rain," "Almost Persuaded," and "Cold Cold Heart"

Rockin' Robin and Other Classics, Pilz, 1995, tracks include "Little Bitty Pretty One," "High Heel Sneakers," "Burning Bridges," "Take Good Care of Her," and "Hearts of Stone"

The Best of Ace Cannon—the Hi Records Years, Capitol Records, 2001, tracks include "Sittin' Tight," "Kansas City," "Prisoner's Song," "Heartbreak Hotel," and "Funny How Time Slips Away"

Various Artists, *Scotty Moore and Friends—Then and Now*, self-released (available at www.scottymoore.net), 2004, tracks include "Matchbox," "The Gambler," "Raunchy," and "You Don't Know Me"

Vinyl

45 rpm Singles

"Tuff" b/w "Sittin' Tight," Hi Records, 1961
"Summer Time" b/w "Hoe Down Rock," Fernwood, 1962
"Sugar Blues" b/w "38 Special," Santo Records, 1962
"Rest" b/w "Big Shot," Santo Records, 1962
"Volare" b/w "Looking Back," Hi Records, 1962
"Blues (Stay Away from Me)" b/w "Blues in My Heart," Hi Records, 1962
"Since I Met You Baby" b/w "Love Letters," Hi Records, 1963
"Swanee River" b/w "Moanin' the Blues," Hi Records, 1963
"Cottonfields" b/w "Mildew," Hi Records, 1963
"Big Shot" b/w "Tie Me to Your Apron Strings Again," Fernwood, 1964
"Empty Arms" b/w "Sunday Blues," Hi Records, 1964
"Searchin'" b/w "Love Letters in the Sand," Hi Records, 1964
"The Great Pretender" b/w "Gone," Hi Records, 1964
"Blue Christmas" b/w "Here Comes Santa Claus," Hi Records, 1964
"Ishapan" b/w "Upshore," Hi Records, 1965
"Sea Cruise" b/w "Gold Coins," Hi Records, 1965
"Funny (How Time Slips Away)" b/w "Saxy Lullabye," Hi Records, 1966
"More" b/w "Spanish Eyes," Hi Records, 1966
"Wonderland by Night" b/w "As Time Goes By," Hi Records, 1966
"Mockingbird Hill" b/w "Dedicated to the One I Love," Hi Records, 1966
"I Walk the Line" b/w "Memory," Hi Records, 1967
"San Antonio Rose" b/w "White Silver Sands," Hi Records, 1967
"Alley Cat" b/w "Cannonball," Hi Records, 1968
"By the Time I Get to Phoenix" b/w "Sleep Walk," Hi Records, 1968
"Down by the Riverside" b/w "Amen," Hi Records, 1969
"Soul for Sale" b/w "If I Had a Hammer," Hi Records, 1969
"Lodi" b/w "Rainy Night in Georgia," Hi Records, 1970
"Ruby, Don't Take Your Love to Town" b/w "I Can't Stop Loving You," Hi Records, 1970
"Drunk" b/w "Chicken Fried Soul," Hi Records, 1971
"Easy Loving" b/w "Misty Blue," Hi Records, 1971
"Me and Bobby McGee" b/w "Sweet Caroline," Hi Records, 1971
"Tuffer Than Tuff" b/w "Green Door," Hi Records, 1972
"Love Sick Blues" b/w "Cold Cold Heart," Hi Records, 1972
"To Get to You" b/w "Wabash Cannonball," Hi Records, 1972
"Ruff" b/w "Baby Don't Get Hooked on Me," Hi Records, 1973
"Country Comfort" b/w "Closin' Time's a Downer," Hi Records, 1973
"Mathilda" b/w "Last Date," Hi Records, 1974
"Tennessee Saturday Night" b/w "There Goes My Everything," Hi Records, 1974
"Peace in the Valley" b/w "Raunchy," Hi Records, 1975
"Malt Liquor" b/w "Walk on By," Hi Records, 1975
"Blue Eyes Crying in the Rain" b/w "I'll Fly Away," Hi Records, 1976

LPs

Tuff, Hi Records, 1962, tracks include "I've Got a Woman," "Kansas City," "Basin Street Blues," "Wabash Blues," and "Cannonball"

Looking Back with Ace Cannon, Hi Records, 1962, tracks include "Someday," "My Blue Heaven," "Jealous Heart," "Foggy River," and "Volare"

The Moaning Sax of Ace Cannon, Hi Records, 1963, tracks include "Prisoner of Love," "I Love You Because," "Singing the Blues," "Last Date," and "The Great Pretender"

Ace Hi, Hi Records, 1964, tracks include "Heartbreak Hotel," "Swanee River," "Gone," "Searchin'," and "You Don't Know Me"

Ace Cannon Plays the Great Show Tunes, Hi Records, 1964, tracks include "A Summer Place," "Love Is a Many Splendored Thing," "Hello Dolly," and "Fascination"

Ace Cannon Live, Hi Records, 1965, tracks include "Yakety Sax," "Moody River," "Memphis," "You Can't Sit Down," and "Honky Tonk"

Nashville Hits, Hi Records, 1965, tracks include "Four Walls," "I'm So Lonesome I Could Cry," "Hey Good Looking," "I've Got a Tiger by the Tail," and "Sweet Dreams"

Sweet and Tuff, Hi Records, 1966, tracks include "Mockinbird Rock," "Goldfinger," "Hang on Sloopy," and "Louie Louie"

Misty Sax of Ace Cannon, Hi Records, 1967, tracks include "When a Man Loves a Woman," "Wonderland by Night," "You'll Never Walk Alone," and "Yesterday"

Memphis Golden Hits, Hi Records, 1968, tracks include "Baby Let's Play House," "Green Onions," "White Silver Sands," "Last Night," and "Haunted House"

Ace of Sax, Hi Records, 1969, tracks include "Down by the Riverside," "Bad Moon Rising," "Alley Cat," and "Proud Mary"

Cool and Saxy, Hi Records, 1971, tracks include "Rainy Night in Georgia," "Let It Be," "Sunny," "Chicken Fried Soul," and "Lodi"

Cannon Country—Ace That Is, Hi Records, 1972, tracks include "Easy Lovin'," "Ramblin' Rose," "Crazy Arms," "Lovesick Blues," and "Cold Cold Heart"

Baby, Don't Get Hooked on Me, Hi Records, 1973, tracks include "Saxy Waltz," "To Get to You," "Tuffer Than Tuff," and "Green Door"

That Music City Feeling, Hi Records, 1974, tracks include "Last Date," "Born to Lose," "Mathilda," "Tuff," and "Tennessee Saturday Night"

Peace in the Valley, Hi Records, 1976, tracks include "One Day at a Time," "Amazing Grace," "I'll Fly Away," "It Is No Secret," and "Why Me"

At His Best, Gusto, 1981, tracks include "Yakety Sax," "Harbor Lights," "Fever," "Frankie and Johnny," and "Night Train"

Ace in the Hole, Allegience, 1984, tracks include "Blue Eyes Crying in the Rain," "Secret Love," "Take Good Care of Her," "Rockin' Robin," and "Alley Cat"

Bobby Crown

CDs

Songs from 1956 to 1966, Texan Records, 2003, tracks include "One Way Ticket," "Fannie Mae," "Shake, Rattle, and Roll," "Sugar Coated," and "Wait a Minute"

Bobby Crown and the Kapers, Collector, 2004, tracks include "That's All Right," "Bouncy Beat," "Chicken Is a Bird," "Thirty Days," and "Baby Let's Play House"

I Think I'm Cool, Lenox, 2005, tracks include "Five O'Clock News," "Your Lover Man," "Sometimes I Cry," "Lookin' for Love," and "Birth of Rock and Roll"

Vinyl

45 rpm Singles

"One Way Ticket" b/w "Your Conscience," Felco, 1959

"Wait a Minute" b/w "I've Never Had a Broken Heart," Manco, 1960

Carl Dobkins, Jr.

CDs

My Heart Is an Open Book, Bear Family Records, 1991, tracks include "Lucky Devil," "Fool Such as I," "Take Time Out," "Love Is Everything," and "My Pledge to You"

Vinyl

45 rpm Singles

"Take Hold of My Hand" b/w "That's Why I'm Asking," Fraternity, 1958

"If You Don't Want My Lovin'" b/w "Love Is Everything," Decca Records, 1958

"Lucky Devil" b/w "In My Heart," Decca Records, 1959

"My Heart Is an Open Book" b/w "My Pledge to You," Decca Records, 1959

"Lovelight" b/w "Take Time Out," Decca Records, 1960

"One Little Girl" b/w "Exclusively Yours," Decca Records, 1960

"A Different Kind of Love" b/w "Genie," Decca Records, 1960

"Sawdust Dolly" b/w "A Chance to Belong," Decca Records, 1961

"Promise Me" b/w "Ask Me No Questions," Decca Records, 1962

"If Teardrops Were Diamonds" b/w "I'm So Sorry Little Girl," Atco, 1964

"A Little Bit Later on Down the Line" b/w "His Loss Is My Gain," Colpix Records, 1965

LPs

Carl Dobkins, Jr., Decca Records, 1959, tracks include "I'm Sorry," "If You Don't Want My Lovin'," True Love," and "For Your Love"

Al Ferrier

CDs

Al Ferrier and His Boppin' Billies, Big Tone Records, 1993, tracks include "Let's Go Boppin' Tonight," "Honey Baby," "My Baby Done Gone Away," "No No Baby," "You Win Again," "I'm the Man," "Hey Baby," "Kiss Me Baby," and "Blues Stop Knocking at My Door"

Legendary Al Ferrier with Louisiana Swamp Cats, Goldband, 1996, tracks include "My Kind of Woman," "Keep the Other Guy," "When the Blues Come Again," and "Nothin' Shakin' (But the Leaves on the Trees)"

I'm the Man: Louisiana Swamp Rockabilly 1955–59, El Toro Records, 2010, tracks include "Indian Rock and Roll," "Hey! Baby," "No No Baby," "My Baby Done Gone Away," "Let's Go Bopping Tonight," "Honey Baby," "Kiss Me Baby," and "I Thought I Found Love"

Various Artists, *Boppin' by the Bayou*, Ace Records, 2012, two tracks by Ferrier—"Kiss Me Baby" and "Indian Rock and Roll"

Vinyl

45 rpm Singles

"No No Baby" b/w "I'll Never Do Any Wrong," Goldband, 1956

"My Baby Done Gone Away" b/w "Too Late Now," Goldband, 1956

"I'm the Man" b/w "Hey! Baby," Excello, 1957

"Let's Go Boppin' Tonight" b/w "What Is That Thing Called Love," Goldband, 1958

"Kiss Me Baby" b/w "I Thought I Found Love," Rocko, 1959

"Chisholm Trail Rock" b/w "Gunsmoke," Zynn, 1959

"Blues Stop Knocking (at My Door)" b/w "She Left Me," Zynn, 1959

"Honey Baby" b/w "Why Doubt My Love," Goldband, 1969

"I'll Try One More Time" b/w "I'm Just a Mender," Goldband, 1969

"78 to Birmingham" b/w "I'll Sin Until I Die," Goldband, 1969

"Last Chance" b/w "Take Two Steps," Goldband, 1970

"Told Her Nobody" b/w "Touch of Mary's Hand," Goldband, 1970

"Yard Dog" b/w "If I Need You (Will I Find You There)," Goldband, 1970

"Seventy-six Dollars a Week" b/w "Two Hungry Eyes," Goldband, 1971

"Rock-a-billy Blues" b/w "Only Sad Songs (Help Me Through the Night)," Goldband, 1971

"All You Need Is a Man" b/w "St. Peter's Call," RPI, 1972

"Be Boppin' Daddy" b/w "You're Humbuggin' Me," Showtime, 1975

"It's My Fault (You're Not Here)" b/w "I'll Take You for a Ride," Showtime, 1975

"The Lonesome Trucker" b/w "Watching the Night Lights Burn," Showtime, 1976

"Hey Baby" b/w "Honey Baby," Showtime, 1976

"I'm Not Drinking More" b/w "Don't Play Blue Eyes Crying in the Rain," Master-Trak, 1980

"Hello Josephine" b/w "I'll Try One More Time," Goldband, 1980

"Every Dog Has a Day" b/w "No Greater Love," Goldband, 1982

LPs

The Birth of Rockabilly, Goldband, 1970, tracks include "No No Baby," "Drip Drop," "Honey Baby," "Sixteen Candles," "Let's Go Boppin' Tonight," and "My Baby Done Gone Away"

From 1955 to 1975: The Back Sound of Rockabilly, Showtime, 1976, tracks include "You're Humbuggin' Me," "Be Boppin' Baby," "Kiss Me Baby," and I'm the Man"

Dixie, Rockhouse, 1987, tracks include "Gone Gone Gone," "No Greater Love," "Rockabilly Blues," and Don't You Know Little Baby"

Rosie Flores

CDs

Rosie Flores, American Beat Records, 1987

Various Artists, *A Town South of Bakersfield, Volumes 1 & 2*, Enigma/Capitol, 1990, one track by Flores—"Heartbreak Train"

After the Farm, Hightone/Shout! Records, 1992

Once More with Feeling, Hightone/Shout! Records, 1993

Rockabilly Filly, Hightone Records, 1995

Honky Tonk Reprise, Rounder Records, 1996

Ronnie Mack, *Born to Rock*, Sunjay, 1996

Rosie Flores and Ray Campi, *Little Bit of Heartache—Honky Tonk Angels*, Watermelon, 1997

Dance Hall Dreams, Rounder Records, 1999

Ray Campi, *Taylor, Texas 1988—Remembering Jimmy Heap*, Bear Family Records, 1999
Various Artists, *Tower Takes Texas by Storm*, Rounder Records, 1999, one track by Flores—"We'll Survive"
Various Artists, *Bozo and Pals: Get Down with the Clown*, Music Little People, 2000, one track by Flores—"Toodleoo"
Speed of Sound, Eminent Records, 2001
Various Artists, *The Bottle Let Me Down: Songs for Bumpy Wagon Rides*, Bloodshot Records, 2002, one track by Flores—"Red, Red Robin"
Various Artists, *Dressed in Black: A Tribute to Johnny Cash*, Dualtone Music Group, 2002, one track by Flores—"Big River"
Bandera Highway, Hightone Records, 2004
Single Rose, Durango Rose Records, 2004
Christmasville, Emergent/92e, 2005
Various Artists, *A T-Rex Named Sue*, Music Little People, 2005, one track by Flores—"T. Rex Boogie"
Various Artists, *Tribute to the Cadillac*, 95 North, 2005, one track by Flores—"Cadillac Ranch"
Girl of the Century, Bloodshot Records, 2009
Patricia Vonne and Rosie Flores, *Austin Rocks*, Bandolera Records, 2009
Working Girl's Guitar, Bloodshot Records, 2012
Janis Martin, *The Blanco Sessions*, Cow Island Music, 2012
After the Farm & Once More with Feeling, Floating World, 2012

Vinyl

45 rpm Singles

"I'm Walkin'" (both sides), Reprise Records, 1986
"Crying Over You" b/w "Midnight to Moonlight," Reprise Records, 1987
"Heart Beats to a Different Drum" b/w "Somebody Loses, Somebody Wins," Reprise Records, 1987
"He Cares" b/w "One Track Memory," Reprise Records, 1988

Four Charms/Joel Paterson

CDs

The Four Charms, *Flatland Boogie*, Hi-Style, 2000
Nick Willett, *Nick Willett*, Styleline, 2002
Down at the Depot, Ventrella Records, 2002
Go Lightnin', Meantone Records, 2005
Devil in a Woodpile, *In Your Lonesome Town*, Bloodshot Records, 2005
Jimmy Sutton's Four Charms, *Triskaidekaphobia*, Hi-Style, 2005
Steve Dawson, *Sweet Is the Anchor*, Undertow Music Collective, 2005
Various Artists, *Viva Las Vegas—Rockabilly Weekend #9*, Viva Las Vegas/Tom Ingram, 2006, two tracks by Jimmy Sutton's Four Charms—"I Gotta Get Another Girl" and "Don't Make Me Beg"
Wee Hairy Beasties, *Animal Crackers*, Bloodshot Records, 2006
Rachel Ries, *Without a Bird*, SoDak, 2007
Steel Is Real, Ventrella Records, 2008
Carl Sonny Leyland, *A Chicago Session*, Ventrella Records, 2008
The Modern Sounds, *Stomp, Stomp!/Hold It Fellas*, Ventrella Records, 2009
The Insomniacs, *At Least I'm Not with You*, Delta Groove Productions, 2009
Steve Dawson, *I Will Miss the Trumpets and the Drums*, Undertow Music Collective, 2009
Various Artists, *Shake the Shack Rockabilly Ball, Volume Five*, KEXP, 2009, two tracks by Jimmy Sutton's Four Charms—"Triskaidekaphobia" and "I Gotta Get Another Girl"
Deke Dickerson and the Modern Sounds, *Live at Duffs*, Major Label Records in association with Ventrella Records, 2010
Eddie Clendening, *Eddie Clendening Is Knockin' at Your Heart*, Ventrella Records, 2010
JD McPherson, *Signs and Signifiers*, Hi-Style, 2010
Cash Box Kings, *I-94 Blues*, Blue Bella, 2010
Cash Box Kings, *Holler and Stomp*, Blind Pig, 2011
The Modern Sounds, *The Modern Sounds Sing and Play for You*, Ventrella Records, 2012
Handful of Strings, Ventrella Records, 2013
Cash Box Kings, *Black Toppin'*, Blind Pig, 2013

Vinyl

45 rpm Singles

The Four Charms, "Sherry Flip" b/w "Midnight at the Mill," Hi-Style, 2000
Joel Paterson and Lester Peabody, "Biscuitboardin'" b/w "Boo-Wah Blues," Goofin' Records, 2011

Four Charms/Jonathan Doyle

CDs

The Mighty Blue Kings, *Come One, Come All*, R-J Records, 1997
The Four Charms, *Flatland Boogie*, Hi-Style, 2000
Pinetop Seven, *Bringing Home the Last Great Strike*, Truck Stop, 2000

Treehouse Project, *Picture Show*, 482 Music, 2002

Various Artists, *Document Chicago: New Jazz and Improvisation*, 482 Music, 2003

Rob Stone, *Just My Luck*, Earwig, 2003

Nick Curran, *Player!*, Blind Pig Records, 2004

Jimmy Sutton's Four Charms, *Triskaidekaphobia*, Hi-Style, 2005

Joel Paterson, *Go Lightnin'*, Meantone Records, 2005

Various Artists, *Viva Las Vegas—Rockabilly Weekend #9*, Viva Las Vegas/Tom Ingram, 2006, two tracks by Jimmy Sutton's Four Charms—"I Gotta Get Another Girl" and "Don't Make Me Beg"

Various Artists, *American Music: The Hightone Records Story* [5 CDs], Shout Factory, 2006

Asylum Street Spankers, *Pussycat Bootleg Series, Vol. 2: Live Rarities 2000–2004*, Spanks a Lot Records, 2006

Nevada Newman, *Why Do It Right?*, Spanks a Lot Records, 2006

Asylum Street Spankers, *Mommy Says No!*, Yellow Dog Records, 2007

Michael Cross, *Blues Lovin' Man*, Diamond Heart Records, 2008

Various Artists, *Shake the Shack Rockabilly Ball, Volume Five*, KEXP, 2009, two tracks by Jimmy Sutton's Four Charms—"Triskaidekaphobia" and "I Gotta Get Another Girl"

Asleep at the Wheel and Willie Nelson, *Willie and the Wheel*, Bismeaux, 2009

Asleep at the Wheel and Leon Rausch, *It's a Good Day*, Bismeaux, 2010

Sunset, *Loveshines but the Moon Is Shining Too*, Autobus Records, 2010

Elizabeth McQueen, *The Laziest Girl in Town*, Freedom, 2010

Nick Curran, *Reform School Girl*, Eclecto Groove, 2010

JD McPherson, *Signs and Signifiers*, Hi-Style, 2010

Shawn Pittman, *Edge of the World*, Delta Groove Music, 2011

Janis Martin, *The Blanco Sessions*, Cow Island Music, 2012

Elizabeth McQueen and Brothers Lazaroff, *Elizabeth McQueen Meet Brothers Lazaroff: The Laziest Remix*, Lazy SOB, 2014

Vinyl

45 rpm Singles

The Four Charms, "Sherry Flip" b/w "Midnight at the Mill," Hi-Style, 2000

JD McPherson, "North Side Gal" b/w "Wolf Teeth," Witchcraft, 2010

Four Charms/Jim Barclay

CDs

The Four Charms, *Flatland Boogie*, Hi-Style, 2000

Cameron McGill, *Stories of the Knife and the Back*, Post-Important, 2003

Brian Deer, *Black Cloud Talk*, CD Baby, 2004

Joel Paterson, *Go Lightnin'*, Meantone Records, 2005

Jimmy Sutton's Four Charms, *Triskaidekaphobia*, Hi-Style, 2005

Various Artists, *Viva Las Vegas—Rockabilly Weekend #9*, Viva Las Vegas/Tom Ingram, 2006, two tracks by Jimmy Sutton's Four Charms—"I Gotta Get Another Girl" and "Don't Make Me Beg"

Various Artists, *Shake the Shack Rockabilly Ball, Volume Five*, KEXP, 2009, two tracks by Jimmy Sutton's Four Charms—"Triskaidekaphobia" and "I Gotta Get Another Girl"

Vinyl

45 rpm Singles

The Four Charms, "Sherry Flip" b/w "Midnight at the Mill," Hi-Style, 2000

Four Charms/Jimmy Sutton

CDs

The Moondogs, *Knocked Out Beat*, Kiaulia

The Moondogs, *Stateside Rockabilly Compilation*, NV Records, 1994

Ronnie Dawson, *Monkey Beat*, No Hit, 1994

Willie "Big Eye" Smith, *Bag Full of Blues*, Blind Pig, 1995

The Mighty Blue Kings, *Meet Me in Uptown*, R-Jay, 1996

The Four Charms, *Flatland Boogie*, Hi-Style, 2000

Nick Willett, *Nick Willett*, Styleline, 2002

Andrew Bird, *Fingerlings*, Grimsey, 2002

Joel Paterson and His Blues Roundup, *Go Lightnin'*, Meantone, 2004

Slink Moss Explosion, *Slink Moss Explosion*, Rattlesnake, 2004

Eddie Clendening, *The Rage of the Teen-Age!*, Wormtone, 2005

Jimmy Sutton's Four Charms, *Triskaidekaphobia*, Hi-Style, 2005

Nick Willett, *Off the Record*, Styleline, 2005

Deke Dickerson, *The Melody*, Major Label, 2005

Various Artists, *Viva Las Vegas—Rockabilly Weekend #9*, Viva Las Vegas/Tom Ingram, 2006, two tracks by Jimmy Sutton's Four Charms—"I Gotta Get Another Girl" and "Don't Make Me Beg"
Koko Taylor, *Old School*, Alligator, 2007
The Del Moroccos, *Blue Black Hair*, Hi-Style, 2008
Eric Noden, *The Original*, Diving Duck, 2008
Kurt Krandall, *Get Wrong with Me*, Yester Year, 2009
Deke Dickerson, *King of the Whole Wide World*, Major Label, 2008
Various Artists, *Shake the Shack Rockabilly Ball, Volume Five*, KEXP, 2009, two tracks by Jimmy Sutton's Four Charms—"Triskaidekaphobia" and "I Gotta Get Another Girl"
Chris Harper, *Four Aces and a Harp*, Swississippi, 2010
Cash Box Kings, *I-94 Blues*, Blue Bella, 2010
Morry Sochat & The Special 20's, *Eatin' Dirt*, Galaxie, 2010
The Del Moroccos, *Rockin' Around Turnhout 15th Anniversary Compilation*, Tombstone, 2010
JD McPherson, *Signs & Signifiers*, Hi-Style, 2010
Cash Box Kings, *Holler and Stomp*, Blind Pig, 2011
JC Brooks and The Uptown Sound, *Want More*, Bloodshot Records, 2011
Cash Box Kings, *Black Toppin'*, Blind Pig, 2013

Vinyl

45 rpm Singles

The Moondogs, "Low Rider" b/w "Layin' Railroad Track," Untouchable Records, 1994
The Four Charms, "Sherry Flip" b/w "Midnight at the Mill," Hi-Style, 2000
JD McPherson, "North Side Gal" b/w "Wolf Teeth," Witchcraft, 2010
JD McPherson, "North Side Gal" b/w "Abigail Blue," Hi-Style, 2012
JD McPherson, "Fire Bug" b/w "A Gentle Awakening," Rounder/Hi-Style, 2013

Billy Hancock

CDs

Joe Stanley, *King of the Honky Tonk Sax*, Wildchild, 1996
On the Jazz, Turkey Mountain Records, 2003
Billy Hancock and Tennessee Rockets Live!, Turkey Mountain Records, 2004
Passions, Turkey Mountain Records, 2005
The Birth of a Billy: The Billy Hancock Anthology 1974–2006, CD Baby, 2006
Out of the Darkness, CD Baby, 2008
For Rockabilly Fans Only—The Lost Tapes, Turkey Mountain Records, 2009
Martí Brom, *Not for Nothin'*, Goofin' Records, 2010
Various Artists, *The Best of Ripsaw Records, Vol. 1*, Part Records, 2010
Anthology 2, CD Baby, 2011

Vinyl

45 rpm Singles

Danny and the Fat Boys, "American Music" b/w "Harlem Nocturne," Aladdin, 1974
"Rootie Tootie" b/w "I Can't Be Satisfied," Ripsaw Records, 1978
Tex Rubinowitz, "Bad Boy" b/w "Feelin' Right Tonight," Ripsaw Records, 1979
"The Boogie Disease" b/w "Knock-Kneed Nellie," Ripsaw Records, 1979
Tex Rubinowitz, "Hot Rod Man" b/w "It Ain't Wrong," Ripsaw Records, 1979
"Redskin Rock 'n' Roll" b/w "Lonely Blue Boy," Ripsaw Records, 1980
"Miss Jessie Lee" b/w "I'm Satisfied," Ripsaw Records, 1980

LPs

Danny and the Fat Boys, *American Music*, Aladdin, 1975
Various Artists, *Waves: An Anthology of New Music—Volume 2*, BOMP, 1980, one track by Hancock—"I Can't Be Satisfied"
Tex Rubinowitz, *Hot Rod Man*, Big Beat Records, 1981
Rockabilly Fever, Big Beat Records, 1981
Shakin' That Rockabilly Fever, Solid Smoke Records, 1981
Hey Little Rock and Roller, Big Beat Records, 1983
Wanted: True Rock 'n' Roll, Ripsaw Records, 1985
Danny Gatton and the Fat Boys, *Vintage Masters 1971–1976, Vol. 1*, Hippo, 1989

Dale Hawkins

CDs

Oh Suzy-Q: the Best of Dale Hawkins, Chess, 1995, tracks include "Little Pig," "Juanita," "Baby Baby," "See You Soon Baboon," "Lulu," and "Ain't That Lovin' You Baby"
Daredevil, Norton Records, 1997, tracks include "Mumbly Peg," "Weep No More," "Susie-Q" (demo version), "Number Nine Train," and "Superman"
Rock 'n' Roll Tornado, Ace Records, 1998, tracks

include "Don't Treat Me This Way," "Lifeguard Man," "Lovin' Bug," "Caledonia," "Boogie Woogie Teenage Girl," "Susie-Q," and "Teenage Dolly"

Wildcat Tamer, Lightyear, 1999, tracks include "Irene," "Country Girl," "Promised Land," "Change Game," and "Goin' Down the Road"

Fool's Paradise, Beveric, 2000, tracks include "Peaches," "Gotta Dance," "Mona Lisa," "Lover Please," "Let the Good Times Roll," "Sixty Minute Man," and "Wildcat Tamer"

L.A., Memphis, & Tyler, Texas, Rev-Ola, 2006, tracks include "Candy Man," "Hound Dog," "Baby What You Want Me to Do," and "Ruby (Don't Take Your Love to Town)"

Dale Rocks, Bear Family Records, 2007, tracks include "Take My Heart," "Susie-Q," "Little Pig," "Tornado," "Number Nine Train," "Sweetie Pie," "Linda," and "Lovin' Bug"

Back Down to Louisiana, Plumtone Records, 2007, tracks include "Bang Bang," "Shake," "This Love of Mine," "Pretty Little Thing," and "New Generation"

Susie Q—the Singles as As and Bs 1956–60, Jasmine Music, 2011, tracks include "Baby Baby," "Little Pig," "Tornado," "See You Soon Baboon," "My Babe," and "Mrs. Merguitory's Daughter"

Rockabilly Madness, Rockabilly, 2012, tracks include "Susie-Q," "See You Soon Baboon," "Who," "Caledonia," "Baby Baby," "Every Little Girl," "Little Pig," and "Teenage Dolly"

Vinyl

45 rpm Singles

"Four Letter Word" b/w "See You Soon Baboon," Checker, July 1956

"Susie-Q" b/w "Don't Treat Me This Way," Checker, May 1957

"Baby, Baby" b/w "Mrs. Merguitory's Daughter," Checker, October 1957

"Tornado" b/w "Little Pig," Checker, April 1958

"La-Do-Dada" b/w "Crossties," Checker, July 1958

"My Babe" b/w "A House, a Car, and a Wedding Ring," Checker, October 1958

"Take My Heart" b/w "Someday One Day," Checker, January 1959

"Yea-Yea (Class Cutter)" b/w "Lonely Nights," Checker, February 1959

"Ain't That Lovin' You Baby" b/w "My Dream," Checker, May 1959

"Lifeguard Man" b/w "Our Turn," Checker, July 1959

"Back to School Blues" b/w "Liza Jane," Checker, September 1959

"Hot Dog" b/w "Don't Break Your Promise to Me," Checker, December 1959

"Every Little Girl" b/w "Poor Little Rhode Island," Checker, February 1960

"Linda" b/w "Who," Checker, October 1960

"I Want to Love You" b/w "Grandma's House," Checker, February 1961

"Money Honey" b/w "The Same Old Way," Tilt, May 1961

"Wish I Hadn't Called Home" b/w "Forbidden Love," Tilt, July 1961

"Hawk Blows, Band Plays (Part I)" b/w "Hawk Blows, Band Plays (Part II)," Tilt, September 1961

"Stay at Home Lulu" b/w "I Can't Erase (You Out of My Heart)," Atlantic, November 1961

"Women—That's What's Happening!" b/w "With a Feeling," Atlantic, June 1962

"Peaches" b/w "Gotta Dance," Zonk, October 1962

"The Flag" b/w "And I Believed You," Abnak (Texas), 1964

"Number Nine Train" b/w "On Account of You," Norton Records, 1997

LPs

Oh! Suzy-Q, Chess, 1958, tracks include "Don't Treat Me This Way," "Little Pig," "Juanita," "Baby Baby," "Take My Heart," "Heaven," and "Wild Wild World"

Let's All Twist at the Miami Beach Peppermint Lounge, Roulette, 1962, tracks include "Hey Hey," "Do the Twist," "Joanne," "Luky Duky," "Someone to Care," and "Goin' Round"

Dale Hawkins, Chess, 1976, tracks include "Susie-Q," "My Babe," "First Love," "Lulu," "Little Pig," and "Take My Heart"

My Babe, Argo Records, 1986, tracks include "Liza Jane," "La-Do-Dada," "Lulu," "Every Little Girl," "Crossties," "Worried About You Baby," and "Gooblie Booblie"

Born in Louisiana, Goofin' Records, 1999, tracks include "Goodnight Irene," "Cute Little Girl," "Hat Trick," "Goodnight Sweetheart Goodnight," "With a Feeling," and "Goin' Down the Road"

Glenn Honeycutt

CDs

Various Artists, *That'll Flat Git It—Vol. 14: Rockabilly from the Vaults of Sun Records*, Bear Family Records, 1999, one track by Honeycutt—"Rock All Night"

Glenn Honeycutt and the Poor Boys, *Mr. All*

Night Rock, Rhythm Bomb Records, 2005, tracks include "Gonna Love You All Over," "Saturday Night," "My Heart," "Tennessee Rockin' Girl," and "Promise Me Love"

Vinyl

45 rpm Singles

"I'll Be Around" b/w "I'll Wait Forever," Sun Records, 1957

"Right Gal, Right Place, Right Time" b/w "You'll Die of Loneliness," Black Gold, 1964

"Tombigbee Queen" b/w "Campus Love," Fernwood, 1964

Glenn Honeycutt and Jimmy Wages, "Rock All Night" b/w "Miss Pearl," Norton Records, 2003

James Intveld

CDs

Various Artists, *A Town South of Bakersfield, Volumes 1 & 2*, Enigma/Capitol, 1990

Various Artists, *Cry-Baby* (Movie Soundtrack), MCA, 1990, four tracks by Intveld—"King Cry Baby," "Doin' Time for Bein' Young," "Teardrops Are Falling," and "High School Hellcats"

Various Artists, *Frankie and Johnny* (Movie Soundtrack), Curb Records, 1991, one track by Intveld—"Frankie and Johnny"

Rosie Flores, *Once More with Feeling*, Hightone Records, 1993

Various Artists, *A Town South of Bakersfield, Vol. 3*, Restless Records, 1993

Dave Alvin, *King of California*, Shout Factory, 1994

Phil Alvin, *County Fair 2000*, Hightone Records, 1994

Rosie Flores, *Rockabilly Filly*, Hightone Records, 1995

Rosie Flores, *Honky Tonk Reprise*, Rounder Records, 1996

Ronnie Mack, *Born to Rock*, Sunjay, 1996

Various Artists, *Turning the World Blue: A Tribute to Gene Vincent*, Skizmatic Records, 1997, one track by Intveld—"Important Words"

Introducing James Intveld, Bear Family Records, 1997

Lester Butler, *13*, Hightone Records, 1997

Grady Champion, *Payin' for My Sins*, Shanachie, 1999

Kid Ramos, *West Coast House Party*, Evidence, 2000

Somewhere Down the Road, Molenaart, 2000

Nelson, *Like Father, Like Sons*, Stone Canyon Records, 2000

Various Artists, *Bozo and Pals: Get Down with the Clown*, Music Little People, 2000, one track by Intveld—"Toodleoo"

Patrick Weathers, *Queen of Tupelo*, Louisiana Red Hot, 2001

Kid Ramos, *Greasy Kid Stuff*, Evidence, 2001

Grady Champion, *2 Days Short of a Week*, Shanachie, 2001

Ray Campi and Tony Conn, *High School Hellcats Reunion*, Part Records, 2002

Various Artists, *Dressed in Black: A Tribute to Johnny Cash*, Dualtone Music Group, 2002, one track by Intveld—"Folsom Prison Blues"

Various Artists, *Billy, Volume 1*, Hepcat Records, 2002, one track by Intveld—"Cryin' Over You"

Dee Lannon, *Vinylly on CD*, Norge Tex, 2004

Rosie Flores, *Single Rose*, Emergent, 2004

Joe Ely, *Settle for Love*, Hightone Records, 2004

Rosie Flores, *Bandera Highway*, Hightone Records, 2004

Various Artists, *A Dirty Shame* (Movie Soundtrack), Watertower Music, 2004, one track by Intveld—"Let's Go Sexin'"

Papa Joe Grappa, *Too White to Sing the Blues*, 2005

Various Artists, *Lowe Profile: A Tribute to Nick Lowe* [2 CDs], Brewery Records, 2005, one track by Intveld—"Lonesome Reverie"

Patrick Weathers, *Hound Dog Diaries*, Louisiana Red Hot, 2005

Various Artists, *Choppertown: The Sinners* (Movie Soundtrack), One World Studio Ltd., 2005, five tracks by Intveld—"Drinkin' Beer and Wrenchin' on Bikes," "Remember Me," "We Gotta Boogie," "One Sweet Letter," and "A Sinner's Prayer"

Various Artists, *Cat'n Around, Volume Three*, Pink 'n' Black, 2006, two tracks by Intveld—"My Heart Is Aching for You" and "Standin' on a Rock"

Various Artists, *Viva Las Vegas—Rockabilly Weekend #10*, Viva Las Vegas/Tom Ingram 2007, one track by Intveld—"Barely Hangin' On"

Have Faith, Molenaart, 2008

Various Artists, *Shake the Shack Rockabilly Ball, Volume Five*, KEXP, 2009, two tracks by Intveld—"Doin' Time for Bein' Young" and "One Sweet Letter"

John Coinman, *This Place Ain't What It Used to Be*, Indie Europe/Zoom, 2009

Tracey K. Houston, *Rockin' Little Angel*, CD Baby, 2010

Nick 13, *Nick 13*, Sugarhill [Country], 2011

Vinyl

45 rpm Singles

James Intveld and the Rockin' Shadows, "My Heart Is Achin' for You" b/w "You're My Baby," 1982

Harold Jenkins a.k.a. Conway Twitty

CDs

The Conway Twitty Collection [4 CDs], MCA Nashville, 1994, tracks include "What Am I Living For," "Such a Night," "I Need Your Lovin'," "Walk Me to the Door," and "Feelins"

Rock 'n' Roll Years [8 CDs], Bear Family Records, 1997, tracks include "Born to Sing the Blues," "Just in Time," "Maybe Baby," "Rock House," "I Need You So," and "Blueberry Hill"

Conway Rocks, Bear Family Records, 2003, tracks include "Mona Lisa," "Double Talk Baby," "Rock House," "Rebound," "Teasin'," "Danny Boy," and "Give Me Some Love"

Conway Twitty and Loretta Lynn, *Definitive Collection*, MCA Nashville, 2005, tracks include "Louisiana Woman, Mississippi Man," "Easy Loving," "After the Fire Is Gone," and "I Can't Love You Enough"

Gold [2 CDs], MCA Nashville, 2006, tracks include "Desperado Love," "Red Neckin' Love Makin' Night," "Happy Birthday Darlin'," "The Rose," "Slow Hand," and "Tight Fittin' Jeans"

Number 1's, MCA Nashville, 2007, tracks include "Lead Me On," "Next in Line," "After the Fire Is Gone," "Linda on My Mind," "Hello Darlin'," and "I Can't Stop Loving You"

Lonely Blue Boy 1957–1959, Jasmine Music, 2010, tracks include "Maybe Baby," "Sentimental Journey," "Star Spangled Heaven," "Lonely Blue Boy," "I Vibrate," and "You'll Never Walk Alone"

Icon, MCA Nashville, 2011, tracks include "Hello Darlin'," "After the Fire Is Gone," "You've Never Been This Far Before," "It's Only Make Believe," and "Tight Fittin' Jeans"

Tell Me One More Time: The MGM Rock and Roll Collection, 101 Distribution, 2011, tracks include "Hallelujah, I Love Her So," "Hey Little Lucy," "You Win Again," "Teasin'," "It's Only Make Believe," and "Mona Lisa"

Essential Recordings [2 CDs], Primo, 2012, tracks include "Lonely Blue Boy," "You Win Again," "Danny Boy," "Shake It Up," "I Need Your Lovin'," "Just Because," and "It's Only Make Believe"

Vinyl

45 rpm Singles

"I Need Your Lovin'" b/w "Born to Sing the Blues," Mercury Records, 1957

"Shake It Up" b/w "Maybe Baby," Mercury Records, 1957

"I'll Try" b/w "It's Only Make Believe," MGM, 1958

"Double Talk Baby" b/w "Why Can't I Get Through to You," Mercury Records, 1958

"Make Me Know You're Mine" b/w "The Story of My Love," MGM, 1959

"Sentimental Journey," "I Vibrate," "The Story of My Love," and "I'll Try," MGM, 1959

"Hey Little Lucy! (Don'tcha Put No Lipstick on)" b/w "When I'm Not with You," MGM, 1959

"Mona Lisa" b/w "Heavenly," MGM, 1959

"Danny Boy" b/w "Halfway to Heaven," MGM, 1959

"Lonely Blue Boy" b/w "Star Spangled Heaven," MGM, 1959

"The Hurt in My Heart" b/w "What Am I Living For," MGM, 1960

"She's Mine" b/w "Is a Blue Bird Blue," MGM, 1960

"Tell Me One More Time" b/w "What a Dream," MGM, 1960

"Teasin'" b/w "I Need You So," MGM, 1960

"Whole Lot of Shakin' Going On" b/w "The Flame," MGM, 1960

"Restless" b/w "Just Because," MGM, 1960

"Hey Miss Ruby" b/w "Foggy River," MGM, 1960

"Platinum High School" b/w "Hallelujah I Love Her So," MGM, 1960

"Don't You Dare Let Me Down" b/w "C'est Ci Bon (It's So Good)," MGM, 1960

"Man Alone" b/w "The Next Kiss (Is the Last Goodbye)," MGM, 1961

"A Million Teardrops" b/w "I'm in a Blue, Blue Mood," MGM, 1961

"It's Drivin' Me Wild" b/w "Sweet Sorrow," MGM, 1961

"Portrait of a Fool" b/w "Tower of Tears," MGM, 1961

"Comfy 'n' Cozy" b/w "A Little Piece of My Heart," MGM, 1962

"There's Something on Your Mind" b/w "Unchained Melody," MGM, 1962

"The Pickup" b/w "I Hope, I Think, I Wish," MGM, 1962

"I Got My Mojo Working" b/w "She Ain't No Angel," MGM, 1963

"She Loves Me (She Don't Love You)" b/w "Go On and Cry," ABC-Paramount, 1963

"My Baby Left Me" b/w "Such a Night," ABC-Paramount, 1964

"Guess My Eyes Were Bigger Than My Heart" b/w "Honky Tonk Man," Decca Records, 1966

"Look into My Teardrops" b/w "If You Were Mine to Lose," Decca Records, 1966

"Don't Put Your Hurt in My Heart" b/w "Walk Me to the Door," Decca Records, 1967

"Funny but I'm Not Laughing" b/w "Working Girl," Decca Records, 1967

"I Don't Want to Be with Me" b/w "Before I'll Set Her Free," Decca Records, 1967

"The Image of Me" b/w "Dim Lights, Thick Smoke," Decca Records, 1968

"Next in Line" b/w "I'm Checking Out," Decca Records, 1968

"To See My Angel Cry" b/w "I Did the Best I Could (with What I Had)," Decca Records, 1969

"That's When She Started to Stop Loving You" b/w "I'll Get Over Losing You," Decca Records, 1969

"Hello Darlin'" b/w "Girl at the Bar," Decca Records, 1970

"Long Black Train" b/w "What a Dream," MGM, 1971

"I Wonder What She'll Think About Me Leaving" b/w "Heartache Just Walked In," Decca Records, 1971

Conway Twitty and Loretta Lynn, "After the Fire Is Gone" b/w "The One I Can't Live Without," Decca Records, 1971

Conway Twitty and Loretta Lynn, "Lead Me On" b/w "Four Glass Walls," Decca Records, 1971

"You've Never Been This Far Before" b/w "You Make It Hard (to Take the Easy Way Out)," MCA Records, 1973

Conway Twitty and Loretta Lynn, "Louisiana Woman, Mississippi Man" b/w "Living Together Alone," MCA Records, 1973

"I'm Not Through Loving You Yet" b/w "Before Your Time," MCA Records, 1974

"Don't Cry Joni" b/w "Touch the Hand," MCA Records, 1975

Conway Twitty and Loretta Lynn, "Feelins'" b/w "You Done Lost Your Baby," MCA Records, 1975

"This Time I've Hurt Her More Than She Loves Me" b/w "She Did-it, Did-I Didn't," MCA Records, 1975

"After All the Good Is Gone" b/w "I Got a Good Thing Going," MCA Records, 1976

"I Can't Believe She Gives It All to Me" b/w "I Can't Help It If She Can't Stop Loving Me," MCA Records, 1976

"Your Love Had Taken Me That High" b/w "My Woman Knows," MCA Records, 1978

"I May Never Get to Heaven" b/w "Grand Ole Blues," MCA Records, 1979

"Happy Birthday Darlin'" b/w "Heavy Tears," MCA Records, 1979

"Tight Fittin' Jeans" b/w "I Made You a Woman," MCA Records, 1981

Conway Twitty and Loretta Lynn, "I Still Believe in Waltzes" b/w "Oh Honey—Oh Babe," MCA Records, 1981

"The Rose" b/w "It's Only Make Believe," Elektra, 1982

"Slow Hand" b/w "When Love Was Something Else," Elektra, 1982

"Hello Darlin'" b/w "Heartache Tonight," Warner Bros., 1983

"Desperado Love" b/w "I Can't See Me Without You," Warner Bros., 1986

"I Want to Know You Before We Make Love" b/w "Snake Boots," MCA Records, 1987

Harold Jenkins, "Rock House" b/w "Crazy Dreams," Norton Records, 2003

LPs

Conway Twitty Sings, MGM, 1959, tracks include "It's Only Make Believe," "Mona Lisa," "You'll Never Walk Alone," "Sentimental Journey," and "My One and Only You"

Saturday Night with Conway Twitty, MGM, 1959, tracks include "Danny Boy," "Goin' Home," "You Win Again," "Restless," and "Hey Little Lucy!"

Lonely Blue Boy, MGM, 1959, tracks include "Just Because," "Heartbreak Hotel," "Trouble in Mind," "Pretty Eyed Baby," and "Eternal Tears"

The Rock and Roll Story, MGM, 1961, tracks include "The Girl Can't Help It," "Treat Me Nice," "Blue Suede Shoes," "Shake, Rattle, and Roll," and "Splish Splash"

Portrait of a Fool, MGM, 1962, tracks include "Sweet Sorrow," "I'm in a Blue, Blue Mood," "Next Kiss," "The Flame," and "What a Dream"

I Love You More Today, Decca Records, 1969, tracks include "Star Spangled Heaven," "Games People Play," "Heartaches by the Number," "Proud Mary," and "Crazy Arms"

Hello Darlin', Decca Records, 1970, tracks include "I'll Get Over Losing You," "Rose,"

"Rocky Top," "Blue Eyes Crying in the Rain," and "I'm So Used to Loving You"

Conway Twitty and Loretta Lynn, *We Only Make Believe*, Decca Records, 1970, tracks include "Take Me," "After the Fire Is Gone," "I'm So Used to Loving You," and "Hangin' On"

I Wonder What She'll Think About Me Leaving, MCA Records, 1971, tracks include "One More Time," "Joy to the World," "Wine Me Up," "I'd Rather Love You," and "A Letter and a Ring"

Conway Twitty and Loretta Lynn, *Lead Me On*, Decca Records, 1971, tracks include "When I Turn Off My Lights," "You're the Reason," "How Far Can We Go," and "Easy Lovin'"

You've Never Been This Far Before, MCA Records, 1973, tracks include "Baby's Gone," "Seasons of My Heart," "Bring It on Home," "Born to Lose," and "I Love You More in Memory"

I'm So Used to Loving You, MCA Records, 1973, tracks include "A Letter and a Ring, "Table in the Corner," "A Little Girl Cried," and "One for the Money"

Honky Tonk Angel, MCA Records, 1974, tracks include "Love Is the Foundation," "Pick Me Up on Your Way Down," "Pop a Top," and "Somewhere Just Out of Her Mind"

Conway Twitty and Loretta Lynn, *Country Partners*, MCA Records, 1974, tracks include "Don't Mess Up a Good Thing," "Two Lonely People," "I Changed My Way," "Country Bumpkin," and "It All Falls Down"

Conway Twitty and Loretta Lynn, *Feelins,'* MCA Records, 1975, tracks include "She's About a Mover," "I'll Never Get Tired of Saying I Love You," "Let Me Be There," and "You Done Lost Your Baby"

Linda on My Mind, MCA Records, 1975, tracks include "Girl from Tupelo," "Roll in My Sweet Baby's Arms," "I'll Get Over Losing You," "Why Me," and "The Fool I've Been Today"

Now and Then, MCA Records, 1976, tracks include "Mona Lisa," "Lonely Blue Boy," "It's Only Make Believe," and "After All the Good Is Gone"

This Time I've Hurt Her More Than She Loves Me, MCA Records, 1976, tracks include "The Race Is On," "She Takes Care of Me," "She Sure Does Make It Hard to Go," and "She Thinks I Still Care"

Mr. T, MCA Records, 1981, tracks include "I Made You a Woman," "Tight Fittin' Jeans," "I'm Already Taken," and "Cheatin' Fire"

By Heart, Warner Bros., 1984, tracks include "All My Life," "Without You," "I Don't Know a Thing About Love," and "A Hard Act to Follow"

Jerry King and the Rivertown Ramblers

CDs

The Sun Sessions, V-8 Records, 2003

Out of This World, V-8 Records, 2004

Various Artists, *Rockabilly Showdown, Volume 1*, Golly Gee Records, 2005, two tracks by Jerry King and the Rivertown Ramblers—"Used to Be" and "I Miss the Ring"

A Date with Jerry King and the Rivertown Ramblers, El Toro Records, 2006

Various Artists, *Wild Records Presents the Wildest* [2 CDs], Wild Records, 2006, two tracks by Jerry King and the Rivertown Ramblers—"I Wanna Love Her" and "Six Feet Deep"

Various Artists, *Best of Fury Rockabilly, Volume 2*, Fury Records, 2006, one track by Jerry King and the Rivertown Ramblers—"Honky Tonk Bop"

Ocala Baby, El Toro Records, 2010

Sleepy LaBeef

CDs

Strange Things Happening, Rounder Records, 1994, tracks include "Playboy," "Waltz Across Texas," "Just Call Me Lonesome," "Stagger Lee," and "Tryin' to Get to You"

Larger Than Life [6 CDs], Bear Family Records, 1996, tracks include "All the Time," "Little Bit More," "Guess Things Happen That Way," "Goodnight Irene," "Turn Me Loose," and "Ain't Got No Home"

Tomorrow Never Comes, M.C. Records, 2000, tracks include "Detour," "Polk Salad Annie," "Wipeout," "Too Much Monkey Business," and "Rolling in My Sweet Baby's Arms"

Rockabilly Blues, Bullseye Blues, 2001, tracks include "Rip It Up," "This Train," "Night Train to Memphis," "Long Tall Sally," "Bottle Up and Go," and "Bright Lights, Big City"

The Human Jukebox, Sun Entertainment, 2002, tracks include "Me and Bobby McGee," "Faded Love," "Boom, Boom, Boom," "Blues Stay Away from Me," and "Raining in My Heart"

The Bull's Night Out/Western Gold, Collectables, 2006, tracks include "Streets of Laredo," "High Noon," "Me and Bobby McGee," "Too Much Monkey Business," "Cool Water," and "Mule Train"

Sleepy Rocks, Bear Family Records, 2008, tracks include "Tore Up," "Little Bit More," "I'm Coming Home," "Ride on Josephine," "Baby Let's Play House," "You're So Easy to Love," and "Home of the Blues"

Roots, Ponk Media, 2009, tracks include "Cotton Fields," "Gotta Travel On," "Amazing Grace," "Detroit City," "What Am I Worth," and "Baby to Cry"

Nothin' but the Truth (Live), Rounder Records, 2009, tracks include "Tore Up," "Ring of Fire," "Milk Cow Blues," "Worried Man Blues," and "Boogie Woogie Country Man"

I'll Never Lay My Guitar Down, Rounder Records, 2009, tracks include "Sweet Thang," "Sick and Tired," "Little Old Wine Drinker Me," "Little Boy Sad," and "Treat Me Like a Dog"

A Rockin' Decade, Snapper UK, 2009, tracks include "Jack and Jill Boogie," "Honky Tonk Man," "Red Hot," "Matchbox," "Honey Hush," "Big Boss Man," and "Blue Moon of Kentucky"

Locomotora Sleepy, Discoloco, 2011, tracks include "Mystery Train," "Who Do You Love," "Pledging My Love," "Tiger by the Tail," and "Goin' Steady"

Vinyl

45 rpm Singles

"I'm Through" b/w "All Alone," Starday, 1957

"I'm Through" b/w "All Alone," Mercury-Starday, 1957

"All the Time" b/w "Lonely," Mercury-Starday, 1957

"Found Out" b/w "Can't Get You Off My Mind," Gulf, 1960

"Turn Me Loose" b/w "Ridin' Fence," Crescent Productions, 1961

"Ride on Josephine" b/w "Walkin' Slowly," Wayside, 1962

"Tore Up" b/w "Lonely," Wayside, 1963

"Drink Up and Go Home" b/w "Teardrops on a Rose," Finn, 1963

"Ride On Josephine" b/w "Lonely," Picture, 1963

"You Can't Catch Me" b/w "Everybody's Got to Have Somebody (to Love)," Columbia Records, 1965

"Blackland Farmer" b/w "Got You on My Mind," Plantation Records, 1965

"A Man in My Position" b/w "Drinking Again," Columbia Records, 1966

"I'm Too Broke (to Pay Attention)" b/w "I Feel a Lot More Like I Do Now," Columbia Records, 1966

"Completely Destroyed" b/w "Go Ahead on Baby," Columbia Records, 1967

"Sure Beats the Heck Outta Settlin' Down" b/w "Schneider," Columbia Records, 1967

"Every Day" b/w "If I Go Right, I'm Wrong," Columbia Records, 1968

"Too Much Monkey Business" b/w "Got You on My Mind," Plantation Records, 1970

"Asphalt Cowboy" b/w "Got You on My Mind," Plantation Records, 1970

"Ghost Riders in the Sky" (both sides), Sun Records, 1975

"There Ain't Much After Taxes" (both sides), Sun Records, 1976

"Good Rockin' Boogie" (both sides), Sun Records, 1978

"Good Rockin' Boogie" b/w "Corine, Corina," Charly UK, 1978

"Flying Saucers Rock and Roll" b/w "Boogie Woogie Country Girl," Sun International, 1979

"Roll Over Beethoven" b/w "Send Me Some Lovin'," Charly UK, 1979

LPs

1977 Rockabilly, Sun Records, 1978, tracks include "You Can Have Her," "Matchbox," "Good Rockin' Tonight," "Baby Let's Play House," "Matilda," and "From a Jack to a King"

Early, Rare, and Rockin' Sides, Baron, 1979, tracks include "Walkin' Slowly," "Turn Me Loose," "Ride on Josephine," "Lonely," "Tore Up," and "Baby Let's Play House"

Rockabilly Heavyweight, Charly UK, 1979, tracks include "Sick and Tired," "Mind Your Own Business," "Lonesome for a Letter," "I'm Feelin' Sorry," and "Honky Tonk Man"

Downhome Rockabilly, Charly UK, 1979, tracks include "I'm a One Woman Man," "Jack and Jill Boogie," "Red Hot," "Mystery Train," "Big Boss Man," and "Boogie Woogie Country Girl"

It Ain't What You Eat, It's the Way How You Chew It, Rounder Records, 1980, tracks include "I'm Ready," "Shake a Hand," "Tutti Frutti," "Let's Talk About Us," and "Satisfied"

Electricity, Rounder Records, 1982, tracks include "Alabam," "Every Day," "I'm Through," "Ain't Got No Home," "These Boots Were Made for Walking," and "Turn Me Loose"

Lil' Esther

CDs

The Bugaloos, *In the Mood*, Rockhouse, 1991

Lil' Esther and her Tinstars, *In the Garden of Love*, Rarity Records, 2002

Lil' Esther and her Tinstars, *Gone Is My Mind*, Empire Records, 2009

Lil' Esther and her Tinstars, *Live, Little, and Loud*, Empire Records, 2010

Vinyl

LPs

The Bugaloos, *The Bugaloos*, Rockhouse, 1990

Lil' Esther and Her Tinstars, *Small Change*, Empire Records, 2007

Robin Luke

CDs

Susie Darlin', Bear Family Records, 1994, tracks include "Five Minutes More," "Who's Gonna Hold Your Hand," "Rotten Love," "Make Me a Dreamer," "So Alone," and "Everlovin'"

Various Artists, *The History of Dot—Volume 1*, Varese Sarabande, 1996, one track by Luke "Susie Darlin'"

Susie Darlin'—The Best of Robin Luke, Master Classic Records, 2012, tracks include "Everlovin'," "Five Minutes More," "School Bus Love Affair," "Bad Boy," and "Poor Little Rich Boy"

Vinyl

45 rpm Singles

"Susie Darlin'" b/w "Living's Loving You," International Records, 1958

"Susie Darlin'" b/w "Living's Loving You," Dot Records, 1958

"Chicka Chicka Honey" b/w "My Girl," Bertram International, 1958

"Chicka Chicka Honey" b/w "My Girl," Dot Records, 1958

"You Can't Stop Me from Dreaming" b/w "Strollin' Blues," Bertram International, 1959

"You Can't Stop Me from Dreaming" b/w "Strollin' Blues," Dot Records, 1959

"Who's Gonna Hold Your Hand" b/w "Five Minutes More," Bertram International, 1959

"Who's Gonna Hold Your Hand" b/w "Five Minutes More," Dot Records, 1959

"Walkin' in the Moonlight" b/w "Make Me a Dreamer," Dot Records, 1959

"Bad Boy" b/w "School Bus Love Affair," Dot Records, 1960

"Everlovin'" b/w "Well Oh, Well Oh (Don't You Know)," Dot Records, 1960

"So Alone" b/w "All Because of You," Dot Records, 1961

"Part of a Fool" b/w "Poor Little Rich Boy," Dot Records, 1961

Robin Luke and Roberta Shore, "Foggin' Up the Windows" b/w "A Wound Time Can't Erase," Dot Records, 1962

LPs

Various Artists, *Young Love*, Dot Records, 1959, one track by Luke—"Susie Darlin'"

Susie Darlin', ABC Records, 1978, tracks include "Poor Little Rich Boy," "Five Minutes More," "Everlovin'," and "Part of a Fool"

Boppin' with Robin, Starfire Records, 1981, tracks include "Strollin' Blues," "Susie Darlin'," "You Can't Stop Me from Dreaming," and "Chicka Chicka Honey"

Ronnie Mack

CDs

Big Jay McNeely and the Ronnie Mack Band, *Welcome to California*, Big J, 1990

Ray Campi, *With Friends in Texas*, Flying Fish Records, 1991

Various Artists, *A Town South of Bakersfield, Vol. 3*, Restless Records, 1993, one track by Mack—"Mama's Reward"

Various Artists, *1975–1995: 20 Years Bear Family Records* (4 CDs), Bear Family Records, 1995 one track by Mack—"The Bare Facts of Life"

Born to Rock, Sunjay, 1996

Various Artists, *Turning the World Blue: A Tribute to Gene Vincent*, Skizmatic Records, 1997, one track by Mack—"Lucky Star"

Ray Campi, *With Friends Along the Way—Austin to L.A.*, Arcade, 2007, two tracks by Mack "Waitin' in School" and "If You've Got the Money, I've Got the Time"

Various Artists, *L.A. Americana Nightlife*, Southern California Sounds, 2013, three tracks by Mack—"Certified Evil," "Legacy," and "You Make Me Wanna Rock"

Vinyl

45 rpm Singles

"I Wanna Dance with You" b/w "You Make Me Wanna Rock," Rollin' Rock, 1982

"Hold Me Tight" b/w "The Usual Thing," Rollin' Rock, 1985

"My Best Friend" b/w "Kentucky Means Paradise," Lonesome Town, 1986

"It Won't Take Much" b/w "My Heart Is Achin' for You," Lonesome Town, 1986

"Lonesome Town" b/w "Brand New Heartache," Lonesome Town, 1989

LPs

The Alley Gators, K-Tel, 1983, tracks by Mack include "Marie, Marie," "Waitin' in School," "I Wanna Dance with You," "You Make Me Wanna Rock," and "Julie"

Jai Malano

CDs

The Royal Rhythmaires, *Shuck and Jive*, Rhythm Bomb Records, 2013

The Royal Rhythmaires, *Talk to Me*, Rhythm Bomb Records, 2014

Mars Attacks

CDs

Run for Your Life, Armadillo Records, 1999
Dirty Tricks, Armadillo Records, 2003
Circle of Love, Blue Lake Records, 2006
Follow Me, Blue Lake Records, 2008
Recaptured!, Part Records, 2011
Blood and Thunder, Sold My Soul Media, 2013

Janis Martin

CDs

The Female Elvis: Complete Recordings 1955–1960, Bear Family Records, 1994, tracks include "My Boy Elvis," "Drugstore Rock and Roll," "Bang Bang," "Cracker Jack," and "All Right Baby"

Here I Am, Hydra Records, 2001, tracks include "Mama He Treats Your Daughter Mean," "Hard Rocking Mama," "Old Time Rock and Roll," "Good Love," "Barefoot Baby," and "Ooby Dooby"

Masters and Studio Outtakes, Bear Family Records, 2006, tracks include "My Boy Elvis," "Cracker Jack," "Ooby Dooby," "Love and Kisses," "My Boy Elvis," and "William"

My Girl Janis, Indie Europe/Zoom, 2009, tracks include "William," "Good Love," "My Confession," "I'll Never Be Free," "My Boy Elvis," "Love and Kisses," "Drugstore Rock and Roll," and "Bang Bang"

Cracker Jack, Snapper Music, 2009, tracks include "My Boy Elvis," "All Right Baby," "Half Loved," "Love and Kisses," "Love Me to Pieces," and "Drugstore Rock and Roll"

The Blanco Sessions, Cow Island Music, 2012, tracks include "It'll Be Me," "Believe What You Say," "Long White Cadillac," "Oh Lonesome Me," and "As Long as I'm Movin'"

My Boy Elvis, Jasmine Music, 2014, tracks include "I Don't Hurt Anymore," "Blues Keep Calling," "Let's Elope Baby," "Here Today and Gone Tomorrow," and "Barefoot Baby"

Vinyl

45 rpm Singles

"Drugstore Rock and Roll" b/w "Will You, Willyum," RCA Victor, 1956
"Ooby Dooby" b/w "One More Year to Go," RCA Victor, 1956
"My Boy Elvis" b/w "Little Bit," RCA Victor, 1956
"Barefoot Baby" b/w "Let's Elope Baby," RCA Victor, 1956
"Two Long Years" b/w "Love Me to Pieces," RCA Victor, 1957
"Love and Kisses" b/w "I'll Never Be Free," RCA Victor, 1957
"All Right Baby" b/w "Billy Boy, Billy Boy," RCA Victor, 1957
"Cracker Jack" b/w "Good Love," RCA Victor, 1958
"Bang Bang" b/w "Please Be My Love," RCA Victor, 1958
"Hard Times Ahead" b/w "Here Today and Gone Tomorrow," Palette, 1960
"Teen Street" b/w "Cry Guitar," Palette, 1961
"I'm Moving On" b/w "Begging to You," Big Dutch Label, 1977
"Barefoot Baby" b/w "Love and Kisses," Sleazy Records, 2011

LPs

Janis Martin and Elvis Presley, *Janis and Elvis*, RCA Victor, 1963, four tracks by Martin—"Ooby Dooby," "Let's Elope Baby," "One More Year to Go," and "Barefoot Baby"

That Rockin' Gal Sings My Boy Elvis, Bear Family Records, 1979, tracks include "Cracker Jack," "Good Love," "Bang Bang," "Little Bit," "Barefoot Baby," and "Will You, Willyum"

That Rockin' Gal Rocks On, Bear Family Records, 1979, tracks include "All Right Baby," "One More Year to Go," "Let's Elope Baby," "Teen Street," "Half Loved," and "Two Long Years"

Janis Martin and Eddie Bond, *Live at the Rockhouse 25*, Rockhouse Records, 1986, seven tracks by Martin—"Ooby Dooby," "Hard Rocking Mama," "My Boy Elvis," "Bang Bang," "Great Balls of Fire," "Let's Elope Baby," and "Barefoot Baby"

Love and Kisses, Bear Family Records, 2003, tracks include "Cracker Jack," "Billy Boy, Billy Boy," "My Boy Elvis," "Love and Kisses," and "Good Love"

Junior Marvel

CDs

Stompin' at the Hillbilly Boogie Barn, Rundell Records, 1999
Early and Unreleased, Rundell Records, 2000
Messin' Around with Junior Marvel, El Toro Records, 2005
The Original Hillbilly Cat Sessions, Volume One, Sleazy Records, 2006
Southern and Rockin', Empire, 2008

Vinyl

45 rpm Records

The Bellhops, "Nickel and a Dime" b/w "Let's Rock," MAC Records, 1990
"Lies, Lies, Lies" b/w "Go Man Go," MAC Records, 1995

LPs

Moon Magic, Marvelous Records, 1996

Big Jay McNeely

CDs

Blow the Wall Down!, Ornament Records, 1990, tracks include "Country Boy," "Summertime," "Pretty Girls," "Tequila," and "Something on Your Mind"
Big Jay McNeely and the Ronnie Mack Band, *Welcome to California*, Big J, 1990, tracks include "There Is Something on Your Mind," "I Can't Stop Loving You," "Chantilly Lace," "Big Jay Shuffle," and "Palomino Ride"
Jay Walkin', ABC, 1991, tracks include "Harlem Nocturne," "Country Boy," "Honky Tonk," "Pretty Girls Everywhere," and "Big Jay Shuffle"
Big Jay McNeely: Live at Birdland, Collectables, 1992, tracks include "Honky Tonk," "Insect Ball," "I Got a Woman," "Flying Home," and "Havana Hop"
Nervous!, Saxophile, 1995, tracks include "Real Crazy Cool," "The Goof," "3-D," and "Nervous Man Nervous"
People Will Be People, Big J, 1996, tracks include "Insect Ball," "You Are My Life," "Big Fat Mama," "Full Moon," and "Deacon's Hop"
Big Jay McNeely and Dana Gillespie, *Cherry Pie*, Big J, 1997, tracks include "Get Up and Boogie," "Watts Up," "You Make Me Feel So Good," and "Jay's Groove"
Central Avenue Confidential, Atomic Theory, 1999, tracks include "Mighty Fine," "Big Jay Shuffle," "You Are My Life" and "Stranger on the Shore"
Big Jay McNeely 1948–1950, Classics, 2001, tracks include "Deacon's Hop," "Wild Wig," "Cherry Smash," "Blow Big Jay," and "Let's Split"
AZ Bootin', Big World (Continental), 2002, tracks include "Young Girl Blues," "Summertime," "Zydeco Stroll," and "Big Jay's Shuffle"
There Is Something on Your Mind, Collectables, 2002, tracks include "Flying Home," "Back Shack Track," "Minnie," "After Midnight," and "Havana Hop"
The Deacon, Unabridged: Vol. 2 1951–1952, Classics, 2003, tracks include "Love from the Heart," "I'll Never Love Again," "Let's Do It," "Don't Cry Baby," and "Insect Ball"
The Go! Go! Go! Man, Swingin', 2007, tracks include "Salt and Pepper," "Body and Soul," "Deacon Blows for Ray," "Real Crazy Cool," and "The Goof"
Axel Zwingenberger and Big Jay McNeely, *Saxy Boogie Woogie*, Vegabond Records, 2008, tracks include "Greasy Groove," "Big Jay's Jungle Jive," "Night Ride," and "Blues Well Done"
King of the Honkin' Sax [2 CDs], JSP Records, 2011, tracks include "Roadhouse Boogie," "Artie's Jump," "Deacon's Hop," "Insect Ball," "Penthouse Serenade," and "Big Jay Shuffle"

Vinyl

45 rpm Singles

Big Jay McNeely with vocals by Jesse Belvin, "All That Wine Is Gone" b/w "Don't Cry Baby," Imperial Records, 1951
"Penthouse Serenade" b/w "Just Crazy," Federal Records, 1952
"Hometown Jamboree" b/w "Teenage Hop," Bayou, 1953
"Catastrophe" b/w "Calamity," Bayou, 1953
"Deacon's Express" b/w "Jet Fury," Imperial Records, 1953
"Let's Work" b/w "Hard Tack," Federal Records, 1954
"Mule Milk" b/w "Ice Water," Federal Records, 1954
"Hot Cinders" b/w "Whipped Cream," Federal Records, 1954
"Beachcomber" b/w "Strip Tease Swing," Federal Records, 1954
"Real Crazy Cool" b/w "Let's Split," Aladdin, 1954
"Big Jay's Hop" b/w "Three Blind Mice," Vee-Jay, 1955
The Delegates/Big Jay McNeely, "The Convention" b/w "Jay's Rock," Vee-Jay, 1956
Big Jay McNeely with vocal by Little Sonny

Warner, "I Got the Message" b/w "Psycho Serenade," Swingin', 1959

Big Jay McNeely with vocal by Little Sonny Warner, "There Is Something on Your Mind" b/w "Back Shack Track," Swingin', 1959

Big Jay McNeely with vocal by Little Sonny Warner, "Minnie" b/w "My Darling Dear," Swingin', 1960

Big Jay McNeely with vocal by Little Sonny Warner, "I Love You, Oh Darling" b/w "Oh What a Fool," Swingin', 1960

"Before Midnight" b/w "After Midnight," Swingin', 1961

"Without a Love" b/w "The Squat," Swingin', 1962

"You Don't Have to Go" b/w "Big Jay's Count," Warner Bros., 1963

"Deacon's Hop" b/w "Blues in G Minor," Modern Oldies, 1968

"Rockin' the Reeds" b/w "California," Big J, 1985

"Zydeco Stroll" b/w "Young Girl Blues," Big J, 1987

LPs

Big Jay McNeely, Federal Records, 1955, tracks include "Big Jay Shuffle," "Whipped Cream," "The Goof," "Mule Milk," and "Ice Water"

Big Jay McNeely Plays a Rhythm and Blues Concert, Savoy, 1955, tracks include "Wild Wig," "Sunday Dinner," "California Hop," and "Cherry Smash"

Big "J" in 3D, Federal Records, 1956, tracks include "Ice Water," "Nervous Man Nervous," "Mule Milk," "Big Jay Shuffle," and "Rock Candy"

Big Jay McNeely: Recorded Live at Cisco's, Manhattan Beach, Calif., Warner Bros., 1963, tracks include "You Don't Have to Go," "Further on Up the Road," "Deacon's Hop," and "Big Boy"

Deacon Rides Again, Imperial Records, 1983, tracks include "Jay Walk," "Blow Blow Blow," "Old Black Mule," "Don't Cry Baby," and "Insect Ball"

Big Jay McNeely: From Harlem to Camden, Ace Records, 1984, tracks include "Harlem Nocturne," "Just Because," "Night Train," "Jumpin' with Jay," and "Strollin' Sax"

Big Jay McNeely Meets the Penguins, Ace Records, 1984, tracks include "Watch Out Big Jay's Loose," "Harlem Nocturne," "Honky Tonk," and "Ooky Ook"

The Best of Big Jay McNeely, Saxophonograph Records, 1985, tracks include "Deacon's Hop," "Big Jay's Hop," "3-D," "Let's Work," and "Nervous Man Nervous"

Big Jay McNeely Direct to Disc, APO APO, 2012, tracks include "Party Time," "There Is Something on Your Mind," "All That Wine Is Gone," and "Country Boy"

Big Jay McNeely with Ray Collins' Hot-Club and Friends, *Life Story*, Brisk, 2012, tracks include "Rock and Roll," "Funky Bug," "Blow Your Brains Out," The Jam," and "Go On"

Miss Mary Ann

CDs

The Ranch Girls and the Ragtime Wranglers, *Rhythm on the Ranch*, Longhorn Records, 1994

The Ranch Girls and Their Ragtime Wranglers, *Hillbilly Harmony*, Goofin' Records, 1997

Miss Mary Ann and the Ragtime Wranglers, *Mad Mama*, Goofin' Records, 2000

The Ranch Girls and the Ragtime Wranglers, *Can You Hear It?*, Homebrew Records, 2001

Miss Mary Ann and the Ragtime Wranglers, *Rock It on Down to My House*, Sonic Rendezvous, 2006

Miss Mary Ann and the Ragtime Wranglers, *Boogie Woogie Santa Claus*, Sonic Rendezvous, 2007

Miss Mary Ann with the Ragtime Wranglers and the Ranch Girls, *Selections: 1992–2008 (15 Years on the Road)*, Sonic Rendezvous, 2009

Miss Mary Ann and the Ragtime Wranglers, *Danger Moved West*, Homebrew Records, 2013

Vinyl

45 rpm Singles

The Ranch Girls and the Hillbilly Boogieman, "Christmas Time's a-Coming" b/w "Christmas Boogie," Homebrew Records, 1994

The Ranch Girls and the Ragtime Wranglers, "Kaw-liga" b/w "I'll Get Him Back," Homebrew Records, 1995

The Orlons

CDs

The Best of the Orlons: 1961–1966, ABKCO Records, 2005, tracks include "South Street," "Don't Hang Up," "The Wah-Watusi," "I'll Be True," and "Not Me"

Cameo Parkway: The Greatest Hits, ABKCO Records, 2006, three tracks by the Orlons—"The Wah-Watusi," "Don't Hang Up," and "South Street"

Vinyl

45 rpm Singles

"I'll Be True" b/w "Heart Darling Angel," Cameo, 1961

"(Happy Birthday) Mr. Twenty-One" b/w "Please Let It Be," Cameo, 1962

"The Wah-Watusi" b/w "Holiday Hill," Cameo, 1962

"Don't Hang Up" b/w "The Conservative," Cameo, 1962

"South Street" b/w "Them Terrible Boots," Cameo, 1963

"Not Me" b/w "My Best Friend," Cameo, 1963

"Crossfire" b/w "It's No Big Thing," Cameo, 1963

"Bon-Doo-Wah" b/w "Don't Throw Your Love Away," Cameo, 1963

LPs

The Wah-Watusi, Cameo, 1962, tracks include "Dedicated to the One I Love," "Let Me In," "Mashed Potato Time," "Over the Mountain, Across the Sea," and "I'll Be True"

All the Hits by the Orlons, Cameo, 1963, tracks include "Don't Hang Up," "Chains," "He's a Rebel," "Big Girls Don't Cry," and "Release Me"

South Street, Cameo, 1963, tracks include "Don't Let Go," "Charlie Brown," "Walk Right In," "Mister Sandman," and "Cement Mixer"

Not Me, Cameo, 1963, tracks include "Something's Got a Hold on Me," "Mama Didn't Lie," "Forever," "Bad Boy," and "He's Sure the Boy I Love"

Down Memory Lane, Cameo, 1963, tracks include "Come Go with Me," "Diamonds and Pearls," "You Cheated," "Let the Good Times Roll," and "Stranded in the Jungle"

Buck Owens

CDs

Collection 1959–90 [3 CDs], Rhino Records, 1992, tracks include "Under Your Spell Again," "Loose Talk," "Sam's Place," "Hot Dog," "Streets of Bakersfield," "Crying Time," and "I've Got a Tiger by the Tail"

The Very Best of Buck Owens, Volume One, Rhino, 1994, tracks include "Under Your Spell Again," "Act Naturally," "Waitin' in Your Welfare Line," "Sam's Place," and "Who's Gonna Mow Your Grass"

The Very Best of Buck Owens, Volume Two, Rhino, 1994, tracks include "Foolin' Around," "Love's Gonna Live Here," "Big in Vegas," "Made in Japan," and "Ruby"

21 #1 Hits—The Ultimate Collection, Rhino, 2006, tracks include "Streets of Bakersfield," "I've Got a Tiger by the Tail," "Johnny B. Goode," "Your Tender Loving Care," and "Together Again"

Act Naturally—The Buck Owens Records 1953–1964 [5 CDs], Bear Family Records, 2008, tracks include "Right After the Dance," "Hot Dog," "Sweethearts in Heaven," "Heartaches by the Number," "Dang Me," and "Truck Drivin' Man"

Open Up Your Heart: The Buck Owens and the Buckaroos Recordings 1965–1968 [7 CDs], Bear Family Records, 2010, tracks include "Steel Guitar Rag," "Cinderella," "I've Got a Tiger by the Tail," "Second Fiddle," "Think of Me," and "Sweet Rosie Jones"

Tall Dark Stranger: The Buck Owens and the Buckaroos 1969–1975 [8 CDs], Bear Family Records, 2012, tracks include "Lonesome Valley," "Nobody but You," "Togetherness," "Bridge Over Troubled Water," and "Wham Bam"

Vinyl

45 rpm Records

Corky Jones, "Down on the Corner of Love" b/w "It Don't Show on Me," Pep, 1956

Corky Jones," "Right After the Dance" b/w "The House Down the Block," Pep, 1956

Corky Jones, "Hot Dog" b/w "Rhythm and Booze," Pep, 1956

Corky Jones and Pauline Parker, "I'd Rather Have You" b/w "My Old Fashioned Heart," Pep, 1956

Corky Jones, "There Goes My Heart" b/w "Sweethearts in Heaven," Pep, 1956

"Come Back" b/w "I Know What It Means," Capitol Records, 1958

"Sweet Thing" b/w "I Only Know That I Love You," Capitol Records, 1958

"I'll Take a Chance on Loving You" b/w "Walk the Floors," Capitol Records, 1958

"Second Fiddle" b/w "My Everlasting Love," Capitol Records, 1959

"Under Your Spell Again" b/w "Tired of Living," Capitol Records, 1959

"Above and Beyond" b/w "Till These Dreams Come True," Capitol Records, 1960

"Excuse Me" b/w "I've Got a Right to Know," Capitol Records, 1960

"Foolin' Around" b/w "High as the Mountains," Capitol Records, 1961

Buck Owens with Rose Maddox, "Loose Talk" b/w "Mental Cruelty," Capitol Records, 1961

"Under the Influence of Love" b/w "Bad Bad Dream," Capitol Records, 1961

"Hot Dog" b/w "Sweethearts in Heaven," New Star, 1961

"Nobody's Fool" b/w "Mirror Mirror on the Wall," Capitol Records, 1962

"Save the Last Dance for Me" b/w "King of Fools," Capitol Records, 1962

"Kickin' Our Hearts Around" b/w "I Can't Stop," Capitol Records, 1962

"You're for Me" b/w "The House Down the Block," Capitol Records, 1962

"Act Naturally" b/w "Over and Over Again," Capitol Records, 1963

Buck Owens with Rose Maddox, "Sweethearts in Heaven" b/w "We're the Talk of the Town," Capitol Records, 1963

"Love's Gonna Live Here" b/w "Getting Used to Losing You," Capitol Records, 1963

"My Heart Skips a Beat" b/w "Together Again," Capitol Records, 1964

"I Don't Care" b/w "Don't Let Her Know," Capitol Records, 1964

"I've Got a Tiger by the Tail" b/w "Crying Time," Capitol Records, 1964

"Before You Go" b/w "No One but You," Capitol Records, 1965

"Gonna Have Love" b/w "Only You," Capitol Records, 1965

"Buckaroo" b/w "If You Want a Love," Capitol Records, 1965

"All I Want for Christmas Dear Is You" b/w "Santa Looked a Lot Like Daddy," Capitol Records, 1965

"Waiting in Your Welfare Line" b/w "In the Palm of Your Hand," Capitol Records, 1966

"Think of Me" b/w "Heart of Glass," Capitol Records, 1966

"Open Up Your Heart" b/w "No More Me and You," Capitol Records, 1966

"Where Does the Good Times Go" b/w "Way That I Love You," Capitol Records, 1966

"Sam's Place" b/w "Don't Ever Tell Me Goodbye," Capitol Records, 1967

"Your Tender Lovin' Care" b/w "What a Liar I Am," Capitol Records, 1967

"It Takes People Like You" b/w "You Left Her Lonely to Go," Capitol Records, 1967

"How Long My Baby Be Gone" b/w "Everybody Needs Somebody," Capitol Records, 1968

"Sweet Rosie Jones" b/w "Happy Times Are Here Again," Capitol Records, 1968

Buck Owens with Buddy Alan, "Let the World Keep on a Turnin'" b/w "I'll Love You Forever and Ever," Capitol Records, 1968

"I've Got You on My Mind Again" b/w "That's Alright with Me," Capitol Records, 1968

"Christmas Shopping" b/w "One of Everything You Got," Capitol Records, 1968

"Things I Saw Happened at the Fountain" b/w "Turkish Holiday," Capitol Records, 1968

"Who's Gonna Mow Your Grass" b/w "There's Gonna Be Some Changes Made," Capitol Records, 1969

"Johnny B. Goode" b/w "Maybe If I Close My Eyes," Capitol Records, 1969

"Tall Dark Stranger" b/w "Sing That Kind of Song," Capitol Records, 1969

"Big in Vegas" b/w "White Satin Bed," Capitol Records, 1969

Buck Owens with Susan Raye, "We're Gonna Get Together" b/w "Everybody Needs Somebody," Capitol Records, 1970

Buck Owens with Susan Raye, "Fallin' for You" b/w "Togetherness," Capitol Records, 1970

"Kansas City Song" b/w "I'd Love to Be Your Man," Capitol Records, 1970

Buck Owens with Susan Raye, "Great White Horse" b/w "Your Tender Loving Care," Capitol Records, 1970

"I Wouldn't Live in New York City" b/w "No Milk and Honey," Capitol Records, 1970

"Bridge Over Troubled Water" b/w "Home," Capitol Records, 1971

"Ruby" b/w "Heartbreak Mountain," Capitol Records, 1971

"Rollin' in My Sweet Baby's Arms" b/w "Corn Liquor," Capitol Records, 1971

Buck Owens with Buddy Alan, "Too Old to Cut the Mustard" b/w "Wham Bam," Capitol Records, 1971

"I'll Still Be Waiting for You" b/w "Full Time Daddy," Capitol Records, 1972

"Made in Japan" b/w "Black Texas Dirt," Capitol Records, 1972

Buck Owens with Susan Raye, "Looking Back to See" b/w "Crying Time," Capitol Records, 1972

"In the Palm of Your Hand" b/w "Get Out of Town Before Sun Goes Down," Capitol Records, 1972

"Big Game Hunter" b/w "That Loving Feeling," Capitol Records, 1973

"Great Expectations" b/w "Let the Fun Begin," Capitol Records, 1974

"Country Singer's Prayer" b/w "Meanwhile Back at the Ranch," Capitol Records, 1975

"Hollywood Waltz" b/w "Rain on Your Parade," Warner Bros., 1976

"California Oakie" b/w "Child Support," Warner Bros., 1976

"Our Old Mansion" b/w "How Come My Dog Don't Bark," Warner Bros., 1977

"Texas Tornado" b/w "Let the Good Times Roll," Warner Bros., 1977

"Do You Wanna Make Love" b/w "Seasons of My Heart," Warner Bros., 1978

"Let Jesse Rob the Train" b/w "Victim of Life's Circumstances, "Warner Bros., 1979

"Moonlights and Magnolias" b/w "Nickels and Dimes," Warner Bros., 1980

"Without You" b/w "Love Don't Make the Bars," Warner Bros., 1981

Buck Owens with Dwight Yoakam, "Streets of Bakersfield" b/w "One More Name," Reprise, 1988

"Put Another Quarter in the Jukebox" b/w "Don't Let Her Know," Capitol Records, 1989

"Gonna Have Love" b/w "Out There Chasing Rainbows," Capitol Records, 1989

"Tijuana Lady" b/w "Brooklyn Bridge," Capitol Records, 1990

LPs

Buck Owens, La Brea, 1960, tracks include "I'm Gonna Blow," "When I Hold You," "Please Don't Take Her from Me," "Country Girl," and "Right After the Dance"

Buck Owens Sings Harlan Howard, Capitol Records, 1961, tracks include "Heartaches by the Number," "Keeper of the Key," "Key's in the Mailbox," "Pick Me up on Your Way Down," and "Foolin' Around"

Buck Owens, Capitol Records, 1961, tracks include "Above and Beyond," "Second Fiddle," "Excuse Me," "Walk the Floor," and "Take Me Back Again"

You're for Me, Capitol Records, 1962, tracks include "Down the River," "Mexican Polka," "Mirror Mirror on the Wall," "Bad Bad Dream," and "Under the Influence of Love"

On the Bandstand, Capitol Records, 1963, tracks include "King of Fools," "Sally was a Good Ole Girl," "Orange Blossom Special," "Kickin' Our Hearts Around," and "Release Me"

The Best of Buck Owens, Capitol Records, 1964, tracks include "Love's Gonna Live Here," "Under Your Spell Again," "Nobody's Fool but Yours," and "Second Fiddle"

Together Again/My Heart Skips a Beat, Capitol Records, 1964, tracks include "Save the Last Dance for Me," "Getting Used to Losing You," "I Don't Hear You," and "Close All the Honky Tonks"

I Don't Care, Capitol Records, 1964, tracks include "Abilene," "Playboy," "Dang Me," "Don't Let Her Know," and "Loose Talk"

I've Got a Tiger by the Tail, Capitol Records, 1965, tracks include "Memphis Tennessee," "Maiden's Prayer," "Crying Time," "Wham Bam," and "Streets of Laredo"

Instrumental Hits, Capitol Records, 1965, tracks include "Steel Guitar Rag," "Buckaroo," "Faded Love," "Mexican Polka," and "Orange Blossom Special"

Roll Out the Red Carpet, Capitol Records, 1966, tracks include "Cajun Fiddle," "Cinderella," "There Never Was a Fool," "After You Leave Me," and "Forever and Ever"

Dust on Mother's Bible, Capitol Records, 1966, tracks include "Pray Every Day," "Bring It to Jesus," "Eternal Vacation," and "Where Would I Be Without Jesus"

Carnegie Hall Concert, Capitol Records, 1966, tracks include "Act Naturally," "Together Again," "Under Your Spell Again," "Waitin' in Your Welfare Line," "My Heart Skips a Beat," and "Above and Beyond"

Open Up Your Heart, Capitol Records, 1966, tracks include "Think of Me," "In the Palm of Your Hand," "You and Only You," "Sam's Place," and "No More Me and You"

In Japan!, Capitol Records, 1967, tracks include "Open Up Your Heart," "We Were Made for Each Other," "Don't Wipe the Tears That You Cry," and "I Was Born to Be in Love with You"

It Takes People Like You, Capitol Records, 1968, tracks include "Where Does the Good Times Go," "I'm Gonna Live It Up," "Long Long Ago," and "I've Got It Bad for You"

Sweet Rosie Jones, Capitol Records, 1968, tracks include "Hello Happiness Goodbye Loneliness," "Happy Times," "Everybody Needs Somebody," "You'll Never Miss the Water," and "If I Had Three Wishes"

I've Got You on My Mind Again, Capitol Records, 1969, tracks include "Let the World Keep on a Turnin'," "Don't Let True Love Slip Away," "That's All Right with Me," and "I Wanna Be Wild and Free"

Tall Dark Stranger, Capitol Records, 1969, tracks include "White Satin Bed," "Darling You Can Depend on Me," "Sing That Kind of Song," and "I Would Do Anything for You"

Buck Owens in London, Capitol Records, 1969, tracks include "Happy Times Are Here Again," "Happening in London Town," "Act Naturally," "Sam's Place," and "Sing Me Back Home"

Big in Vegas, Capitol Records, 1970, tracks include "Lodi," "Maybe If I Close My Eyes," "Catfish Capers," "Along Came Jones," and "We're Gonna Let the Good Times Roll"

Your Mother's Prayer, Capitol Records, 1970, tracks include "Old Time Religion," "Great Judgment Day," "In God I Trust," "My Savior Leads the Way," and "Lonesome Valley"

Buck Owens and Susan Raye, *We're Gonna Get*

Together, Capitol Records, 1970, tracks include "Together Again," "Crying Time," "Foolin' Around," "Love Is Strange," and "Togetherness"

The Kansas City Song, Capitol Records, 1970, tracks include "Full Time Daddy," "Amsterdam," "Bring Back My Peace of Mind," and "I'd Love to Be Your Man"

Buck Owens and Susan Raye, *The Great White Horse*, Capitol Records, 1970, tracks include "Think of Me," "Your Tender Loving Care," "Tennessee Bird Walk," and "High as the Mountain"

I Wouldn't Live in New York City, Capitol Records, 1970, tracks include "Reno Lament," "Down in New Orleans," "Houston Town," "Big in Vegas," and "Kansas City Song"

Live in Scandinavia, Capitol Records, 1970, tracks include "I've Got a Tiger by the Tail," "Six Days on the Road," "Buckaroo," "Up on Cripple Creek," and "Okie from Muskogee"

Bridge Over Troubled Water, Capitol Records, 1971, tracks include "Within My Loving Arms," "I'm Goin' Home," "Catch the Wind," and "I Am a Rock"

Ruby, Capitol Records, 1971, tracks include "Corn Liquor," "Rollin' in My Sweet Baby's Arms," "Rocky Top," and "Heartbreak Mountain"

Live at the John Ascuga's Nugget, Capitol Records, 1972, tracks include "Mountain Dew," "Ruby Are You Mad," "Help Me Make It Through the Night," "Lookin' Out My Back Door," and "Nugget Lament"

Live at the White House, Capitol Records, 1972, tracks include "Act Naturally," "Streets of Laredo," "Truck Drivin' Man," "Gentle on My Mind," and "Crying Time"

Buck Owens and Buddy Allen, *Too Old to Cut the Mustard*, Capitol Records, 1972, tracks include "Wham Bam," "Beautiful Morning Glory," "Forever and Ever," and "You're a Real Good Friend"

In the Palm of Your Hand, Capitol Records, 1973, tracks include "There Goes My Love," "I Love You So Much It Hurts," "Arms Full of Empty," and "Sweethearts in Heaven"

Ain't It Amazing Gracie, Capitol Records, 1973, tracks include "Your Monkey Won't Be Home Tonight," "Long Hot Summer," "I Know That You Know," and "When You Get to Heaven"

Arms Full of Empty, Capitol Records, 1973, tracks include "Loving You," "Happy Hour," "That Loving Feeling," and "I Won't Be Needing You"

It's a Monster's Holiday, Capitol Records, 1974, tracks include "Amazing Love," "Meanwhile Back at the Ranch," "Kiss an Angel Good Mornin'," "Great Expectations," and "Pass Me By"

16 Big Hits, Trip Top, 1976, tracks include "Blue Love," "Rollin' in My Sweet Baby's Arms," "I'm Gonna Blow," "Waiting in Your Welfare Line," and "Country Girl"

Buck 'Em, Warner Bros., 1976, tracks include "Child Support," "Lady Madonna," "Hollywood Waltz," "Love Don't Make the Bars," and "California Oakie"

Our Old Mansion, Warner Bros., 1977, tracks include "Let the Good Times Roll," "Cinderella," "Texas Tornado," and "Feel Good Again"

Hot Dog!, Capitol Records, 1988, tracks include "Memphis Tennessee," "Summertime Blues," "Don't Let Her Know," "Put a Quarter in the Jukebox," and "Under Your Spell Again"

Act Naturally, Capitol Records, 1990, tracks include "Tijuana Lady," "Gonna Have Love," "I Was There," "Brooklyn Bridge," and "Playboy"

The Paladins

CDs

The Paladins, Wrestler Records, 1990

Let's Buzz, Alligator Records, 1990

Years Since Yesterday, Alligator Records, 1990

Various Artists, *Genuine Houserockin' Music III*, Alligator Records, 1990, one track by the Paladins—"Years Since Yesterday"

Genuine Houserockin' Music IV, Alligator Records, 1990, one track by the Paladins—"I Don't Believe"

Various Artists, *Blues: The New Breed*, K-Tel, 1990, one track by the Paladins—"I've Been Down Before"

Various Artists, *The Alligator Records 20th Anniversary Collection* [2 CDs], Alligator Records, 1991, one track by the Paladins—"Going Down to Big Mary's"

Ticket Home, Sector 2, 1994

Million Mile Club, Warner Bros/Wea, 1996

Various Artists, *Hootenanny Compilation: The Best of*, Foil Records, 1998, one track by the Paladins—"Elvis' Sister"

Slippin' In, Ruf, 1999

Rejiveinated, Foil Records, 1999

Various Artists, *Where Blues Crosses Over*, Ruf Records, 1999, one track by the Paladins—"Slippin' In"

Various Artists, *The 10th Anniversary East Coast Blues and Roots Music Festival 1999*, Shock, 1999, one track by the Paladins—"Let's Buzz"

Various Artists, *Live at the Hootenanny, Vol. 1*, Time Bomb, 2000, one track by the Paladins—"Slowdown"
Palvoline No. 7, Ruf, 2001
El Matador, Lux Records, 2003
Power Shake: Live in Holland [2 CDs], Rounder Europe/Continental Blue Heaven, 2007
Various Artists, *Crucial Rockin' Blues*, Alligator Records, 2007, one track by the Paladins—"Follow Your Heart"
Various Artists, *Wild Guitar Instrumental Rockers*, Collector/Wht Label, 2007, one track by the Paladins—"Party Time"
Hollywood Fats and the Paladins Live: 1985, Topcat Records, 2008

Clyde Stacy

CDs

Pleasant Jamboree: There's a Good Rockin' Tonight with Clyde Stacy, Eagle Records, 1993, tracks include "Hoy Hoy," "Nobody's Darlin'," "Return to Me," "So Young," "Summertime Blues," "Sittin' Down Crying," "Baby Shame," "I Sure Do Love You Baby," and "Honky Tonk Hardwood Floor"
Various Artists, *Rockabilly Cats*, Buffalo Bop, 2001, one track by Stacy—"Honky Tonk Hardwood Floor"
Hoy Hoy: Gonna Shake This Shack Tonight, Bear Family Records, 2011, tracks include "Summertime Blues," "Hoy Hoy," "Baby Shame," "So Young," "Live and Learn," "Honky Tonk Hardwood Floor," "I Sure Do Love You Baby," "You Want Love," and "You're Satisfied"

Vinyl

45 rpm Singles

"Hoy Hoy" b/w "So Young," Candlelight, 1957
"Dream Boy" b/w "A Broken Heart (Is So Hard to Mend)," Candlelight, 1957
"Baby Shame" b/w "Nobody's Darlin'," Bullseye, 1958
"Honky Tonk Hardwood Floor" b/w "I Sure Do Love You Baby," Bullseye, 1958
"Baby Shame" b/w "You Want Love," G&H, 1958
"Once in a While" b/w "You Want Love," G&H, 1958
"So Young" b/w "A Broken Heart," Argyle, 1959
"Sit'in Down Crying" b/w "You're Satisfied," Len, 1961

LPs

Big Al Downing, *Big Al Downing and His Friends*, Collector, 1971, two tracks by Stacy—"Hoy Hoy" and "Baby Shame"

Big Al Downing, *Big Al Downing and the Poe-Kats*, Jumble, 1987, two tracks by Stacy—"You're Satisfied" and "Sittin' Down Crying"

Dodie Stevens

CDs

Various Artists, *Rockin' Little Christmas*, MCA Records, 1986, one track by Stevens—"Merry Merry Christmas Baby"
Various Artists, *Great Ladies of Rock and Roll: The 50's*, Collectables, 2002, one track by Stevens—"Pink Shoe Laces"
Ultimate Collection, Marginal, 2013, tracks include "Only You," "Candy Store Blues," "Pink Shoe Laces," "Too Young," "Mairzy Doats," "Sailor Boy," and "Poor Butterfly"

Vinyl

45 rpm Singles

"Pink Shoe Laces" b/w "Coming of Age," Crystalette, 1959
"The Five Pennies" b/w "Yes-Sir-Ee," Crystalette, 1959
"Mairzy Doats" b/w "Steady Eddy," Dot Records, 1959
"Miss Lonely Hearts" b/w "Poor Butterfly," Dot Records, 1959
"Amigo's Guitar" b/w "Candy Store Blues, Dot Records, 1960
"Am I Too Young" b/w "So Let's Dance," Dot Records, 1960
"No" b/w "A Tisket a Tasket," Dot Records, 1960
"Yes I'm Lonesome Tonight" b/w "Too Young," Dot Records, 1960
"Merry Christmas Baby" b/w "Jingle Bells," Dot Records, 1960
"(The Story of) the In Between Years" b/w "Trade Winds, Trade Winds," Dot Records, 1961
"Let Me Tell You 'Bout Johnny" b/w "You Are the Only One," Dot Records, 1961
"I Fall to Pieces" b/w "Turn Around," Dot Records, 1961
"Pink Shoe Laces" b/w "Yes-Sire-Ee," Dot Records, 1962
"I Cried" b/w "Dancing on the Ceiling," Dot Records, 1962
"Hello Stranger" b/w "For a Little While," Imperial Records, 1963
"Don't Send Me Roses" b/w "Daddy Couldn't Get Me One of Those," Imperial Records, 1963
"I Wore Out Our Record" b/w "You Don't Have to Prove a Thing to Me," Dolton Records, 1963

"Sailor Boy" b/w "Does Goodnight Mean Goodbye," Dolton Records, 1963

LPs

Dodie Stevens, Dot Records, 1960, tracks include "Only You," "Poor Butterfly," "Twilight Time," "My Prayer," and "Cry"

Over the Rainbow, Dot Records, 1960, tracks include "Where or When," "Meet Me in St. Louis," "The Trolley Song," "Someone to Watch Over Me," and "You Made Me Love You"

Pink Shoelaces, Dot Records, 1961, tracks include "Just a Dream," "Mairzy Doats," "To Know Him Is to Love Him," "Turn Around," and "Poor Butterfly"

Billy Swan

CDs

Choice Cuts, Sony, 1998, tracks include "Matchbox," "Go on Home Girl," "I Hear You Knockin'," and "My Little Girl"

Like Elvis Used to Do, Audium Entertainment, 2000, tracks include "Blue Moon of Kentucky," "Mystery Train," "Love Me Tender," "Too Much," and "Viva Las Vegas"

Best of Billy Swan, Epic Europe, 2003, tracks include "Lover Please," "I Can Help," "You're the One," "Stranger," and "Shake, Rattle, and Roll"

Presents the Mighty Handful, Belle Meade Records, 2007, tracks include "Reconsider Baby," "I'm Ready," "Let the Good Times Roll," and "Since I Met You Baby"

Rock on with the Rhythm, rpm–Retro, 2007, tracks include "Your True Love," "Smokey Places," "Undying Love," "Pardon Me," and "Don't Kill Our Love"

Vinyl

45 rpm Singles

"Friendship" b/w "You Got Me Laughin'," Rising Sons, 1966

"Breakin' Up" b/w "Out of Her System," Monument Records, 1966

"I've Got to Have You" b/w "Below Average Everyday," Monument Records, 1966

"Chances Are" b/w "Then Came the Lover," Elf, 1968

"El Paso" b/w "The Sweet Sound of Your Name," MGM Records, 1968

"Wedding Bells" b/w "P.M.S. (Post Mortem Sickness)," Monument Records, 1974

"I Can Help" b/w "Ways of a Woman in Love," Monument Records, 1974

"Don't Be Cruel" b/w "Vanessa," Monument Records, 1974

"I'm Her Fool" b/w "I'd Like to Work for You," Monument Records, 1975

"Come By" b/w "(You Just) Woman Handled My Mind," Monument Records, 1975

"Everything's the Same (Ain't Nothing Changed)" b/w "Overnite Thing (Usually)," Monument Records, 1975

"Just Want to Taste Your Wine" b/w "Love You Baby to the Bone," Monument Records, 1976

"Vanessa" b/w "Number One," Monument Records, 1976

"Ms. Misery" b/w "You're the One," Monument Records, 1976

"Shake, Rattle, and Roll" b/w "I Got It for You," Monument Records, 1976

"Swept Away" b/w "California Song," Monument Records, 1977

"No Way Around It (It's Love)" b/w "Forever in Your Love," A&M Records, 1978

"Hello Remember Me" b/w "Never Go Lookin' Again," A&M Records, 1978

"Don't Be Cruel" b/w "Vanessa," Monument Records, 1979

"I'm into Lovin' You" b/w "Not Far from Forty," Epic Records, 1981

"Do I Have to Draw a Picture" b/w "I Want to Change Your Life," Epic Records, 1981

"Stuck Right in the Middle of Your Love" b/w "Soft Touch," Epic Records, 1981

"Your Picture Still Loves Me (and I Still Love You)" b/w "Give Your Lovin' to Me," Epic Records, 1982

"With Their Kind of Money (and Our Kind of Love)" b/w "Lay Down and Love Me Tonight," Epic Records, 1982

"Rainbows and Butterflies" b/w "Only Be You," Epic Records, 1983

"Yes" b/w "I Can't Stop Writing Love Songs," Epic Records, 1983

"You Must Be Lookin' for Me" b/w "Three Chord Rock and Roll," Mercury Records, 1986

"I'm Gonna Get You" b/w "Three Chord Rock and Roll," Mercury Records, 1987

LPs

Billy Swan, Monument Records, 1974, tracks include "Number One," "I Got It for You," "Your True Love," and "Lucky"

I Can Help, Monument Records, 1974, tracks include "Lover Please," "Shake, Rattle, and Roll," "Queen of My Heart," and "Don't Be Cruel"

Rock and Roll Moon, Monument Records, 1975, tracks include "Stranger, "You're the Pain (in

My Heart), "Ubangi Stomp," and "Home of the Blues"
Four, Columbia Records, 1977, tracks include "Pardon Me," "Me and My Honey," "Swept Away," and "Don't Kill Our Love"
You're Okay, I'm Okay, A&M Records, 1978, tracks include "You Make My Soul Rock and Roll," "Bloodstream," "Please Help Me I'm Falling," and "Lonely Avenue"
At His Best, Monument Records, 1978, tracks include "I Can Help," "Lover Please," "Don't Be Cruel," "Number One," and "Vanessa"
I'm into Lovin' You, Epic Records, 1981, tracks include "Do I Have to Draw a Picture," "What's Our Love Coming To," "Win You Over," and "Stuck Right in the Middle of Your Love"

Vernon Taylor

Vinyl

45 rpm Singles

"I've Got the Blues" b/w "Losing Game," Dot Records, 1957
"Why Must You Leave Me" b/w "Satisfaction Guaranteed," Dot Records, 1958
"Today Is a Blue Day" b/w "Breeze," Sun Records, 1958
"Mystery Train" b/w "Sweet and Easy to Love," Sun Records, 1959
"Your Lovin' Man" b/w "This Kind of Love," Sun International, 1976
"I Ain't Never" b/w "Young Love," NBT, 1991
"The Great Big Rock and Roll Show" b/w "Fredericksburg Jam," NBT, 2001

LPs

Sun Recordings—Country Rock Sides, Charly Records, 1985, tracks include "Mystery Train," "Your Lovin' Man," "This Kind of Love"
Various Artists, *Sun Records: The Rocking Years* (12 LP box set), Charly Records, 1987, seven tracks by Taylor—"Mystery Train," "Sweet and Easy to Love," "Your Lovin' Man," "Today Is a Blue Day," "Breeze," "Hey Little Girl," and "This Kind of Love"

CDs

Various Artists, *The Sun Collection: Rock and Roll Originals, Volume 8*, Charly Records, 1990, two tracks by Taylor—"Sweet and Easy to Love" and "Mystery Train"
There's Only One ... Your Lovin' Man, Eagle Records (Germany), 1995, tracks include "Your Lovin' Man," "Dinah Lee," "Sweet and Easy to Love," "Losing Game," and "Satisfaction Guaranteed"
Daddy's Rockin', Hepcat Records, 1999, tracks include "Lonesome for a Letter," "Your Lovin' Man," "Sugaree," "The Fool," and "Big River"
Now and Then, self-released, 2001, tracks include "Why Must You Leave Me," "Infatuation," "You Better Leave," and "The Great Big Rock and Roll Show"

Leroy Van Dyke

CDs

The Auctioneer, Bear Family Records, 1994, tracks include "I'm Movin' On," "One Heart," "Chicken Shack Boogie," "Poor Boy," "Leather Jacket," and "Honky Tonk Song"
Walk on By, Bear Family Records, 1994, tracks include "Black Cloud," "Happy to Be Unhappy," "Night People," "Faded Love," and "My World Is Caving In"
Various Artists, *Pure Country Classics: The #1 Hits*, UTV Records, 2003, one track by Van Dyke—"Walk on By"
Cowboy Country, Sun Record Company, 2008, tracks include "The Hanging Tree," "Moonlight Gambler," "Rio Colorado," and "Rawhide"

Vinyl

45 rpm Singles

"Auctioneer" b/w "I Fell in Love with a Pony-Tail," Dot Records, 1956
"Honky Tonk Song" b/w "The Pocket Book Song," Dot Records, 1957
"One Heart" b/w "Every Time I Ask My Heart," Dot Records, 1957
"Leather Jacket" b/w "My Good Mind Went Bad," Dot Records, 1958
"Walk on By" b/w "My World Is Caving In," Mercury Records, 1961
"Faded Love" b/w "Big Man in a Big House," Mercury Records, 1961
"If a Woman Answers (Hang Up the Phone)" b/w "A Broken Promise," Mercury Records, 1962
"Dim Dark Corner" b/w "The Life You Offered Me," Mercury Records, 1962
"Black Cloud" b/w "Five Steps," Mercury Records, 1962
"How Long Must You Keep Me a Secret" b/w "I Sat Back and Let It Happen," Mercury Records, 1962
"Wrong Side of the Track" b/w "What Are the Lips of Janet," Mercury Records, 1963

"Be a Good Girl" b/w "The Other Boys Are Talking," Mercury Records, 1963

"Happy to Be Unhappy" b/w "Now I Lay Me Down," Mercury Records, 1964

"Night People" b/w "Baby (Where Can You Be)," Mercury Records, 1964

"Afraid of a Heartache" b/w "Your Money," Mercury Records, 1964

"Poor Guy" b/w "Anne of a Thousand Days," Mercury Records, 1964

"I'm Not Sayin'" b/w "Your Daughter Cried All Night," Warner Bros., 1965

"It's All Over Now, Baby Blue" b/w "Just a State of Mind," Warner Bros., 1965

"Roses from a Stranger" b/w "Before I Change My Mind, Warner Bros., 1966

"Almost Persuaded" b/w "Less of Me," Warner Bros., 1966

"What Am I Bid" b/w "I'll Make Up to You," Warner Bros., 1967

"I've Never Been Loved" b/w "Less of Me," Warner Bros., 1967

"Louisville" b/w "There's Always Tomorrow," Warner Bros., 1968

"You May Be Too Much for Memphis" b/w "Road of Love," Kapp, 1968

"The Long Drive Home" b/w "Lonesome Is," Kapp, 1968

"One Minute More of Lonely" b/w "A Lonely Thing," Kapp, 1968

"Goin' Back to Boston" b/w "The Straw," Kapp, 1969

"Crack in My World" b/w "We'll Try a Little Bit Harder," Kapp, 1969

"People Gonna Turn You Off" b/w "Mister Professor," Decca Records, 1970

"An Old Love Affair, Now Showing" b/w "Belle," Kapp, 1970

"Party Girl" b/w "I Get Lonely When It Rains," Decca Records, 1971

"Birmingham" b/w "What Am I Gonna Tell 'Em Now," Decca Records, 1971

"I'll Be Around (in All the Old Places)" b/w "Yesterday Will Come Again Tonight," Decca Records, 1972

"My Mind Is on You" b/w "I'd Rather Be Wantin' Love," Decca Records, 1972

"Unfaithful Fools" b/w "What Will You Do Now, Mrs. Jones?," ABC Records, 1975

"Who's Gonna Run the Truck Stop in Tuba City When I'm Gone?" b/w "There Ain't No Roses in My Bed," ABC Dot Records, 1976

"Texas Tea" b/w "Las Vegas Girl," ABC Records, 1977

LPs

Walk on By, Mercury Records, 1962, tracks include "Big Man in a Big House," "Heartaches by the Number," "The Image of Me," "Take Good Care of Her," and "Funny How Time Slips Away"

Movin' Van Dyke, Mercury Records, 1962, tracks include "Don't Let the Stars Get in Your Eyes," "Lonely Street," "Honeycomb," "I Need You Now," and "I Almost Lost My Mind"

Songs for Mom and Dad, Mercury Records, 1964, tracks include "These Hands," "Family Bible," "Home," "Mom and Dad's Waltz," and "Mama Sang a Song"

At the Trade Winds, Mercury Records, 1964, tracks include "Walk on By," "Black Cloud," "Time Has Just Slipped Away Too Fast," "Auctioneer," and "I'm Glad You Didn't Walk on By"

Out of Love, Mercury-Wing Records, 1965, tracks include "I'm a Fool to Care," "Born to Lose," "Just Out of Reach," "Am I That Easy to Forget," and "When Two Worlds Collide"

The Leroy Van Dyke Show, Warner Bros., 1965, tracks include "Tennessee Waltz," "King of the Road," "Just a State of Mind" and "Ol' Man Mose"

Country Hits, Warner Bros., 1966, tracks include "Distant Drums," "Flowers on the Wall," "I'm So Lonesome I Could Cry," "Make the World Go Away," and "The Race Is On"

Lonesome Is..., Kapp, 1968, tracks include "Big Bad City," "She Called Me Baby," "A Lonely Thing," "Road of Love," and "Honey"

Just a Closer Walk with Thee, Kapp, 1969, tracks include "How Great Thou Art," "Peace in the Valley," "Beyond the Sunset," "If I Can Help Somebody, and "Suppertime"

I've Never Been Loved Before, Harmony Records, 1969, tracks include "What Am I Bid," "I'm Not Sayin'," "Louisville," and "Less of Me"

Rock Relics, Plantation, 1978, tracks include "Put Your Head on My Shoulder," "Wake Up Little Susie," "Teen Angel," "Runaround Sue," and "Young Love"

Alvis Wayne

CDs

Various Artists, *Cat Music*, Hightone, 1998, two tracks by Wayne—"Lay Your Head on My Shoulder" and "I Wanna Eat Your Pudding"

Rockabilly Daddy, Rollin' Rock, 2000, tracks include "One Woman Man," "Here I Am," "Alone with You," "Back to the 50's," and "You Can Have Her"

Proud of My Rockabilly Roots, Rollin' Rock, 2008, tracks include "Thanks a Lot," "Sugar Coated Love," "You Better Take My Life," "Going Down to the River," and "Don't Go"

Various Artists, *Texas Tornados: Rock 'n' Roll from the Lone Star State*, Fantastic Voyage, 2012, one track by Wayne—"Sleep Rock-a-Roll Rock-a-Baby"

Rockabilly Dynamite [40 CDs], Documents, 2013, three tracks by Wayne—"Don't Mean Maybe, Baby," "Swing Bop Boogie," and "Sleep Rock-a-Roll Rock-a-Baby"

Vinyl

45 rpm Singles

"Swing Bop Boogie" b/w "Sleep Rock-a-Roll Rock-a-Baby," Westport, 1956

"Don't Mean Maybe, Baby" b/w "I'd Rather Be with You," Westport, 1957

"Lay Your Head on My Shoulder" b/w "You Are the One," Westport, 1958

"I Wanna Eat Your Pudding" b/w "It's Your Last Chance to Dance Tonight," Rollin' Rock, 1974

LPs

Various Artists, *Texas Rockabilly*, Esoldun, 1986, five tracks by Wayne—"Sleep Rock-a-Roll Rock-a-Baby," "Swing Bop Boogie," "I Gottum," "Don't Mean Maybe, Baby," and "Lay Your Head on My Shoulder"

Swing Bop Boogie, Pink 'n' Black, 1994, tracks include "I Gottum," "You Are the One," "Lay Your Head on My Shoulder," and "Sleep Rock-a-Roll Rock-a-Baby"

Don Woody

CDs

Tha'll Flat Git It—Volume 2: Rockabilly from the Vaults of Decca Records, Bear Family Records, 1992, three tracks by Woody—"You're Barking Up the Wrong Tree," "Bird-Dog," and "Make Like a Rock and Roll"

You're Barking Up the Wrong Tree, Bear Family Records, 2010, tracks include "Morse Code," "A Lesson in Love," "Bigelow 6-200," "Bird-Dog," and "Make Like a Rock and Roll"

Vinyl

45 rpm Singles

"You're Barking Up the Wrong Tree" b/w "Bird-Dog," Decca Records, 1957

"Not I" b/w "Red Blooded American Boy," Arco, 1958

LPs

Various Artists, *Rare Rockabilly*, MCA Records, 1975, four tracks by Woody—"Barking Up the Wrong Tree," "Make Like a Rock and Roll," "Bird-Dog" and "Morse Code"

Rusty York

CDs

Early Bluegrass (1950's and 1960's), Jewel Records, 2002, tracks include "Little Rosewood Casket," "Pretty Polly," "Roving Gambler," "Doin' My Time," and "East Virginia Blues"

Rusty Rocks, Bear Family Records, 2004, tracks include "A Fallen Star," "Tore Up Over You," "Sugaree," "Great Balls of Fire," "Mean Woman Blues," and "Love Struck"

Vinyl

45 rpm Singles

"Shake 'Em Up Baby" b/w "Peggy Sue," King Records, 1957

"Sugaree" b/w "Red Rooster," PJ, 1958

"Sugaree" b/w "Red Rooster," Note, 1959

"The Lock on Your Heart" b/w "Don't Do It," Starday, 1959

"Sugaree" b/w "Red Rooster," Chess Records, 1959

"Sadie-Mae" b/w "Margaret Ann," Sage, 1960

"That's What I Need" b/w "Just Like You," New Star, 1961

"Love Struck" b/w "Goodnight Cincinnati, Goodmorning Tennessee," King Records, 1961

"That's What I Need" b/w "Just Like You," Capitol Records, 1961

"Tore Up Over You" b/w "Tremblin'," King Records, 1962

"I Might Just Walk Right Back Again" b/w "Sally Was a Good Old Girl," New Star, 1963

"I Might Just Walk Right Back Again" b/w "Sally Was a Good Old Girl," Gaylord, 1963

"Big Man, Big House" b/w "Crazy," Afco, 1966

"Sugaree–66" b/w "Sing the Girls a Song, Bill," Jewel Records, 1966

"Sweet Love" b/w "The Girl Can't Help It," Twin Spin Records, 2011

LPs

Rock and Roll Memories, Jewel Records, 1979, tracks include "Sugaree," "Great Balls of Fire," "Shake Em Up Baby," "Peggy Sue," "Sadie-Mae," and "The Girl Can't Help It"

Sweet Love, Eagle Records, 1990, tracks include "Sugaree," "The Girl Can't Help It," "A Fallen Star," and "Mean Woman Blues"

Chapter Notes

Chapter One

1. Portions of this profile appeared in Sheree Homer, "Dale Hawkins' Legacy Is More Than Just 'Susie-Q,'" *Keep Rockin'* magazine, February 2010. Phone interviews by Sheree Homer with Dale Hawkins conducted May 15, 2002, and November 17, 2009. All quotes that follow are from the same interviews, unless otherwise noted.
2. Ken Burke, "Dale Hawkins," Gale Musician Profiles, http://www.answers.com/topic/dalehawkins, accessed December 2, 2013.
3. Kip Lornell and Tracey E.W. Laird, *Shreveport Sounds in Black and White* (Jackson: University Press of Mississippi, 2008), 274.
4. *Ibid.*, 277.
5. Stan Lewis, phone interview by Sheree Homer, 11 August 2010. All quotes that follow are from the same interview.
6. Lornell and Laird, *Shreveport Sounds in Black and White*, 289.
7. Burke, "Dale Hawkins."
8. Bob Sullivan, phone interview by Sheree Homer, 27 February 2010. All quotes that follow are from the same interview.
9. Lornell and Laird, *Shreveport Sounds in Black and White*, 124.
10. Sonny Trammell, phone interview by Sheree Homer, 11 August 2010.
11. Burke, "Dale Hawkins."
12. *Ibid.*
13. Allen Harris, phone interview by Sheree Homer, 27 October 2010. All quotes that follow are from the same interview.
14. Dean Mathis, phone interview by Sheree Homer, 5 August 2014. All quotes that follow are from the same interview.
15. Lornell and Laird, *Shreveport Sounds in Black and White*, 288.
16. Burke, "Dale Hawkins."
17. Portions of this profile appeared in Sheree Homer, "Big Jay McNeely Reigns Supreme as the King of the Honking Saxophone," *Blue Suede News*, Winter 2009/2010. Phone interview by Sheree Homer with Big Jay McNeely conducted May 5, 2009. All quotes that follow are from the same interview.
18. Stephen Caldwell, phone interview by Sheree Homer, 27 September 2009. All quotes that follow are from the same interview.

Chapter Two

1. Portions of this profile appeared in Sheree Homer, "Clyde Stacy's 'Hoy Hoy' Put Tulsa, Oklahoma on the Map," *Blue Suede News*, Winter/Spring 2011. Phone interview by Sheree Homer with Clyde Stacy conducted June 23, 2010. All quotes that follow are from the same interview.
2. Portions of this profile appeared in Sheree Homer, "Al Ferrier Strikes Gold with Rockabilly Fans," *Blue Suede News*, Fall 2009. Phone interview by Sheree Homer with Al Ferrier conducted May 11, 2009. All quotes that follow are from the same interview.
3. Rusty York, phone interview by Sheree Homer, 1 September 2006. All quotes that follow are from the same interview, unless otherwise noted.
4. "Rusty York," Rockabilly Hall of Fame, http://www.rockabillyhall.com/rustyyork1.html, accessed October 12, 2014.
5. Bill Griggs and Jim O'Brien, "Cincinnati Rock and Rusty York," *Rockin' '50s* magazine, June 1990, 10.
6. *Ibid.*, 11.
7. Portions of this profile appeared in Sheree Homer, "Don Woody Ain't Barking Up the Wrong Tree Now ... Songwriter Makes Good as Singer," *Blue Suede News*, Spring 2010. Phone interview by Sheree Homer with Don Woody conducted May 4, 2009. All quotes that follow are from the same interview.
8. Bobby Crown, phone interview by Sheree Homer, 12 August 2006. All quotes that follow are from the same interview, unless otherwise noted.
9. Steve Kelemen, "Bobby Crown," Rockabilly Hall of Fame, http://www.rockabillyhall.com/BobbyCrown.html, accessed October 17, 2014.
10. Alvis Wayne, phone interview by Sheree

Homer, 24 April 2009. All quotes that follow are from the same interview.
11. *Welcome to the Club: The Women of Rockabilly*, prod. and dir. Beth Harrington, 95 minutes, M2k, 2004, DVD.
12. *Ibid.*
13. *Ibid.*
14. Howard A. DeWitt, "Janis Martin: The First Lady of Rockabilly," *Blue Suede News*, Winter 2007/2008, 13.
15. *Ibid.*, 14.
16. *Welcome to the Club: The Women of Rockabilly*.
17. Bob Allen, liner notes for *The Female Elvis: Complete Recordings: 1956–1960* (Bear Family Records, 1987).
18. DeWitt, "Janis Martin: The First Lady of Rockabilly," 15.
19. *Ibid.*
20. Greg Milewski, "Cat Talkin' with ... Janis Martin," *Roctober Magazine*, http://www.roctober.com/roctober/greatness/janis.html, accessed October 14, 2013.
21. *Welcome to the Club: The Women of Rockabilly*.
22. Mary A. Bufwack and Robert K. Oermann, *Finding Her Voice: The Saga of Women in Country Music* (New York: Crown, 1993), 223.
23. Greg Milewski, "Cat Talkin' with ... Janis Martin."
24. Rosie Flores, phone interview by Sheree Homer, 11 December 2012.
25. DeWitt, "Janis Martin: The First Lady of Rockabilly," 16.
26. Rosie Flores, phone interview by Sheree Homer, 11 December 2012.
27. Ray Campi, phone interview by Sheree Homer, 18 July 2014. All quotes that follow are from the same interview.

Chapter Three

1. Glenn Honeycutt, phone interview by Sheree Homer, 31 July 2006. All quotes that follow are from the same interview.
2. Jimmy Harrell, phone interview by Sheree Homer, 17 August 2006. All quotes that follow are from the same interview.
3. Alton Lott, phone interview by Sheree Homer, 29 August 2006. All quotes that follow are from the same interview.
4. Sleepy LaBeef, phone interview by Sheree Homer, 31 July 2006. All quotes that follow are from the same interview, unless otherwise noted.
5. Martin Hawkins, liner notes for *Sleepy Rocks* (Bear Family Records, 2008), 20.
6. Peter Guralnick, *Lost Highway: Journeys and Arrivals of American Musicians* (Boston: Little, Brown, 1999), 165.
7. Hawkins, liner notes for *Sleepy Rocks*, 25.
8. Bob Mehr, "Rockin' Daddy: Musician and Show Business Impresario, Eddie Bond Helped Launch Legends and Secure His Own," *The Commercial Appeal*, http://www.commercialappeal.com/go-memphis/rockin-daddy-musician-and-show-business-eddie, accessed October 19, 2014.
9. Eddie Bond, phone interview by Sheree Homer, 28 August 2006. All quotes that follow are from the same interview.
10. Andy Anderson, phone interview by Sheree Homer, 5 September 2006. All quotes that follow are from the same interview, unless otherwise noted.
11. Andy Anderson and Erika Celeste, *Memoirs of the Original Rolling Stone* (Bloomington, IN: AuthorHouse, 2010), 116.
12. "History," Andy Anderson Official Homepage, http://andyanderson.com/history.htm, accessed July 6, 2014.
13. Anderson and Celeste, *Memoirs of the Original Rolling Stone*, 16.
14. Vernon Taylor, phone interview by Sheree Homer, 5 November 2013. All quotes that follow are from the same interview.
15. Ken Burke, "'Tuff' and Tales from the Bill Black Combo: The Ace Cannon Interview," *Blue Suede News*, Winter 2008, 5.
16. Gary James, "Interview with Ace Cannon," classicbands.com, http://www.classicbands.com/AceCannonInterview.html, accessed May 17, 2014.
17. Ace Cannon, phone interview by Sheree Homer, 9 March 2004. All quotes that follow are from the same interview, unless otherwise noted.
18. Burke, "'Tuff' and Tales," 5.
19. *Ibid.*, 6.
20. Gary James, "Interview with Ace Cannon."
21. Burke, "'Tuff' and Tales," 6.
22. *Ibid.*, 7.
23. *Ibid.*, 5.

Chapter Four

1. Colin Escott, *All Roots Lead to Rock: Legends of Early Rock 'N' Roll, a Bear Family Reader* (New York: Schirmer, 1999), 195.
2. Richard Carlin, *The Big Book of Country Music: A Biographical Encyclopedia* (New York: Penguin, 1995), 468.
3. Alanna Nash, *Behind Closed Doors: Talking with the Legends of Country Music* (New York: Alfred A. Knopf, 1988), 504–505.
4. Escott, *All Roots Lead to Rock*, 196.
5. Allen Harris, phone interview by Sheree Homer, 27 October 2010. All quotes that follow are from the same interview.
6. Billy Weir, phone interview by Sheree Homer, 16 August 2010. All quotes that follow are from the same interview.
7. Jimmy Ray Paulman, phone interview by

Sheree Homer, 17 August 2010. All quotes that follow are from the same interview.
  8. Sheree Homer, *Catch That Rockabilly Fever: Personal Stories of Life on the Road and in the Studio* (Jefferson, NC: McFarland, 2009), 39.
  9. *Ibid.*
  10. *Ibid.*
  11. Ace Collins, *The Stories Behind Country Music's All-Time Greatest 100 Songs* (New York: Boulevard, 1996), 214.
  12. Richard Carlin, *The Big Book of Country Music: A Biographical Encyclopedia* (New York: Penguin, 1995), 469.
  13. Nash, *Behind Closed Doors*, 507.
  14. *Ibid.*, 485.
  15. *Ibid.*, 492.
  16. Billy Swan, phone interview by Sheree Homer, 7 August 2006. All quotes that follow are from the same interview, unless otherwise noted.
  17. Ken Burke, "Mr. 'I Can Help': The Billy Swan Interview," *Blue Suede News*, Fall 2004, 8–9.
  18. *Ibid.*, 7.
  19. *Ibid.*, 8.
  20. *Ibid.*
  21. Leroy Van Dyke, phone interview by Sheree Homer, 21 January 2013. All quotes that follow are from the same interview.
  22. Willie Cantu, phone interview by Sheree Homer, 29 April 2013. All quotes that follow are from the same interview.
  23. "Buck Owens' Ranch Party, Volume 2," The Video Beat! 1950s and 1960s Rock 'n' Roll Movies, http://www.thevideobeat.com/modmovies/buck-owens-ranch-show-vol2.html, accessed July 30, 2014.

Chapter Five

  1. Dodie Stevens, phone interview by Sheree Homer, 24 January 2013. All quotes that follow are from the same interview, unless otherwise noted.
  2. Andrew Merey, "Dodie Stevens: Rock and Roll Class of 1959," *Blue Suede News*, Winter 2008/2009, 12.
  3. *Ibid.*
  4. Mark Marymont, "Robin Luke: 'Susie Darlin,'" *Blue Suede News*, Summer/Fall 2012, 18.
  5. Robin Luke, phone interview by Sheree Homer, 21 October 2010. All quotes that follow are from the same interview, unless otherwise noted.
  6. Marymont, "Robin Luke," 20.
  7. Carl Dobkins, Jr., email interview by Sheree Homer, 19 January 2013. All quotes that follow are from the same interview, unless otherwise noted.
  8. Michael Jack Kirby, "Carl Dobkins, Jr.: My Heart Is an Open Book," Way Back Attack, http://www.waybackattack.com/dobkinscarljr.html, accessed October 14, 2013.
  9. Scott Preston, "Interview with Carl Dobkins, Jr.," Cincy Groove, http://www.cincygroove.com/?p=5899, accessed October 14, 2013.
  10. Greg Evans, "The Cincinnati Sound: Dig Deep Enough and You'll Find the Roots of Rock and Roll," *Cincinnati Magazine*, June 1986, 77.

Chapter Six

  1. Jimmy Sutton, phone interview by Sheree Homer, 21 May 2004. All quotes that follow are from the same interview.
  2. Joel Paterson, phone interview by Sheree Homer, 26 April 2012. All quotes that follow are from the same interview.
  3. Jim Barclay, email interview by Sheree Homer, 10 January 2013. All quotes that follow are from the same interview.
  4. Jonathan Doyle, email interview by Sheree Homer, 12 February 2013. All quotes that follow are from the same interview.
  5. Ronnie Mack, phone interview by Sheree Homer, 19 July 2010. All quotes that follow are from the same interview.
  6. Sheree Homer, *Rick Nelson: Rock and Roll Pioneer* (Jefferson, NC: McFarland, 2012), 129.
  7. *Ibid.*, 130.
  8. *Ibid.*, 129.
  9. *Ibid.*, 130.
  10. James Intveld, in-person interview by Sheree Homer, 27 August 2010. All quotes that follow are from the same interview, unless otherwise noted.
  11. "Bio," James Intveld Official Homepage, http://jamesintveld.com/bio, accessed November 15, 2013.
  12. Sheree Homer, *Rick Nelson*, 125.
  13. *Ibid.*
  14. *Ibid.*
  15. *Ibid.*
  16. *Ibid.*
  17. *Ibid.*
  18. *Ibid.*
  19. Jim Washburn, "James Intveld: A Shadow Returns to OC on Saturday Night," OC Weekly Contributor, http://blogs.ocweekly.com/heardmentality/2013/07/james_intveld_a_shadow_returns_to_oc.php, accessed July 24, 2013.
  20. *Ibid.*
  21. *Ibid.*
  22. Marc Bristol, "Rosie Flores," *Blue Suede News*, Winter 2012/2013, 7.
  23. Rosie Flores, phone interview by Sheree Homer, 11 December 2012. All quotes that follow are from the same interview.
  24. Sheree Homer, *Catch That Rockabilly Fever*, 56.
  25. *Ibid.*
  26. Eddie Angel, phone interview by Sheree Homer, 3 August 2006. All quotes that follow are from the same interview.

27. Homer, *Catch That Rockabilly Fever*, 202.

28. Billy Hancock, phone interview by Sheree Homer, 24 April 2012. All quotes that follow are from the same interview.

29. Tapio Väisänen, liner notes for *Shakin' That Rockabilly Fever* (Bluelight Records, 2001).

30. Dave Gonzalez, phone interview by Sheree Homer, 19 December 2012. All quotes that follow are from the same interview, unless otherwise noted.

31. "The Paladins," Rockabilly Hall of Fame, http://www.rockabillyhall.com/Paladins1.html, accessed August 21, 2014.

32. *Ibid.*

33. Ken Burke, "History of the Paladins: The Dave Gonzalez Interview," Rockabilly Hall of Fame, http://www.rockabillyhall.com/DrlPaladins.html, accessed August 21, 2014.

34. Jerry King, phone interview by Sheree Homer, 2 August 2006. All quotes that follow are from the same interview, unless otherwise noted.

35. Jeremiah Brockman, phone interview by Sheree Homer, 7 March 2004. All quotes that follow are from the same interview.

36. Jerry King, email interview by Sheree Homer, 31 May 2014.

37. Jai Malano, phone interview by Sheree Homer, 5 December 2013. All quotes that follow are from the same interview.

Chapter Seven

1. Junior Marvel, email interview by Sheree Homer, 8 June 2013. All quotes that follow are from the same interview.

2. Martin Telfser, email interview by Sheree Homer, 13 March 2013. All quotes that follow are from the same interview, unless otherwise noted.

3. Roland Riedberger, email interview by Sheree Homer, 8 April 2013. All quotes that follow are from the same interview, unless otherwise noted.

4. Sheri Bomb, "Interview: Mars Attacks," http://www.sheribomb.com.au/2012/05/interviewmarsattacks.html, accessed June 12, 2014.

5. *Ibid.*

6. Lil' Esther, email interview by Sheree Homer, 14 January 2013. All quotes that follow are from the same interview, unless otherwise noted.

7. Fred "Virgil" Turgis, "Lil' Esther," Jumpin' from 6 to 6, http://www.jumpingfrom6to6.com/itv_lil_esther.htm, accessed June 10, 2014.

8. *Ibid.*

9. Jerry King, email interview by Sheree Homer, 31 May 2014.

10. Jack Baymoore, email interview by Sheree Homer, 5 March 2013. All quotes that follow are from the same interview.

11. Miss Mary Ann, email interview by Sheree Homer, 10 December 2012. All quotes that follow are from the same interview.

Bibliography

Books

Anderson, Andy, and Erika Celeste. *Memoirs of the Original Rolling Stone*. Bloomington, IN: AuthorHouse, 2010.

Bufwack, Mary A., and Robert K. Oermann. *Finding Her Voice: The Saga of Women in Country Music*. New York: Crown, 1993.

Carlin, Richard. *The Big Book of Country Music: A Biographical Encyclopedia*. New York: Penguin, 1995.

Collins, Ace. *The Stories Behind Country Music's All-Time Greatest 100 Songs*. New York: Boulevard, 1996.

Escott, Colin. *All Roots Lead to Rock: Legends of Early Rock 'n' Roll, A Bear Family Reader*. New York: Schirmer, 1999.

Guralnick, Peter. *Lost Highway: Journeys and Arrivals of American Musicians*. Boston: Little, Brown, 1999.

Homer, Sheree. *Catch That Rockabilly Fever: Personal Stories of Life on the Road and in the Studio*. Jefferson, NC: McFarland, 2009.

_____. *Rick Nelson: Rock and Roll Pioneer*. Jefferson, NC: McFarland, 2012.

Lornell, Kip, and Tracey E.W. Laird. *Shreveport Sounds in Black and White*. Jackson: University Press of Mississippi, 2008.

Nash, Alanna. *Behind Closed Doors: Talking with the Legends of Country Music*. New York: Alfred A. Knopf, 1988.

Film

Welcome to the Club: The Women of Rockabilly. Produced and directed by Beth Harrington. 95 minutes. M2k, 2004. DVD.

Interviews by the Author

Anderson, Andy. 5 September 2006.
Angel, Eddie. 3 August 2006.
Barclay, Jim. 10 January 2013.
Baymoore, Jack. 5 March 2013.
Bond, Eddie. 28 August 2006.
Brockman, Jeremiah. 7 March 2004.
Caldwell, Stephen. 27 September 2009.
Campi, Ray. 18 July 2014.
Cannon, Ace. 9 March 2004.
Cantu, Willie. 29 April 2013.
Crown, Bobby. 12 August 2006.
Dobkins Jr., Carl. 19 January 2013.
Doyle, Jonathan. 12 February 2013.
Ferrier, Al. 11 May 2009. Portions published in *Blue Suede News*, Fall 2009, pp. 24–25.
Flores, Rosie. 11 December 2012.
Gonzalez, Dave. 19 December 2012.
Hancock, Billy. 24 April 2012.
Harrell, Jimmy. 17 August 2006.
Harris, Allen. 27 October 2010.
Hawkins, Dale. 15 May 2002 and 17 November 2009. Portions published in *Keep Rockin'*, February 2010, pp. 40–44.
Honeycutt, Glenn. 31 July 2006.
Intveld, James. 27 August 2010.
Junior Marvel. 8 June 2013.
King, Jerry. 2 August 2006 and 31 May 2014.
LaBeef, Sleepy. 31 July 2006.
Lewis, Stan. 11 August 2010.
Lil' Esther. 14 January 2013.
Lott, Alton. 29 August 2006.
Luke, Robin. 21 October 2010.
Mack, Ronnie. 19 July 2010.
Malano, Jai. 5 December 2013.
Mathis, Dean. 5 August 2014.
McNeely, Big Jay. 5 May 2009. Portions published in *Blue Suede News*, Winter 2009/2010, pp. 17–18.
Miss Mary Ann. 10 December 2012.
Paterson, Joel. 26 April 2012.
Paulman, Jimmy Ray. 17 August 2010.
Riedberger, Roland. 8 April 2013.
Stacy, Clyde. 23 June 2010. Portions published in *Blue Suede News*, Winter/Spring 2011, pp. 6–8.
Stevens, Dodie. 24 January 2013.
Sullivan, Bob. 27 February 2010.
Sutton, Jimmy. 21 May 2004.

Swan, Billy. 7 August 2006.
Taylor, Vernon. 5 November 2013.
Telfser, Martin. 13 March 2013.
Trammell, Sonny. 11 August 2010.
Van Dyke, Leroy. 21 January 2013.
Wayne, Alvis. 24 April 2009.
Weir, Billy. 16 August 2010.
Woody, Don. 4 May 2009. Portions published in *Blue Suede News*, Spring 2010, pp. 19–20.
York, Rusty. 1 September 2006.

Liner Notes

Allen, Bob. *Janis Martin, the Female Elvis: Complete Recordings: 1956–1960*. Bear Family Records, 1987.
Hawkins, Martin. *Sleepy LaBeef: Sleepy Rocks*. Bear Family Records, 2008.
Väisänen, Tapio. *Billy Hancock: Shakin' That Rockabilly Fever*. Bluelight Records, 2001.

Periodicals

Bristol, Marc. "Rosie Flores." *Blue Suede News* (Winter 2012/2013): 7–12.
Burke, Ken. "Mr. 'I Can Help': The Billy Swan Interview." *Blue Suede News* (Fall 2004): 7–13.
———. "'Tuff' and Tales from the Bill Black Combo: The Ace Cannon Interview." *Blue Suede News* (Winter 2008): 5–11.
DeWitt, Howard A. "Janis Martin: The First Lady of Rockabilly." *Blue Suede News* (Winter 2007/2008): 13–16.
Evans, Greg. "The Cincinnati Sound: Dig Deep Enough and You'll Find the Roots of Rock and Roll." *Cincinnati Magazine* (June 1986): 71–78.
Griggs, Bill, and Jim O'Brien. "Cincinnati Rock and Rusty York." *Rockin' '50s* magazine (June 1990): 9–13.
Marymont, Mark. "Robin Luke: 'Susie Darlin'." *Blue Suede News* (Summer/Fall 2012): 18–20.
Merey, Andrew. "Dodie Stevens: Rock and Roll Class of 1959." *Blue Suede News* (Winter 2008/2009): 12–15.

Websites

AllMusic. http://www.allmusic.com/.
Amazon. http://www.amazon.com.
Andy Anderson Official Homepage. http://andyanderson.com/history.htm, accessed July 6, 2014.
Bob Mehr. http://www.commercialappeal.com/go-memphis/rockin-daddy-musician-and-show-business-eddie, accessed October 19, 2014.
CD Universe. http://www.cduniverse.com.
Dot Album Discography. http://www.bsnpubs.com/dot/dotc.html.
eBay. http://www.ebay.com.
45cat. Discographies, discussions, discoveries, http://www.45cat.com/.
Fred "Virgil" Turgis. http://www.jumpingfrom6to6.com/itv_lil_esther.htm, accessed June 10, 2014.
Gary James. http://www.classicbands.com/AceCannonInterview.html, accessed May 17, 2014.
Greg Milewski. http://www.roctober.com/roctober/greatness/janis.html, accessed October 14, 2013.
James Intveld Official Homepage. http://jamesintveld.com/bio, accessed November 15, 2013.
Jim Washburn. http://blogs.ocweekly.com/heardmentality/2013/07/james_intveld_a_shadow_returns_to_oc.php, accessed July 24, 2013.
Ken Burke. http://www.answers.com/topic/dale-hawkins, accessed December 2, 2013.
———. http://www.rockabillyhall.com/DrIPaladins.html, accessed August 21, 2014.
LP Discography. Covers and Lyrics, http://www.lpdiscography.com/.
Michael Jack Kirby. http://waybackattack.com/dobkinscarljr.html, accessed October 14, 2013.
PragueFrank's Country Music Discography. http://countrydiscography.blogspot.com/.
Rockabilly Hall of Fame. http://www.rockabillyhall.com/Paladins1.html, accessed August 21, 2014. http://www.rockabillyhall.com/rustyyork1.html, accessed October 12, 2014.
The Rock and Country Encyclopedia and Discography. http://www.rocky-52.net.
Rockin' Country Style. http://rcs-discography.com/rcs/index.html.
Scott Preston. http://www.cincygroove.com/?p=5899, accessed October 14, 2013.
Sheri Bomb. http://www.sheribomb.com.au/2012/05/interview-mars-attacks.html, accessed June 12, 2014.
Steve Kelemen. http://www.rockabillyhall.com/BobbyCrown.html, accessed October 17, 2014.
US and UK Hits Charts. http://www.musicvf.com/.
The Video Beat! 1950s and 1960s Rock 'n' Roll Movies, http://www.thevideobeat.com/modmovies/buck-owens-ranch-show-vol2.html, accessed July 30, 2014.
Wang Dang Dula. Discographies, http://koti.mbnet.fi/wdd/fifties.htm.

Index

Numbers in ***bold italics*** indicate pages with photographs.

"A-V8 Boogie" 189–190
"Act Naturally" 109, 111, 113
Acuff, Roy 70, 80, 83, 85
Adams, Carl 13–14
"Ain't Got a Thing" 61, 183
"All Night Rock" 60–62
Alton and Jimmy 63–68, ***64***
Alvin, Dave 52, 141, 143–144, 150
American Bandstand 12–13, 22, 28, 30, 37, 50, 55, 76, 82, 86, 88, 116, 122, 129, 141, 153
Anderson, Andy 67–68, 76–81, ***77***, 186
Anderson, Bill 70, 107
Andy Anderson and the Rolling Stones 63, 79
Angel, Eddie 158–161, ***159***, 165
Arnold, Eddy 46, 48, 122–124
Atkins, Chet 28, 42, 49–51, 72, 90
"Auctioneer" 103, 105–107
Austin City Limits 58, 137, 140, 153
Autry, Gene 25, 72, 82, 100–101, 104
Avalon, Frankie 31, 37, 116, 118–119, 122, 126, 144

"Baby, Let's Play House" 45, 70, 93
"Bad Boy" 126, 165
The Bad Boys 159, 162
Baker, LaVern 49, 177–178
Bakersfield Sound 109, 113
"Ballad of a Teenage Queen" 75, 86
Ballard, Hank 36–37
The Bandits 187–189
Barclay, Jim 130–131, 135–138
Bare, Bobby 34, 37–38
The Barnstompers 183, 185
Barry, Len 22–23
Baymoore, Jack 187–191, ***189***
The Beach Boys 140, 155
Bear Family Records 38, 150, 155
The Beatles 115, 135, 153, 155, 158–159, 167
Bechtel, Perry 123–124
Beck, Jeff 91, 137, 154
Beckham, Bob 102–103
Belew, Carl 66, 70
The Bellhops 180–181
Benton, Brook 22, 95
Bernero, Johnny 60, 90

Berry, Chuck 9, 13, 38, 54, 62, 70, 80, 92, 95, 101, 113, 124, 127, 154, 159, 167, 172
Big C Jamboree 132, 135
Big D Jamboree 41–42, 46, 75
Big Sandy 143–144, 180, 187, 190
"Bigelow 6-200" 38–39
Bill Black Combo 88–91
"Bird-Dog" 38–39
Black, Bill 43, 70, 79, 89–91, 101–102, 160, 173
Black, Buddy 105–106
"Black Slacks" 139, 192
The Blasters 58, 132, 138–139, 147–150, 156
"Blue Moon of Kentucky" 45, 63, 74, 78, 83
Bob Wills and His Texas Playboys 41, 44–46
Bond, Eddie 71–76, ***73***, 165, 181
Boone, Howard 64, 80
Boone, Pat 50, 125
"Bouquet of Roses" 122, 124
Bradley, Owen 38, 51, 97, 127, 129
Brent, Carl 80–81
Brewer, Teresa 61, 128
Brickley, Shirley 22–24, 26
Broadley, Whit 165, 167–168
Brockman, Jeremiah 171–175
Brody-Thompson, Raina 191–192
Brom, Martí 48, 52, 157
Brown, Johnny Mack 57, 60
Brown, Ruth 49, 177–178
Brumley, Tom 112, 114–115
Buchanan, Roy 7, 14–15, 164
Buck Owens and the Buckaroos 109–115, ***110***
The Buckaroos 109–110, 112–113, 115
Buckel, Steve 173, 175
The Buddy Deane Show 87–88
The Bugaloos 186–187, 192
Burgess, Sonny 61, 68, 91, 95–97, 133, 155, 157, 160, 170, 173, 181, 183, 185
Burnette, Billy 139, 149, 152
Burnette, Johnny 155, 167, 181, 184–185
Burns, Carl 116–117
Burton, James 7, 9–10, 12–13, 17–18, 63, 113, 140
Bush, Alan 141–142
Byrd, Charlie 83, 162

Index

Caldwell, Stephen 22–27
Cameo-Parkway Records 22–25
Campbell, Glen 69, 144
Campbell, Scott 168–169
Campi, Harvey 53, 58
Campi, Ray 47, 52–59, *53*, 139–144, 150, 155, 181
Cannon, Ace 88–91, *89*, 170
Cannon, Ed 176, 178
Cantu, Willie 109, 111–115
Capitol Records 109, 112
Carroll, Joe 84–85
Carroll, Johnny 44, 46, 57
Carson, Martha 70, 161
The Carter Family 49, 83
Cash, Johnny 33, 37, 46, 54, 62, 70, 74–75, 80, 85–86, 91, 100, 126, 155, 181, 183–184, 188, 190
"Caterpillar" 54, 56, 58
Charles, Ray 22, 64, 178, 182
Checker, Chubby 25, 90, 119
Checker Records 10, 15–16
Chess, Leonard 10, 12–16
Chess Records 10–13, 16–18, 34, 37, 184
Clark, Chewy 172, 174
Clark, Dick 13, 24–25, 34, 37, 127, 129
Clark, Roy 84–86, 115
Clement, Jack 60–62, 75, 78, 86, 94, 96
Cline, Patsy 31, 82, 85–87, 119, 143, 187, 191
The Clovers 9, 11, 164
Club 88 138–139, 147
Clyde Leoppard and His Snearly Ranch Boys 72, 88
The Coasters 86, 142
Cochran, Eddie 12, 143, 146, 155, 181, 188
Cochran, Jackie Lee 57, 140–141
Cole, Nat King 20, 30, 96, 141
Collins, Larry 67, 144
Collins, Lorrie 67, 191
The Collins Kids 31, 67, 144, 191
Columbia Records 70, 127
Conn, Tony 57, 140
Continental Club 44, 168, 170
Corneille, Roger 180, 182
Count Basie 132, 167
Covington, Billy 78, 80
Cowboy Copas 49, 162
Cramer, Floyd 50, 85, 96
The Cramps 159, 172
Creedence Clearwater Revival 7, 12, 155
Crown, Bobby 41–44, *42*
Cruise Inn 185, 192
Cry-Baby 144, 149
"Cryin' Over You" 141, 150–151, 156
"Crying Time" 112–113
Crystalette Records 116–118
Cuoghi, Joe 88, 91
Curtis, Mac 44, 46–47, 57, 160, 173

"Daddy's Home" 22–23
Danny and the Fat Boys 163–164
"Danny Boy" 96, 98
Darin, Bobby 16, 31
The Dave and Deke Combo 68, 144
Davis, Mac 116, 119–121
Davis, Marlena 22–27

The Dawnbreakers 76, 80
Dawson, Ronnie 52, 133, 160–161
"Deacon's Hop" 19–20
Dean, James 77, 151–152
Decca Records 38–39, 97, 127–129, 184
The Delmore Brothers 54, 63–64, 66
Depp, Johnny 144, 149
Dickens, Little Jimmy 62, 72
Dickerson, Deke 68, 133, 190
Diddley, Bo 16, 80
Dixon, Willie 15–16, 21, 133
Dobkins, Carl, Jr. 127–129, *128*
Domino, Fats 16, 33, 54, 70, 91, 95, 101, 141–142, 146, 164, 183
"Don't Be Cruel" 90, 95, 103, 158, 183
"Don't Hang Up" 22, 24–25
Dot Records 55, 57, 82, 85–86, 105–106, 118–119, 122, 125–126
The Dovells 22, 24–25
"Down the Line" 67, 78
Doyle, Jonathan 130–131, 133–134, 136–138
"Drugstore Rock and Roll" 49–51
Dylan, Bob 154–155, 164

Eagle's Nest 89, 160
The Ed Sullivan Show 88, 153
Eddy, Duane 16, 37, 90
Estes, Roy 78–80
The Everly Brothers 13, 63, 101, 125, 137, 141–142, 186–187

Fabian 90, 116, 118–119, 122
Fahey, Brian 169–170
Feathers, Bubba 173, 175
Feathers, Charlie 71, 87, 160, 163–165, 173, 175, 189
Feathers, Wanda 173, 175
Fein, Art 139, 144
Felts, Narvel 87, 91, 95, 101, 109, 185
Fender, Freddy 21, 99
Ferrier, Al 32–34, *33*
Fitzgerald, Ella 153, 187
The Five Americans 7, 17
Flatt and Scruggs 8, 35–36, 82, 141
Flores, Rosie 48, 51–52, 141–144, 150–151, 153–158, *154*, 168, 185
Foley, Red 38, 70, 104, 106
Fontana, D.J. 7, 14–16, 91, 170
"Fools Rush In" 139, 143
"For Your Love" 23, 27
The Four Charms 130–138, *131*
Franklin, Aretha 117, 177–178
Franks, Tillman 56, 66
Freed, Alan 13, 16, 21, 30
Frizzell, Lefty 37, 45, 54, 63, 70, 145–146, 162
Funicello, Annette 37, 119
Fuqua, Harvey 14, 18

Gaffney, Chris 169–170
Garland, Hank 50, 74, 85, 107, 128
Garland, Judy 80, 119
Gatton, Danny 162–163
"Give That Love to Me" 55, 57
Glen Echo Ballroom 85–86

"Go Fast" 172, 174
Godfrey, Arthur 123, 127
Gonzalez, Dave 165–170
"Good Rockin' Tonight" 143, 173
Gordon, Robert 139, 161–162, 188
Grand Ole Opry 30, 35, 44, 68–69, 72, 75, 77, 79, 83, 92, 98, 107, 114, 152–153, 161, 170
Grandpa Jones 53–54, 85
Green Mill 130, 134, 137–138
Griffin, Gus 165, 167–169
Grimes, Tiny 130, 134
Grindle, Steve 147–148

Haggard, Merle 37, 109, 112, 151, 167
Haley, Bill 10, 63, 100, 128, 173, 181, 183
Hancock, Billy 162–165, **162**
"(Happy Birthday) Mr. Twenty One" 23–24
Hardy, Al 45–46
Harman, Buddy 50, 74, 79, 85, 107, 128
Harrell, Jimmy 63–68, 81
Harris, Allen 10, 12–15, 18, 93, 97–100
Harris, Bill 93–94
Harris, Emmylou 142, 161
Hawkins, Coleman 19, 133
Hawkins, Dale 7–18, **8**, 63, 85, 133, 164
Hawkins, Jerry 7, 18
Hawkins, Ronnie 7, 94–96
"Heaven" 13–14
Hee Haw 88, 115
"Hello Mary Lou" 139, 143
Hemsby Rock 'n' Roll Weekender 28, 32, 38, 47, 62, 81–82, 87, 160, 186
Hernandez, Alex 176, 178
Heslinga, Sietse 191–192
The Hi-Flyers 182–183
Hi Records 90–91
High Noon 173, 180
HighTone Records 156, 170
Hightower, Rosetta 22–24, 26
"Hit the Road Jack" 22–23
Holland, W.S. 74, 87, 96, 136
Holly, Buddy 12, 21, 28–29, 36, 43–44, 55, 70, 100–101, 124, 128, 141–143, 146, 154–155, 163–164, 166, 172
Holly, Doyle 110–111, 113–115
Honeycutt, Glenn 60–62, **61**
Hooker, John Lee 18, 70, 76
Horton, Billy 177–178
Horton, Johnny 13, 17, 31, 46, 63, 66, 71–72, 173, 181, 191
"Hound Dog" 36, 178
Hound Dog Man 116, 119
"A House, a Car, and a Wedding Ring" 15–16
Houston, David 56, 115
Houston Jamboree 68–69
Howlin' Wolf 70, 76
"Hoy Hoy" 28, 30–32
Husky, Ferlin 38, 107

"I Can Help" 100, 102–103
"I Can't Be Satisfied" 164–165
"I Don't Care" 112–113
"I Got a Feeling" 142–143

"I Wanna Dance with You" 139–141
"I'll Be True" 23–24
"I'll Never Be Free" 50–51
"I'll Try" 95–96
Intveld, James 58, 138, 140–141, 143–153, **146**, 155–156, 158, 168, 180
Intveld, Ricky 138, 140, 142, 145, 147–148, 168
"It Ain't Me" 55, 57
"It's Only Make Believe" 92, 95–96, 98
"I've Got a Tiger by the Tail" 112–113
"I've Got the Blues" 85–86

Jackson, Wanda 31, 86, 109, 131, 155–157, 160, 166, 187
James, Elmore 7, 76, 184
James, Etta 21, 176–178
James, Sonny 49, 55, 109, 115
James Intveld and the Rockin' Shadows 138, 147
Janes, Roland 61, 66–68, 86
Jennings, Waylon 28, 102, 115, 155
Jerry King and the Rivertown Ramblers 38, 170–175, **171**
Joel Paterson Trio 130, 134
Johnnie and Jack 100–101
"Johnny B. Goode" 115, 154, 167, 185
"Johnny Valentine" 76–79, 81
Johnson, Dave 174–175
Jones, Al 12, 14
Jones, George 42, 70, 86, 115, 137, 155
Jones, Sonny 9–10, 12, 14
Jordan, Louis 130, 153, 162, 181
The Jordanaires 50, 79, 85, 96, 142, 152
"Juanita" 13–14
The Jungle 77–78
Junior Marvel 180–183, **181**, 185
"Just Because" 82, 135
Justis, Bill 67, 100

Kilgore, Merle 9, 13–14, 17
King, B.B. 9, 21, 65, 76, 154–155, 167, 169
King, Freddie 134, 167
King, Jerry 170–175, 187
King Records 36–37, 54, 128, 171
Knox, Buddy 129, 165
Kristofferson, Kris 100, 102
KWKH 10, 13, 15, 17, 69

"La-Do-Dada" 15, 164
LaBeef, Sleepy 58, 68–71, **69**, 131, 140, 189
Landon, Michael 31, 56
"Lawdy Miss Clawdy" 36, 93
Led Zeppelin 135, 154–155
Lee, Brenda 38–39, 90, 116, 155
Lenz, Kim 48, 172
The LeRoi Brothers 58, 140
Les Paul and Mary Ford 85, 186
Lester, Jimmy 159–161
"Let's Go Boppin' Tonight" 32–33
Levan, John D. 30, 32
Levi Dexter and the Rockats 147, 155, 168
Lewis, Jerry Lee 31, 38, 54, 62, 66–67, 78, 80, 85, 89–91, 100–103, 137, 148, 155, 171, 188
Lewis, Joe 95–98

Lewis, Margaret 14–15, 18
Lewis, Ronnie 10, 14
Lewis, Stan 9–12, 17
Lightnin' Chance 74, 96
Lightnin' Hopkins 8, 54, 134
Ligon, Scott 136–137
Lil' Esther 185–187, *186*, 191–192
Lit, Hy 16, 26
"Little Pig" 13–14
Little Richard 21, 54–55, 62–63, 70, 95, 177–178, 188
London Records 77–79
"Lonely Blue Boy" 96, 165
"Lonesome Town" 139, 142
Los Lobos 141, 156, 166
Los Straightjackets 158, 160–161
"Losing Game" 85–86
Lott, Alton 63–68, 81
Louisiana Hayride 8–9, 11, 14, 46, 56, 63, 66–70, 71, 75
The Louvin Brothers 186, 191
"Love and Kisses" 50–51
"Love Me to Pieces" 50–51
"Lover Please" 100–101
"Love's Gonna Live Here" 111, 113
Luke, Robin 37, 122–127, *123*
Luman, Bob 13, 44, 46, 55, 70, 102
Lynn, Loretta 97–99, 102, 115, 120–121

Mack, Ronnie 58, 138–144, *140*, 149
Maddox, Duke 85, 87
Maddox, Rose 56, 58, 143
"Make Like a Rock and Roll" 39–40
Malano, Jai 175–179, *176*
Mann, Carl 65, 96, 100–101, 189
Maphis, Joe 56, 67
Maphis, Rose Lee 56, 67
"Marie, Marie" 58, 140, 148
Mars Attacks 183–185, *184*
Martin, Dean 36, 128, 145, 153
Martin, Grady 39, 50, 79, 95, 107, 184
Martin, Janis 48–52, *49*, 144, 155–157, 186–187
The Marvelettes 22, 25
Maslon, Jimmie Lee 57, 141
Masters, Rip 57–59, 140, 144
Mathis, Dean 13–16
Mathis, Marc 13–15
The Mavericks 115, 151
"Maybellene" 9, 92, 95
Mays, Tim 167–168
McDonough, Casey 136–137
McNeely, Big Jay 18–21, *19*, 144, 176
McPhatter, Clyde 9, 100–101
McPherson, JD 32, 136
McVoy, Carl 90–91
"Mean Little Mama" 172, 174
Mercury Records 72, 74–75, 92, 94, 101, 106–107
Mess Around 180, 182
MGM Records 92, 95, 97
Midnight Jamboree 152, 158
Milburn, Amos 162, 164
"Milkcow Blues Boogie" 142–143
Miller, Roger 37, 75
The Miller Sisters 61, 186

Millet, Lou 189–190
The Mills Brothers 77, 153
The Milt Grant Show 12, 87
Milton, Roy 130, 162
Mirt Mirley and the Rhythm Steppers 100–101
Miss Mary Ann 185–187, 191–192, *192*
The Modern Sounds 135, 137
"Molly Darling" 122, 124
Monroe, Bill 7, 70, 82
Monroe, Marilyn 103, 105
Moor, Huey 182, 192
Moore, Bob 50, 79, 107, 128, 173
Moore, Scotty 7, 16, 63–64, 70, 79, 87, 89, 91, 102, 134, 159–160, 170, 184
Moreno, Sue 158, 165, 185
"My Babe" 15–16
"My Heart Is Achin' for You" 142, 147–148
"My Heart Is an Open Book" 127, 129
"My Heart Skips a Beat" 111, 113
"Mystery Train" 36, 63, 82–83, 87, 102, 139, 158

Nader, Richard 142, 148
Nance, Jack 95, 97
Nashville Now 88, 153
Neill, Mark 168–169
Nelson, Ricky 65, 115–116, 119, 125–126, 138–139, 141–145, 147–148, 152, 164
Nelson, Willie 80, 136–137
The Nighthawks 84–86
The Nitecaps 28–30
"No More Crying the Blues" 63, 66–68
Nobles, Gene 10–11
"Not I" 39–40

Old Dominion Barn Dance 48–49
"One Hand Loose" 173, 175
"One Way Ticket" 41–44
"Ooby Dooby" 50, 63
Orbison, Roy 41, 43, 61–62, 65, 70, 74–75, 78–79, 87, 91, 94, 134, 146–147, 167, 172–173
The Orlons 22–27, *23*
Osborn, Joe 7, 15, 17–18
Otis, Johnny 19, 162
Owens, Buck 109–115, 137, 143, 167
Owens, Don 84–86
Ozark Jubilee 38–40, 50, 106

The Pacers 91, 95
Page, Patti 39, 128
The Paladins 68, 147, 165–170, *166*
Palomino Club 58, 139–140, 143–144, 148–149, 155
Parker, Colonel Tom 50–51, 55, 89
Parsons, Gram 142, 155
Paterson, Joel 130–132, 134–138
Paul, Les 134, 137
Paulman, Jimmy Ray 93–95
"Peggy Sue" 29, 36, 124, 127
Perkins, Carl 21, 33, 37–38, 43, 46, 50, 54, 59, 63, 65, 74–75, 80, 91, 96, 100–101, 126, 156, 163, 167, 171, 173, 183–185
Phillips, Dewey 65, 74, 76
Phillips, Sam 33, 60–61, 66–67, 74, 78–79, 86–88, 94, 96

Phillips International Records 64, 68, 96
Pierce, Webb 30, 45–46, 56, 72, 75, 100–101, 162
Pilgrim, Denny 83–85
"Pink Shoelaces" 116–119, 122
The Planet Rockers 68, 158, 160–161
"Play It Cool" 54, 58
Prease, Roger 83–84
Presley, Elvis 16, 28, 30, 33, 36, 41, 43–46, 48, 50, 54–55, 62–63, 65–68, 70, 72–75, 77- 80, 83, 87, 89, 92–95, 100–103, 105, 120, 128–129, 132, 134–135, 141, 144–146, 155–156, 158–161, 163, 166–167, 170–174, 177, 180–181, 183, 188, 190
Price, Lloyd 17, 164
Price, Ray 30, 34, 109
Prima, Louis 108, 153

Quaintance, Jack 83–85

Raitt, Bonnie 58, 140
Rall, Lorne 152–153
The Ranch Girls 187, 191–192
Raney, Wayne 8, 53
"Rawhide" 100, 159
Ray, Johnny 61, 180
Ray Campi and the Rockabilly Rebels 57, 139–140
RCA Records 17, 37, 48, 50–51, 63
"Red Blooded American Boy" 39–40
"Red Headed Woman" 157, 183
"Red Hot" 89, 149
"Red Rooster" 34, 36
Reed, Jimmy 8, 16, 101
Reeves, Jim 10, 43, 50, 109
Reverend Horton Heat 133, 166, 172
Rhode, Storm, IV 152–153
Rhythm Bomb Records 62, 178
Rich, Charlie 67, 86, 91, 100
Rich, Don 109–115
Richards, Keith 91, 154
Riedberger, Roland 183, 185
Riley, Billy Lee 61–62, 65–66, 79, 86, 89, 95, 100, 146, 170, 173, 185
Ripsaw Records 158, 162, 164–165
Ritter, Tex 34, 60, 107
Robbins, Marty 30, 36, 43, 48, 62, 72, 75, 173, 191
Rock and Roll Hall of Fame 7, 52, 157
The Rock and Roll Trio 155, 168, 182
Rockabilly Filly 51, 153, 156
Rockabilly Hall of Fame 43, 129
Rockabilly Rave 180, 183, 186, 192
"Rockhouse" 41, 93–94
The Rockhousers 92–94
"Rockin' Daddy" 72, 74–75
Rodgers, Jimmie 7, 33, 37, 45
Roeper, Jason 172, 174–175
Rogers, Kenny 69, 99
Rogers, Melvin 14–15
Rollin' Rock Records 47, 57, 138–142
The Rolling Stones (Andy Anderson) 76, 78, 80
The Rolling Stones (England) 79, 153–155, 167
Ronnie Mack's Barn Dance 143–144
Ronstadt, Linda 102, 144
"Rootie Tootie" 164–165
The Royal Rhythmaires 175–178

Rubinowitz, Tex 158–159, 162, 165
Ruby and the Romantics 22, 25
Russell, Leon 30, 32
Rydell, Bobby 37, 116, 119, 122

Sample, Beau 52, 137
Sands, Tommy 70, 96, 109
"Satisfaction Guaranteed" 85–86
Scott, Jack 37, 63
Screamin' Rockabilly Weekender 180, 182
Seat, Don 92–95
"Shake, Rattle, and Roll" 43, 63–64
Shakin' Stevens 58, 188
Shakin' That Rockabilly Fever 162, 164–165
Sharpe, Ray 37, 41, 133
"She'll Be Coming 'Round the Mountain" 100, 145
The Shirelles 117–118
Sholes, Steve 49–51
Simmons, Gene 67, 75, 90
Sims, Ray 105, 107
Sinatra, Frank 103, 141, 153, 180
Singleton, Shelby 70, 81, 87, 101, 106
Sixpack, Joe 186, 191–192
Skinner, Jimmie 36, 70
Skyway Club 12, 14
Sleepy Eyed John 74, 89
"Slip, Slip, Slippin' In" 72, 76
Smith, Bryan 158, 164
Smith, Carl 30, 62, 75, 151
Smith, Curley 84–85
Smith, Kevin 170–171, 173
Smith, Warren 65, 74, 89, 146
"Smokie" 89–90
Snow, Hank 43, 50, 54, 56, 77, 85, 104, 161–162
Snowden, Gene 54, 58
"So Young" 28, 30, 32
"Someday, One Day" 15–16
"South Street" 22, 26
The Southerners 84, 86
Southgate House Revival 172, 175
Spelling, Aaron 80–81
Springsteen, Bruce 142, 164
Stacy, Clyde 28–32, **29**
Stampley, Joe 17–18
Stan's Record Shop 9–11
Starday Records 36, 68, 70, 85
The Stardevils 172–173
Starr, Kay 141, 187
Steel Pier 92, 164
Stevens, Dodie 116–122, **117**
The Stompers 72, 75
The Stray Cats 132, 159, 166, 172, 188
"Sugaree" 34, 36–37
Sullivan, Bob 10–11, 14, 18
Summers, Gene 175–176
Sun International Records 70–71
Sun Records 37, 49, 60–61, 63, 66–68, 74, 78–79, 81–82, 86–88, 92, 94, 96, 103, 171, 183–184, 190
Sun Studio 62, 66–67, 74, 77–78, 86–87, 93, 103, 126, 170, 174
"Susie Darlin'" 122, 124–125, 127
"Susie-Q" 7, 9–13, 18, 63, 85
Sutton, Jimmy 130, 132–138, 178

Swan, Billy 100–103, *101*, 170
"Swing Bop Boogie" 45–46, 48

Tail Records 188–189
Taylor, Koko 21, 169
Taylor, Skip 80–81
Taylor, Vernon 82–87, *83*
"Teardrops Are Falling" 144, 149
Telfser, Martin 183–185
The Tennessee Rockets 158, 162, 164–165
Terry and the Pirates 85–86
Tharpe, Sister Rosetta 15, 70
"That's All Right" 45, 63, 65, 74, 78, 180
"There Is Something on Your Mind" 19, 21
Thompson, Hank 46, 70, 88, 162
Thornton, Big Mama 65, 177–178
Tillis, Mel 75, 102
The Tinstars 185, 187, 192
"Together Again" 111–113
"Tore Up" 57, 69
"Tornado" 13–14
"Tough, Tough, Tough" 76, 78, 80–81
Travis, Dave 62, 75, 81, 87
Travis, Merle 54, 134
Travis, Randy 150, 156
Trimble, Bobby 40, 52
Tubb, Ernest 33, 49, 70, 72, 153
Tubb, Joe 78–80
"Tuff" 88–90
Tuminello, A.J. 9–10
Turk 57, 113
Turner, Big Joe 21, 70–71, 153, 164, 181, 184, 188
Twitty, Conway 31, 92–100, *93*, 102, 115, 146

"Unchained Melody" 55, 62
"The Usual Thing" 139, 142–143

Van Dyke, Leroy 97, 103–109, *104*
Van Eaton, JM 61, 66, 86, 95
Vaughn, Stevie Ray 166, 169
Vincent, Gene 12, 21, 42, 55, 57, 65, 109, 128, 140, 143, 146, 155, 159, 163–164, 167, 181
Viva Las Vegas Weekender 18, 28, 32, 40, 47, 63, 76, 81, 131, 137, 174–175, 177

"The Wah-Watusi" 22–24, 27
"Walk on By" 103, 106–107
Walker, Gary 39–40, 106–107
Wallace, Slim 60–61
Warner Bros. Records 151, 156
Waters, John 144, 149
Waters, Muddy 11, 16, 22, 26, 65, 70, 76, 79, 134, 155, 167, 184
Wayne, Alvis 44–48, *45*

Weir, Billy 93–95
Weiser, Ronny 47, 52, 56–58, 138–140, 142
West, Mae 56–57
"Western Union" 7, 17
What Am I Bid? 107–108
"What's the Use" 66–67
"White Silver Sands" 89–90
Whitman, Slim 10, 45–46
"Whole Lotta Shakin' Goin' On" 36, 100
"Why Must You Leave Me" 84–86
The Wilburn Brothers 72, 161
Wildcat Tamer (album) 7, 17
Wildfire Willie (Jan Svensson) 43–44, 58
Wildfire Willie and the Ramblers 41, 43, 47
"Will You, Willyum" 49–50
Willett, Nick 130, 134–137, 159
William Morris Agency 80–81
Williams, Hank, Sr. 7–8, 29–30, 45–46, 48, 54, 58, 62, 72, 100–101, 137, 141, 143, 145–146, 152, 162, 181, 184, 188, 190
Williams, Hank, III 152, 159
Williams, Lew 44, 173, 189
Willis, Martin 87, 89, 94–95
Willman, Dave 172, 174
Wills, Bob 70, 109
Wilson, Jackie 16, 22
Wilson, Jimmy 61, 86
Wilson, Kim 168–169
Winchester, Marc 160–161
Wink Martindale's Dance Party 76, 88
Winski, Colin 57–58, 149
Woodward, Patrick 140, 147–148
Woody, Don 38–40, *39*
Wray, Link 159, 161

X 147, 156, 166

The Yardbirds 154–155
Yearsley, Thomas 165, 167–170
Yoakum, Dwight 115, 144, 149–150, 156, 169
York, Rusty 34–38, *35*, 189
"You Are My Sunshine" 7, 90, 128
"You Make Me Wanna Rock" 139–141
"You Shake Me Up" 76, 80
"You Want Love" 29–31
Young, Faron 50, 56, 72, 100, 107, 109
Young, Lester 19, 133
Young, Reggie 72, 74–75, 90
"Your Conscience" 42–43
"Your Lovin' Man" 84, 87
"Your True Love" 101, 163
"You're Barking Up the Wrong Tree" 38–40

Zoom, Billy 56, 147

www.ingramcontent.com/pod-product-compliance
Ingram Content Group UK Ltd.
Pitfield, Milton Keynes, MK11 3LW, UK
UKHW050533150426
5217IPUK00026B/1916